PATHWAYS TO OUTSTANDING LEADERSHIP

A Comparative Analysis of Charismatic, Ideological, and Pragmatic Leaders

PATHWAYS TO OUTSTANDING LEADERSHIP

*A Comparative Analysis of Charismatic,
Ideological, and Pragmatic Leaders*

Michael D. Mumford
University of Oklahoma

 LAWRENCE ERLBAUM ASSOCIATES, PUBLISHERS
2006   Mahwah, New Jersey   London

LEA's SERIES IN APPLIED PSYCHOLOGY

Edwin A. Fleishman, *George Mason University*
Jeanette N. Cleveland, *Pennsylvania State University*
Series Editors

Gregory Bedny and David Meister
The Russian Theory of Activity: Current Applications to Design and Learning

Michael T. Brannick, Eduardo Salas, and Carolyn Prince
Team Performance Assessment and Measurement: Theory, Research, and Applications

Jeanette N. Cleveland, Margaret Stockdale, and Kevin R. Murphy
Women and Men in Organizations: Sex and Gender Issues at Work

Aaron Cohen
Multiple Commitments in the Workplace: An Integrative Approach

Russell Cropanzano
Justice in the Workplace: Vol. 1. Approaching Fairness in Human Resource Management

Russell Cropanzano
Justice in the Workplace: Vol. 2. From Theory to Practice

David V. Day, Stephen Zaccaro, and Stanley M. Halpin
Leader Development for Transforming Organizations: Growing Leaders for Tomorrow

James E. Driskell and Eduardo Salas
Stress and Human Performance

Sidney A. Fine and Steven F. Cronshaw
Functional Job Analysis: A Foundation for Human Resources Management

Sidney A. Fine and Maury Getkate
Benchmark Task for Job Analysis: A Guide for Functional Job Analysis (FJA) Scales

J. Kevin Ford, Steve W. J. Kozlowski, Kurt Kraiger, Eduardo Salas, and Mark S. Teachout
Improving Training Effectiveness in Work Organizations

Jerald Greenberg
Organizational Behavior: The State of the Science, Second Edition

Uwe E. Kleinbeck, Hans-Henning Quast, Henk Thierry, and Hartmut Häcker
Work Motivation

Ellen Ernst Kossek and Susan J. Lambert
Work and Life Integration: Organizational, Cultural, and Individual Perspectives

Martin I. Kurke and Ellen M. Scrivner
Police Psychology Into the 21st Century

Lawrence Erlbaum Associates, Inc., Publishers
10 Industrial Avenue
Mahwah, New Jersey 07430
www.erlbaum.com

Cover design by Tomai Maridou

Library of Congress Cataloging-in-Publication Data

Mumford, Michael D.
Pathways to outstanding leadership : a comparative analysis of charismatic, ideological,
and pragmatic leaders / by Michael D. Mumford.
p.   cm.
Includes bibliographical references and index.
ISBN 0-8058-5110-0 (hardcover)
ISBN 0-8058-5111-9 (pbk.)
1. Leadership—Psychological aspects.   I. Title.

BF637.L4M75   2006
158'.4—dc22   2005049475
                                                                        CIP

Books published by Lawrence Erlbaum Associates are printed on acid-free paper,
and their bindings are chosen for strength and durability.

Printed in the United States of America
10 9 8 7 6 5 4 3 2 1

*To Quin, who reminds me daily
of the importance of leadership
for our future.*

Contents

Series Foreword

Series Editors

Edwin A. Fleishman
George Mason University

Jeanette N. Cleveland
Pennsylvania State University

There is a compelling need for innovative approaches to the solution of many pressing problems involving human relationships in today's society. Such approaches are more likely to be successful when they are based on sound research and applications. This Series in Applied Psychology offers publications that emphasize state-of-the-art research and its applications to important issues of human behavior in a variety of social settings. The objective is to bridge both academic and applied interests.

The topic of leadership has been a subject of continuing interest to researchers in the behavioral and social sciences, as well as practitioners who deal with such issues as identifying leadership potential, selecting and training individuals for leadership positions in organizations, and assessing leadership performance. However, the subject of leadership needs to be studied in a broader context, since the leadership of others plays a major role in the fabric of our society and impacts our daily lives and our future prospects. This book, *Pathways to Outstanding Leadership: A Comparative Analysis of Charismatic, Ideological and Pragmatic Leaders*, focuses on the study of outstanding leadership in this broader context.

The book describes an intensive developmental study of leaders in a wide variety of historical contexts. The author, Michael D. Mumford, is particularly qualified to deal with this topic in a comprehensive manner. He is the current Senior Editor of the journal *Leadership Quarterly*, was the senior author of the book *Patterns of Life History: The Ecology of Human Individuality* and of *The Biodata Handbook*, and has directed major research projects on the relations between problem-solving creativity, cognitive skills, and high-level leader effectiveness.

Pathways to Outstanding Leadership describes the developmental/historical study of 120 historically notable leaders, selected by means of a careful sampling strategy. Unlike previous studies of leader biographies, this work is based on a careful foundation of empirically derived leadership theory and utilizes well-developed statistical procedures and controls and psychometric methods, within a framework called the historiometric method. The latter is a form of meta-analysis allowing cumulation of data across historic cases or biographies. The results are compelling and interpreted in terms of expanded and clarified constructs of *charismatic, ideological, and pragmatic* leadership. The components of these constructs, their development, and consequences, their distinctions from one another, and their explanatory value in the study of leadership are among the many important contributions of the book.

The book is a landmark publication in the study of leadership and will be a valuable addition to the literature on the nature and understanding of leadership. It will certainly be of interest to researchers and students in this field and useful for advanced courses in organizational psychology, research methodology, and related fields.

Preface

Like many of my colleagues who study leadership, I have been fascinated with the impact outstanding, historically notable leaders have had on our lives, yet when I read the biographies of leaders, a hobby to which I devote much of my spare time, I have been left with a question: Do our current models of outstanding leadership really account for what we know about the lives and behavior of these notable leaders?

Clearly, the dominant model of outstanding leadership may be found in charismatic and transformational theories. Charismatic and transformational theories do seem to provide a good model for understanding the careers of Franklin Roosevelt and Lee Iacocca. They had a vision, they had impact, and they articulated a better and brighter future. By the same token, however, it is difficult to see in Dwight Eisenhower or John D. Rockefeller a vision and inspiration. Nonetheless, Rockefeller and Eisenhower have shaped our world as much as Roosevelt and Iacocca.

This rather straightforward observation posed to me the question that underlies this book: Are there other ways of exhibiting outstanding leadership aside from the charismatic style that has received so much attention as of late? A few years ago, my graduate students and I began a series of studies intended to establish the potential existence of two other styles of outstanding leadership—styles we refer to as pragmatic and ideological leadership. Although our initial research provides some evidence for the existence of these alternative styles, we have not conducted the kind of comprehensive comparative study needed to fully establish the similarities and differences among charismatic, ideological, and pragmatic leaders. This book represents our attempt to fill this gap.

We hope, however, that by calling scholars' attention to the existence of these alternative styles we will provide a theory of outstanding leadership more in tune with the realities of the 21st-century world. It is difficult to envision a charismatic leader directing our forthcoming flight to Mars. In a world where rejection of globalization has led to the emergence of ideological leaders, such as Usama bin Laden, we need to understand how ideological leaders think and act. Hopefully, this book will help readers envision the implications of these different types of leadership and reconsider the relative merits of charismatic, ideological, and pragmatic leadership in the world of the 21st century.

—*Michael D. Mumford*

Acknowledgments

This book is the result of the efforts of many people, colleagues, students, friends, and family. First, and foremost, I would like to thank our graduate students in the Industrial and Organizational Psychology program at the University of Oklahoma. Not only did they play an instrumental role in preparation of many of the chapters presented in this book, they volunteered for many of the more onerous tasks involved in preparation of any book—checking and formatting tables, proofreading draft text, and tracking down obscure references.

In particular, thanks are due to Jill Strange and Ginamarie Scott. Jill and Gina took on the essential, but essentially thankless, tasks of tracking down the relevant source material, scheduling the distribution of this material, recruiting raters, and ensuring the quality of the rater-training programs. Without the work they put into developing the technical infrastructure underlying this project, it is doubtful this book could have been completed.

In addition, Katrina Bedell and Sam Hunter, despite being overloaded with thesis and project work, agreed to take on the chore of fact checking, reference checking, and table formatting. Any errors that appear in this book are mine. I can assure the reader they have performed an amazing job in final assembly. With regard to assembly of this book, I must also recognize the contributions of Kathryn Paine, my administrative assistant at the University of Oklahoma. Kathryn somehow managed multiple changes in multiple chapters, keeping track of drafts and changes while making sure that changes were consistent and the final drafts were "good to go."

Unlike many research projects, the present effort required the support of a rather large number of undergraduates who agreed to serve as judges. My thanks go out to the undergraduate psychology students and the psychology club (Psi Chi) at the University of Oklahoma. The effort these outstanding undergraduates devoted to this project provides a shining example of what undergraduates can do if the graduate students and faculty get them involved in projects.

The Psychology Department at the University of Oklahoma not only provided critical undergraduate support, but they also provided course releases to support the research underlying this book and preparation of the manuscript. My colleagues in the Psychology Department—Shane Connelly, Claudia Cogliser, Eric Day, Jorge Mendoza, Bob Cox, and Eugenia Cox-Fuenzalida—not only provided invaluable feedback and statistical support, they also provided the administrative backup that made it possible to prepare the book at an unusually busy time in my career.

Finally, I would like to thank my family, Shane and Quin, who created the time and space that allowed me to write this book. Their unselfish support is ultimately the true foundation on which this project was built.

About the Author

Michael Mumford, Ph.D., University of Georgia 1983, is currently a professor of psychology at the University of Oklahoma where he is director of the graduate program in Industrial and Organizational Psychology and Director of the Center for Applied Social Research. Prior to joining the faculty at the University of Oklahoma, he held faculty positions at the Georgia Institute of Technology and George Mason University. His current research interests focus on leadership, creativity, planning, and integrity. Dr. Mumford is currently the senior editor of *The Leadership Quarterly*. He serves on the editorial boards of the *Creativity Research Journal*, the *Journal of Creative Behavior*, and *IEEE Transactions on Engineering Management*. Dr. Mumford is a fellow of the American Psychological Association (Divisions 3, 5, & 14), the American Psychological Society, and the Society for Industrial and Organizational Psychology. He is the recipient of the Society for Industrial and Organizational Psychology's M. Scott Myers award for applied research in the workplace. Projects directed by Dr. Mumford include ones sponsored by the National Institute of Health, the Office of Naval Research, the Army Research Institute, the U.S. Department of Labor, the U.S. Department of State, and a number of industrial organizations.

I

EXAMINING DISTINCT PATHWAYS TO OUTSTANDING LEADERSHIP

1

Introduction—Charismatic, Ideological, and Pragmatic Leaders: Are They Really Different?

Michael D. Mumford
Jill M. Strange
Katrina E. Bedell
The University of Oklahoma

When one mentions the word *leadership*, images come to mind of historic greats. We think of Mohandas Gandhi, Franklin Roosevelt, and John Kennedy. We think of William Paley, Andrew Carnegie, and Henry Ford. We think of George Patton, Erich Ludendorff, and Dwight Eisenhower. We think of Pope John Paul, Billy Graham, and the Ayatollah Khomeini. Across domains of human endeavor, politics, religion, business, and the military, leadership is, in our minds, linked to those people who have had a disproportionate impact on the institutions in which they work and the broader world in which we live (H. Gardner, 1993a). It is those leaders we refer to when we use the term outstanding leadership (Bass, 1985).

Outstanding leaders do not just influence others; although they may be masters at the exercise of influence, they shape the fabric of our world. Europe as we know it today would not exist without the efforts of George Marshall. The suburban landscape, which shapes much of our day-to-day existence, is in part the creation of William Leavitt. The conditions under which we work are, in many ways, the creation of the Roosevelts, both Theodore and Franklin, who advocated the passage of fair labor laws.

Given their manifest impact on our lives, one might expect that the study of outstanding leaders would be a major preoccupation of students of leadership. If one considers leadership studies to include the study of leaders' lives, it is clear that substantial effort has been devoted by historians (e.g., Hirshon, 2002), journalists (e.g., Halberstam, 1986), and political scientists (e.g., Morris, 2001) to the study of outstanding leaders. Enter any bookstore or library and one will find hundreds, if not thousands, of carefully wrought, thoroughly researched, biographies that examine the lives of historically notable leaders.

From the standpoint of those scholars whose concern is the *empirical* investigation of leadership, these biographies, however compelling, do little more than fill space on library shelves. In fact, scholars who study leadership within the tradition of the behavioral sciences have devoted little effort to the study of outstanding leadership. Three key considerations, considerations that are implicit assumptions within the positivist tradition of modern social science (Lasch, 1991), have led leadership researchers to discount the value of biographical work and, more generally, the study of outstanding leaders.

First, behavioral science has been concerned with establishing general "laws" of human behavior. Because outstanding leadership is a non-normative event, it is open to question whether an examination of the lives of these leaders is an appropriate basis for framing scientific investigations. Second, outstanding leadership is a rare event, and it has been notoriously difficult to apply the statistical methods of the social sciences to the study of rare events (Simonton, 1990). Third, people's lives, especially the lives of outstanding leaders, are highly complex. The complexity of people's lives, however, makes it difficult to identify the critical factors that operate in shaping leader behavior. Without the ability to identify these critical causal variables, it is difficult to see how studies of outstanding leaders can contribute much to the science of leadership.

Although these considerations, taken in total, represent an argument, indeed a compelling argument, against the study of outstanding leadership, one is likely to feel uncomfortable with the conclusion that invariably unfolds. It is a conclusion that leads us to ignore the most significant manifestations of leadership in social settings, bringing to question the relevance or real-world utility of our theories and findings. More centrally, however, studies of outstanding leadership may reveal important new facets of leadership—facets that must be incorporated in our models if we are to develop a truly comprehensive understanding of leadership. One illustration of this point may be found in Mumford, Zaccaro, Harding, Jacobs, and Fleishman (2000). Their findings indicated that when one examines upper-level leaders, new skills, skills such as creative thinking skills and system thinking skills, come to fore as important influences on performance.

Apparently, there is good reason to study outstanding leaders. Recognizing the rarity of outstanding leadership and the difficulty in gaining access to outstanding leaders (they are busy people who have better things to do than serve as guinea pigs for leadership theorists) a new question comes to fore. How are we to go about studying outstanding leadership in a systematic quantitative fashion—a fashion that allows identification of critical causal variables?

One approach to this question would be to apply an idiographic approach, following a particular leader and changes in his or her behavior over time (S. Dionne & K. Jaussi, personal communication, April 15, 2003; Mumford & Van Doorn, 2001). Another approach would be to conduct in-depth interviews with a limited number of leaders (McGourty, Tarshis, & Dominick, 1996). Still another approach would involve examination and analysis of public-record documents such as speeches (House, Spangler, & Woycke, 1991; Winter, 1987). Although all of these approaches have value, a more compelling approach may be found in the historiometric method (Deluga, 2001; O'Connor, Mumford, Clifton, Gessner, & Connelly, 1995; Simonton, 1990). Historiometric methods may be viewed as a form of meta-analysis, admittedly a specialized form, where general conclusions are obtained by cumulating results across studies—specifically historic cases or biographies. Essentially, the problem of rare events is addressed by aggregation of cases over time. In the study of outstanding leadership, this approach is attractive because a large body of well-documented biographical evidence is available.

Moreover, select portions of this biographical material can be abstracted from the relevant text, focusing on certain behaviors of interest. Judgmental appraisal of these behaviors with respect to a select set of theoretically specified variables can then be used to describe the leaders under consideration, thereby providing a systematic structured framework for observation. These judgmental evaluations, in turn, provide the basis for drawing general conclusions.

In this book, we present a historiometric analysis of outstanding leadership. We compare and contrast three types of outstanding leaders with respect to their impact on institutions as well as the behavior they evidence in problem solving, leader–follower interactions, communication, and politics. Additionally, the variables that give rise to these three leadership types are discussed. The three types of leaders that are considered in this historiometric investigation are charismatic, ideological, and pragmatic leaders.

TYPES OF OUTSTANDING LEADERSHIP

Charismatic Leadership

As noted earlier, studies of leadership have for the most part focused on understanding more routine, day-to-day, forms of leadership. One set of studies along these lines has sought to identify the behaviors required in leadership roles with behaviors indicative of consideration, initiating structure, participation, and change management consistently emerging across investigations (Fleishman & Harris, 1962; Hunt, 2004; Yukl, 2002). Other studies have sought to identify the conditions that place more emphasis on certain dimensions. Thus, Hersey and Blanchard (1984) provided evidence indicating that initiating structure is more important under conditions where followers lack expertise. Participation and change management are, however, at a premium when followers have substantial expertise. Still other studies have sought to identify the skills—social skills, planning skills, and so forth—that make effective expression of these behaviors possible (Marta, Leritz, & Mumford, 2005; Zaccaro, Gilbert, Thor, & Mumford, 1991).

We do not wish to dispute the value of this research. Nonetheless, it is difficult to see how the kind of variables identified in these studies can account for the powerful impact of outstanding leaders on their followers. In other words, can variables such as consideration and initiating structure really account for the impact Franklin Roosevelt and Adolf Hitler had on their followers? The followers of outstanding leaders ascribe to the leader heroic, almost mythic, status. They are willing to take actions outside the bounds of anything they have done before. They are willing to invest inordinate effort in projects advocated by the leader.

To account for the remarkable impact outstanding leaders have on followers, Bass (1985) and House (1977), drawing on the earlier work of Burns (1978) and Weber (1924), proposed the theories of charismatic and transformational leadership. Although theories of charismatic and transformational leadership differ from each other in some notable ways, they are based on a similar proposition. Both theories hold that the marked impact of outstanding leaders on followers can be attributed to the leaders' effective articulation of a vision—an emotionally evocative image of an idealized future (Conger & Kanungo, 1988, 1998; Deluga, 2001; House, 1995; Shamir, House, & Arthur, 1993). Theories of charismatic leadership, however, hold that attributes of the leader that serve to magnify the impact of the vision being articulated, for example, apparent self-sacrifice, manifest confidence, interpersonal attractiveness, and communication skills, should also be considered in accounting for the impact of outstanding leaders (Hunt, Boal, & Dodge, 1999; Yorges, Weiss, & Strickland, 1999). Theories of transformational leadership, in contrast, hold that leaders' interaction with followers should be considered. Thus transformational theories stress the importance of intellectual stimulation, individualized consideration, and inspirational motivation as well as vision (Antonakis & House, 2002; Avolio, Howell, & Sosik, 1999; Bass, 1997).

Even bearing in mind these differences in charismatic and transformational theories, the impact of outstanding leaders ultimately lies in the vision being articulated. This observation, in turn, broaches the question: Why is vision such a powerful mechanism for the exercise of influence? In fact, the power of vision lies in the multiple ways vision articulation affects followers. First, vision appears to provide followers, and the group as a whole, with a sense of personal meaning that both explains events and helps establish a sense of identity (Meindl, 1990; Shamir et al., 1993). Second, visioning involves articulation of emotionally evocative images that not only motivates followers but also allows followers to create a shared experience and a shared future (Klein & House, 1998). Third, vision, as a positive image of the future, suggests a path that will allow resolution of current social problems and tensions (Erikson, 1959). Fourth, as followers apply a vision they will begin to make decisions in a manner consistent with the vision, resulting in the institutionalization of the vision through norms, culture, and standard operating procedures (Jacobsen & House, 2001).

Although there is reason to suspect that vision can have powerful effects, the kind of effects that would explain the impact of outstanding leaders, the question remains as to whether vision, in fact, explains these effects in real-world settings. In one study intended to assess the effects of transformational leadership, Sosik, Kahai, and Avolio (1999) manipulated the statements made by confederate leaders as business students worked on an electronic brainstorming task. In accordance with current theory, they found that leaders evidencing transformational behavior induced higher levels of motivation in followers. In another experimental study, Kirkpatrick and Locke (1996) used actors to simulate behaviors linked to two key aspects of charisma—visioning and an expressive communication style. They found that visioning and expressive communication had a positive effect on follower performance by leading followers to evidence higher self-efficacy and set more difficult goals.

Evidence pointing to the impact of charismatic leadership on performance is not, however, limited to experimental studies, although these studies have proven useful in demonstrating motivational effects. For example, Dvir, Eden, Avolio, and Shamir (1999) conducted a workshop intended to provide training in transformational leadership tactics for noncommissioned officers in the military. They found that those noncommissioned officers who participated in training were better leaders of their squads, as compared to no-training controls, on criterion measures examining motivational effects such as follower self-efficacy, independent thinking, and extra effort.

Bass and Avolio (1990) designed a behavior description measure intended to assess followers' perceptions of transformational behavior on the part of leaders. This measure is referred to as the Multifactor Leadership Questionnaire (MLQ). In a meta-analytic study examining the relationship of scores on this measure to various indices of group and organizational performance obtained in 39 studies, Lowe, Kroeck, and Sivasubramaniam (1996) found that appraisals of transformational leadership obtained from the MLQ were related to indices of leader effectiveness.

However, the Lowe et al. (1996) study also indicated that the magnitude of these relationships varied as a function of criteria and setting. Specifically, stronger positive relationships were obtained in government as opposed to business settings and stronger positive relationships were obtained for motivational as opposed to performance criteria. Similar findings have been reported in a more recent study by Yammarino and Tosi (in press). They obtained senior executives' (e.g., vice presidents) appraisals of chief executive officers' (CEOs) charisma and correlated these appraisals with indices of organizational performance. They found that charismatic CEOs received better compensation but that charisma did not necessarily result in better performance in business organizations.

The findings of Lowe et al. (1996) and Yammarino and Tosi (2004) are noteworthy in part because they remind us that our identification of the charismatic/ transformational type may not have provided us with one true way for understanding outstanding leadership. Apparently, in some settings charisma does not work (Hunt et al., 1999; Mumford & Licuanan, 2004). Moreover, charismatic leadership, while encouraging motivation, does not necessarily ensure organizational performance. These observations, in turn, beg the question as to whether there are other types of outstanding leadership. In fact, Weber (1924), in his discussion of charisma, reminded us that there exist at least two other pathways to outstanding leadership, the ideological and the bureaucratic or pragmatic paths.

Ideological Leadership

A few scholars, notably Gerring (1997), Mills (1967), and Rejai (1991), have extended Weber's (1924) observations concerning the nature and significance of ideological leadership. Nonetheless, studies of ideological leadership have been few and far between. Perhaps the most thorough recent examination of ideological leadership may be found in Strange and Mumford (2002).

In Strange and Mumford's (2002) view, ideological leadership, like charismatic leadership, represents a form of vision-based leadership. Ideological leaders, in contrast to charismatic leaders, however, do not articulate a vision of the future. Ideological leaders instead articulate a vision, again an emotionally evocative vision, that appeals to the virtues of the past rather than the future. For ideological leaders, this vision is framed in terms of the values and standards that must be maintained in order to build a just society.

In an initial attempt to provide evidence bearing on the meaningfulness of the ideological type, Strange and Mumford (2002) conducted a historiometric study. In this study, a sample of 60 historically notable leaders was obtained and these leaders were classified as ideological (e.g., Charles de Gaulle, Ronald Reagan), charismatic (Winston Churchill, J.P. Morgan) or mixed (e.g., Theodore Roosevelt, Emma Goldman). Academic biographies describing the leaders' lives were obtained and the rise-to-power and pinnacle-of-power chapters were identified. Content coding was conducted using the information presented in each chapter by applying a behavioral observation approach. In this approach, judges were asked to review the leader behaviors presented in each chapter and indicate whether they reflected one of 30 charismatic behaviors (e.g., the leader acted according to a vision that specifies a better future) or 29 ideological behaviors (e.g., the leader has a limited set of extreme, consistent, strongly held beliefs).

It was found that the charismatic, ideological, and mixed-type leaders could be distinguished from each other based on the frequency with which they expressed these behaviors. More specifically, ideological, charismatic, and mixed-type leaders were distinguished from each other by behaviors indicative of value commitment and value autonomy. Interestingly, the three leader types did not, however, differ on markers of performance—a finding suggesting that ideological leadership may prove as effective as charismatic leadership under certain conditions.

In another study examining this distinction between charismatic and ideo-logical leadership, Strange and Mumford (2005) examined the process of vision formation. In this study, undergraduates were asked to form a vision for a new experimental school under conditions where they were asked to (a) reflect or not reflect on prior personnel experience, (b) consider good and poor school models, and (c) analyze goals or causes. The quality and originality of the result-ing vision statements were evaluated by judges drawn from different "stake-holder" groups (e.g., parents, teachers, students). In accordance with the char-acterization of ideological and charismatic leaders, it was found that analysis of goals resulted in better vision statements when people were presented with poor models (an ideological strategy for vision formation) whereas analysis of causes resulted in better vision statements when people were presented with good models (a charismatic strategy for vision formation).

Pragmatic Leadership

Although ideological leadership apparently represents a form of outstanding leadership that can be distinguished from charismatic leadership, both these pathways to outstanding leadership involve articulation of a vision. The exis-tence of these two pathways to outstanding leadership, and their basis in vi-sion, however, begs a question: Is it possible to be an outstanding leader lack-ing vision?

One potential answer to this question may be found in a series of studies by Mumford and his colleagues (e.g., Connelly et al., 2000; Mumford, Marks, Connelly, Zaccaro, & Reiter-Palmon, 2000; Mumford, Zaccaro, Harding, et al., 2000). In these studies, measures of the skills needed to understand and solve problems in complex social systems were developed to assess judgment skills, creative processing skills, and system thinking skills. These measures were ad-ministered to 1,818 army officers at varying levels of seniority. It was found that high-performing senior officers typically evidenced better social judgment and system thinking skills along with a complex form of situated creative thought.

These findings, along with similar findings reported by Jacques (1976), led Mumford and Van Doorn (2001) to suggest that a third path to outstanding leadership might exist, which they referred to as pragmatic leadership. In Mumford and Van Doorn's view, pragmatic leadership does not require vision-ing although it may call for some related attributes such as communication skills. Instead, pragmatic leaders exert their influence through an in-depth un-derstanding of the social system at hand and the causal variables that shape sys-tem operations. Pragmatic leaders are skilled not only at identifying socially sig-nificant problems but also at devising actions that allow them to manipulate current situations in such a way as to bring about efficient practical solutions to significant system problems.

In an initial study intended to demonstrate the potential existence of this pragmatic type, Mumford and Van Doorn (2001) conducted a qualitative analysis of 10 incidents of outstanding leadership attributed to Benjamin Franklin (e.g., the founding of subscription libraries, the introduction of paper currency, and the development of the Albany Plan of Union). They found that Franklin's success in leading these ventures depended on an unusual sensitivity to significant social problems, exceptional skill at identifying the causes of these problems, and skill at marshaling the social and fiscal resources needed to leverage understanding into an effective problem solution. Furthermore, no broader vision appeared to underlie these efforts. In a study of Smith's tenure as CEO of General Motors, Hunt and Ropo (1995) reached a similar conclusion, finding that his success was largely attributable to skill at identifying and structuring solutions to critical system problems.

Socialized and Personalized Leaders

Outstanding leadership, whether charismatic, ideological, or pragmatic, does not ensure positive social outcomes. As Conger (1989) pointed out, in the pursuit of their vision, charismatic and ideological leaders may at times drive people and institutions to pursue dangerous, potentially destructive, actions simply through undue self-confidence and the narrowness of focus associated with their vision. A more pervasive, and more dangerous, characteristic of outstanding leadership, however, arises from the fact that outstanding leadership simply involves the exercise of influence—nothing is said about the direction of influence. In other words, outstanding leaders are a force—potentially a force for evil (witness Adolf Hitler) as well as a force for good (Beyer, 1999; Yukl, 1999).

To account for the direction of influence, and the impact of outstanding leaders on society, House and Howell (1992) drew a distinction between socialized and personalized leaders. Socialized leaders seek to enhance others and the broader social system by building capabilities in others that transcend the leader. Personalized leaders frame actions in terms of there own self-aggrandizement, seeking to enhance their power and control regardless of the costs to others and the broader social system.

In one study intended to assess the meaningfulness, or validity, of the distinction drawn between socialized leaders (e.g., Franklin Roosevelt) and personalized leaders (e.g., Adolf Hitler), O'Connor, Mumford, Clifton, Gessner, and Connelly (1995) obtained biographies for 80 historically notable 20th-century leaders. The "rise to power" chapters included in these biographies were content coded to assess the expression of characteristics, such as narcissism, fear, outcome uncertainty, power motives, object beliefs, and negative life themes, held to distinguish socialized and personalized leaders. An analysis of the "summary" chapters presented in these biographies was used to assess the outcomes of the leader's exercise of influence. Not only was it found that socialized and personalized leaders could be distinguished based on the leader's differential expression of these characteristics, it was found that leaders expressing personalized characteristics such as narcissism often had a negative impact on society.

In an extension of this study, Strange and Mumford (2002) found that the socialized-versus-personalized distinction could be applied to both ideological and charismatic leaders with similar negative social outcomes being observed for both personalized ideologues and personalized charismatics. However, personalized ideologues were most likely to manifest their destructive tendencies through behaviors linked to object beliefs whereas personalized charismatics were most likely to manifest their distinctive tendencies through behaviors linked to narcissistic manipulation. Though evidence is lacking, based on these findings, it does seem plausible to argue that this distinction between personalized and socialized leaders can also be applied to pragmatic leaders—a point attested to by comparing the careers of William Paley (socialized) and David Sarnoff (personalized) as leaders in the broadcasting industry.

Summary

Taken as a whole, it appears that one can plausibly argue that at least six distinct types of outstanding leaders might exist: (a) socialized charismatics, (b) personalized charismatics, (c) socialized ideologues, (d) personalized ideologues, (e) socialized pragmatics, and (f) personalized pragmatics. By the same token, however, evidence bearing on the ideological and pragmatic types that serves to clearly delineate how these leaders differ from charismatics is lacking. Our primary goal in the present effort was to provide such evidence focusing on key behaviors relevant to the behavior of people occupying upper-level leadership roles.

Before turning to the key behaviors characterizing charismatic, ideological, and pragmatic leaders, it may be useful to provide some concrete examples. Figures 1.1, 1.2, and 1.3 present biographical material bearing on a critical event occurring in the careers of a charismatic leader, Henry Ford, an ideological leader, W.E.B. DuBois, and a pragmatic leader, Thomas Watson Sr. (Note: The sources for the biographical material used in this and all other chapters are listed in the Appendix.)

The biographical material presented for Henry Ford examines his behavior when he took the landmark step of raising the wages of manufacturing workers to $5 a day—a huge increase in salary given the wages for factory work at the time. Note that the decision was not phrased in economic terms but rather, when proposing this vision, Ford referred to the broader conditions of workers' lives—a theme common in Ford's thoughts, even in his design of the Model T. This vision was phrased in emotionally evocative terms (e.g., "a generation of children undernourished and underdeveloped morally as well as physically") to bring about a radical change in employment conditions. As is common with charismatics, however, the focus is on this future-oriented vision. The pragmatic consequences of this vision, a stampede at the gate, were apparently of little interest to Ford.

Ford's behavior stands in stark contrast to the behavior of Thomas Watson Sr., a pragmatic leader, in dealing with a problem arising in his business. The problem of poor sales of punch cards is not addressed in emotional terms or with respect to a broader vision. Instead, Watson discussed the future in terms of product line and market growth, noting inherent limitations of one business

Henry Ford

Yet Ford was worried. For the first time in its ten-year life, the company could not hold onto workers. Rapid labor turnover retarded manufacture. Ford instructed John R. Lee, head of employment, to find out how other automotive companies coped with it. . . .

Examines characteristics of majority of followers

On Sunday, January 3, 1914, Ford convened a directors' meeting to discuss a better division of profits between stockholders, executives, customers, and labor. "Our workers are not sharing in our good fortune," he began. "There are thousands out there in the shop who are not living as they should. Their homes are crowded and unsanitary. Wives are going out to work because their husbands are unable to support the family. They fill up their homes with roomers and boarders in order to help swell their income. It's all wrong—all wrong. It's especially bad for the children. By underpaying men we are bringing on a generation of children undernourished and underdeveloped morally as well as physically." Everyone agreed the company could afford to raise the workers' pay. Ford walked to a blackboard he had in his office, and wrote out figures he had asked one of his executives to prepare: materials, overhead, and labor. They showed that as production rose, costs fell and profits went up. Transferring figures from the profits column to labor costs, he figured what $3.00 a day for each worker would cost the company (workers currently got $2.34 for a nine-hour day); then $3.50, $3.75, $4.25, $4.50, $4.75, and finally $5.00. Why not a five-dollar day? He asked. Most objected strenuously; to double wages in one stroke would ruin the company, they asserted. Ford suggested that everyone go home and think about it. On January 5 he called another directors' meeting. "The plan was gone over at considerable length," the minutes stated. Couzens, as enthusiastic about the idea as Ford, worked on dissenting directors until they acquiesced. Later that day Ford and Couzens summoned reporters from three Detroit newspapers, the *Free Press*, and *News*, and the *Journal*. Couzens did most of the talking. Beginning January 12, the Ford Motor Company would pay a minimum wage of five dollars a day, and would reduce that day from nine hours to eight, thereby converting the factory to a three shift day. The announcement, made in the middle of a national depression, hit the local newspapers late Tuesday afternoon. Within hours telegrams and cables from wire services and newspapers poured into Detroit from all over the world. By the morning of January 6, every daily newspaper in America and thousands of papers abroad carried the story.

Most papers were ecstatic. They pointed out that a new economic era had begun. Previously profit had based on payment of wages as low as a worker would take, and on pricing as high as the traffic would bear. Ford, on the other hand, practiced low pricing for the widest market and then met the price by volume and efficiency. The *Michigan Manufacturer and Financial Record* wrote that "it is the most generous stroke of policy between a captain of industry and worker" that the scheme had "all the advantages and none of the disadvantages of socialism."

The mere mention of socialism put dread in the hearts of Ford's fellow industrialists. The Employers Association of Detroit accused Ford of undermining the structure of the capitalist system. A Detroit socialite and heir to one of Michigan's lumber fortunes declared that the five-dollar day would permanently undermine the peace and contentment of the lower classes; by increasing wages, Ford created millions of dissatisfied workers who would breed revolution. Another prominent businessman predicted the newly affluent workers would drown themselves in dissolution, would fall prey to agitators, and would lose respect for work; pay a worker twice what he needed for a minimum existence, and he would show up for work only every other day. All local businessmen criticized Ford for not having consulted other employers before taking such a radical step.

Alvin Macauley, President of Packard Motor Car Company, telephoned Charles Sorenson, a top Ford executive, demanding, "What are you fellows trying to do? We got the news while we were having a board meeting. It was so astonishing that

Well-articulated, future-oriented vision that uses eloquence and focuses on follower

Uses emotionally persuasive vision to gain consensus

Uses imagery to order information

Generates ideas radically different from status quo

FIG. 1.1.   *(Continued)*

we broke up the meeting. We all felt, what is the use; we can't compete with an organization like the Ford Motor Company."

"Of course, Mr. Macauley," Sorenson replied, "you don't have to follow our example unless you want to. Perhaps you have an advantage over us if you don't pay as much wages as we do."

"That would be fine," Macauley responded, "but how are we going to avoid paying those wages once you start paying them here in Detroit? We are not running a philanthropic business like you."

"There is no philanthropy about it," the Ford executive answered. "If you will take the time to come and have a look at what we are doing, I'll explain it in a way that you will understand and not assume it is philanthropy."

Alvin Macauley was not alone in labeling the five-dollar day misplaced altruism; *The Wall Street Journal* called it blatant immorality—a misapplication of "Biblical principles" in a field "where they do not belong." Yet Ford always insisted that the five-dollar wage was pure business. He scoffed at his friend John Burroughs, the naturalist, who once called the five-dollar day a marvelous humanitarian gesture. Ford said it simply gave him the pick of the workers. Within less than a year it became evident that the new wage accounted for skyrocketing profits. The magic maneuver was simple, Ford declared. Keyed by higher wages, his men produced more efficiently and for less money per unit of work performed. Nevertheless, businessmen denounced Ford as a quack, a visionary, a glory-seeker.

[margin note: Examines strengths of idea in terms of how it will impact the future]

While everyone argued the pros and cons of the five-dollar day, hordes of the unemployed flocked to Highland Park's hiring office on Manchester Street. The first day after the announcement 10,000 came. The next day, despite public notices that there were no more jobs available, 15,000 crowded the streets surrounding the huge factory . . .

The next day under the headline, "Icy Fire-Hose Deluge Stops Twelve Thousand in Riotous Push for Ford's Jobs," the *Journal* described the scene in these words: "Three thousand men were soaked, it is estimated. With the temperature hovering close to the zero mark and a biting blast coming across the field from the northwest, they were as unenviable lot as they hurried away to find some place to thaw out. Their clothes froze the moment after they encountered the business end of the hose." Police Chief Seymour of Highland Park defended his method of dealing with the near-riot by blaming Ford management for making such a dramatic disclosure without devising some way to control the inevitable stampede.

[margin note: Does not plan for macrolevel issues that are not vision focused]

FIG. 1.1. Illustration of charismatic-leader behavior. From *Henry Ford: The Wayward Capitalist,* by C. Gelderman (1981, pp. 52–55). New York: Dial Press.

line. Rational persuasion is used to build support for this shift in business strategy—arguments build up based on careful analyses of the business, the technology, and the market.

Watson's dispassionate arguments, however, were not in any way similar to the behavior of W.E.B. DuBois, an ideological leader in founding the Niagara Movement. In founding this movement, DuBois clearly articulated an emotionally evocative vision. This vision, however, was ultimately rooted in the wrongs of the past, the pragmatic accommodation of Booker T. Washington, and the need to restore the sense of Black dignity and equality that had been lost with the imposition of segregation. Support for this vision, however, was not built upon the image of a better future but rather upon the shared values and shared concerns of Black professionals. It was through like-minded Black professionals that DuBois exercised his influence.

These case examples are noteworthy for two reasons. First, they provide some tangible support for the distinctions we have drawn among charismatic, ideological, and pragmatic leaders. Second, they indicate that charismatic, ideological, and pragmatic leaders do, in fact, evidence marked differences in their behavior across a range of domains held to represent critical aspects of

W.E.B. DuBois

From 1903 until 1910, DuBois took some time from his duties at the university to devote himself to his new program of direct agitation. As professor of sociology, he continued to train part of the Talented Tenth and to issue sociological reports. But as spokesman for the "radical" wing of the Negro race, he took on new responsibilities.

Searches for others who share values

To mobilize articulate Negroes ready to fight for their rights, DuBois in 1905 sent out a summons for the first convention of what became known as the Niagara Movement. Several of Dubois's "radical" associates had for some time been urging him to organize a national committee of Negroes representing their views. Two of them, F. L. McGhee and C. C. Bentley, drew up a plan for the new group: a nation-wide organization with committees assigned to definite Negro problems, local organizations of militant Negroes, and an annual convention to plan and to generate enthusiasm. In response to DuBois's appeal, twenty-nine professional men from thirteen states and the District of Colombia met at Niagara Falls, Ontario. These were to be the nucleus of the "very best class of Negro Americans." For Dubois, the movement's executive officer, the Niagara Movement was to serve two functions: in the white world, its annual manifestoes would periodically call attention to the Negro's complaint; among Negroes, the movement would whip up indignation against the injustices of white America. Both purposes hinged on Booker T. Washington: the steady barrage of protest would contradict his soothing assurances to the whites, and the movement would offer dissident Negroes a medium for opposition to him.

Shares direction of group with key lieutenants

Identifies violations of standards or morals

Vision is emotionally persuasive

A "Declaration of Principles," largely written by Trotter and Dubois, was dramatically "submitted to the American people, and Almighty God" after the first convention. It indicated the broad sweep of the Negro "radical" protest with which DuBois now associated himself. Demands for suffrage and civil rights headed the list, followed by complaints against "peonage and virtual slavery" in the rural South and against the prejudice "helped often by iniquitous laws" that created difficulties in earning a decent living. Two classes of men deserved public excoriation, it said: employers who imported ignorant Negro American laborers in emergencies, and then afforded them "neither protection nor permanent employment" (an elaborate circumlocution for "strike breakers"); and labor unions which excluded "their fellow toilers, simply because they are black." Free and compulsory education through the high-school level was set as a universal minimum, and college training, instead of being the "monopoly" of any class or race, should, the statement continued, be open to talent. Trade schools and higher education were both listed as essential. In the courts the Negro wanted upright judges, juries selected without reference to color, and equal treatment both in punishment and in efforts at reformation. Some of Dubois's old complaints appeared: "We need orphanages and farm schools for dependent children, juvenile reformatories for delinquents, and the abolition of the dehumanizing convict-lease system." Any discrimination along the color line was said to be a relic of "unreasoning human savagery of which the world is and ought to be thoroughly ashamed." The Niagara group expressed astonishment at the increase of prejudice in the Christian church, and labeled the third-class accommodations of Jim Crow cars as an attempt "to crucify wantonly our manhood, womanhood, and self-respect." They pleaded for health—the opportunity to live in decent localities with a chance to raise children in "physical and moral cleanliness."

Vision based on key aspects that all potential followers share

Scans environment for dissenting ideas or violators of solution

Vision focus is on personal needs of followers

Defines problems using black-and-white standards of right and wrong

To right the wrongs, the small band urged national aid to education, especially in the South, a return to the "faith of the fathers," and legislation to secure power enforcement of the War Amendments. Rejecting the "cowardice and apology" of the current Negro leadership, it called for "persistent manly agitation" as the road to liberty, for "to ignore, overlook, or apologize for these wrongs is to prove ourselves unworthy of freedom." To accomplish its ends, the Niagara group appealed for the cooperation of men of all races.

Generates ideas that evoke strong affective responses

The past decade, the Niagara band said, had shown "undoubted evidences of progress": the increase in intelligence and in the ownership of property, the decrease in crime, the uplift in home life, the advance in literature and art, and the demonstration of executive ability in religious, economic, and educational institutions. However, in the face of the "evident retrogression of public opinion on human brotherhood," only loud and insistent complaint could hold America to its professed ideals.

FIG. 1.2. Illustration of ideological-leader behavior. From *W.E.B. DuBois: Negro Leader in a Time of Crisis*, by F. L. Broderick (1959, pp. 75–77). Copyright © 1959 by the Board of Trustees of the Leland Stanford Jr. University, renewed 1987 by the author. Used with the permission of Stanford University Press.

14

Thomas Watson, Sr.

Watson didn't dream up only big concepts for punch card machines; he paid attention to surprisingly minute aspects. From the reports of servicemen in the field, Watson noticed that punch card machines tended to break down more in damp weather. He encouraged the engineers to come up with a heating lamp that could be fitted inside a machine, so the lamp could keep parts dry. Whether the engineers thought this was the best solution, they carried it out.

Punch card machines—how to improve them, how to apply them, and how to sell more of them—ate up an increasing share of Watson's time. What occupied Watson would occupy the rest of the company. He appropriated more executive time, more engineering manpower, and more money to punch card machines. In 1924, Bryce sent Watson a two-page engineering report. The first page-and-a-half detailed new punch card machine products and improvements. By contrast, about one-third of a page was devoted to Time Recording developments. The scale division got two sentences. A laboratory report a few years later showed IBM spending, in six months, $83,411 on developing tabulating machine products, $13,393 on scales, and $9,850 on time clocks.

On Monday, October 17, 1927, Watson called a meeting in the IBM boardroom. Braitmayer, Bryce, and Nichol took seats, as did 12 other executives from the top levels of the company. Watson, looking older, his hair nearly white, the skin on his cheekbones beginning to sag, began the session by stating: "The object of this meeting is to talk about the future."

He made his leanings clear. The scale division got nothing but his disgust. "There is absolutely no common sense in this scale business going along and making no money."

The Time Recording division was well managed and making a profit, but the potential for growth seemed limited. IBM's marketers couldn't find many new ways to apply time clocks, and engineers could improve the products only incrementally. Time Recording's managers ran a steady, decent business, but it was not explosive. "The time clock business is a little harder problem than anything else," Watson told the men, sounding apologetic about the static nature of what was once the centerpiece of C-T-R. "There isn't very much there we can give the men in the way of anything new."

Watson then pointed to where he wanted IBM to go. "There isn't any limit for the tabulating business for many years to come," he said. "We have just scratched the surface in this division. I expect the bulk of [increased business] to come from the tabulating end, because the potentialities are greater, and we have done so little in the way of developing our machines in this field."

Underneath that statement lay a number of reasons—other than the thrill of new technology—why Watson zeroed in on the punch card business. When seen together, the reasons click like a formula for total domination. IBM would never be able to make sure it was the world leader in scales or time clocks, but it would make certain that it was the absolute lord of data processing.

The formula began with the patents. Watson had learned the value of patents while at NCR and from Kettering. Inventions would drive sales, and patents could keep competitors at bay by preventing them from introducing similar inventions. It's a formula in full boil in the technology industry of the 2000s. From the beginning at C-T-R, Watson was aware of the value of the patents that Hollerith held. Bryce later pushed Watson to become aggressive about patents. Bryce's lab generated many of IBM's patents; Watson acquired more by buying upstart competitors. For instance, IBM bought J. Royden Peirce's fledgling punch card machine company to get Peirce's patents—and to get Peirce, who would go on to win more patents as an IBM engineer. Controlling the key patents on tabulating systems helped make life difficult for the competition because competitors would have to invent entirely new technology or license IBM's patents, which IBM could refuse to do.

Another ingredient in the formula was the punch card. The rectangular pieces of thin cardboard, seven and three-eighths by three and one-quarter inches, were the data storage devices for tabulating machines—the equivalent of a hard drive on a twenty-first-century computer. By the late 1920's, IBM had embraced Clair Lake's new and patentable card design . . . To fit all 960 spaces on card, Lake made the holes narrow and rectangular, instead of round, as they were previously.

Lake's new IBM cards only worked on IBM machines. IBM offered a reproducing device that transferred information on old punched cards to the new versions. Once an IBM customer put all of its old information on IBM's proprietary cards, and stored more and more of its new information on those cards, the customer became locked in. Switching to a competing data processing company would require transferring the information on millions of cards to that company's cards. Some insurance companies, for instance, literally had entire floors devoted to the storage of punched cards. The cost of transferring all those cards would have been prohibitive; so the cards coerced IBM customers to remain IBM customers.

FIG. 1.3. Illustration of pragmatic-leader behavior. From *The Maverick and His Machine*, by K. Maney (2003, pp. 98–100). Copyright © 2003 by Wiley. Reprinted with permission of John Wiley & Sons, Inc.

leader behavior including problem solving, communication, and leader–follower interactions.

BEHAVIORS

To establish the existence of these types it is necessary to show that they evidence differences, substantially meaningful differences, with respect to the expression of relevant behaviors. In fact, given the complexity of the information presented in leader biographies, it becomes essential to examine differences among types using a priori dimensions derived from theoretical taxonomies examining behavioral domains critical to outstanding leadership (Fleishman & Quaintance, 1984; Mumford, Stokes, & Owens, 1990). In this section, we examine the behavioral domains, and dimensions of behavior within these domains, that might be used to validate the distinctions we have drawn between charismatic, ideological, and pragmatic leaders.

With regard to the specification of these behavioral domains, however, a critical methodological point must be considered. Regardless of their orientation, socialized or personalized, charismatic, ideological, and pragmatic leaders are successful, in fact unusually successful, leaders. As a result, one would not necessarily expect these three types of outstanding leaders to differ with respect to the behaviors commonly used to distinguish leaders and nonleaders. For example, intelligence, extraversion, and social skills are attributes of leaders in general (Bass, 1990; Zaccaro et al., 1991). Therefore, these dimensions are unlikely to have much value in describing different types of outstanding leaders.

These observations, of course, pose a question—indeed a question critical to the present study: What types of behaviors, or behavioral domains, are likely to prove useful in describing the similarities and differences among charismatic, ideological, and pragmatic leaders? One strategy for identifying these domains is to focus on the kind of behaviors likely to be important to the exercise of outstanding leadership. In the present effort, we examine the similarities and differences among charismatic, ideological, and pragmatic leaders with respect to five domains: (a) performance, (b) creative problem solving, (c) leader–follower interactions, (d) political tactics, and (e) communication strategies.

Performance

Performance is perhaps the most intuitively attractive basis for distinguishing among different types of outstanding leaders. In this regard, however, it is important to recognize that outstanding leaders, be they charismatic, ideological, or pragmatic leaders, will, as outstanding leaders, display good performance on standard indices of leader effectiveness—indices such as follower motivation, clarification of paths to goal attainment, and interpersonal reactions to the leader (Yukl, 2002). It is possible, however, that charismatic, ideological, and pragmatic leaders will differ on performance indices tailored to the unique nature of outstanding leadership. Thus, Strange and Mumford (2002), in contrasting charismatic and ideological leaders, assessed performance in terms of social outcomes such as the number of institutions established and the leader's long-term contributions to society.

Although these macrolevel impact markers provide a plausible basis for assessing performance differences among outstanding leaders, it is open to question whether performance differences will consistently be observed in comparing charismatic, ideological, and pragmatic leaders. In their comparison of charismatic and ideological leaders, Strange and Mumford (2002) did not observe marked differences in performance on social-impact criteria. Mumford and Van Doorn (2001), in their study of Benjamin Franklin's contributions, did obtain some evidence suggesting that pragmatic, as opposed to charismatic and ideological leaders, might display better performance on the social-impact measures. Given the method applied in the Mumford and Van Doorn study, however, this observation, at best, provides only initial tentative evidence bearing on potential performance differences. Clearly, this finding should be replicated in a larger sample where explicit comparisons of multiple pragmatic, ideological, and charismatic leaders have been made with respect to multiple markers of social outcomes.

Attempts to contrast the performance of charismatic, ideological, and pragmatic leaders are complicated by a broader pattern of findings. Prior studies of outstanding leadership by O'Connor et al. (1995) and Strange and Mumford (2002) indicated that most variation in historic-outcome markers of performance was accounted for by House and Howell's (1992) distinction between socialized and personalized leadership. These findings are of some importance not only because they suggest that integrity, as reflected in the socialized-versus-personalized distinction, is a critical aspect of performance for outstanding leaders, but also because they suggest that attempts to examine cross-type performance differences must take this distinction into account.

Creative Problem Solving

All leaders, due to the unique nature of leadership roles, must make decisions—decisions that require solving problems bearing on task performance and group maintenance (Hackman & Walton, 1986; Mumford, Zaccaro, Harding, et al., 2000). As leaders move into the kind of roles where outstanding leadership is possible, the nature of the problems that are posed changes. One set of changes involves an extension of the time frame over which problems, and their solutions, unfold (Jacobs & Jaques, 1991; Jacques, 1976). Another set of changes, however, involves the nature of the problems that leaders must address. In upper-level leadership roles, the type of roles where outstanding leadership occurs, problems become more complex and more ill-defined or poorly structured.

Moreover, a greater value is placed on the generation of novel, or original, solutions to these problems. These characteristics of the problems encountered in upper-level leadership roles indicate that outstanding leaders will be confronted with problems calling for creative thought (Lubart, 2001; Mumford & Gustafson, 1988; Mumford, Strange, Scott, & Gaddis, 2004; Sternberg, Kaufman, & Pretz, 2003).

Although creative thought is a complex phenomenon involving both motivation and expertise, studies of creativity stress the importance of information-processing activities (Runco, 2003). In a review of prior studies intended to describe the key cognitive processes involved in creative thought (e.g., Amabile, 1988; Finke, Ward, & Smith, 1992; Merrifield, Guilford, Christensen, & Frick, 1962; Sternberg, 1988a), Mumford and his colleagues (Mumford, Mobley, Uhlman, Reiter-Palmon, & Doares, 1991; Mumford, Peterson, & Childs, 1999) identified eight core processes commonly used in creative problem solving: (a) problem identification, (b) information gathering, (c) concept selection, (d) conceptual combination, (e) idea generation, (f) idea evaluation, (g) implementation planning, and (h) solution monitoring.

Although these processes are commonly involved, in one way or another, in most creative problem-solving efforts, different solutions may arise in a number of ways. People may define the problem differently and they may emphasize different skills, or processes, in their approach to problems. Observations of this sort led Perkins (1992) to argue that different stylistic approaches may emerge in creative problem-solving efforts. In fact, there is reason to suspect that outstanding leaders display kinds of stylistic differences in this regard whereas information search and idea generation appear to play a critical role in creative problem solving among pragmatic leaders (Mumford, 2002). For example, problem identification and idea generation appear to play a critical role in creative problem solving among charismatic leaders (Jenkins, 2001). Given these observations, it seems plausible to argue that creative problem-solving processes represent one set of attributes that might be used to distinguish charismatic, ideological, and pragmatic leaders.

Leader–Follower Interactions

All leaders have followers. However, in the case of lower-level leaders, for example, a first-line supervisor in a manufacturing facility, followers are assigned to the leader. These followers, vis-à-vis sharp power differentials and normative constraints, typically have a rather circumscribed relationship with their leader. In contrast, in upper-level leadership roles, the leadership roles occupied by outstanding leaders, leader–follower relationships are far less circumscribed. The followers of outstanding leaders are, in fact, often notable leaders in their own right—consider the relationship between Dwight Eisenhower and George Marshall. Leader–follower relations at this level are not structural givens but must be actively constructed through the interactions of the parties involved in a reciprocal exchange. These observations, in turn, suggest that a form of leader–member exchange (LMX) might have value in describing the similarities and differences among charismatic, ideological, and pragmatic leaders.

A number of scholars have examined how leaders create effective exchange relationships with followers (Yukl, 2002). The key proposition underlying most models of LMX is that leaders create a unique exchange relationship with each individual follower (Dansereau, Graen, & Haga, 1975; Graen & Uhl-Bien, 1998). Variation in the nature and quality of these relationships (positive vs. negative grammar relationships) has been shown to be related to both group and follower performance (Liden, Sparrowe, & Wayne, 1997; Schreisheim, Castro, & Cogliser, 1999). Given these performance outcomes, it seems reasonable to ask what behaviors characterize positive exchange relationships. The findings obtained in studies examining the quality of exchange relationships indicate that positive exchange relationships depend on mutual respect for capabilities, trust, and shared commitments (Graen & Uhl-Bien, 1998). However, other dimensions such as investment in the relationship may also be required for positive exchange relationships (Yukl, 2002).

In the case of outstanding leadership, by virtue of the issues at hand, and the positions of followers, a number of other dimensions might be used to characterize the quality of exchange relationships. For example, positive exchange relationships may be reflected in support for the follower's organization or the leader's willingness to publicly support the follower during periods of conflict and controversy. Moreover, there is reason to suspect that the dimensions characterizing exchange relationships will differ across the three types of outstanding leaders. For example, in the case of ideological leaders, shared commitment may be a particularly important influence on the quality of exchange relationships, whereas in the case of pragmatic leaders, respect for capabilities may be a particularly important influence on the quality of exchange relationships.

Political Tactics

Leadership, of course, is not simply a matter of establishing relationships; it also involves the exercise of influence. Although the exercise of influence is required in all leadership roles, the ways in which influence is exercised may vary across roles. In upper-level leadership roles, the leader is required to interact with groups or institutions external to the organization where the action of these groups or institutions might influence organizational performance (Mintzberg, 1979). Moreover, in upper-level leadership roles, leaders are confronted with multiple competing groups within the organization where they somehow must bring about coordinated action on the part of the parties involved. These observations about cross-organizational coordination and within-organization integration have an important, albeit commonly overlooked, implication. Outstanding leadership is likely to involve political behavior.

Although in the popular mind political behavior is held to be a part, a critical part, of outstanding leadership, surprisingly few discussions of political behavior have appeared in the literature (Ferris, Adams, Kolodinsky, Hochwarter, & Ammeter, 2002). In recent years, however, we have seen a new interest in political behavior in general and leader political behavior in particular (Ammeter, Douglas, Gardner, Hochwarter, & Ferris, 2002). Some political behavior on the part of leaders, particularly personalized behaviors such as self-promotion and "going along to get ahead" (Kacmar & Ferris, 1991), appear to have a negative impact on leader effectiveness and group performance. Often more socialized forms of political behavior, such as consensus building and strategy definition, however, appear not only necessary but potentially beneficial (Yukl, 2002).

Not only can socialized and personalized leaders be expected to differ with respect to characteristic political behavior, one might expect to see differences in the political tactics employed by charismatic, ideological, and pragmatic leaders. For example, in Mumford and Van Doorn's (2001) study of Benjamin Franklin it was found that selective presentation of information, structuring of situations, and demonstration of economic gains were common political tactics used by one pragmatic leader. Charismatic and ideological leaders, however, appear to rely on other tactics such as emotional arousal and affective symbols.

Communication Strategies

Political behavior, of course, often involves communication and persuasion. In fact, all models of outstanding leadership agree on this one basic point. Outstanding leaders, regardless of type, tend to be unusually skilled at the art of communication (Bass, 1985, 1990). Outstanding leaders are people who, through their communications, can change other attitudes, create understanding, and engage others in the projects being advocated by the leader. What is perhaps most remarkable about outstanding leaders is that their mass communications, for example, speeches and interviews, can have a marked impact on people's behavior. In fact, we may not know much about leaders but we remember their words. Even a decade later, Ronald Reagan is remembered for his use of the phrase "evil empire" when describing the Cold War conflict between the United States and Russia. Martin Luther King, half a century later, is still remembered for his "I have a dream" speech.

Though outstanding leaders all tend to be unusually effective communicators, communication is, in its own right, a highly complex phenomenon. Communication may differ along dimension of style (e.g., articulation of positive vs. negative affect, personalization vs. objectification of issues) and content (e.g., economic arguments, social arguments). What should be noted here, however, is that charismatic, ideological, and pragmatic leaders may differ in the style and content of their communications. Thus, Mumford and Van Doorn (2001) found that pragmatic leaders relied on objective information and economic arguments. Charismatic and ideological leaders, however, typically seem to rely on a more emotionally evocative style, often emphasizing personal and social implications of events (Deluga, 2001).

Summary

These observations about behavior are noteworthy because they indicate that at least five domains exist where one might expect to see noteworthy differences in the characteristic behavior of charismatic, ideological, and pragmatic leaders. These domains, all domains that appear critical to outstanding leadership given the requirements imposed by upper-level leadership roles, include: (a) performance, (b) creative problem solving, (c) leader–follower interactions, (d) political tactics, and (e) communication strategies. In the present effort, taxonomies describing the key dimensions, or kinds of behavior, falling into each of these five domains are developed. The dimensions included in these taxonomies, vis-à-vis assessment of biographical data, are used to conduct a comparative analysis of charismatic, ideological, and pragmatic leaders.

DEVELOPMENT

If the expected differences in behavior emerge in our comparison of charismatic, ideological, and pragmatic leaders, then some noteworthy evidence will have been accrued pointing to the existence of alternative pathways to outstanding leadership. The existence of these distinct pathways, however, broaches two more questions: How do the careers of charismatic, ideological, and pragmatic leaders unfold over time? And, what leads people to pursue one pathway as opposed to another? Both of these questions, questions critical to understanding the implications of the distinction we have drawn between charismatic, ideological, and pragmatic leaders, are, at their core, questions bearing on the development of outstanding leadership.

Although there is a need to understand how the careers of outstanding leaders unfold over time, development has not been a major focus in studies of outstanding leadership. A notable exception to this rule of thumb may be found in Erikson (1959). Erikson examined the development of one outstanding leader: Martin Luther, the founder of the Protestant movement. In a qualitative analysis of historic material, Erikson found that even early in his life Luther evidenced a profound spirituality—a spirituality that served as a vehicle for the resolution of personal turmoil. Luther's conflicts, however, were seen, at least in Erikson's analysis, as a reflection of the society in which Luther was living, a society that was moving from the medieval to the modern period, and his early experiences as the child of a family at the cusp of this change. Luther's personal resolution of this conflict provided the basis for his charismatic vision.

Developmental Change

The role of crisis in shaping the emergence of charismatic leaders has received some attention in the literature (Hunt et al., 1999; Strange & Mumford, 2002). Less attention has been given to the kind of changes likely to be observed in leader behavior as roles change and experience grows over the course of a career. In a rare investigation along these lines, Mumford, Marks, et al. (2000) contrasted army officers in junior, midlevel, and more senior leadership roles to identify changes in leader skills and the experiences contributing to change in these skills. They found that as leaders moved into more senior positions, growth was observed in certain creative problem-solving skills. Specifically, growth was observed in those creative problem-solving skills that involved contextual appraisal of ideas with respect to broader system requirements. The growth of these skills, moreover, appeared to be linked to exposure to novel problems, responsibility for complex system problems, and the growth of tacit knowledge.

The Mumford, Marks, et al. (2000) study illustrates one approach to the study of leader development—how changes in behavior over time, as a function of change in roles and experience, are used to draw inferences about development. In fact, one might expect to see similar patterns of growth and change as outstanding leaders move through their careers. Thus Strange and Mumford (2002) found that ideological and charismatic behaviors shifted as a function of the career point being examined in biographical material (e.g., "rise to power" vs. "pinnacle of power"). Value articulation and credentialing proved important to outstanding leaders, both ideological and charismatic leaders, early, but not later, in their careers.

In this regard, however, it is important to bear in mind a final point. Some patterns of developmental change may characterize outstanding leaders in general. Other patterns of developmental change, however, may be specific to the particular type of leader, charismatic, ideological, and pragmatic, under consideration. For example, charismatic leaders may, as a function of experience, show more growth and change in communication skills than pragmatics for the simple reason that effective communication of vision is critical to the success of charismatic leaders. Some evidence pointing to the potential existence of these type-specific patterns of change and growth has been provided by Mumford, Zaccaro, Johnson, et al. (2000).

Developmental Direction

One way to study development is to look for changes in behavior at different points in leaders' careers. Another way one might study development is to examine the early environmental events that start outstanding leaders moving along a particular developmental path (Mumford, Wesley, & Shaffer, 1987). In fact, Erikson (1959) in his study of Luther stressed the importance of these formative, or crystallizing, events—events that shape the path leaders take through life. A similar point was made by Mumford and Manley (2003), who argued that leaders understand their world, and act on their world, by reference to select life events that provide touchstones for appraisal of the self and others.

The life events that people use to understand their world, however, are not isolated entities. Instead, people appear to organize these events into an autobiographical narrative or life story (Habermas, 2001; Habermas & Bluck, 2000; McAdams, 2001; Oyserman & Markus, 1990; Singer & Bluck, 2001). This autobiographical narrative or life story not only is used to understand prior events but acts as a plan. The plan embedded in this narrative is used to frame future actions, forecast the consequences of action in new situations, and guide the selection of alternative actions (Nelson, Plesa, & Henseler, 1998). As a result, the life stories people create based on their experiences shape the direction of development and the paths pursued through life. Presumably, similar phenomena shape the paths pursued by charismatic, ideological, and pragmatic leaders.

These autobiographical narratives, or life stories, appear to be built around select types of events that serve to define the content and structure of the narrative (Pillemer, 2001). The keystone events used to define these narratives include: (a) originating events (events tied to the definition of long-term goals and action plans), (b) anchoring events (events that illustrate fundamental beliefs and values), (c) turning point events (events leading to noteworthy modifications in goals and plans), (d) analogous events (events used as preferred case models for behavior in different situations), (e) redemptive events (apparently negative events with positive downstream consequences), and (f) contaminating events (apparently positive events with negative consequences).

One intriguing implication of these event types is that charismatic, ideological, and pragmatic leaders may build the narratives they apply around different kinds of events. For example, anchoring events may be particularly important in shaping the careers of ideological leaders whereas originating events may be particularly important in shaping the careers of pragmatic leaders. Charismatic, ideological, and pragmatic leaders, however, may not only differ with respect to the emphasis placed on certain kinds of events in narrative formation, they may also differ with respect to the typical content of these events. Thus, spiritual and enculturation experiences may loom large in the anchoring events that shape the careers of ideological leaders whereas achievement and growth experiences may loom large in the anchoring events that shape the careers of charismatic leaders.

Summary

In addition to establishing the differences observed between charismatic, ideological, and pragmatic leaders in various behavioral domains critical to outstanding leadership, there is a need to understand the origins of these pathways to outstanding leadership and how the behaviors of charismatic, ideological, and pragmatic leaders change over time. In this book, we examine the development of charismatic, ideological, and pragmatic leaders through two approaches. In the first approach, we look at changes observed in leader behavior, for example, creative problem solving and political tactics, as leaders move through the "rise to power," "pinnacle of power," and "fall from power" career periods. In the second approach, we examine the kind of early life events that start leaders moving along a charismatic, ideological, or pragmatic path.

ORGANIZATION

This book, a book examining the nature and development of charismatic, ideological, and pragmatic leaders, is organized in three parts. In the first part, we describe the general approach applied in this investigation of outstanding leadership. The first chapter in Part I presents a general theoretical model, a model based on characteristic mental models and sensemaking activities, that can be used to account for the behavior and development of charismatic, ideological, and pragmatic leaders. The second chapter in Part I presents the general method used to test this model. Not only does this chapter consider the historiometric method in general, it examines how this method applied in the present study considering issues such as the selection of leaders, the selection of biographies, content-coding methods, and control studies.

Part II of this book focuses on the behaviors characterizing charismatic, ideological, and pragmatic leaders and changes in these behaviors as leaders move through their careers. This part contains five chapters examining performance, creative problem solving, leader–follower interactions, political tactics, and communication strategies. In each of these chapters, we begin with a section considering "study"-specific methods and development of the behavioral dimensions and content-coding scheme that were used to contrast charismatic, ideological, and pragmatic leaders. Subsequently, the results obtained in this comparison are presented and their implications for studies of outstanding leadership, specifically the charismatic, ideological, and pragmatic pathways, are discussed.

The third part of this book begins with an examination of the life events shaping the careers of charismatic, ideological, and pragmatic leaders. In Part III, we consider differences across leader types in the nature and content of relevant life events observed during the leader's early life. The next chapter in Part III also focuses on development, examining how differences in life events are related to the leader's later behavior. The final chapter presents the overall conclusions flowing from the present effort. The findings obtained with respect to the model of outstanding leadership presented and the distinction drawn between charismatic, ideological, and pragmatic leaders are discussed. We also consider certain limitations of the present study and potential directions for future research.

2

Theory—Charismatic, Ideological, and Pragmatic Leaders: How Do They Lead, Why Do They Lead, and Who Do They Lead?

Michael D. Mumford
Ginamarie Scott
Samuel T. Hunter
The University of Oklahoma

Theories of outstanding leadership, and indeed there are many, have typically been built around one crucial issue. How do outstanding leaders evidence such large effects on followers? Thus, Shamir et al. (1993) stressed the role of vision in providing a vehicle of expression of followers' feelings, values, and self-concepts. In Bass' (1997) model, outstanding leaders exercise influence through a set of behaviors that contribute to motivational and intellectual engagement on a set of tasks.

We do not wish to dispute these, and the other available models of outstanding leadership, which attempt to understand outstanding leadership in terms of motivation and influence. Undoubtedly, the mechanisms through which outstanding leaders exercise influence to induce follower motivation must be considered in any discussion of outstanding leadership. Indeed, we return to this topic later on in this chapter. One must, however, recognize that influence and motivation provide only one framework that might be used to understand outstanding leadership. For example, one might attempt to understand it in terms of follower attributions and the willingness of followers to respond to influence attempts (Den Hartog, House, & Hanges, 1999). Alternatively, one might seek to understand it in terms of the effects leaders have on follower beliefs about themselves and their world (Shamir & Howell, 1999). Still another approach involves understanding the conditions that give rise to a need for outstanding leadership (Hunt et al., 1999).

Though all of these models have value, substantial value, in understanding the nature and origins of outstanding leadership, they do not directly address two critical questions—questions fundamental to the present effort: Why are there multiple alternative pathways to outstanding leadership? And, why do charismatic, ideological, and pragmatic leadership represent frequently traveled paths to outstanding leadership?

In this chapter, we argue that the origins of the charismatic, ideological, and pragmatic leadership result from the conceptual system people apply to make sense of the crisis commonly associated with the emergence of outstanding leaders. We argue, furthermore, that these conceptual systems display a complex pattern of differences—differences in time frame, assumptions about causation, and reference models, which give rise to the pathways we have labeled charismatic, ideological, and pragmatic leadership. After presenting this theory of leader types, we consider how these conceptual frameworks shape the exercise of influence and set boundary conditions on the emergence and likely effectiveness of charismatic, ideological, and pragmatic leaders. Additionally, the implications of this model for understanding the origins of charismatic, ideological, and pragmatic leaders are considered along with its implications for the differences likely to be observed between charismatic, ideological, and pragmatic leaders with respect to performance, creative problem solving, leader–follower relationships, political tactics, and communication strategies.

MODEL

Crises

Although leadership scholars differ in the theories they use to understand outstanding leadership, there are certain facts about outstanding leadership that are not contested. One of these core observations holds that outstanding leaders emerge when social systems are experiencing a crisis (Rivera, 1994). In one study along these lines, Strange and Mumford (2002), in a historiometric study of 60 notable 20th-century leaders, contrasted the behaviors and experiences characterizing outstanding leaders early in their careers, during their "rise to power," and later in their careers, when they were at their "pinnacle of power." They found that crises played an important role in the emergence of outstanding leaders—both charismatic and ideological leaders.

Evidence pointing to the importance of crisis in the emergence of outstanding leaders is not limited to historiometric studies. For example, Hunt et al. (1999) had groups of students work on a task involving the actions to be taken to improve a university's ranking. Crises were created as the groups worked on this task under conditions where confederate leaders executed scripts involving the expression of charismatic, visionary, exchange, and expressive leadership behavior. It was found that visionary and charismatic leaders were perceived more favorably in crisis as opposed to the no-crisis condition.

Although there seems good reason to believe that outstanding leaders emerge under crisis conditions, these findings broach a critical substantive question: Why are crises associated with the emergence of an outstanding leader? To begin answering this question, one must consider exactly what is meant by the term *crisis*.

We tend to think of a crisis as a single precipitating event, typically an event associated with extreme outcomes (Jick & Murray, 1982). Whereas our common use of the term crisis stresses episodic high-risk events, in studies of leadership, the term crisis often carries a broader connotation. It refers not just to a single precipitating event, but instead to a set of events creating turbulence in organizations, institutions, or social systems where this turbulence places the organization at risk due to suboptimal performance and the loss of stakeholder support. In other words, crises are events, typically negative change events, that threaten the existence and effective functioning of certain social institutions. Thus we speak of the crisis of the Civil War—a crisis associated with the unresolved conflict over slavery in the United States, or the crisis of the Great Depression—a crisis involving reexamination of the social contract in the age of capitalism.

When one considers this definition of the term crisis, it becomes apparent why outstanding leaders emerge in times of crisis. Turbulence and change disrupt the ways in which people understand their world, making it unclear how people should act. Not only is it unclear what should be done, confusion will surround crises based on the differing positions of different stakeholders. Moreover, in this confusion and conflict, the stakes are high for individuals, groups, and institutions. Under these conditions, there is a need for an individual, a leader, who can define, and gain acceptance for, a strategy for dealing with the crisis event. The subsequent successful execution of this strategy, in turn, gives rise to attributions of outstanding leadership.

Though it seems reasonably clear why outstanding leaders emerge during times of crisis, it is less clear exactly what leaders do in resolving crises. This ambiguity about requisite leadership activities is underscored by the point that leaders may not always have a "hands-on" role in solving the problems posed by a crisis—at times, in fact, the leader may be a rather distant figure (Mumford & Van Doorn, 2001). Some important clues about what leaders must do in guiding responses to crises may be found in a series of studies by Drazin, Glynn, and Kazanjian (1999) and Kazanjian, Drazin, and Glynn (2000). In an in-depth qualitative study of a large-scale, long-term, technical development effort the design of a new aircraft, they found that crises emerged frequently and that resolution of these crises was a critical aspect of leader performance. The role of the leader in crises resolution, however, involved sensemaking activities. These sensemaking activities involved anticipating the origins of the crisis, identification of the causes of the crisis, and analysis of the actions to be taken vis-à-vis these causes to resolve the crisis. In others words, leader sensemaking provides followers with a framework, or strategy, for crisis resolution.

What should be recognized here, however, is that the kinds of crises confronting outstanding leaders are highly complex. Under conditions of change, it may not be clear exactly what the problem is or what the origins of the crisis were. Moreover, with multiple causes multiple parties will in one way or another be involved. This uncertainty is noteworthy because it suggests that crises are highly ambiguous events. This ambiguity in crisis definition allows for multiple alternative ways of making sense of the situation at hand. In other words, crises may be interpreted or construed in different ways—a phenomenon giving rise to the potential for multiple different types of outstanding leadership if leaders differ in the conceptual frameworks they apply in sensemaking.

More centrally, however, there is a reason to suspect that sensemaking is a critical aspect of outstanding leadership regardless of the type of outstanding leader under consideration (Keller, 2003). For example, earlier we noted that vision appears to be a key attribute of charismatic and ideological leadership. Vision formation, however, appears to involve sensemaking activities on the part of the leaders. One illustration of this point may be found in Ellis' (2001) examination of one archetypical vision statement. Specifically, he examined the vision statement articulated by George Washington in his "farewell address." In this letter Washington articulated two key principles, principles he believed to be integral to the success of the young republic: (a) unity at home and (b) independence abroad. What is notable in Ellis' analysis is that these two principles emerged from Washington's reflection on the causes of success in the American War of Independence where unity, holding the continental army together, was more important than battlefield success and realism was more important than the ideological enthusiasms that captivated other countries.

Sensemaking activities, however, are not the exclusive provenance of charismatic and ideological leaders. For example, in their study of Benjamin Franklin, a pragmatic leader, Mumford and Van Doorn (2001) found that sensemaking was an important feature of virtually all the notable incidents of outstanding leadership in which he was involved. One illustration of this point may be found in Franklin's efforts to introduce paper currency. Arguing for the introduction of paper currency as a response to the economic crisis resulting from a lack of coinage, he carefully evaluated the reasons for prior failure in attempts to introduce paper currency, enumerating key causes such as counterfeiting, confidence, and so on, but noting that the key cause appeared to be a failure to tie paper currency to a tangible asset. This insight allowed Franklin to propose a unique solution to the crisis at hand by tying paper currency to land values. Along similar lines, in the establishment of volunteer fire departments, Franklin based his approach on careful analysis of the causes of fires, the distance between houses, unclean chimneys, and so forth, building his approach around a few key controllable causes—a want of organization in responding to fires and a lack of knowledge.

Examples of such sensemaking activities are not, however, limited to the founders of the United States. In the case of J.P. Morgan his efforts in founding modern corporations such as General Electric, U.S. Steel, and Southern Rail were guided by a belief that disruptive economic cycles and limitations on growth were attributable to ruinous and wasteful competition (Strouse, 1999). Similarly, George Patton's success in World War II is in part attributable to his careful analysis of the role of mobility in modern warfare.

Although there is apparently ample reason to suspect that sensemaking is a key to understanding outstanding leadership, it seems reasonable to ask why sensemaking would prove such a powerful mechanism of influence. Crises, of course, are threatening, anxiety-producing, events. Leader sensemaking takes on unique importance in this context because it provides a framework for understanding the threat, thereby reducing anxiety and permitting effective action. Sensemaking activities on the part of leaders, moreover, serve to articulate goals and potential paths to goal attainment at a time when followers are actively seeking such direction (House, 1971). Finally, sensemaking provides people with a sense of control or empowerment, allowing an effective response to the crisis while at the same time motivating followers by increasing their feelings of efficacy (Tierney & Farmer, 2002).

Mental Models

If it is granted that sensemaking is a critical component of outstanding leadership, then a new question comes to fore: How do leaders go about making sense of crisis situations? As noted earlier, crisis situations are complex, ambiguous, evolving situations where multiple causes, causes of varying significance, will be operating. Leaders, as a result, like people in general (Hogarth, 1980), cannot work with all of these causal variables. Instead, they must simplify the situation, boiling things down to the causes that influence valued aspects of system performance. This observation, in turn, suggests that in their sensemaking activities leaders are applying some kind of mental model.

The term *mental models* refers to a particular type of cognitive representational system (Johnson-Laird, 1983). Within this cognitive framework, a mental model is held to involve a conceptual representation of interactions among the entities involved in a system that is used to both understand the operations of a system and guide action in response to change (Sein & Bostrom, 1989). These conceptual representations identify key causal events that engender action and bring about goal attainment within a system articulating associations, or causal linkages, among causal concepts along with variables that influence the status and operation of these causes (Holyoak & Thagard, 1997; Largan-Fox & Code, 2000). These mental models, as abstractions of past experience, develop over time as a function of a person's exposure to system operations (Mumford, Feldman, Heir, & Nago, 2001; Zaccaro, Gualatieri, & Minionis, 1995) and are used in both identifying salient events and guiding adaptive responses to these events (Rouse, Cannon-Bowers, & Salas, 1992; Volpe, Cannon-Bowers, Salas, & Spector, 1996).

Mental models provide a description, or representation, of the system as it is. Leaders, however, in responding to crises must be able to move beyond a description of current system operations to describe the system as it might be. This observation led Mumford and Strange (2002) to argue that ultimately leaders' sensemaking activities are based not on descriptive mental models but rather on a prescriptive mental model constructed through the analysis of descriptive mental models. Figure 2.1 illustrates Mumford and Strange's theory of how leaders construct the prescriptive mental models applied in sensemaking.

Essentially, Mumford and Strange's (2002) theory holds that prescriptive mental models arise from reflection on, and analysis of, extant descriptive mental models in relation to (a) the goals that should be pursued by the organization, (b) the causes of goal attainment, and (c) other alternative models that might be used to understand the system under consideration. This analysis, an analysis often initiated by perceived deficiencies in current system operations (Zhou & George, 2001), gives rise to conceptual combination and reorganization activities intended to build a crisis-responsive model. In conceptual combination and reorganization, key causes and key goals are identified and the relationships among these causes and goals are restructured (Baughman & Mumford, 1995; Mumford, Connelly, & Gaddis, 2003) to create a model describing how the system should operate to resolve the crisis at hand. The resulting prescriptive mental model provides the leader with the conceptual framework needed to guide sensemaking. These prescriptive mental models with refinement, follower feedback, and the articulation of personal and interpersonal meaning, in turn, provide the foundation for formation of the visions held to be involved in some forms of outstanding leadership.

In an initial attempt to test this model, and the proposition that prescriptive mental models underlie the visions articulated by charismatic and ideological leaders, Strange and Mumford (2005) conducted an experimental study intended to asses whether three key elements held to be involved in inducing movement from descriptive mental models to prescriptive mental models influenced the production of higher quality vision statements by the occupants of leadership roles. In their study, 212 undergraduates were asked to assume the role of a principal taking responsibility for a new experimental school. After reading through background information, reading a consultant's report, and working through a set of exercises, the undergraduates were asked to prepare a speech to be given to students, parents, and teachers describing their vision for the school. One manipulation was made through the consultant's report, where either good or poor models for alternative curriculum were presented. The second manipulation, a search activation manipulation, occurred through the

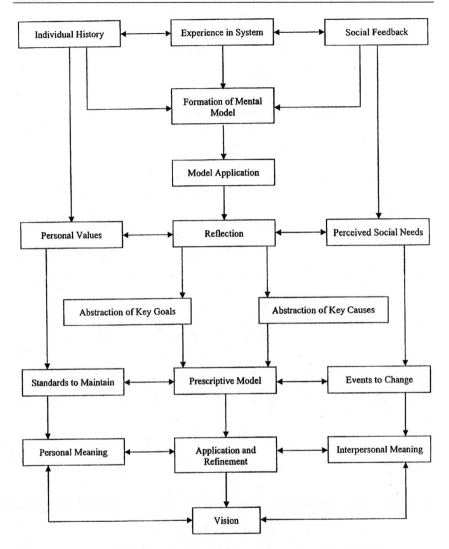

FIG. 2.1. Variables influencing construction of prescriptive mental models. Reprinted from *Charismatic and Transformational Leadership*, by B. J. Avolio and F. J. Yammarino (Eds.), "Vision and Mental Models," pp. 140–142, Copyright © 2002, with permission from Elsevier.

worksheet exercises, where participants were asked to identify key goals in the models, key causes of performance, both, or neither. The third manipulation, an instructional manipulation, asked some but not other participants to reflect on their own secondary-school experiences. The resulting vision statements were evaluated by panels of students, teachers, and parents with respect to affective reactions and motivation.

It was found that reflection per se contributed little to the production of vision statements. However, when reflection occurred in the context of abstraction of goals and causes better, more evocative, vision statements were obtained. More specifically, reflection on goals when poor models were presented led to the production of particularly compelling vision statements whereas reflection on causes when good models were presented led to the production of particularly compelling vision statements. Not only do these findings provide some support for Mumford and Strange's (2002) model, they suggest that goals can be abducted from poor models (a characteristic of ideological leaders) but that identification of causes and their use in vision formation requires exposure to sound models (a characteristic of charismatic leaders).

In another study intended to test this model, Scott, Lonergan, and Mumford (2005) sought to determine whether the combination and reorganization of available models or cases were, in fact, related to vision formation. In this study, 192 undergraduates were asked to work on the curriculum-generation task described earlier. In this study, however, the number and similarity of the model curriculum presented were varied. In addition, in combining these models to create a new curriculum, half the participants were presented with principles and asked to apply the analogical reasoning heuristics (e.g., feature search and mapping) and half the participants were presented with case summaries and asked to apply case-based reasoning heuristics (e.g., strengths and weaknesses analysis, forecasting, etc.). It was found that both these strategies could be used in conceptual combination but that a case-based, or model, approach led to better performance when only a limited amount of material was available with which to work. Thus there is some reason to suspect that conceptual combination plays a role in the formation of prescriptive mental models and that these combination and reorganization efforts can be based on experiential case models.

Summary

Taken as a whole, it appears that some evidence is available that outstanding leadership, the kind of leadership evidenced by charismatic, ideological, and pragmatic leaders, involves sensemaking activities. These sensemaking activities allow outstanding leaders to help groups and organizations respond to system crises. The basis of this sensemaking activity, however, is a prescriptive mental model constructed by the leaders based on experience, reflection, and analysis of relevant goals and causes applying to the crisis situation at hand. Given the basis of outstanding leadership in the development and application of prescriptive mental models, it seems reasonable to argue that differences in the prescriptive mental models applied will provide a cornerstone for understanding the similarities and differences among charismatic, ideological, and pragmatic leaders.

LEADER TYPES

Model Differences

The prescriptive mental models that provide the basis for sensemaking on the part of outstanding leaders take on particular significance within the context of the present effort because they provide a framework for understanding the emergence of charismatic, ideological, and pragmatic leaders as well as the socialized and personalized variants on these three basic types. More specifically, it appears that charismatic, ideological, and pragmatic leaders differ in the nature, content, and structure of the prescriptive mental models applied in sensemaking. These differences cause charismatic, ideological, and pragmatic leaders to construe and respond to crises in qualitatively different ways, evidence different behaviors, and emerge under different conditions. In this section, we examine the key features of these differences in prescriptive mental models that serve to differentiate charismatic, ideological and pragmatic leaders.

Broadly speaking, there appear to be seven basic features of prescriptive mental models that can be used to distinguish charismatic, ideological, and pragmatic leaders. These seven features include (a) time frame, (b) type of experience available, (c) nature of outcomes sought, (d) type of outcomes sought, (e) focus in model construction, (f) locus of causation, and (g) controllability of causation. Table 2.1 summarizes these attributes of prescriptive mental models with respect to the differences likely to be observed among charismatic, ideological, and pragmatic leaders.

One way that charismatic, ideological, and pragmatic leaders differ is in the time frame that provides a reference point for construction of a prescriptive mental model. In other words, the key causes and goals used in model construction might be selected and organized to reflect the future, the present, or the past. Typically, it is held that the vision being articulated by charismatic leaders is oriented toward the future (Conger & Kanungo, 1988, 1998). Ideological

TABLE 2.1
Differences Among Charismatic, Ideological,
and Pragmatic Leaders in Prescriptive Mental Models

	Charismatic	Ideological	Pragmatic
Time Frame	Future	Past	Present
Type of Experience Used	Positive	Negative	Both
Nature of Outcomes Sought	Positive	Transcendent	Malleable
Number of Outcomes Sought	Multiple	Few	Variable
Focus in Model Construction	External	Internal	External
Locus of Causation	People	Situations	Interactive
Controllability of Causation	High	Low	Selective

leaders, in contrast, appear to organize the elements of their prescriptive mental models around an idealized past (Strange & Mumford, 2002). Pragmatic leaders, however, seem to ground their sensemaking activities in the known features of the present situation (Mumford & Van Doorn, 2001).

These differences in temporal orientation have some potentially noteworthy implications for understanding the similarities and differences observed among charismatic, ideological, and pragmatic leaders (Bluedorn, 2002; Halbesleben, Novicevic, Harvey, & Buckley, 2003; Mainemelis, 2002). Clearly, construal of prescriptive models in terms of a past system will limit flexibility, and indeed, rigidity often seems to characterize ideological leaders. The orientation of charismatic and pragmatics toward the future or present will induce greater flexibility but a flexibility that requires ongoing environmental scanning. By this same token, however, a strong future orientation will result in charismatics creating prescriptive mental models that are fuzzy—models that will lack the clarity of those articulated by ideologues and pragmatics.

Though ideologues reference their prescriptive mental models to an idealized past, the cases available for construction of a prescriptive mental model are, more often than not, negative. One implication of this statement is that comparison of the present and past will play a pivotal role in the thought of ideological leaders. Another implication of this statement is that failures in the current system will shape ideological thought. Charismatic leaders, in contrast, will tend to seek positive models, particularly models that can be readily adapted to change (Keane, 1996). This use of positive case models allows charismatic leaders to apply causes rather than goals in formulating their prescriptive mental models (Strange & Mumford, 2002). Use of key causes in model construction allows charismatics to operate as change agents. Pragmatics, by virtue of their use of both positive and negative models, escape the error of overconfidence endemic to charismatic leaders (Conger, 1989). More centrally, however, by virtue of the ability to compare positive and negative models, pragmatics will have the ability to cut to the heart of an issue.

These observations about the kind of experience used in constructing prescriptive models, of course, also have implications for the goals or outcomes likely to be emphasized by charismatic, ideological, and pragmatic leaders. Charismatic leaders can be expected to frame prescriptive mental models in terms of multiple positive goals. Ideological leaders, however, must frame prescriptive models in terms of a limited number of transcendent goals—goals that obviate the mistakes and failure evident in current available case models. Unlike charismatic and ideological leaders, pragmatic leaders will see goals as malleable with the number and nature of the goals to be pursued being dictated by the exigencies of the situation at hand.

Of course, the malleability and flexibility of pragmatic leaders with respect to goals permits an opportunistic implementation of plans but may lead to the perception of a lack of consistency or direction. Ideological leaders, in contrast, will evidence a consistency, and an apparent integrity, that allows little deviation with regard to their select set of transcendent goals. By the same token, however, other potentially viable goals may be ignored, leading to a kind of tunnel vision. The pursuit of multiple positive goals on the part of charismatic leaders offers the option of shifting goals and proposing goals likely to be appealing to different stakeholders. This pursuit of positive goals at times, however, may prove detrimental if charismatic leaders fail to come to grips with potential negative outcomes associated with the pursuit of certain goals.

The tendency of ideological leaders to focus on a limited number of transcendent goals has an important, albeit often overlooked, implication. More specifically, because goal definition requires evaluation, one can expect that the focus in model construction will, among ideological leaders, tend to be internally oriented (Sternberg et al., 2003). This inward focus may make it difficult for ideological leaders to construct prescriptive mental models that have broad appeal. Yet for those who find this model appealing, it may prove unusually powerful because it provides a unique, distinctive, highly personal vehicle for imposing meaning on events—potentially providing people with a sense of identity. The linkage of prescriptive mental models to personal identity, moreover, will make possible truly exceptional sacrifice. Charismatic and pragmatic leaders, leaders who will construct prescriptive models based on external demands, may not be able to call for similar levels of sacrifice. However, the prescriptive mental models constructed by these two types may be better suited for dealing with crises emerging from the operation of broader social forces.

In considering the internal focus of ideological leaders, it is easy to extend this argument to the idea that ideological leaders see people as the locus of causation. In this regard, however, it is important to bear in mind a point made earlier—ideological leaders focus on transcendent goals derived from negative models. As a result, ideological leaders are more likely to see situations as opposed to individuals, as the key causal forces that must be considered in the construction of prescriptive mental models. Charismatic leaders will, in part, due to the use of more positive models, tend to stress the importance of people, and their efforts, as central causal variables. One obvious implication of these statements is that charismatic leaders will be more concerned with motivating followers whereas ideological leaders will be more concerned with changing the system. Pragmatic leaders, by virtue of their use of an interactional approach, will focus on how the situation effects people and their behavior (Mumford & Van Doorn, 2001).

These differences across leader types in beliefs about the locus of causation are also associated with differences in beliefs about the controllability of causation. As one might expect based on our foregoing observations, charismatics will tend to see causes as being under the leader's control whereas ideologues will tend to see them as under the control of external forces. Pragmatics on the other hand will tend to see causes as differing with regard to the potential for control. The tendency of pragmatics to construct prescriptive mental models around a limited number of key controllable causes may provide them with a powerful lever for inducing change (Isenberg, 1986; Mumford & Van Doorn, 2001; Thomas & McDaniel, 1990) despite certain disadvantages with regard to motivation.

The differences between charismatics and pragmatics with regard to locus of causation are of interest in part because they help explain an anomaly—an anomaly commonly noted in studies of outstanding leadership. More specifically, it may be inwardly oriented people, people such as Lenin or Thatcher, who understand and act on crises based on system considerations. More outwardly focused leaders, for example, Kennedy, may be more likely to understand and act on crises based on the people involved.

Influence Mechanisms

Our foregoing observations with respect to the nature of the prescriptive mental models used by charismatic, ideological, and pragmatic leaders are of interest for a number of reasons. These differences in prescriptive models tell us something about the characteristic behavior of charismatic, ideological, and pragmatic leaders. These differences, moreover, have some noteworthy implications about the boundary conditions shaping the emergence of a given leader type. In this section, however, we examine the implications of these prescriptive mental models with respect to a key attribute of outstanding leaders—the exercise of influence.

Charismatic leaders, like all outstanding leaders, exercise influence through sensemaking activities. These sensemaking activities, as noted earlier, will be based on the prescriptive mental model being applied. In the case of charismatic leaders, however, the application of this prescriptive mental model will typically occur through the vision of the future being articulated by the leader. Because the prescriptive mental model being applied by charismatics involves multiple, positive, future outcomes, charismatic leaders have the ability to formulate a vision likely to prove attractive to multiple groups that differ in terms of operative goals. In other words, some goals will appeal to one group and other goals to other groups. Thus the ability of charismatic leaders to articulate multiple future goals allows them to build consensus among stakeholders as to how to cope with a crisis. With the emergence of consensus and adoption of the vision, this appeal to multiple groups will create powerful normative pressures—normative pressures that will serve to reinforce acceptance of the vision being articulated (Klein & House, 1998).

The creation of a new consensus, particularly when groups have been experiencing the anomie that accompanies turbulence in the social environment and change in social systems, will prove to be a particularly powerful influence mechanism because it provides direction—a shared sense of direction that reduces anxiety about the future. More centrally, however, under conditions of turbulence and change, people, and groups, will lose their old sense of identity. The vision being articulated by a charismatic leader, given their ability to build consensus around this vision, will provide followers with a new sense of identity (Shamir et al., 1993). Moreover, the sense of identity provided by charismatics' vision will prove particularly powerful because it is shared by multiple stakeholders.

Charismatic influence, however, is not simply a matter of creating shared social identity. As noted earlier, charismatic leaders frame their understanding of causation in terms of people and people's ability to affect their world. This point is of some importance because it suggests that the vision being articulated by charismatic leaders will prove empowering for people and relevant stakeholder groups (Conger & Kanungo, 1988, 1998). When this empowerment is accompanied by the initiation of projects, successful projects, that in one way or another symbolize the ability to cope with change through the vision being articulated, it will serve to build feelings of efficacy and commitment and thus follower motivation. In fact, in the careers of charismatic leaders, Franklin Roosevelt, John Kennedy, Adolf Hitler, and Joseph Stalin, one sees symbolic projects being used as a motivational mechanism. These successful projects, along with the sense of efficacy and commitment they develop, will help charismatics weather setbacks and the disappointments that occur when the future turns out to be more complicated than one might expect based on the leader's vision.

Ideological leaders, in contrast to charismatic leaders, will not generally be able to build a broad new consensus. The inability of ideological leaders to build consensus may be traced to the nature of the prescriptive mental models used in vision formation. Because ideological leaders construct the models around a few transcendent goals, it becomes difficult for ideological leaders to articulate a vision that will appeal to a broad range of people and multiple stakeholder groups. The difficulty ideological leaders have in appealing to a range of people and groups will be compounded by two other characteristics of the prescriptive mental models applied in vision formation: (a) their tendency to frame models and visions in terms of negative events because negative events will typically prove less attractive than positive events, and (b) their tendency to frame models and visions in terms of transcendent goals because the use of transcendent goals will lead to the discounting of others' views.

Taken at face value, these characteristics of ideological leaders might lead one to conclude that it is difficult for ideological leaders to exercise much influence. What one must remember here, however, is that ideological leaders frame their vision in terms of beliefs and values already held by certain groups, stressing the transcendent goals evident in an idealized past. As a result, ideological leaders can exercise substantial influence if they appeal to fundamental traditional values (Lalonde, 2003). This appeal will prove to be a particularly effective basis for the exercise of influence when the crisis at hand threatens these values and when these values are integral to the identity of a relatively large number of people.

When it proves possible to apply this approach, an approach most likely to prove effective when a leader is working in a society or institution characterized by a strong, as opposed to a weak, culture, then ideological leaders may articulate an unusually compelling vision. One reason ideological leaders can exert such a powerful influence is that their analysis of the crisis, an analysis arising from the prescriptive mental model being applied, will vis-à-vis cultural/histori-cal familiarity, prove intuitively appealing. Another reason ideological leaders can exercise unusual influence is that the core identity of followers is reflected in the vision being articulated. As a result, ideological leaders may provide fol-lowers, admittedly at times often a relatively small band of followers, with a stronger sense of identity than charismatic leaders (Barreto, Spears, & Ellemers, 2003). This strongly shared identity will allow ideological leaders to create highly cohesive groups that serve to reinforce and maintain the vision be-ing articulated by the leader (Post, Ruby, & Shaw, 2002).

The impact of ideological leaders will be amplified by two other characteris-tics of the prescriptive mental models applied in vision formation. First, when crises have been prolonged it will be difficult for people to see how positive, fu-ture-oriented change is possible. As a result, the use of situational explanations and a focus on the personal internal will prove particularly compelling. Second, when people or groups are in conflict, and conflict often accompanies social change, victimization may occur. Ideological leaders can capitalize on the nega-tive models provided by the victimization to reinforce the vision being articu-lated. Thus, ideological leaders can, and often do, appeal to injustice despite the fact that this appeal may result in ideological leaders proving to be a divisive force in society (Post et al., 2002).

When compared to charismatic and ideological leaders, pragmatic leaders seem to have few tools available for the effective exercise of influence. What should be recognized here, however, is that the prescriptive mental model ap-plied by pragmatics will often provide a balanced view of the crisis at hand. In sensemaking, pragmatic leaders will provide a framework for understanding the crisis where a more complex set of crises is considered, both positive and nega-tive outcomes of actions are taken into account, and goals are adjusted to take into account changes in the situation. As a result, one would expect that prag-matic leaders will form more effective strategies for addressing crises with their performance in handling crises providing a basis for the exercise of influence (Mumford & Van Doorn, 2001).

The ability of pragmatic leaders to exercise influence by providing superior models for sensemaking, problem solving, and crisis resolution is, of course, contingent on there being a reasonable level of agreement about what the problem is in the first place. When this condition is met, three other charac-teristics of the prescriptive mental models applied by pragmatics will contrib-ute to the effective exercise of influence. First, the malleability of pragmatic leaders and their more sophisticated view of causation permits the negotia-tion and persuasions needed to bring multiple groups "to the table." Second, negotiation and persuasion allow pragmatics to work with multiple diverse groups in crisis resolution. Third, because pragmatic leaders can more readily identify key causes, it becomes possible for them to identify the leverage points that must be manipulated to induce effective change (Isenberg, 1986; Thomas & McDaniel, 1990).

Along related lines, one must also remember that the focus of pragmatic leaders on sensemaking rather than vision articulation may not always prove to be a disadvantage. The arousal of affect through vision articulation can, at times, cloud analysis of the origins and implications of a crisis. Moreover, by allowing followers the autonomy to construct their own image of the situation, pragmatic leaders provide followers with the capability to make unique contributions to crisis resolution (Mumford & Licuanan, 2004; Mumford, Scott, Gaddis, & Strange, 2002). In other words, pragmatic leadership will promote the creative thought needed for solving complex social problems.

Boundary Conditions

One implication of our observations about the exercise of influence is that the effectiveness of the influence that is applied by charismatic, ideological, and pragmatic leaders will vary as a function of certain conditions. Accordingly, one might expect to see differences in the conditions giving rise to the emergence of charismatic, ideological, and pragmatic leaders. For example, due to their basis in tradition, ideological leaders can be expected to emerge from religious institutions. Due to the need for consensus building, charismatic leaders will often emerge from political institutions. The conditions that shape leader emergence and performance, however, are not solely a matter of institutional type. Instead, these institutional effects are a manifestation of a broader phenomenon. Here, of course, we refer to boundary conditions (Eisenhardt, 1989), specifically those boundary conditions that represent situational constraints on the effective use of different influence tactics.

One of the boundary conditions that shape the likely emergence and acceptance of pragmatic leadership was mentioned earlier. More specifically, pragmatic leadership is contingent on broader agreement about the nature and significance of the crisis at hand. Although it is possible that a broad social consensus will at times allow for the operation of pragmatic leadership, more often than not pragmatic leadership will emerge when a discrete problem is at hand that can be defined and understood primarily in terms of objective considerations.

Another boundary condition that shapes the potential impact, and likely emergence, of pragmatic leaders involves the feasibility of control. One strength of pragmatic leaders is that they have the ability to identify and manipulate the key leverage points needed to induce change in complex social systems. This ability, however, is unlikely to prove of much value if pragmatic leaders cannot exert influence over the actions occurring at these leverage points. This observation is of some importance both because it suggests that pragmatic leadership requires substantial experience working in the social system at hand and because it suggests that pragmatic leaders will need the authority to influence system operations. These requirements, of course, in accordance with the earlier observations of Weber (1924), indicate that pragmatic leadership will often be the preferred from of leadership in bureaucracies and business organizations.

Still another boundary condition that shapes the emergence and performance of pragmatic leaders is people's affective investment in the issue under consideration. When affective investment in an issue is high, valued, personally valued, outcomes become salient. The activation of affective outcomes undermines causal analysis, thereby limiting the impact of pragmatic leadership. As a result, the effectiveness, and thus likely emergence, of pragmatic leaders will depend on whether the crisis at hand can be framed in objective terms. Indeed, pragmatic leaders will go to unusual lengths to frame crises objectively in an attempt to create conditions where the effective exercise of influence is possible.

When strong affect is attached to a crisis the visionary forms of outstanding leadership, charismatic and ideological leadership, will prove more effective. Charismatic leadership, however, depends on the existence, or the leader's creation of, shared beliefs among relevant stakeholders about the desirability of outcomes. Thus the emergence and performance of charismatic leaders will depend on a shared sense of the "collective good." This contingency, moreover, suggests that charismatic leadership will prove most effective when the crisis at hand places most people in a similar position—conditions that make it possible for charismatic leaders to appeal to the "common good."

Earlier, we noted that charismatic leadership is a leadership of empowerment in that charismatic leaders exercise influence through people and their ability to act on the situation. The need for effective action by people implies that charismatic leadership will prove less effective when the conditions at hand are such that people prove difficult to communicate with and/or are not easily mobilized through persuasive communication. As a result, charismatic leadership will depend on image building and the creation of an aura of credibility (Yorges et al., 1999) as well as access to and control over mass-communication channels— witness Franklin Roosevelt's "fireside chats." This emphasis on image and communication, moreover, may, in part, explain why charismatic leadership often emerges in political forums (Weber, 1924).

The fact that charismatic leaders exercise influence through people and their ability to act on the situation gives rise to another boundary condition shaping leader emergence and performance. More specifically, the impact of charismatic leaders depends on whether followers will accept the proposition that a better future is possible through collective action. As a result, charismatic leaders are unlikely to emerge when prolonged demoralization and endemic ongoing conflict have made it impossible for people to believe that collective action will result in positive outcomes for themselves and society (Mumford & Marcy, 2004).

The effects of demoralization and conflict, though militating against the emergence of charismatic leaders, may contribute to the emergence of ideological leaders (Blank, 2003; Post et al., 2002). Prolonged demoralization and endemic uncompromising conflict will lead people to find the transcendent goals articulated by ideological leaders attractive and create conditions where an emphasis on external in prescriptive models is seen as plausible and realistic. Whereas demoralization and conflict represent boundary conditions needed for the emergence of ideological leaders, the likely success of ideological leaders will be determined by two other conditions.

First, as noted earlier, the vision being articulated by ideological leaders entails an appeal to an idealized past. Accordingly, ideological leadership requires a strong collective culture in the society or institutions of concern. This requirement, in turn, suggests that ideological leaders will be unlikely to emerge in settings where individual autonomy and cultural diversity are evident. Moreover, because ideological leadership is a leadership of tradition (Weber, 1924), when tradition has proven ineffective in handling relevant crises, ideological leadership will be undermined.

Second, to exert influence with respect to tradition, the ideological leader must understand and be engaged in this tradition. This point is of some importance because it suggests that ideological leaders are unlikely to emerge from the fringes of a culture. Thus, ideological leadership may be the province of the middle and upper-middle class (e.g., Ronald Reagan, Osama bin Laden). More centrally, however, ideological leadership will require an intense personal engagement in the tradition of relevant groups. In fact, given the inward-focus characteristic of ideological leaders, it seems unlikely that a viable, attractive vision can be formulated without this kind of personal cultural engagement.

Summary

In this section we have presented a theory of outstanding leadership that holds that the differences observed among charismatic, ideological, and pragmatic leaders can be traced to the nature and structure of the prescriptive mental models leaders use to make sense of crises. These differences in the nature and structure of the prescriptive mental models applied in sensemaking result in qualitative differences among charismatic, ideological, and pragmatic leaders in both how influence is exercised and the conditions that permit the effective exercise of influence. These conditions shaping the effective exercise of influence, in turn, condition the emergence of charismatic, ideological, and pragmatic leaders.

BEHAVIOR AND EXPERIENCES

Behavior

Our observations about influence and boundary conditions are of interest in part because they suggest that the prescriptive mental models being applied by charismatic, ideological, and pragmatic leaders will be associated with differences across types with respect to behavior. In fact, it can be argued that one reason boundary conditions are observed, conditions influencing the emergence of charismatic, ideological, and pragmatic leaders, is that the behaviors required under certain conditions cannot be effectively executed by people pursuing a given pathway to outstanding leadership. Accordingly, in this section we examine the behaviors, key behaviors commonly required of people holding the upper-level positions where outstanding leadership is possible, that characterize charismatic, ideological, and pragmatic leadership.

Performance. The emergence of charismatic, ideological, and pragmatic leaders under certain select conditions provides one explanation for why prior studies have failed to reveal marked differences among charismatic, ideological, and pragmatic leaders with respect to performance. With regard to this statement, however, two provisions should be borne in mind. First, prior studies contrasting outstanding leaders with respect to general social criteria (e.g., how many institutions were established by the leader, how many positive contributions were made by the leader, and how long these contributions lasted) compared only charismatic and ideological leaders (Strange & Mumford, 2002). Thus, as noted earlier, the possibility remains that performance differences might emerge in comparing pragmatic leaders to ideological and charismatic leaders. Given the fact that the prescriptive mental models applied by pragmatics often provide a more complex and sophisticated framework for understanding crises, there is reason to suspect that performance differences, performance differences favoring pragmatics, might be observed.

The differences observed among charismatic, ideological, and pragmatic leadership with respect to boundary conditions and influence tactics, however, suggest that a more complex pattern of performance effects might also be observed. More specifically, charismatic, ideological, and pragmatic leaders might emphasize different forms of performance—performances appropriate to the conditions associated with leader emergence and the kind of influence tactics being applied. In other words, one might expect to see differences among leader types on more specific dimensions of performance.

For example, charismatic and ideological leaders by virtue of the use of vision as an influence mechanism might start more mass movements than pragmatic leaders. Pragmatic leaders, however, may differ from ideological and charismatic leaders by providing more efficient and "lower cost" crisis resolution strategies. Ideological leaders, due to the importance of group identity as an influence mechanism, can be expected to maintain closer relationships with followers than either charismatic or pragmatic leaders, with their followers displaying a greater willingness to make sacrifices for the leader. Although other examples of this sort might be provided, the foregoing examples are sufficient to make our basic point that there is a need to examine performance differences among charismatic, ideological, and pragmatic leaders on discrete criteria as well as overall social-impact criteria.

In this discussion of performance, however, one must consider a point made earlier. More specifically, the available evidence indicates that the performance differences observed among outstanding leaders are closely tied to leader orientation—socialized versus personalized (House & Howell, 1992; O'Connor et al., 1995; Strange & Mumford, 2002). The theory of leader types sketched out previously suggests why orientation exerts such strong effects on performance. Leaders use prescriptive mental models to guide action. When leaders build these models around negative assumptions about others and their interactions, leaders will exercise influence and take actions, especially during times of crisis where threat is high, that serve to protect both the group and their own position within the group. These self-protective actions will, in turn, give rise to socially destructive behavior (Mumford, Connelly, & Leritz, 2005). This point is nicely illustrated by considering the impact two ideological leaders, Joseph McCarthy and Vladimir Lenin, have had on the world.

What should be recognized here, however, is that the way these self-protective tendencies are expressed will be contingent on the influence tactics being applied and the boundary conditions shaping leader emergence and performance. In keeping with this proposition, Strange and Mumford (2002), in their comparison of charismatic and ideological leaders, found that charismatic and ideological leaders differed in their behavioral expression of a personalized orientation. Personalized charismatics tended to evidence narcissistic behavior whereas personalized ideologues tended to evidence behaviors associated with object beliefs or the belief that others can be used as "tools" (O'Connor et al., 1995). The self-aggrandizement associated with narcissism is, of course, consistent with the expansive, future-oriented perspective mental models used by charismatics. Similarly, the tendency to view others as "tools" is consistent with the ideological focus on transcendent goals. These observations, of course, suggest that charismatic, ideological, and pragmatic leaders will evidence personalized and socialized behaviors in different ways, and for different reasons, with these differences, at least potentially, being associated with performance differences on certain discrete criteria.

Creative Problem Solving. Not only will the prescriptive mental models being applied by charismatic, ideological, and pragmatic leaders result in differential expressions of personalized and specialized behaviors, it seems likely that application of these models will result in differences in the other key behaviors required for those occupying positions where outstanding leadership is possible. Earlier, we noted that the prescriptive mental models applied by charismatics stress multiple future-oriented goals. Thus future-goal framing suggests that problem construction or problem identification skills will prove crucial to effective charismatic leadership (Mumford, Reiter-Palmon, & Redmond, 1994; Okuda, Runco, & Berger, 1991). The use of a prescriptive mental model where *multiple* positive goals are being articulated will, moreover, encourage the application of generative or divergent thinking skills. Thus in charismatic leaders it is not uncommon to find exceptional conceptual combination and idea-generation skills (Mumford, Strange, Scott, & Gaddis, 2004).

More centrally, it can be expected that ideological leaders will differ from charismatics with respect to the problem-solving skills used. Ideological leaders do not try to create a new future, a generative activity, but instead argue for a return, admittedly with modification, to an idealized past. This tendency, along with the tendency of ideologues to stress current differences in formation of their prescriptive mental models, suggests that the evaluative aspects of problem solving, for example, information gathering and idea evaluation, will be emphasized in the thought and actions of ideologues.

In contrast to ideological and charismatic leadership, problem solving is a particularly important influence on the emergence and performance of pragmatic leaders. One implication of this statement is that more, and more effective, problem-solving behavior should be observed in comparing pragmatic leaders with charismatic and ideological leaders (Mumford & Van Doorn, 2001). Another implication of this statement derives from the prescriptive mental models applied by pragmatics. Because pragmatics' prescriptive mental models entail a balanced view of causation that takes into account both positive and negative outcomes, one would expected to see more balance between generative and evaluative problem-solving activities as well as a greater emphasis on the use of problem-solving skills, such as idea evaluation and planning, contributing to idea implementation.

Leader–Follower Relations. Just as the application of different prescriptive models gives rise to differences in problem-solving strategies, the differences in the prescriptive mental models applied by charismatic, ideological, and pragmatic leaders are associated with differences in characteristic patterns of leader–follower interactions. In the case of charismatic leaders, where issues are framed in terms of people and their empowerment, one would expect to see relationships characterized by trust, mutual influence, participation, and high levels of contact and collaboration (Dansereau et al., 1975; Graen & Cashman, 1975). Our stereotypic view of ideological leaders is that they are cold, distant, rather aloof people. What should be recognized here, however, is that ideological leaders rely on a group that shares and reinforces the transcendent goals being articulated. As a result, ideological leaders will maintain close relationships with followers. However, tight group boundaries and the oppositional character of ideologues' prescriptive mental models suggests that trust, loyalty, and attitudinal similarity will prove particularly important to ideological leaders.

As might be expected based on our foregoing observations, pragmatic leaders, in comparison with ideological leaders, can be expected to place a greater emphasis on performance in interactions with followers while allowing followers greater autonomy in how the work gets done. In keeping with this pattern of leader–follower exchange, and the key characteristics of the prescriptive mental models applied by pragmatics, leader–follower relationships will typically be characterized by a greater emphasis on negotiation, an emphasis of shared out-comes, and respect for followers' unique concerns.

Political Tactics. Given the effects of prescriptive mental models on the ways in which charismatic, ideological, and pragmatic leaders exercise influ-ence, one would expect differences to emerge in examining the political tactics and power bases employed by leaders following these three pathways. In the case of pragmatic leaders, where expertise and performance in crisis resolution are at a premium, political tactics stressing control through expertise, informa-tion, and resources will be emphasized. Pragmatic leaders, however, by virtue of the malleability of goals, will also tend to rely on negotiation as a vehicle for the exercise of influence (Mumford & Van Doorn, 2001). Finally, because prag-matic leaders apply a balanced view of causation, they may, vis-à-vis charis-matic and ideological leaders, be better able to exercise control through the ma-nipulation of situational contingencies.

On the other hand, charismatic and ideological leaders tend to exercise con-trol though vision. The arousal attached to effective articulation of a vision, along with the role of vision in relational definition, suggests that charismatic and ideological leaders will differ from pragmatic leaders in that social relation-ships and affective arousal will often provide a basis for the effective exercise of influence (Deluga, 2001). Because, however, the visions articulated by charis-matic and ideological leaders are derived from different types of prescriptive mental models, charismatic and ideological leaders will evidence differences with respect to their preferred influence tactics. For example, as a result of the use of multiple future goals, charismatic leaders are better able and more likely to apply coalition tactics. The construction of prescriptive mental models based on negative events and transcendent goals will cause ideological leaders to ex-ercise control through both personal commitment and aggression.

Communication Strategies. The existence of differences in political tactics, moreover, suggests that differences will also be observed among charis-matic, ideological, and pragmatic leaders in persuasion or the strategies used in mass communication (C. Fitzgerald & Kirby, 1997; Yrle, Hartman, & Galle, 2002; Yukl, 2001). One obvious difference likely involves comparison of the communication strategies used by charismatic and ideological leaders with those used by pragmatic leaders. More specifically, charismatic and ideological leaders are likely to stress emotion and imagery in their communications whereas pragmatic leaders are likely to place a greater emphasis on rational per-suasion, position clarification, and description of paths to goal attainment (Baum, Locke, & Kirkpatrick, 1998; Fiol, Harris, & House, 1999).

In this regard, however, it should be recognized that charismatic and ideo-logical leaders may display some noteworthy differences with regard to the con-tent and style of their communications. The tendency of ideologues to focus on negative events and situational forces in construing prescriptive mental models suggests that their communications will be characterized by negative affect, audience confrontation, and skilled use of propaganda. Charismatic leaders' communications, in contrast, are more likely to be characterized by positive affect and humor (Avolio et al., 1999) as well as an attempt to build consensus through the articulation of multiple positive goals that might be attained through collective action.

Experiences

Events.   The prescriptive mental models applied by charismatic, ideological, and pragmatic leaders arise, in part, from reflection on system performance, institutional or organizational, in relation to personal experience. The role of reflection and personal experience on the construction of prescriptive mental models has an important, albeit often overlooked, implication for understanding outstanding leadership. Outstanding leadership, and the individual's tendency to apply a charismatic, ideological, or pragmatic strategy, will be influenced by both the narratives people use to understand events in their lives (Habermas, 2001) and the events that provide a basis for the formation of these narratives (Pillemer, 2001).

In fact, salient life events, the events used to construct life narratives, may influence the prescriptive mental models applied by charismatic, ideological, and pragmatic leaders in three ways. First, in reflection, crises will be framed and understood in terms of their personal consequences for the leader involved. Thus, a crisis is not a purely objective event. Instead, crises represent events that are interpreted and appraised in terms of the individual's life narrative. This point is of some importance because it suggests that the events used to define a life narrative will influence how crises are appraised. These appraisals will, in turn, influence construction of a prescriptive mental models (Popper, 2000; Popper & Mayseless, 2002).

Second, reflection, particularly reflection on personal experience, will activate central, salient life events used in construction of a life narrative. Activation of these powerful personal experiences is noteworthy because new events, particularly the kind of novel, complex, and ill-defined events reflected in leadership crises, will tend to be understood and interpreted by reference to, or comparison with, these salient life events (Keller, 2003). As a result, these life events will provide key content used in combination and reorganization activities to help people construct a new prescriptive mental model for understanding the crisis at hand (Mumford et al., 2003).

Third, the events used to construct life narratives provide people with what might be viewed as a set of reference cases for understanding events in their lives. The use of life events as a set of reference cases is noteworthy because it suggests that case-based reasoning will be used in formation of prescriptive mental models. Cases, including life event cases, represent a highly complex form of knowledge (Scott et al., 2005) incorporating information about resources, applicable restrictions, relevant contingencies, and key actions (Hammond, 1990; Hershey, Walsh, Read & Chulef, 1990; Kolodner, 1993; Xiao, Milgram, & Doyle, 1997). The content of the material contained in life events therefore provides a basis for identifying relevant goals and causes for use in formation of the prescriptive mental models applied by charismatic, ideological, and pragmatic leaders in making sense of social crises.

Event Types.   Although there is reason to suspect that life events shape the nature and structure of the prescriptive mental models constructed by charismatic, ideological, and pragmatic leaders, the question at hand in this chapter is more specific: How can differences in the events used in constructing life narratives be used to describe the similarities and differences among charismatic, ideological, and pragmatic leaders? One way leaders and their prescriptive mental models might differ is attributable to differences in the kind of events used to construct life narratives. McAdams (2001) and Pillemer (2001) argued that a number of different kinds of life events may be used in the construction of life narratives: (a) orientating events, (b) anchoring events, (c) turning point events, (d) analogical events, (e) contaminating events, and (f) redemptive events. Mumford and Manley (2003) argued that differences among leaders in the kind of events used to construct life narratives may, in turn, lead to differences in the prescriptive mental models constructed, and thus differences in the behaviors arising from application of these prescriptive mental models.

For example, ideological leaders stress the importance of certain transcendent goals. Because anchoring events define long-term goals, one might expect to see anchoring events predominantly in the life narratives applied by ideological leaders. Along similar lines, contaminating events (apparently positive events with negative downstream consequences) can be expected to emerge with some frequency in the life narratives of ideological leaders, perhaps causing ideologues to stress negative events in the formation of prescriptive mental models. In contrast, given their tendency to construct prescriptive mental models around multiple positive future goals, it seems plausible to argue that redemptive events (apparently negative events with positive downstream consequences) will frequently be observed in the lives of charismatic leaders. Moreover, the future orientation of charismatics suggests that originating events may be viewed as a salient experience shaping their later lives. Pragmatic leaders, given their focus on the present, seem more likely to emphasize analogous and turning point events (both case models involving adaptation to change).

Event Content.   In addition to differences in the kind of events that shape the prescriptive mental models applied by charismatic, ideological, and pragmatic leaders, differences may arise in the content of these events. For example, the events defining the life narratives and prescriptive mental models of charismatics may stress the importance of achievement, the need for persistence in the pursuit of goals, and the feasibility of managing crises through positive role modeling (Conger, 1999; House & Howell, 1992; Hunt et al., 1999). The focus of ideological leaders on transcendent goals, however, suggests that life events stressing the importance of spirituality, moralism, justice, and a commitment to traditional values will prove influential in both definition of a life story and the construction of prescriptive mental models (Beeghley, Bock, & Cochran, 1990; Hogan & Dickstein, 1972). Events illustrating the value of spirituality and tradition, however, seem unlikely to be evident in the lives of pragmatic leaders. Instead, the events shaping the lives and the prescriptive mental models applied by pragmatics seem more likely to emphasize the value of observation, analysis, and joint problem-solving efforts.

The content of life events may prove useful not only in distinguishing charismatic, ideological, and pragmatic leaders, but also in distinguishing socialized and personalized leaders. When key life events involve loss, fear, distrust, and uncertainty with respect to others' actions, the tendency to apply these events in the construction of prescriptive mental models can be expected to result in a personalized orientation due to the threat to self implied by others' actions in these events (Gessner, O'Connor, Clifton, Connelly, & Mumford, 1993; O'Connor et al., 1995). Moreover, when these events illustrate the value of self-protection, self-promotion, and power as a means for coping with threat, then the kind of prescriptive mental models that characterize personalized leaders seem especially likely to emerge. Conversely, when salient life events stress the value of trust, concern, commitment, and sacrifice, one can expect a more socialized model to emerge and leadership behavior indicative of a socialized orientation.

Summary

In this section, we have examined the implications of the differences in structure and content held to characterize the prescriptive mental models applied by charismatic, ideological, and pragmatic leaders in sensemaking with respect to resultant behavior. In fact, it appears that the differences observed among charismatic, ideological, and pragmatic leaders in prescriptive mental models are associated with differences in problem-solving processes, leader–follower relations, political tactics, and communication strategies. These differences, moreover, may be linked to different performance emphases as well as the tendency of charismatic, ideological, and pragmatic leaders to emerge from, and perform well in, different settings. The emergence, or development of, charismatic, ideological, and pragmatic leaders, in turn, appears to depend on the nature of the content of the life events shaping people's images of their lives and the impact of these events on the kind of prescriptive mental models leaders create in their attempts to make sense of relevant crises.

CONCLUSIONS

Before turning to the broader conclusions emerging from this chapter, certain limitations should be noted. To begin, we have in our examination of the development of charismatic, ideological, and pragmatic leaders focused on the life events influencing construction of prescriptive mental models. As a result, little attention has been given to other potential influences on the development of outstanding leadership such as personality and general cognitive ability (Bass, 1990; Mumford, Zaccarro, Harding, et al., 2000). Along similar lines, our examination of the events influencing development stressed how the prescriptive mental models held to characterize a particular type of outstanding leader emergence. As a result, little attention was given to changes in prescriptive mental models and the transformation of leader types (e.g., the emergence of charisma in pragmatic leaders), although at least some evidence is available indicating that, though rare, these transformations may occur from time to time (Mumford & Marcy, 2004).

Second, with regard to theory development, it should be recognized that the theory formulated in the present chapter is most directly relevant to understanding socialized and personalized charismatic, ideological, and pragmatic leaders. This point is of some importance because other pathways to outstanding leadership might exist (Dansereau, Kim, & Kim, 2002). In this regard, however, it seems likely that if other forms of outstanding leadership are eventually identified, they may be accounted for by relatively simple extensions of the general theory presented in the present chapter.

In the present chapter, we have argued that outstanding leadership is a form of leadership that emerges in response to crisis where crises are seen as complex unfolding events involving suboptimal performance in social systems. Under these conditions, the leader's job does not require that he or she resolve the crisis at hand. Instead, we have argued that the leader's role under crisis conditions is to provide followers with a structure that will help them make sense of events. These leader sensemaking activities both direct and motivate followers, permitting a collective response to the crisis.

Within the theoretical model, leaders' sensemaking activities are held to be contingent on an in-depth understanding of and tangible experience with the social system at hand. Without this kind of expertise, leaders cannot formulate viable mental models reflecting current operations of the social system under consideration. Understanding of current system operations, however, was not held to be sufficient for outstanding leadership. Instead, extant descriptive models must be reconfigured through a conceptual combination and reorganization process to create a prescriptive mental model reflecting requirements for optimal performance given the crisis at hand. The construction of these prescriptive mental model was held to depend on reflection on experience, including the leader's personal experience, to identify the key goals and key causes operating in the situation that might be used to direct action. In some, but not all cases, the construction of viable prescriptive mental models will provide a basis for vision formation.

The differences observed among charismatic, ideological, and pragmatic leaders were held to be a result of the nature and structure of the prescriptive mental model being applied by leaders in their various sensemaking activities. More specifically, we argued that the nature and structure of the prescriptive mental models created by charismatic, ideological, and pragmatic leaders will differ with respect to seven major attributes: (a) time frame, (b) type of experience used, (c) nature of outcomes sought, (d) number of outcomes sought, (e) focus in model construction (internal vs. external), (f) locus of control, and (g) controllability of causation.

These differences in the nature and structure of prescriptive mental models were held to be associated with the use of different strategies for the exercise of influence and differences in the conditions giving rise to, and successful performance by, charismatic, ideological, and pragmatic leaders. More centrally, these differences in the nature and structure of the prescriptive mental models applied by charismatic, ideological, and pragmatic leaders were held to lead to differences in five major domains of behavior associated with outstanding leadership: (a) performance and integrity, (b) problem-solving processes, (c) leader–follower relationships, (d) political tactics, and (e) strategies. In the later sections of this book, we use a historiometric approach to examine whether these behavioral differences are, in fact, observed in contrasting charismatic, ideological, and pragmatic leaders.

Another noteworthy implication of the theory we have developed in the present chapter is that reflection on prior life events, specifically the types of events people use to construct life narratives, will also influence the kind of prescriptive mental models constructed and thus the pathways people pursue to outstanding leadership. These life events provide reference cases used in interpreting crises, thereby influencing the kind of prescriptive mental models constructed by charismatic, ideological, and pragmatic leaders. Accordingly, after examining behavioral differences, we apply a historiometric approach to examine the type and content of the life events related to the emergence of both socialized and personalized charismatic, ideological, and pragmatic leaders.

3

General Method: What History Remembers and Predicts for Outstanding Leaders

Michael D. Mumford
Blaine Gaddis
Jill M. Strange
Ginamarie Scott
The University of Oklahoma

In the preceding chapter, we presented a theory describing the nature and origins of outstanding leadership. This theory holds that outstanding leadership emerges from sensemaking during times of crisis. The basis for these sensemaking activities is a prescriptive mental model constructed by the leader based on his or her understanding of the social system under consideration. Differences in the content and structure of these prescriptive mental models are held to give rise to different pathways to outstanding leadership—pathways we have labeled charismatic, ideological, and pragmatic leadership.

Not only does this theory provide an explanation of the emergence of alternative pathways to outstanding leadership, it leads to a series of propositions, really hypotheses, about the kind of behavioral differences likely to be observed among charismatic, ideological, and pragmatic leaders. These behavioral differences, moreover, were held to be evident in key domains, domains critical to performance in upper-level leadership roles such as problem solving, follower interactions, communication strategies, and political tactics. In addition, these behavioral differences, and differences in the prescriptive mental models held to underlie these behaviors, were held to be influenced, or shaped, by the life narratives used by leaders to understand themselves and their world. As a result, it was held that charismatic, ideological, and pragmatic leaders would differ with respect to the nature and content of the events around which they constructed their life narratives.

Our intent in the present effort is, broadly speaking, to accrue some evidence for the validity, or meaningfulness, of the distinction we have drawn between charismatic, ideological, and pragmatic leaders by showing that leaders evidencing these types, in fact, evidence the expected behavioral and developmental differences. To determine whether these behavioral and developmental differences are observed, we apply a historiometric approach. The historiometric approach applied herein involves a series of content analytic investigations, investigations based on available biographical evidence, intended to examine the behavioral and developmental differences characterizing charismatic, ideological, and pragmatic leaders. Before turning to the specific methods applied in the present set of investigations, however, it would seem germane to briefly consider the various methodological strategies commonly applied in studies of outstanding leadership.

METHODOLOGICAL STRATEGIES

Major Methodological Approaches

Any study of outstanding leadership must confront two problems. First, outstanding leadership is a rare event. Because we cannot bring leaders such as Abraham Lincoln, Theodore Roosevelt, and John Kennedy together to complete a battery of psychological measures, it is difficult to apply the methods commonly used in other areas of the social sciences. Second, outstanding leadership is an unusually complex phenomenon unfolding over time in relation to a multifaceted and dynamic social setting. The complex conditions that surround outstanding leadership make it difficult to draw strong inferences, or unambiguous conclusions, about the causes of leader emergence and performance—a point attested to in the opinion-editorial pages of our newspapers. Students of outstanding leadership attempt to deal with the problems posed by rarity and complexity through one of four alternative methods: (a) dimensional approximation, (b) experimental simulation, (c) qualitative case analysis, and (d) quantitative case analysis.

Perhaps the most widely applied approach in studies of outstanding leadership is dimensional approximation. In dimensional approximation theory, qualitative observations are used to identify a set of attributes, constructs or dimensions, that seem to pull outstanding leaders apart from more "run of the mill" leaders. Thus, Bass and Avolio (1990), in their theory of transformational leadership, argued that the impact of outstanding leaders is attributable to their expression of attributes such as idealized influence (vision), intellectual stimulation, and inspirational communication. To test these models, measures are developed intended to capture differences across people in their expression of these attributes—typically behavior description measures (e.g., my leader sets challenging goals, my leader is concerned with my personal development). Leaders, and/or followers, are then asked to complete these measures under the assumption that leaders who are more likely to manifest behaviors held to characterize outstanding leadership will have followers who evidence greater motivation, performance, cohesion, creativity, and so on (e.g., Jung, Cho, & Ul, 2003; Lowe et al., 1996).

Although few scholars would dispute the value of the dimensional approximation approach, it does suffer from certain problems. First, the behavioral report measures commonly applied in dimensional approximation studies are subject to multiple potential biases (e.g., method bias, attraction/attribution biases, social-desirability bias, etc.). Second, in the dimensional approximation approach, outstanding leadership is studied in samples that may not, and often do not, contain outstanding leaders—under the assumption that similar behaviors will produce similar results. The problem with this approach, of course, is that certain unique aspects of outstanding leadership may be lost and that expression of relevant dimensions may differ in studies of outstanding leaders. Third, this approach will tend to ignore, or discount, distinctions among different types of outstanding leaders by virtue of its focus on distinguishing outstanding leaders from more run-of-the-mill leaders.

The experimental simulation approach is, in principle, similar to the behavioral-approximation approach in that it relies on a priori theoretical specification of the dimensions, and their associated behaviors, that can be used to distinguish outstanding leaders from their more run-of-the-mill counterparts. In a typical experimental simulation study (e.g., Kirkpatrick & Locke, 1995; Sosik et al., 1999), confederates, people acting out leadership scripts, are asked to act out different scripts where variation in script content is used to simulate behavioral differences on select dimensions. For example, Sosik et al. (1999) asked confederate leaders to follow scripts where different levels of transformational attributes were varied through behaviors evident in communications sent by the "leader" of a group working on an electronic brainstorming task. They found that transformational behaviors resulted in higher follower motivation.

The experimental approach is attractive both because it allows for tight control with respect to measures and potential confounds (extraneous influences on outcomes), and because it allows for the systematic examination of situational influences, interpersonal processes, and individual processes (Hunt et al., 1999; Strange & Mumford, 2005). By the same token, however, the experimental-simulation approach is plagued by the assumptions that similar behaviors produce similar results. Moreover, experimental simulations, though providing control, also result in a loss of real-world complexity, thereby limiting the generality of conclusions.

The qualitative case analysis approach is intended to address the generality problem noted earlier. In the qualitative case analysis approach, a wide variety of descriptive material is collected for a single outstanding leader or a small set of outstanding leaders. This descriptive material, often quite extensive, may include interview transcripts, setting or event descriptions, historic records, and the like. Expert analysis of this material, typically analyses guided by theory in relation to the setting at hand (Eisenhardt, 1989), is used to draw conclusions about the nature and origins of outstanding leadership (H. Gardner, 1993a). One example of the application of this approach may be found in the Mumford and Van Doorn (2001) study cited earlier. Here a qualitative analysis of Franklin's leadership activities was used to demonstrate the existence of a pragmatic leadership type and articulate some key aspects of this type.

This kind of in-depth qualitative analysis of a limited number of cases is typically feasible due to the voluminous material available for many outstanding leaders. Moreover, the qualitative case analysis approach apparently leads to conclusions that evidence real-world relevance. Nonetheless, application of this approach suffers from two noteworthy problems. First, the kind of qualitative data applied in these studies is highly complex. Thus, a certain amount of subjectivity creeps into *both* the selection and interpretation of relevant material. Second, by virtue of the limited number of cases under consideration, it becomes difficult to provide the kind of evidence needed to warrant general conclusions, demonstrate repeatability, and establish the relative importance of different variables in shaping the nature of outstanding leadership.

The quantitative case analysis approach, as broadly construed, can be understood as an attempt to overcome the generality problem evident in the qualitative analysis of a single case (Kazdin, 1980; Simonton, 1990). In this approach, qualitative data is obtained for *multiple* cases. This qualitative data is then content analyzed by judges who evaluate each case on a standard set of metrics or rating scales (e.g., Deluga, 2001; House et al., 1991). The relationships observed between those metrics and relevant performance indices are used to draw general conclusions about the variables influencing the behavior of outstanding leaders (Strange & Mumford, 2002).

Although the quantitative case approach permits the formation of general conclusions about the nature of outstanding leadership in real-world settings, including notably comparative statements about different types of outstanding leaders, this approach, like the other approaches described previously, has its limitations. First and foremost, this approach, by focusing on outstanding leaders, does not allow strong statements about how outstanding leaders differ from more run-of-the-mill leaders. Second, the complexity of the qualitative data used in these studies implies that the results obtained will depend on the quality, the reliability and validity, of the coding procedures being applied. Third, due to the difficult, time-consuming nature of coding, there will be some significant limitations in practice on the size of the sample that can be examined.

Historiometric Methods

The historiometric method represents a specific instantiation of the quantitative analysis of multiple cases (Mumford & Threlfall, 1992). In historiometric studies, however, the data applied in the analysis of multiple cases are obtained through available historic records (Simonton, 1990). Historic record data, of course, come in many forms. For example, one might examine the time an event occurred, the nature of a certain event, or the outcomes of an event. This kind of hard, or objective, data is often preferred in historiometric studies because its objectivity lends credence to the reliability of measures and the validity of resulting inferences (Tyler, 1964). In fact, early historiometric studies (e.g., Cox, 1926) were commonly criticized because they drew inferences about underlying psychological variables, for example, intelligence and defense mechanisms, which were not warranted based solely on objective events.

One can argue on the other hand, however, that underlying psychological variables are of interest precisely because they are associated with some form of overt behavior. In fact, most psychological variables are defined in terms of a set of overt behavioral markers. Thus, the historiometric approach can be, and indeed has been, extended to capture unobservable variables, such as motives (Winter, 1987) and personality characteristics (Deluga, 2001), by framing the content analysis of historic records in terms of observable behaviors, making the underlying variables of concern.

Though application of a behavioral marker strategy allows historiometric studies to address a wider range of phenomena, successful application of this approach requires that at least four other issues be taken into account. First, historiometric studies are clearly contingent on the accuracy of the behavioral observations provided by the historic documents used as a basis for coding. This point is of some importance because historic documents vary in quality and are subject to certain interpretive and reporting biases. As a result, historiometric studies of outstanding leadership are likely to prove most successful when (a) based on high-quality verified material stressing behavioral markers and (b) content analysis focuses on behavior per se rather than broader contextual interpretations and subjective evaluations.

Second, historic records, like most qualitative material, provide a rich, albeit unusually complex, dataset. The complexity of historic record data is, in fact, clearly evident when outstanding leaders are under consideration because multiple observations, by multiple people, extending over the entire course of a leader's career are commonly available. The complexity of this material, in turn, implies that historiometric studies of outstanding leadership are most likely to prove successful when the career time frames used in drawing inferences are clearly specified and sound operational definitions are developed concerning the kind of behaviors that will, and will not be, considered in coding.

Third, it should be remembered that the historic record, however rich, is rarely complete. Moreover, historic data tend to vary with respect to the kind of behaviors for which accurate, reasonably complete, data are available. For example, "private behavior," such as family relationships and spousal relationships, is not typically described with a high degree of accuracy or consistency. Other behaviors, however, typically behaviors occurring as part of the leader's public role, are more accurately and consistently recorded. Similarly, life events, including early life events, tend to be accurately and consistently described. These observations are of some importance because they suggest that historiometric studies of outstanding leadership should focus on either life events or behaviors occurring as part of public leadership roles.

Fourth, although outstanding leadership is a relatively rare event, over the course of history there have been tens of thousands of outstanding leaders. Of course, given the demands imposed by systematic content analyses, this observation indicates that historiometric studies of outstanding leadership will require construction of a viable sampling plan—a plan appropriate for the inferences to be drawn. One consideration that will influence the development of a viable sampling plan involves the desired generality of the inferences to be drawn. For example, are inferences to be drawn about men, women, or both men and women as the occupants of leadership roles? Another consideration, one unique to historiometric studies, is the accuracy of available data because there is little point in sampling data for leaders where the historic record is weak.

METHOD

Sample

The present set of studies was based on a sample of 120 historically notable leaders. Given the broad intent of the present set of studies, specifically to distinguish charismatic, ideological, and pragmatic leaders, the leaders included in this sample were expressly selected because they were held to manifest, unambiguously manifest, a charismatic, ideological, or pragmatic type. Additionally, to control for orientation, socialized versus personalized (House & Howell, 1992), half of the leaders selected within each type were chosen because they were held to display a socialized orientation whereas the remaining half of the leaders selected within each type were chosen because they were held to display a personalized orientation. Thus, 20 leaders were selected for examination in each of the following categories: (a) socialized charismatics, (b) personalized charismatics, (c) socialized ideologues, (d) personalized ideologues, (e) socialized pragmatics, and (f) personalized pragmatics. Table 3.1 provides a list of leaders included in the present set of studies listed by category assignment.

With regard to this sample, three points should be noted. First, 120 was not an arbitrary number. Instead, the size of this sample was specified to provide sufficient power to detect differences among charismatic, ideological, and pragmatic leaders taking into account the demands made by content coding. Second, the sample applied herein was restricted to 20th-century leaders due to the need for objective, verifiable biographical material—typically, biographies written prior to this period were subject to less rigorous evaluation. Third, use of 20th-century leaders was attractive because, although time was available to

TABLE 3.1
Leaders, Types, and Orientations

	Type		
Orientation	Ideological	Charismatic	Pragmatic
Socialized	1. Jane Addams	1. Mustafa K. Atatürk	1. Warren Buffett
	2. Susan B. Anthony	2. David Ben-Gurion	2. Richard Daley
	3. Dietrich Bonhoeffer	3. Cesar Chavez	3. Walt Disney
	4. Michael Collins	4. Winston Churchill	4. John Foster Dulles
	5. Eugene V. Debs	5. Henry Ford	5. Alfred Dupont
	6. John Dewey	6. Samual Gompers	6. Dwight D. Eisenhower
	7. W.E.B. DuBois	7. Lee Iacocca	7. Felix Frankfurter
	8. Betty Friedan	8. John F. Kennedy	8. Berry Gordy
	9. Indira Gandhi	9. Jomo Kenyatta	9. Katharine Graham
	10. Mohandas Gandhi	10. Martin Luther King, Jr.	10. Oliver W. Holmes
	11. Charles de Gaulle	11. Fiorello H. La Guardia	11. George Marshall
	12. Emma Goldman	12. Douglas MacArthur	12. Mikhail Gorbachev
	13. Dag Hammarskjöld	13. Louis B. Mayer	13. Thomas Watson
	14. John L. Lewis	14. J.P. Morgan	14. George H. Rickover
	15. Kwame Nkrumah	15. Edward R. Murrow	15. Erwin Rommel
	16. Ronald W. Reagan	16. Gamal Abdel Nasser	16. George Soros
	17. Eleanor A. Roosevelt	17. Sam Rayburn	17. Josip B. Tito
	18. Theodore Roosevelt	18. Franklin D. Roosevelt	18. Harry S. Truman
	19. Lech Walesa	19. Anwar Sadat	19. Sam Walton
	20. Woodrow T. Wilson	20. Margaret Thatcher	20. Booker T. Washington
Personalized	1. Lavrenti Beria	1. Idi Amin	1. Al Capone
	2. Fidel Castro	2. Neville Chamberlain	2. Andrew Carnegie
	3. Georges Clemenceau	3. John De Lorean	3. Otis Chandler
	4. Ferdinand Foch	4. Porfirio Diaz	4. Lyndon B. Johnson
	5. Francisco Franco	5. François Duvalier	5. Al Dunlap
	6. Marcus Garvey	6. Hermann Göring	6. Henry Ford II
	7. Warren Harding	7. Assad Hafaz	7. Carlo Gambino
	8. Rudolf Hess	8. Adolf Hitler	8. Leslie Groves
	9. Heinrich Himmler	9. Jimmy Hoffa	9. Leona Helmsley
	10. Ho Chi Minh	10. Herbert R. Hoover	10. Reinhard Heydrich
	11. Vladimir Lenin	11. J. Edgar Hoover	11. Horatio Kitchener
	12. Joe McCarthy	12. Huey P. Long	12. Alfred Krupp
	13. Pol Pot	13. Ferdinand Marcos	13. Robert Moses
	14. John D. Rockefeller	14. Benito Mussolini	14. Rupert Murdoch
	15. Josef Stalin	15. Manuel Noriega	15. George Patton
	16. Leon Trotsky	16. Eva Perón	16. Jackie Presser
	17. Kaiser Wilhelm II	17. Juan Perón	17. Richard M. Nixon
	18. Deng Xiaoping	18. Rafael Trujillo	18. David Sarnoff
	19. Emiliano Zapata	19. W. C. Westmoreland	19. Martha Stewart
	20. Mao Ze-dong	20. Malcolm X	20. Lew Wasserman

fully assess the outcomes of the leaders' efforts, leadership could still be examined in the context of modern institutional settings. Fourth, an attempt was made to include in this sample leaders working in different fields (e.g., business, politics, nonprofit organizations, and the military). No attempt was made, however, to ensure equal representation of leaders drawn from different domains in the six categories under consideration due to the tendency of charismatic, ideological, and pragmatic leaders to gravitate to different fields. Nonetheless, an attempt was made to ensure that each category under consideration included leaders drawn from multiple fields.

The procedures used to identify the leaders included in this sample involved a number of steps. Initially, a list of candidate leaders, leaders who were candidates for inclusion in the sample, was developed. Development of this candidate list began with a review of general history texts and biographical Web sites to identify historically notable 20th-century leaders for whom at least one "academic" biography was available. Thus, leaders who had only been immortalized by the "popular" press were not considered for inclusion in this study. In initial formation of the candidate list, an attempt was made to draw leaders from multiple fields. Preference was given to leaders for whom multiple biographies were available because (a) the availability of multiple biographies provided additional evidence of the impact of the leader and (b) the availability of multiple biographies allowed for the selection of biographies providing material appropriate for the present set of investigations. Application of these procedures resulted in the identification of 221 twentieth-century leaders who were plausible candidates for inclusion in the sample.

Once the pool of 221 candidates had been identified, it was necessary to screen this pool in an attempt to reduce the list of leaders to be studied to 120. This screening began with the assignment of leaders to the categories under consideration. To classify leaders with respect to orientation, socialized versus personalized, the criteria suggested by O'Connor et al. (1995) were applied. More specifically, three psychologists were asked to review the summary material obtained from the text and Web site searches. Based on this material, judges, all doctoral candidates in industrial and organizational psychology, were to classify a leader as socialized if they initiated action for the betterment of people, society, or institutions regardless of personal consequences (e.g., Gerald Ford), or as personalized if they initiated action to acquire, maintain, and enhance power (e.g., Joseph McCarthy).

These judges were also asked to classify leaders, based on this behavioral material, as charismatic, ideological, or pragmatic. In accordance with the observations of Strange and Mumford (2002), a leader was classified as charismatic if they articulated a vision based on perceived social needs and the requirements for effective, future-oriented change (e.g., J.P. Morgan). A leader was classified as ideological when they articulated a vision based on strongly held personal beliefs (e.g., Ronald Reagan). Mumford and Van Doorn's (2001) study was used as a basis for identifying pragmatic leaders with leaders being classified as such if their efforts were focused on the solution of immediate social problems (e.g., Benjamin Franklin).

Application of these criteria resulted in the three judges agreeing on more than 70% of their assignments of a leader to one of the six categories. In cases where the judges disagreed in their assignments to a category, the leader was dropped from the candidate list. This point is of some importance for two reasons. First, by dropping cases where there was disagreement, the sampling plan applied herein efficiently prohibited examination of mixed-type leaders (e.g., leaders evidencing both charismatic and ideological behavior). Second, by dropping cases where there was disagreement, it became impossible for the present effort to say much about alternative pathways to outstanding leadership outside the charismatic, ideological, and pragmatic pathways of concern herein.

To further reduce this candidate list, the three judges were asked to review the available descriptive material pertaining to the leaders falling into the six categories under consideration (e.g., socialized and personalized charismatic, ideological, and pragmatic leaders). The final set of leaders to be examined was determined vis-à-vis application of the following criteria: (a) the volume of biographical material available for the leader, (b) representation of multiple fields (e.g., business, politics, nonprofit organizations, the military) in each category, (c) representation of non-Western leaders, and (d) representation of women.

Application of these criteria led to the final list of leaders to be examined— the list presented in Table 3.1. Given the conditions influencing access to leadership roles throughout most of the 20th century, it is not surprising that the majority of the leaders included in this sample were men. Nonetheless, a few women were identified who could be included in the sample. In examining the leaders assigned to the charismatic, ideological, and pragmatic categories, another noteworthy trend comes to fore. More specifically, political and nonprofit leaders tend to be found in the ideological category, and business leaders tend to be found in the pragmatic category, whereas a rather diverse group of leaders, with respect to field of endeavor, tend to be found in the charismatic category. Given our earlier observations, this pattern of assignments is not surprising and provides some evidence pointing to the validity of this sampling procedure.

Some further evidence bearing on the meaningfulness of the sampling procedures applied, and assignment of leaders to the categories under consideration, may be obtained by comparing the leader assignments made in the present study with those made in earlier studies by O'Connor et al. (1995) and Strange and Mumford (2002). Bearing in mind the point that these earlier studies did not consider pragmatic leaders, it is evident that a fairly high degree of overlap emerged with respect to leader assignment to either the socialized or personalized charismatic categories or the socialized or personalized ideological categories. This convergence in assignments of leaders to categories provides some evidence pointing to the validity, or meaningfulness, of the selection and assignment process applied in the present set of studies.

Biography Selection

The historic data that provided the basis for the present set of studies were drawn from biographies describing the careers of the selected leaders. Because these biographies provided the data used as a basis for content coding, some attention was given to the selection of appropriate biographies. Identification of the biographies used in the various content analyses was carried out through application of the following procedures.

Initially, a reference search was conducted to identify biographies published describing the careers of each of the selected leaders. Although in a few cases (less than 10% of the total sample) only one biography was available, in most cases a number (three or more) biographies were available describing the careers of the selected leaders. When multiple biographies were available, a Web search and a library search were conducted to obtain reviews of the available biographies. Any biography that received unfavorable scholarly reviews, particularly with respect to the comprehensiveness and accuracy of the material presented, was eliminated.

The reviews available for the remaining biographies were then examined to identify the two or three biographies that appeared to provide the best available descriptions of the leader's career. These more-promising biographies were obtained and reviewed by three psychologists with respect to the following five criteria:

1. Did the biography stress accurate and detailed reporting of the leader's behavior and key events he or she encountered over the course of his or her career?
2. Did the biography expressly focus on behaviors of concern with respect to the present set of investigations (e.g., leader–follower interactions, communication strategies, etc.)?
3. Did the biography provide a reasonably detailed account of the leader's early life?
4. Did the biography provide a clear and reasonably objective summary of the leader's accomplishments?
5. Was there evidence of adequate scholarly work as indicated by citations provided and sources examined?

Of the available biographies, the biography that best satisfied these five criteria was retained for use in the various content analysis studies.

With regard to the general procedure just sketched out, two further points are worthy of note. First, if only one biography was available for a leader and this biography did not satisfy the aforementioned criteria, then this leader was dropped and replaced by a comparable leader with respect to type (e.g., charismatic) and orientation (e.g., socialized) drawn from the candidate list. Second, if none of the biographies selected for review, in cases where multiple biographies were available, satisfied these criteria then a search for an alternative biography was initiated. If an adequate alternative biography could not be obtained, then this leader was also dropped from the sample and replaced by a comparable leader with respect to type and orientation for whom adequate biographical material was available. In all cases, adequate biographies were obtained following these substitutions.

The Appendix presents the reference list for the biographies applied in the present set of investigations. The majority of the biographies (more than 75%) had been published within the last 25 years. A typical biography was over 500 print pages with many biographies presenting more than 600 pages of text. Most biographies presented this material in 15 to 20 chapter segments with these chapters averaging 30 to 40 pages in length.

To help guide subsequent content analyses, these chapters were classified into the following categories: (a) early-career chapters describing the leader's life before they began to assume the kind of leadership roles for which they would eventually become noted, (b) rise-to-power chapters examining the period in which the leader began moving into the leadership roles for which they would eventually become noted, (c) pinnacle-of-power chapters examining the leader's career in the roles where he or she exercised the greatest influence, (d) fall-from-power chapters examining the leader's behavior and experiences as they lost position and influence, and (e) "summary" chapters, commonly prologue or epilogue chapters, where the biographer summarized the leader's accomplishments.

All biographies under consideration had chapters falling into all of these categories. Assignment of a chapter to one of these categories was based on a psychologist's review of chapter content in relation to the classification scheme just provided. Because a pilot study indicated that there was virtually no disagreement among judges when assigning chapters to these categories, a single psychologist made the assignment of chapters to categories. Although biographies differed with respect to the number of chapters falling into a category, most biographies devoted more chapters to the early-career, rise-to-power, and pinnacle-of-power periods than the fall-from-power period or summarizations of accomplishments.

Summary

In this section we have described the sample of leaders applied in the present set of investigations and the procedures used to identify the biographies to be applied in describing the careers of these leaders. The present set of investigations is based on a sample of 120 twentieth-century leaders where these leaders were expressly selected to include both socialized and personalized charismatic, ideological, and pragmatic leaders. Academic biographies were obtained describing the careers of these leaders. These biographies were expressly selected based on the accuracy and comprehensiveness of the material presented. The material presented in these biographies provided the basis for the content analyses to be conducted in the various studies under consideration herein.

CONTENT CODING

Materials

As noted earlier, biographies, like other forms of historic records, provide a rich, albeit complex, source of descriptive data. As a result, the successful use of this material in various content analyses depends, at least in part, on the procedures used to draw career events from this large, complex body of material. Selection of material to be applied in content coding proceeded in two distinct steps. First, the chapters from which relevant behaviors or events were to be drawn were identified. Second, procedures were developed for identifying and sampling relevant behaviors, or events, within these chapters.

   Chapter Selection.   Identification of the chapters (e.g., "rise to power," "pinnacle of power") to be applied in a given content analytic study was based on two considerations: (a) the substantive questions to be addressed in a particular content analysis study and (b) the typical presentation of relevant material in biographies.

   In the study of the communication strategies used by charismatic, ideological, and pragmatic leaders, the primary concern at hand was how these three different types of leaders exercised influence through mass communication. Accordingly, comparison of charismatic, ideological, and pragmatic leaders in this regard seemed to require a focus on the communication strategies applied when they exercised their greatest influence. As a result, pinnacle-of-power chapters were to be applied in the study of differences among charismatic, ideological, and pragmatic leaders with respect to communication strategies. Along similar lines, the study of LMX requires examination of how leaders interacted with followers when they were in a position of power. In keeping with this observation, it was concluded that the study of leader–follower relationships should examine how leaders interacted with followers when they were at their ultimate position of influence. Hence in the study of leader–follower relationships, the pinnacle-of-power chapters were to provide the material applied in content coding.

   Problem-solving activities and political tactics, in contrast to communication strategies and leader–follower relationships, are not manifest in a prototypic form at a particular point in leaders' careers. Instead, differences in problem-solving activities and political tactics can be appropriately assessed at different points in the careers of charismatic, ideological, and pragmatic leaders. In this regard, furthermore, it should be recognized that both problem-solving strategies and political tactics change as leaders move through their career due to individual development and shifts in role demands (Mumford, Zaccaro, Harding, et al., 2000). As a result of these considerations, chapters examining the leader's "rise to power" and "fall from power" as well as their behavior at the "pinnacle of power" were examined in the content analyses contrasting charismatic, ideological, and pragmatic leaders with respect to problemsolving strategies and political tactics.

The developmental study was concerned with identifying the kind of early experiences shaping the life narratives, and thus presumably the prescriptive mental models applied by, outstanding leaders. Because the available evidence indicates that people begin constructing life narratives in late childhood or early adolescence (Habermas & Bluck, 2000), it seemed clear that the early-career chapters, the chapters examining the leader's early life before they began their rise to power, should be applied in this study. However, early-career chapters focusing on family and family context were not considered in this analysis because chapters examining this background material typically had little to say about the *leader's* early experiences.

The final set of comparisons to be made among charismatic, ideological, and pragmatic leaders concerned their performance. Although performance-relevant information may be gleaned from many of the chapters included in biographies, this information is typically presented in summary form in the prologue or epilogue chapters. Application of the prologue, or epilogue, chapters, the "summary" chapters, moreover, avoided the problems posed by drawing predictor information (e.g., communication strategies, political tactics) and criterion information (e.g., number of institutions established) from the same chapters. Accordingly, only the information presented in the summary chapters was used to contrast charismatic, ideological, and pragmatic leaders with respect to performance.

Identifying and Sampling Material.   Having specified the chapters to be applied in the various content analyses, it was then possible to abstract from these chapters the material to be applied in a given content analysis study. The systematic abstraction of select material from relevant chapters was necessary for three reasons. First, by abstracting select portions of the material presented in a chapter, judges were not presented with evaluative and contextual information about the leader that might color, or bias, appraisals in the content analysis. Second, prior abstraction of relevant material allowed systematic procedures to be applied in sampling behaviors, or events, to be appraised in the content analysis. Third, prior abstraction of select material served to reduce the complexity of the material presented and thus the burden placed on judges during content coding.

For the study of communication strategies, the approach used to draw material from the relevant pinnacle-of-power chapters was quite straightforward. Initially, a psychologist reviewed the material presented in the pinnacle-of-power chapters to identify speeches, testimony, public letters, and other forms of mass communications that were described in the text, and described in some detail (half a page or more), under the assumption that these detailed descriptions are provided only for noteworthy communications. Subsequently, this material, along with accompanying material describing the development, delivery, and outcomes of the communication, were abstracted from the relevant chapters. It is of note that all communications meeting this extended substantive analysis criteria were applied in the content analysis. Typically, 6 to 10 communications met this extended analysis criteria with most relevant text abstracts averaging three to four pages in length. Table 3.2 presents a typical text abstract for a communication used in content coding.

To examine leader–follower relationships, it was necessary to apply a different strategy in identifying and sampling relevant behaviors. Initially, three judges, all doctoral candidates in industrial and organizational psychology, reviewed the pinnacle-of-power chapters. They were asked to reach a consensus decision concerning who were the leader's three closest followers. A "close" follower was defined as a person holding a high official, or unofficial, role in the organization the leader was responsible for and with whom the leader frequently interacted. The index of the biography was then used to identify the places in the pinnacle-of-power chapters where noteworthy interactions occurred, and meaningful interactions were abstracted for use in content coding. A "meaningful interaction" was defined as an exchange between the leader and follower

TABLE 3.2
Incident of Leader Communication

Andrew Carnegie

Carnegie took his mother to Cresson in hopes the fresh air would revive her. In June, he came down from the mountains to preach at Pittsburgh's Curry Commercial College. The title of his sermon was "The Road to Business Success." From his experiences, he delivered unto them some of his most oft-quoted axioms:

> The rising man must do something exceptional, and beyond the range of his special department. HE MUST ATTRACT ATTENTION . . . Always break orders to save owners. There never was a great character who did not sometimes smash the routine regulations and make new ones for himself. . . . Boss your boss just as soon as you can; try it on early. There is nothing he will like so well if he is the right kind of boss; if he is not, he is not the man for you to remain with—leave him whenever you can, even at a present sacrifice, and find one capable of discerning genius. . . . "Don't put all your eggs in one basket" is all wrong. I tell you "put all your eggs in one basket, and then watch that basket." . . . Look out for the boy how has to plunge into work direct from the common school and who begins by sweeping out the office. He is the probable dark horse that you had better watch.

That dark horse was Carnegie, of course. To soothe any painful memories from his struggle to escape poverty, he'd become sentimental about those early years. From his lofty pedestal, however, he failed to explain to the students that it took him a good ten years to put all the eggs in one basket and that he still owned a wide variety of railroad and insurance stocks, among others, as well as land and properties. (He owned stock and bonds in some twenty companies that were not directly related to his iron, steel, and bridge manufacturing, or to his newspaper syndicate.)

Note. From *Carnegie*, by P. Krass (2002, pp. 197–198). Copyright © 2002 by John Wiley & Sons, Inc. Reprinted with permission of John Wiley & Sons, Inc.

where the interaction was described in some detail and entailed significant outcomes for both the leader and the follower. It is of note that a reliability check conducted using three judges working with 12 biographies resulted in 85% agreement in the meaningful incidents of leader–follower interactions identified using these procedures. The material describing these interactions was half a page to a page and a half long with 8 to 10 such interactions being abstracted from a leader biography for use in content coding. Table 3.3 presents a sample of the material identified using these procedures.

In the studies of problem-solving behavior and political tactics, the number of chapters under consideration, and the rather complex nature of the incidents providing illustrations of problem-solving behavior and political tactics, dictated application of a different set of procedures for abstracting the material to be applied in content coding. Here abstraction of the relevant material began with an explicit definition of the kind of biographical incidents held to reflect problem-solving behavior and political tactics. Problem-solving behavior was held to be reflected in incidents where the *leader* had to address a complex, novel issue where a number of alternative courses of action were possible given the situation at hand and the success of the actions taken had significant implications for organizational outcomes (Mumford, Zaccaro, Harding, et al., 2000). Political behavior was held to be reflected in incidents where the leader exercised influence to induce changes in others' behavior or obtain the support and compliance needed to carry out some activity associated with significant organizational or personal outcomes (Ammeter et al., 2002).

TABLE 3.3
Incidents of Leader–Follower Relationships

Rudolf Hess

Hess's chief of staff was a thirty-three-year-old man, heavyset and somewhat bull-like, who had been a party member since 1927. He proved to be a good bookkeeper, rude in handling subordinates but completely honest in money matters and a veritable workhorse with an astonishingly precise memory. He was assigned to the deputy's staff in July 1933 and Hess was happy to have him as his chief of staff, the "deputy's deputy." Hess trusted him because he never forced his way into the limelight, and gradually he gave the man more power.

Margaret Thatcher

Whitelaw and Parkinson, however, had something else in common: a particularly personal relationship with their leader. During both the preparations and the war itself, they could offer her a special kind of solace. They felt a desire to protect her. . . . Whitelaw, with his Military Cross as proof of sometime gallantry in the Scots Guards, saw it as part of his job to remind this inexperienced lady, who had no first-hand knowledge of gunfire, that she must steel herself for casualties, prepare for bloodiness, not imagine that it could be a painless victory.

Note. Hess is from *Rudolf Hess: The Last Nazi*, by W. Schwarzwaller (1988, p. 138). Copyright © 1988 by National Press, Inc. Thatcher is from *One of Us: A Biography of Margaret Thatcher*, by H. Young (1989, p. 269). Copyright © 1989 by Macmillan UK. Reprinted by permission.

Once these definitions had been formulated, definitions appropriate for identifying manifestations of problem-solving and political behavior among outstanding leaders, three psychologists were presented with two leader biographies and were asked to apply these definitions to identify incidents involving problem-solving and political behavior in the pinnacle-of-power chapters. They then compared their selections, discussed any discrepancies in incident selection, and repeated this process on a new set of biographies until a 90% agreement criterion was reached with respect to the incidents of problem-solving and political behavior identified.

After they had met this criterion for incident identification, these psychologists were asked to review one rise-to-power chapter, one pinnacle-of-power chapter, and one fall-from-power chapter in each biography. They were to select three to five incidents of problem-solving behavior and three to five incidents of political behavior with these incidents being spread throughout the chapters under consideration. The material describing this incident along with material describing the content of the incident and the outcome of the leader's behavior were to be abstracted from the text and used as a basis for content coding. These incidents were generally two to four text pages in length. Table 3.4 illustrates an incident of problem-solving behavior whereas Table 3.5 illustrates an incident of political behavior.

Identification of the life events to be used in the developmental studies required application of a rather elaborate set of procedures in event identification to permit subsequent comparison of charismatic, ideological, and pragmatic leaders with respect to the kind of events involved in the formation of life narratives. Here four undergraduates, unfamiliar with the intent of the present study, received a 16-hour training program, extended over 2 weeks, where they were taught how to identify and abstract key life events. This training program began by familiarizing these undergraduates with the definitions of the six types of life events under consideration: (a) originating events, (b) anchoring events, (c) analogous events, (d) turning point events, (e) redemptive events, and (f) contaminating events (Pillemer, 2001). Subsequently, they practiced identifying these events using the early-career chapters drawn from five biographies. Feedback was provided concerning identification of events, classification of events, and discrimination of event types. This practice continued until these undergraduates reached an 80% agreement criterion with respect to both event identification and event classification.

Following training, these undergraduates were asked to review the early-career chapters applying to the 120 leaders under consideration in the present set of studies. They were asked to identify and abstract any events falling into the six event categories under consideration and classify the event into *one* of these six categories. An examination of the reliability of these classifications, using a kappa index, indicated that adequate interrater agreement coefficients were obtained; originating events ($r = .89$), anchoring events ($r = .75$), analo-

TABLE 3.4
Incident of Leader Problem-Solving Behavior

Woodrow Wilson

Wilson had one more task before making the electoral appeal that was to lift the campaign of 1912 to the level of a great national debate: had to clarify in his mind and come to terms with the nature of the economic problem confronting the United States. On August 28 he was visited in Trenton by the progressive Boston lawyer Louis D. Brandeis, long a champion of the small businessman and a foe of monopolistic restrictions in all forms. The two men conferred for several hours. Brandeis was well impressed by Wilson. "It seems to me," he wrote a friend, "that he has all the qualities for an ideal President—strong, simple, and truthful, able, open-minded, eager to learn and deliberate." As for Wilson, he had come in those few illuminating hours to revise his own approach to the problem of the trusts.

Brandeis defined with sharp contrast the difference between the Democratic and Progressive parties in regard to monopoly. The Democrats insisted that competition be maintained, and if necessary created and enforced, in all branches of private industry. The Progressive Party, on the other hand, accepted private monopoly as inevitable in some branches of industry; it maintained that in such cases existing trusts should not be broken up or dismembered, but should be regulated so as to moralize them and prevent them from doing evil. "This difference in the economic policy of the two parties," Brandeis wrote in a subsequent memorandum to Wilson, "is fundamental and irreconcilable." The approach of Roosevelt and his Progressive Party meant constant regulation and control by big government; the approach of the Democrats meant a regime of liberty, once the conditions of a free market had been established and enforced.

The idea of establishing a free market by deliberate government action was far from new to Wilson. The classical economist had not denied that some degree of human intervention was necessary before their "invisible hand" could bring about the benefits of unhampered competition. Indeed, Wilson's economics professor during his undergraduate years, the highly conservative Lyman H. Atwater, had recognized a free market to be a purposeful creation of law, needing to be constantly and subtly regulated. Wilson was clear on the principle, now that Brandeis had argued it forcibly and applied it to the trust. But he was still uncertain in regard to its application, and later in the campaign telegraphed Brandeis somewhat frantically asking him "please [to] set forth as explicitly as possible the actual measures by which competition can be effectively regulated." Brandeis's reply seemed too detailed and technical for use in speeches. But Wilson did not really need details. He had gotten hold of a central idea which he could develop in his own way. The idea liberated him once and for all from thinking that the only alternative to concentrated economic power was restored to the power of big government.

His capacity to absorb advice, to grasp its implications, and to fit it into his own philosophy never was better proven than in the days following the encounter with Brandeis. Busy as he was with the practical details of the campaign, besieged by callers and driven by speaking engagements, he managed to recast overnight his approach to industrial problems, and in doing so to give his argument a new precision and depth. In Buffalo, four days after the talks at Trenton, he got his campaign under way with an effective Labor Day address in which for the first time he defined the existence of the trusts as the result of deficient competition within an unregulated market. Lack of competition, he asserted, "has permitted . . . men to do anything that they chose to do to squeeze their rival's out and to crush their rivals to the earth." And he forcefully described the kind of massive and pervasive control that, under his rival's approach, would be necessary to keep the existing monopolies in line.

In later speeches Wilson's imagination was fired by these concepts; he saw the full establishment of a free market as underlying his belief in the capacities and the opportunities of the common man. He had felt increasingly during the Princeton battles that it was the "man on the make," the man fighting against the tide, the man rising by his skills and ardor from the mass, who gave democracy its special character. In Lincoln he had found his ideal. Basing his campaign upon the elimination of monopoly in all forms, he rose to the kind of popular eloquence first exemplified in the Pittsburgh speech in 1910. More than that, he came to see the major reforms of banking and the tariff as means to eliminate the privileges, the nooks of entrenched interest and advantages, which distorted visionary zeal in even the most workaday policies of the state.

Note. From *Woodrow Wilson: A Biography*, by A. Heckscher (1991, pp. 256–257). Copyright © 1991 by August Heckscher. Reprinted with the permission of Scribner, an imprint of Simon & Schuster Adult Publishing Group.

TABLE 3.5
Incident of Political Behavior

Sam Walton

When Sam bought 12½ acres—with a railroad siding—about a mile from downtown Bentonville on which to erect his new headquarters, he was far more interested in creating a distribution center through which those thousands of cardboard cartons containing appliances, hardware, shoes and dresses, and the like could move out expeditiously and efficiently on his own trucks to his stores.

So Ferold Arend and Jim Henry cut the office space down to 12,000 square feet and put the other 60,000 into warehouse space.

It also is axiomatic that to create the eventual Wal-Mart miracle, Sam went at distribution backward. Traditionally retailers build warehouses to serve existing outlets, but Walton built the warehouses first, then the stores were spotted around it. Initially Sam only opened stores within a radius of 300 miles from Bentonville headquarters. That meant that his trucks could deliver fresh inventory to any Wal-Mart within five or six hours. And if he knew anything about running a store, he didn't show sales growth when what the customer wants to buy is not on his shelves. Grudgingly, Sam later extended the radius to 350 miles, perhaps 400. But when the stores began to spread out all across the Sunbelt, he insisted on building a flock of new distribution centers to keep the truck travel within the five- to six-hour drive time.

Arend and Jim Henry proved to be pretty good designers in the first place; within three years Sam was forced to double the initial office space at his Bentonville complex. Naturally, at the same time he had to add 64,000 more square feet to the original warehouse, which would now cover an area as large as three football fields. The Wal-Mart distribution operation was already unloading two to three railroad cars a week, and four or five full trailers a day.

Note. From *Sam Walton*, by V. Trimble (1990, pp. 119–120). Copyright © 1990 by Vance H. Trimble. Used by permission of Dutton, a division of Penguin Group (USA) Inc.

gous events ($r = .98$), turning point events ($r = .92$), redemptive events ($r = .64$), and contaminating events ($r = .78$). Typically, these events were a half to one page in length with 20 to 30 events across categories being identified for each leader. The material abstracted describing these events is presented in Table 3.6, which presents events lying in each of the six categories under consideration. These event abstracts provided the material used in content coding.

Content Coding

Once the material describing relevant behavior or events had been abstracted from relevant portions of the biographies, it provided a basis for the various content analysis studies. A similar set of general procedures was applied in the various content analysis efforts. Initially, four to six judges were recruited—judges who had not participated in selection of the material to be used in coding. These judges were a mix of undergraduates and graduate students pursuing degrees in psychology. A total of 24 judges participated in at least one of the various content analyses. The judges, eight in all, participating in multiple analyses were, of course, rotated to minimize the potential for spurious overlap.

TABLE 3.6
Incident of Leader Development

Fidel Castro

In what Fidel calls, "a decisive moment in my life," Angel Castro decided during the boys' summer holiday after the fourth grade that they would not go back to school. . . . But Fidel [Castro] was determined to return to school. As he tells the story, "I remember going to mother and explaining to her that I wanted to go on studying; it wasn't fair not to let me go to school. I appealed to her and told her I would set fire to the house if I wasn't sent back . . . so they decided to send me back. I'm not sure if they were afraid or just sorry for me, but my mother pleaded my case."

Fidel was learning quickly that absolute and uncompromising stubbornness was a powerful weapon. This may have been the most important lesson he had drawn from his young years at the *finca* and at the Santiago schools, and he never forgot it.

Note. From *Fidel: A Critical Portrait*, by T. Szulc (1986, p. 112), New York: William Morrow and Company, Inc.

Prior to the start of a content analysis study, the judges participating in this effort were required to complete a 2-week training program involving 8 to 12 hours of instruction. In this training, the judges were familiarized with the nature of the stimulus material—the material abstracted from the biographies that would be used in coding. Subsequently, they were presented with definitions of the dimensions on which this material would be evaluated. These definitions, for example, definitions of problem construction and idea generation in the problem-solving study, were cast in concrete operational terms and the similarities and differences between the various dimensions under consideration in a given study were discussed. After clarifying the nature of the dimensions to be applied, they were presented with behavioral illustrations of varying levels of expression of the attributes, or dimensions, of interest.

Once the judges had been familiarized with the dimensions and their behavioral manifestations, they were presented with the rating scales to be applied in the content analysis. This rater training described not only how the rating scales were to be applied, but also common errors to be avoided in making ratings generally (e.g., halo, leniency errors) and specific errors that must be avoided in the analysis of biographical material (e.g., a focus on evaluative statements rather than on behaviors or events, overinterpretation of context, imposition of personal assumptions on text). Following rater training, the judges were provided with instruction for applying the relevant rating scales. Broadly speaking, these instructions boiled down to the requirement to read through the material abstracted to describe an incident of leader behavior or experience. And, after reading through this material, evaluate the material provided considering only the material presented in the incident under consideration.

Following rater training, the judges participating in a particular study were presented with a sample of biographical material abstracted from the pertinent chapters. They were asked to evaluate this material using the rating scales provided. After making their own independent ratings, the judges reconvened as a panel to compare their ratings and discuss any observed discrepancies. At this time, feedback was provided to clarify dimensional definitions and application of the relevant rating scales. These practice sessions continued until the judges evidenced adequate agreement—an average interrater agreement coefficient above .70.

In making ratings, judges were presented with a binder containing a subset of the relevant stimulus materials abstracted from the biographies. The stimulus material contained in a binder was structured in such a way that it contained material drawn from multiple biographies where the leader involved in the incident was not expressly identified. Moreover, material applying to a given leader was distributed across binders. These steps were taken to minimize potential set and evaluative biases. These binders were rotated across judges so that different judges evaluated different material at different levels of practice.

The ratings applied in the various content analysis studies differed depending on the nature of the material being evaluated. For the leader–follower relationships and communication strategies studies, 5-point Likert rating scales were applied in evaluating the relevant material. In the studies examining leader problem-solving activities and political tactics, evaluation of the stimulus material was based on the frequency with which various behaviors were evident in the incident under consideration. These frequency evaluations were based on a modified checklist approach. A modified Q-sort approach was applied to assess the content of the developmental events. Greater detail concerning the nature of these rating scales, along with evidence bearing on their reliability and validity, is provided in the chapters examining the results obtained in the various content analysis studies.

Summary

In this section, we have examined the basic procedures applied in the content analysis of the biographies describing the careers of charismatic, ideological, and pragmatic leaders. The methods applied in these content analyses involved two distinct operations. First, select material was abstracted from relevant portions of the biographies to sample relevant behaviors or events. This abstraction process was used both to focus the content analysis on material directly relevant to the inferential questions at hand and to reduce rater burden. Second, multiple judges, all of whom had received extensive training, were asked to review the material abstracted from the biographies, only abstracted material and not full chapters, and evaluate this material using a set of rating scales intended to allow appraisal of the dimensions being assessed in the content analysis. These ratings were to be used in comparing the behaviors and developmental experiences characteristic of charismatic, ideological, and pragmatic leaders.

CRITERIA AND CONTROLS

Criteria

Earlier, we noted that charismatic, ideological, and pragmatic leaders *might* differ in terms of performance. Prior studies, furthermore, have indicated that marked differences in performance are commonly observed in studies contrasting socialized and personalized leaders (O'Connor et al., 1995). To examine cross-type differences in performance, and examine how various aspects of leader behavior being assessed in the content analyses were related to performance, a set of criterion, or outcome, measures were drawn from the summary chapters presented in the various biographies under consideration.

Based on the earlier findings of Strange and Mumford (2002), 12 general criterion measures were drawn from these summary chapters intended to provide an overall appraisal of performance with respect to social impact. The first five criterion measures, all based on the biographers' observations, were counts examining: (a) the number of positive contributions made by the leader, (b) the number of negative contributions made by the leader, (c) the number of different types of positive contributions made by the leader, (d) the number of different types of negative contributions made by the leader, and (e) the number of institutions established by the leader. In addition to these counts of points mentioned, a psychologist was asked to rate seven additional criteria based on the material presented in the summary chapters. These ratings, made on a 5-point scale, examined:

1. How much did the leader contribute to society?
2. How long did these contributions last?
3. How many people did the leader affect?
4. Did the leader initiate mass movements?
5. Was the leader's agenda maintained when they left power?
6. Were institutions established by the leader still in existence?
7. What was the biographer's evaluation of the leader?

The reliability of these outcome assessments was established in a small-scale study. In this study, three judges, all doctoral candidates in industrial and organizational psychology, were asked to evaluate the performance of 18 leaders using the aforementioned scales and the information presented in the relevant summary chapters. Using the procedures suggested by Shrout and Fleiss (1979), an average interrater agreement coefficient of .83 was obtained across the 12 rating scales under consideration. In a second study, intended to provide some evidence for the validity, or meaningfulness, of these evaluations, a second, high-quality biography was obtained for five leaders. The outcome evaluations derived from the summary chapter presented in this second biography were contrasted with the outcome evaluations derived from the summary chapters presented in the first biography. The agreement coefficient obtained in this comparative analysis was 84%. Thus, some evidence is available for the convergent validity of these evaluations across biographical sources.

In addition to these general criteria, a separate set of criteria was drawn from the summary chapters expressly intended to focus on outcomes directly linked to the behavioral domain under consideration in a given study. In the case of the study of leader–follower relationships, two domain-specific outcomes were assessed using the information presented in the summary chapter:

1. To what extent did the leader remain in contact with followers after they left power?
2. To what extent did the leader maintain a positive relationship with followers after they left power?

The specific criteria applied in the communications study included:

1. To what extent do people continue to quote the leader's communications or speeches?
2. Are the leader's speeches considered landmark events?
3. Do the leader's communications continue to influence others?
4. To what extent are the ideas presented in these communications still considered relevant?
5. Did the leader's communications lead to institutional change?
6. Are the leader's communications or speeches still read today on special occasions?
7. Do people still discuss the ideas presented in the leader's communications?

In contrast to communications, the summary chapters typically contained relatively little information bearing on leader performance in problem solving. It did, however, prove possible to evaluate performance using the material presented in the chapter describing significant incidents of problem-solving activity. More specifically, it proved possible to develop context appropriate measures of solution quality and originality. More was said in the summary chapters bearing on the effects of the leader's political activities. Accordingly, ratings were obtained on a 5-point scale examining: (a) the degree of divisiveness arising from the leader's actions, (b) maintenance over time of arrangements brought about by the leader's political behavior, (c) institutionalization of the leader's base of influence, and (d) establishment of positive relations with other groups. Examination of the interrater agreement coefficients obtained for these domain-specific criteria resulted in an average interrater agreement coefficient of .80 using the procedures suggested by Shrout and Fleiss (1979).

Controls

A number of additional measures were also obtained as part of the biographical analyses. These measures were intended to provide requisite controls with respect to the inferences being drawn. Again, a set of general controls was obtained applicable to all the studies under consideration. The first set of covariate control measures was intended to take into account temporal, cultural, and historic effects. Thus, the following control measures were obtained through judgmental evaluations:

1. Was the leader a pre– or post–World War II leader?
2. Was the leader from a Western or non-Western country?
3. Was the leader's country industrialized or nonindustrialized?
4. Was the leader's biography translated into English?

The second set of control measures examined attributes of the leader and their role: (a) type of leadership role (e.g., business, political, nonprofit organization, military), (b) political conflict in the leader's organization, (c) years in power, and (d) elected or appointed versus leadership positions seized by force.

In addition to these general controls, a select set of control measures was formulated bearing on the inferences to be made in a particular content analysis study. The control measures obtained for the developmental studies included: (a) presence of theoretical assumptions about the nature of developmental influences (Freudian, educational, etc.), (b) amount of information available about developmental events, (c) number of developmental events abstracted, (d) age at rise to power, (e) amount of documentation provided for developmental events, (f) source of external information about developmental events (teachers, siblings, friends, etc.), and (g) number of leader recollections used as a basis for describing developmental events.

For the study of leader–follower relationships, three study-specific control measures were obtained based on information presented in the leader's biography. These study-specific controls examined: (a) the number of close followers identified, (b) demographic similarity of the leader with close followers, and (c) demographic similarity of the leader to more distant followers. The study-specific controls developed for the communications strategy study focused on the amount and quality of the material available for coding: (a) total number of identified communications, (b) frequency of major communications during the period when the leader was in power, (c) amount of material quoted in the biography, (d) need for translation of speeches, (e) amount of input others had into preparation of the communications, and (f) size of the leader's audience.

For the problem-solving study, a total of 10 study-specific control measures were obtained. These measures examined social-situational factors that might affect the leader's problem-solving behaviors, including: (a) whether the problem was social or nonsocial in nature, (b) public or private problem solving, (c) the number of people affected by the problem, (d) the number of people involved in problem solving, (e) the number of institutions affected by the problem, (f) individual versus group problem solving, (g) the amount of time required to solve the problem, (h) the length of problem descriptions, (i) the amount of time spent solving the problem, and (j) the effectiveness of the problem solution apart from the leader's efforts.

For the political study, a total of eight study-specific control measures were obtained. Typically, these control measures examined situational variables that might act to condition the application of certain political tactics, including: (a) the number of actors involved, (b) the amount of risk for the leader apparent in the incident, (c) implications of the issue at hand for the institutions under consideration, (d) the amount of trust the parties involved had in the leader, (e) the amount of conflict surrounding the event, (f) public or private political behavior, (g) the number of targets of the political behavior, (h) length of the descriptions of political behavior, and (i) biographer's reactions to political tactics.

The rating scales and counts applied in evaluating the biographies with respect to these control variables necessarily varied as a function of the question under consideration. Some ratings and counts, moreover, reflected overall evaluations drawn from the summary chapters. Other ratings and counts, however, were obtained as part and parcel of the content coding of relevant descriptive material. Because these covariate control measures, regardless of the measurement scales applied, tended to focus on relatively objective events, it was not surprising that they proved to be reasonably reliable. The average interrater agreement coefficient, obtained using the procedures suggested by Shrout and Fleiss (1979), was .94. Again, examination of the correlations among these control measures using the data applied in the present set of studies indicated that these measures displayed adequate convergent and discriminant validity.

Summary

In this section, we have examined the criteria and controls to be applied in the various content analysis studies examined in the remaining portions of this book. Broadly speaking, the criteria and controls applied in these studies were formulated using a two-fold strategy. Some criteria and controls represented general measures—measures to be applied across all of the various content analysis studies. Other criteria and controls represented specific measures—measures of concern only with respect to the inferences to be drawn in a specific content analysis study.

The criteria and controls applied in these studies, however, display two other noteworthy characteristics. First, because a range of criteria or outcome measures were drawn from the summary chapters, it was possible to obtain a reasonably comprehensive assessment of the performance of charismatic, ideological, and pragmatic leaders. Second, the range of control measures available not only allowed competing explanations for the observed differences among charismatic, ideological, and pragmatic leaders to be ruled out, it allowed relevant methodological issues to be taken into account in drawing conclusions about the similarities and differences among charismatic, ideological, and pragmatic leaders.

ANALYSES

General Approach

The analyses conducted using the data derived from the various content-coding efforts were relatively straightforward. These analyses flow directly from the structure of the sample under consideration and key questions of concern in the present set of investigations. More specifically, the question underlying all these studies was, "How did the three hypothesized types of outstanding leaders, charismatic, ideological, and pragmatic, differ with respect to the various behavior and experiences being examined in the content analyses?"

Accordingly, the first set of analyses conducted were a series of multivariate analyses of covariance. In these analyses, leader type (charismatic, ideological, and pragmatic) and leader orientation (socialized vs. personalized) were treated as independent variables whereas the dimensions being examined in a given content analysis study were treated as dependent variables. The covariates applied in these analyses included both the general, cross-study set of covariate controls along with the covariate controls applicable to the study at hand. It is of note in this regard that only those covariates that proved significant ($p < .05$) with the dependent variables of concern were applied in a given set of analyses assuming they met the sphericity assumption. Thus, inferences about behavioral or developmental differences across leader types were made only after taking into account requisite controls.

The second set of analyses was intended to provide a summary description of how charismatic, ideological, and pragmatic leaders differed from each other in terms of the various dimensions being examined in a given study. Thus, when significant differences ($p < .05$) or marginally significant differences ($p < .10$) were obtained for type, orientation, or the type-by-orientation interaction in the multivariate analyses of covariance, a discriminant-function analysis was conducted to identify the underlying variable, or variables, best able to account for these differences.

The discriminant-function scores obtained in this second set of analyses provided the basis for the third set of analyses. In this third set of analyses, leaders' scores on the applicable discriminant functions were obtained. Subsequently, scores on the various criterion measures applying in a given study, the general criteria and the appropriate set of study-specific criteria, were correlated with and regressed on the scores on the discriminant-function variables intended to summarize the differences observed in the dimensions being examined in a given content analysis study. In conducting these regressions, however, it should be noted that the significant ($p < .05$) covariates identified in the multivariate analyses of covariance were entered as the first block of predictors to ensure that statements made about the implications of observed differences took into account requisite controls.

Supplemental Analyses

In addition to the general analyses sketched out in the preceding subsection, a number of study-specific analyses were conducted. These study-specific analyses typically occurred because the nature of the data being collected in a given study, or the inferential issues at hand, required extending the general analytic framework. For example, in the study of developmental events, there was a need to examine cross-type differences in the frequency of event exposure through a chi-square analysis. Similarly, in the performance study, the correlations among criteria were obtained to provide some additional content and construct validity evidence for the criteria being applied.

Not only were certain supplemental analyses necessary, at times it was necessary to modify this basic analytic paradigm given the issues to be addressed in a particular study. Thus, in the case of the problem-solving and political-tactics studies, where a time variable was examined ("rise to power," "pinnacle of power," and "fall from power"), the multivariate analyses of covariance was extended to include a temporal grouping variable. In the case of the study examining the influence of developmental events on leader behavior (problem solving, communication strategies, leader–follower relationships, and political tactics), a correlational approach was necessarily applied.

The nature of these supplemental analyses is examined in greater detail in the relevant chapters describing the results obtained in each of the specific studies. Additionally, in the study-specific analyses sections presented in these chapters, more information is provided on scoring as well as the reliability and validity of the rating scales applied in the various content analysis studies.

CONCLUSIONS

In this chapter, we have examined the general method applied in contrasting charismatic, ideological, and pragmatic leaders, both socialized and personalized leaders, with respect to behavior and developmental experiences. We began this chapter by noting that outstanding leadership can be, and indeed has been, studied using a number of methodological approaches—the most common approaches being dimensional approximation, experimental simulation, qualitative case studies, and quantitative case studies. Although each of these approaches evidences certain strengths and limitations, we argued that the quantitative analyses of multiple case studies provides a particularly attractive vehicle for studies of outstanding leadership concerned with identifying alternative pathways to outstanding leadership.

In the course of this discussion, we noted that one way to implement the quantitative case study method is to apply historic data—a historiometric approach. In the case of studies of outstanding leadership, this approach is attractive for two reasons. First, a rich, well-established body of historic data is available describing the careers of outstanding leaders. Second, these historic data are available in the form of leader biographies. Although the application of biographical analyses provides an attractive strategy for the study of outstanding leadership, at least under certain conditions, the success of efforts along these lines requires that studies be designed with five conditions in mind.

First, the leaders to be examined in the study must be selected based on a well-defined sampling strategy—a strategy that considers both statistical and inferential issues. Second, the behavior and experiences to be examined must be appropriate with respect to the material commonly presented in biographies. Third, biographies must be carefully selected to ensure the accuracy and comprehensiveness of the information to be examined in the content analyses. Fourth, content analyses should not be based on overall subjective appraisals, but rather on select sets of stimulus material abstracted from the biography that expressly focuses on description of relevant behavior or events. Fifth, systematic procedures for conducting the content analysis must be developed.

In this chapter, we have examined how each of these issues was addressed within the context of the present investigation—a set of studies intended to elucidate the behavioral and developmental differences evidenced by charismatic, ideological, and pragmatic leaders. More specifically, these studies were to be based on a sample of 120 historically notable 20th-century leaders where this sample was structured to include both socialized and personalized charismatic, ideological, and pragmatic leaders. Not only were the behavioral and experiential domains under consideration those commonly examined in biographies (e.g., political tactics, significant life events), but also substantial effort was devoted to identification of high-quality biographies. The procedures used to abstract material from these biographies were, moreover, designed to ensure that only "relevant" material, material expressly focused on describing the leader's behavior and experiences, was applied in the content analysis. Finally, the content analysis of this material was conducted by trained judges who were asked to apply a carefully designed set of rating scales when evaluating the relevant material.

One attractive feature of this approach is that the content analysis does not rely on subjective impressions derived from a highly complex set of material. Instead, the content analysis is focused on a well-defined set of behavioral samples where a priori dimensions could be applied in the content analysis. Another attractive feature of this approach, however, is that it permits control measures to be applied, both general and study-specific controls, that permit stronger inferences to be drawn concerning the similarities and differences observed in contrasting charismatic, ideological, and pragmatic leaders.

In the following chapters of this book, we examine the results obtained in the various studies contrasting charismatic, ideological, and pragmatic leaders. We contrast charismatic, ideological, and pragmatic leaders with respect to differences in their early development and their later behavior in the areas of problem solving, leader–follower relationships, communication strategies, and political tactics—all areas of critical interest in studies of outstanding leadership. Before turning to the findings obtained in these studies, however, we examine the differences observed among charismatic, ideological, and pragmatic leaders with respect to the various performance indices drawn from the summary chapters presented in the relevant biographies.

II

BEHAVIORALLY DISTINCT PATHWAYS TO OUTSTANDING LEADERSHIP

4

Performance: Who Masters the Art of Influence? Charismatic, Ideological, or Pragmatic Leaders?

Michael D. Mumford
Jill M. Strange
Blaine Gaddis
Brian Licuanan
Ginamarie Scott
The University of Oklahoma

We study leadership not only to understand the nature of leadership as a social phenomenon; we also hope that our understanding of leadership will lead to interventions that will enhance leader performance. The focus of leadership research on practical performance issues is illustrated in the various techniques that have been proposed to facilitate leader development (Day, 2000) and the widespread use of assessment center techniques (Campbell & Bray, 1993). In fact, given the apparent impact of leaders' actions on the institutions they are responsible for (Zaccaro & Klimoski, 2001), there would seem to be ample justification for studies of leader performance.

When one turns to studies of outstanding leadership, the exercise of exceptional influence, the issue of performance becomes an especially important concern. Outstanding leaders, by virtue of their ability to exercise influence, have unusually profound effects on both institutions and society (Bass, 1985). Consider just a few examples. Franklin Roosevelt reshaped the social compact between employers and American workers, making possible a "middle class" society. Mikhail Gorbachev made possible the transition of Russia from a totalitarian to an open society. John Kennedy provided the impetus not only for the American space program but also for our continued involvement in Vietnam.

Our observations with regard to John Kennedy point to a broader issue—an issue that warrants attention in any study of outstanding leadership. Outstanding leaders exercise influence but the exercise of influence may be for good or may be for ill. In the case of outstanding leaders, these ill effects may be devastating—consider the cases of Vladimir Lenin and Adolf Hitler. Accordingly, our intent in the present chapter is to examine the differences among charismatic, ideological, and pragmatic leaders with respect to their manifest performance, taking into account House and Howell's (1992) distinction between socialized and personalized leaders.

PERFORMANCE

Conceptions of Performance

When one attempts to study the performance of outstanding leaders, some unique problems, problems not necessarily apparent in other studies of leadership, come to fore. To begin, in studies of outstanding leadership, one is examining performance, and presumably performance differences, in a restricted sample—a sample where all the leaders under consideration have proven unusually effective in the exercise of influence. As a result, the motivational criteria commonly applied in studies of leadership are unlikely to prove of much value (Yukl, 2001).

To complicate matters further, outstanding leaders tend to arouse intense affect on the part of others—both followers and nonfollowers (Conger & Kanungo, 1998; Shamir et al., 1993). Though affective arousal may be an important component of outstanding leadership, especially in differentiating outstanding leadership from more routine forms of leadership, it causes a further problem in the appraisal of leader performance. More specifically, people's evaluations of leaders will be colored by these intense affective reactions, making it difficult to apply the kind of judgmental performance appraisal criteria commonly applied in other studies of leader performance.

To complicate matters even further, the settings in which outstanding leaders operate make it difficult to obtain viable evaluations of performance. As noted earlier, outstanding leaders emerge in response to typically highly complex institutional crises where change is required. These conditions are noteworthy because they suggest that the ambiguity and complexity of the issues involved will make it difficult to assess performance over the short run. Rather, performance can be assessed only after the effects of leaders' actions have had the time needed to become apparent. These effects of ambiguity and complexity are compounded by the fact that outstanding leaders are often, although not always, responsible for large, complex organizations. And, in organizational settings, it is often difficult to separate the effects of the leaders' actions from the broader social influences.

Taken at face value, our foregoing observations would seem to suggest that it is impossible to adequately appraise the performance of outstanding leaders. Implicit in our foregoing observations, however, are a number of suggestions about how one might go about appraising performance in studies where the focus is on outstanding leadership as opposed to contrasting outstanding leaders with more run-of-the-mill leaders. First, and perhaps foremost, the criteria applied to appraise performance must focus not on influence, but rather on success in resolving the crises that give rise to leader emergence. In other words, the criteria applied must examine how the leader affected their world and the people and institutions that make up this world.

Second, it must be recognized that the effects of leaders' actions on people and institutions will not necessarily be immediately apparent. This observation, in turn, suggests that attempts to appraise the performance of outstanding leaders will require the passage of time—passage of sufficient time to allow the consequences of the leader's exercise of influence in a complex system to become apparent. These attempts to appraise the performance of outstanding leaders will, in one fashion or another, require a historic approach.

Third, in appraising performance, one must remember that people have opinions, often strong, emotional opinions, about outstanding leaders. This point is of some importance because it suggests that preference should be given to more objective, at least potentially verifiable, criteria in attempts to assess the performance of outstanding leaders. For example, how many institutions did the leader establish? And, are these institutions still in existence? Application of these more objective outcome measures serves to minimize the impact of opinion and cultural stereotypes in appraisals of leader performance.

In fact, these conclusions have led students of outstanding leadership to stress historic-outcome criteria in attempts to appraise the performance of outstanding leaders. In one study along these lines, a study focusing on charismatic leaders in business settings, Yammarino and Tosi (2004) used indices of corporate financial performance. In another study along these lines, Strange and Mumford (2002), using leaders drawn from a variety of domains, domains where financial criteria were not necessarily applicable, applied an alternate strategy. They assessed leader performance using social-impact measures examining the number of institutions established, the maintenance of these institutions, and the number of positive and negative social contributions. Thus, there appears some reason to suspect that historic organizational performance criteria can be effectively applied in studies of outstanding leadership.

Leader Performance

If it is granted that it is possible to assess the performance of outstanding leaders using a historic-outcome approach, then a new question comes to fore: Is there reason to suspect that performance differences will be observed among outstanding leaders? With regard to the distinction drawn between socialized and personalized leaders by House and Howell (1992), there is, in fact, substantial reason to expect that performance differences, marked performance differences, will be observed among outstanding leaders (O'Connor et al., 1995).

The distinction drawn between socialized and personalized leaders, along with the related distinction drawn by Bass and Steidelmier (1999) with respect to authentic and inauthentic transformational leaders, is based on the assumption that all outstanding leaders exercise influence. *Differences* in performance are held to arise from the intent underlying the exercise of influence as manifest in the goals being pursued by the leader. Thus, in the case of socialized leaders, influence is exercised for the enhancement of others or social institutions. In the case of personalized leaders, influence is exercised to increase *the leader's* power and control.

Some critical support for this argument may be found in O'Connor et al. (1995). Using a historiometric approach, they content coded the "rise to power" chapters found in the biographies of some 80 outstanding, historically notable, leaders for behaviors indicative of personality attributes commonly linked to the pursuit of personal power including narcissism, fear, negative life themes, and power motives. They found not only that expression of these personality characteristics would distinguish socialized and personalized leaders but that expression of these characteristics was related to objective historic indices of performance producing multiple correlations in the .50s.

If it is granted that the distinction drawn between socialized and personalized leaders is indeed meaningful and is related to observed performance, then another question comes to fore: Why does a socialized versus personalized orientation exert effects, apparently rather strong effects, on the performance of outstanding leaders? One explanation for these effects is quite straightforward. Solutions to the crises associated with the emergence of outstanding leadership are likely to prove effective in a societal sense only when the goal is institutional enhancement rather than personal positioning. However, it should be recognized that a socialized versus personalized orientation may exert a number of other effects on performance. First, the performance of outstanding leaders has been linked to the time frame applied in crisis resolution with application of longer time frames leading to better performances (Jacques, 1976). As a result, the ability of socialized leaders to apply a longer time frame may contribute to their performance vis-à-vis personalized leaders. Second, due to their focus on personal concerns, personalized leaders may fail to adequately define causes and the requirements for effective crisis resolution. Third, because personalized leaders fail to look beyond their own concerns, they may have difficulty identifying the events or actions most likely to allow the leader to induce effective change in a complex social system.

Though both theory and findings would lead one to expect performance differences among socialized and personalized leaders, it is less clear whether performance differences will be observed among charismatic, ideological, and pragmatic leaders. In one of the few studies, perhaps the only study contrasting leader types with respect to objective historic markers of performance, Strange and Mumford (2002) found that charismatic and ideological leaders displayed similar performance. As noted earlier, however, the question remains as to whether pragmatic leaders display similar performance with respect to charismatic and ideological leaders.

Although one might argue that charismatic, ideological, and pragmatic leaders will differ with respect to performance, there is also reason to expect that such differences might not emerge, at least when the distinction between socialized and personalized leaders is taken into account. Where charismatic, ideological, and pragmatic leaders understand crises in different ways and apply different strategies in their attempts to resolve these crises, it is possible that these alternative strategies may prove equally effective. Thus, it is possible that one might resolve crises by motivating people to work toward a better future (a charismatic strategy) or alternately by working with elites to resolve this crisis as an objective problem (a pragmatic strategy). What differs as a result is not overall performance but rather the conditions giving rise to a charismatic, ideological, or pragmatic leader (Mumford & Van Doorn, 2001).

These differences in strategy are noteworthy in part, however, because they suggest that charismatic, ideological, and pragmatic leaders might differ on more specific criteria—criteria bearing on the differences among charismatic, ideological, and pragmatic leaders with respect to the strategy or approach being applied. For example, one might expect charismatic and ideological leaders to produce more evocative communications than pragmatic leaders. Along similar lines, one might expect pragmatic leaders to employ less divisive political tactics than ideological leaders.

Summary

Our intent in the present chapter is to examine the performance characteristics of different types of outstanding leaders in terms of objective historical markers of performance. In the course of this chapter, we consider both differences between socialized and personalized leaders and differences between charismatic, ideological, and pragmatic leaders. We begin by considering the similarities and differences among these various types of outstanding leaders with respect to general performance criteria. Subsequently, we go on to consider the similarities and differences observed among these leaders with respect to criteria bearing on leader–follower relationships, communication strategies, political tactics, and problem-solving strategies.

GENERAL CRITERIA

Measures

The general performances measures applied were drawn from the relevant prologue or epilogue chapters of the biographies describing the careers of the 120 leaders under consideration. A total of 12 general performance measures were drawn from these chapters. Of these measures, five reflected counts of the material presented in the prologue or epilogue chapters: (a) the number of positive contributions made by the leader, (b) the number of negative contributions made by the leader, (c) the number of different types of positive contributions made by the leader, (d) the number of different types of negative contributions made by the leader, and (e) the number of institutions established by the leader. The remaining seven measures were derived from ratings, on a 5-point scale, made by psychologists after reviewing the material presented in the prologue or epilogue chapter:

1. How much did the leader contribute to society?
2. How long did these contributions last?
3. How many people did the leader affect?
4. Did the leader initiate mass movements?
5. Was the leader's agenda maintained after they left power?
6. Were institutions established by the leader still in existence?
7. What was the biographer's evaluation of the leader?

These evaluations of performance outcomes not only displayed adequate agreement across judges, but adequate agreement was obtained when different biographies were used as a basis for evaluating the leader with respect to these performance measures. More detail concerning these reliability and validity studies may be obtained by consulting chapter 3.

Table 4.1 presents the mean and standard deviation of scores on the measures within the sample of 120 outstanding leaders under consideration in the present investigation. More centrally, Table 4.1 presents the correlations among scores on these 12 general indices of leader performance. Perhaps the most clear-cut pattern of findings to emerge from this analysis was that correlations of uniformly high magnitude ($\bar{r} \leq .50$) were not obtained. Thus, it seems reasonable to conclude that a general method bias factor was unlikely to have exerted much influence on these evaluations of leader performance. Some further support for this conclusion may be found in contrasting the correlations of the count and rating measures, which were found to yield comparable correlations despite differences in scoring format.

More centrally, the pattern of the relationships observed among these measures of leader performance provides some rather compelling evidence for their construct validity. As might be expected, the number of positive contributions was positively related to the number of different types of positive contributions ($\bar{r} = .76$) whereas the number of negative contributions was positively related to the number of different types of negative contributions ($\bar{r} = .81$). However, the number and type of positive contributions were negatively related to the number and type of negative contributions ($\bar{r} = -.12$). It is of note that this weak negative correlation reflects the fact that as leaders

TABLE 4.1
Means, Standard Deviations, and Correlations for General Measures of Leader Performance

	$\bar{X}$	SD	1	2	3	4	5	6	7	8	9	10	11	12
1. Number of positive contributions	5.30	5.07	1.00	-.12	.76	-.14	.28	.45	.42	.23	.13	.31	.39	.5
2. Number of negative contributions	3.68	4.64		1.00	.13	.81	.05	.02	.25	.15	.11	-.38	-.26	-.49
3. Number of different types of positive contributions	2.88	2.81			1.00	-.05	.31	.37	.25	.19	.05	.20	.28	.38
4. Number of different types of negative contributions	2.22	2.52				1.00	-.04	.06	-.26	.18	.13	-.33	-.34	-.42
5. Number of institutions established by the leader	2.46	2.54					1.00	.15	.21	.07	.09	.43	.26	.12
6. Amount of leader contribution to society	2.84	1.35						1.00	.56	.62	.43	.51	.36	.36
7. Length of time contribution lasted	3.34	1.50							1.00	.39	.19	.68	.69	.51
8. Number of people affected by leader	3.10	1.25								1.00	.24	.30	.22	.30
9. Mass-movement initiation	2.14	1.41									1.00	.37	.01	.10
10. Long-term agenda maintenance	3.01	1.53										1.00	.50	.52
11. Degree institutions established still in existence	2.98	1.72											1.00	.42
12. Biographer's evaluation of leader	3.57	1.35												1.00

Note. $r \geq .18$ significant beyond .05 level.

engage in more activity, a greater chance occurs of both positive and negative contributions.

Along similar lines, it was found that evaluations of how long a leader's contribution lasted was, as expected, strongly positively related to the number of institutions established and whether these institutions were still in existence ($\bar{r} =$ .49). Apparently, outstanding leaders, in accordance with the observations of Jacobsen and House (2001), exert ongoing influence by establishing viable institutions. Moreover, the ongoing influence through the creation of viable institutions apparently influences biographers' evaluations of the leader ($\bar{r} = .39$), along with the number of positive contributions and the number of different types of positive contributions ($\bar{r} = .44$).

Differences in Performance

If it is granted that a valid, substantively meaningful, set of performance measures were obtained from the prologue and epilogue chapters, it is now appropriate to consider the similarities and differences observed among the various leader types on these measures. To address this issue, a multivariate analysis of covariance was conducted where leader orientation (socialized vs. personalized) and leader type (charismatic, ideological, and pragmatic) were treated as independent variables that might be used to account for differences among leaders on these performance measures. The covariate control measures (e.g., Western/non-Western leader, type of organization, elected vs. appointed leader, etc.) included in this analysis, all general covariate controls, were those that were significant beyond the .05 level. Table 4.2 summarizes the results obtained in this analysis.

TABLE 4.2
Multivariate Analysis of Covariance Results Contrasting
Leaders With Respect to Performance

	F	df	p	η^2
Covariates				
Elected and appointed versus force	3.22	12, 98	0.001	0.283
Type of position	2.53	12, 98	0.006	0.237
Organizational size	2.61	12, 98	0.005	0.242
Pre– versus post–World War II	3.80	12, 98	0.001	0.317
Time in power	2.43	12, 98	0.008	0.229
Main Effects				
Orientation (socialized or personalized)	6.23	12, 98	0.001	0.433
Type (charismatic, ideological, pragmatic)	1.74	12, 99	0.070	0.174
Interactions				
Orientation * Type	1.80	12, 99	0.058	0.179

Note. F = F-ratio; df = degrees of freedom; p = significance level using Roy's Largest Root; η^2 = effect size.

Before turning to the effects of orientation (socialized vs. personalized) and the effects of the leader type (charismatic, ideological, pragmatic), the effects of the various covariate control variables should be briefly summarized. Typically, the longer leaders were in power, the longer their contributions lasted, and the more likely it was that institutions they established were still in existence. If the leader was responsible for a large institution, they contributed more to society, affected more people, and were more likely to make a greater number of positive and negative contributions. Post–World War II leaders were more likely to have established institutions that were still in existence, a relationship simply reflective of recency effects. Business and military leaders, as opposed to political and nonprofit leaders, tended to produce both fewer positive and fewer negative contributions while having less effect on society as a whole. These relationships, of course, reflect the more circumscribed domain of operations that characterizes military and business leadership as opposed to political and nonprofit leadership. Finally, as might be expected, leaders who attained their position through force rather than election or appointment evidenced more negative contributions.

Although none of these finding is especially surprising, they do provide some further evidence bearing on the validity of the performance measures. Moreover, it should be remembered that by virtue of their failure to produce significant effects, it can be assumed that the conclusions drawn herein generalize over culture (Western vs. non-Western), types of economy (industrialized vs. nonindustrialized), and source language of the biography (written in English vs. translated into English).

When the requisite relevant covariate controls were taken into account, consistent with earlier studies by O'Connor et al. (1995) and Strange and Mumford (2002), leader orientation (socialized vs. personalized) had a significant effect $[F(12, 98) = 6.23; p \leq .001]$. As might be expected, the significant effects ($p \leq .05$) obtained in the univariate analyses indicated that socialized leaders, in comparison to personalized leaders, made more positive contributions ($\overline{X} = 7.36, SE = .60$ vs. $\overline{X} = 3.29, SE = .60$) (note: SE means standard error), more different types of positive contributions ($\overline{X} = 4.03, SE = .32$ vs. $\overline{X} = 1.74, SE = .32$), established more institutions ($\overline{X} = 2.43, SE = .32$ vs. $\overline{X} = 1.98, SE = .32$), established institutions that were more likely to still be in existence ($\overline{X} = 3.67, SE = .17$ vs. $\overline{X} = 2.28, SE = .17$), contributed more to society ($\overline{X} = 3.24, SE = .14$ vs. $\overline{X} = 2.43, SE = .14$), made more lasting contributions ($\overline{X} = 3.97, SE = .16$ vs. $\overline{X} = 2.70, SE = .16$), made contributions that were more likely to be maintained over time ($\overline{X} = 3.60, SE = .17$ vs. $\overline{X} = 2.41, SE = .17$), and finally were likely to be more positively viewed by the author of the biography ($\overline{X} = 4.3, SE = .15$ vs. $\overline{X} = 2.85, SE = .15$). Taken as a whole, it appears that socialized leaders evidence substantially better performance than do personalized leaders.

In keeping with this pattern of findings, the significant effects obtained in the univariate analyses indicated that personalized leaders, in comparison to socialized leaders, obtained higher scores on only two measures. Personalized leaders made more negative contributions ($\overline{X} = 5.55, SE = .52$ vs. $\overline{X} = 1.79, SE = .52$) and more different types of negative contributions ($\overline{X} = 3.07, SE = .27$ vs. $\overline{X} = 1.36, SE = .27$). In fact, only on criteria examining influence, how many people did the leader effect and did the leader start mass movements, did significant differences fail to emerge in contrasting socialized and personalized leaders.

As might be expected based on our foregoing observations, when the performance measures were used to discriminate socialized and personalized leaders, the resulting discriminant function was significant ($\chi^2(13) = 92.04, p < .001$). The canonical correlation was .75. Thus, socialized and personalized leader appear to differ markedly in their performance. The performance measure yielding the largest loadings on this function was the number of positive contributions ($\beta = .51$) and the number of different types of positive contributions ($\beta = .50$).

Whereas orientation exerted strong effects on leader performance, leader type exerted weaker effects. In the overall multivariate analysis of covariance, the type variable (charismatic, ideological, and pragmatic) produced a marginally significant [$F(12, 93) = 1.71; p < .10$] main effect. A marginally significant [$F(12, 93) = 1.61; p \leq .10$] interaction was also obtained between the type and orientation variables. Examination of the univariate effects, however, indicated that only one measure produced significant differences across the types. More specifically, significant differences [$F(2, 93) = 5.63, p \leq .005$] were observed on the item examining whether the leader types differed with respect to initiation of mass movements. As might be expected based on the mental models and influence tactics being applied, ideological ($\overline{X} = 2.64, SE = .27$) and charismatic ($\overline{X} = 2.24, SE = .25$) leaders were more likely to initiate mass movements than pragmatic ($\overline{X} = 1.62, SE = .27$) leaders with personalized pragmatics being somewhat less likely to initiate mass movements than socialized pragmatics ($\overline{X} = 1.70, SE = .27$ vs. $\overline{X} = 1.46, SE = .28$).

Summary

Taken as a whole, it does appear that objective historic-outcome measures may be used as a basis for assessing leader performance. The differences observed among outstanding leaders with respect to performance, however, appeared most closely linked to House and Howell's (1992) distinction between socialized and personalized leaders. Although the distinction drawn between socialized and personalized leaders, or alternatively authentic and inauthentic transformational leaders, is most commonly linked to integrity, in the case of leadership it appears that integrity and prosocial behavior are integral to leader performance as evident in the historic outcomes of leaders' actions.

When people who are capable of exercising unusual influence act, and indeed all the leaders under consideration herein appear capable of exercising exceptional influence, the effects of their actions will be pronounced. When actions are taken for the enhancement of others or the social institutions that outstanding leaders build, leaders are able to make the sustained long-term contributions for which they are eventually recognized. When, however, leaders act to protect their position and power, they apparently forgo building institutions and instead destroy extant institutions, resulting in the kind of negative contributions observed in the present study.

What should be recognized here, however, is that the effect of this orientation is apparently quite complex. In the present study socialized leaders did some harm, although they did more good for society. Personalized leaders did some good, although they did more harm. This ambiguity in outcomes can be expected whenever people are asked to deal with complex emerging crises. However, application of a personalized orientation apparently makes it more likely that negative outcomes will emerge from the exercise of influence. These negative outcomes may result, in part, from intent but also potentially more subtle influences, such as difficulty in working through problems objectively or application of short time frames, associated with a personalized orientation. This intimate linkage of integrity and performance among outstanding leaders is aptly illustrated by considering the case information summarized in Table 4.3, which examines the career accomplishments of a socialized and a personalized leader.

TABLE 4.3
Examples of Socialized and Personalized Leader Performance Outcomes

Mohandas Gandhi—Socialized Leader

On 21 January 1914, a provisional agreement was arrived at between General Smuts and Gandhi, and Satyagraha was suspended. Satyagrahis were gradually released from jail. In the meantime the commission set to work, but only a few witnesses on behalf of Indians appeared before it. This virtual boycott of the commission shortened its work and the report was published at once. It recommended that the main Indian demands should be accepted.

Meetings were held at various places and Gandhi was able to persuade the Indians to approve the terms of the agreement. Smuts, for his part, pleaded with the Members of Parliament to approach the problem "in a non-controversial spirit." On 30 June, Gandhi and Smuts finally exchanged letters confirming the terms of a complete agreement. This document was then incorporated into the Indian Relief Bill and submitted to Union Parliament.

Under the new legislation, all monogamous Indian marriages solemnized by Hindu, Muslim, and Parsi traditions were recognized as valid, and the £3 tax was abolished and arrears cancelled. A domicile certificate bearing the holder's thumbprint was made sufficient evidence of right to enter the Union, although the main provisions of the Black Act still remained in force—Indians were not permitted to move freely from one province to another, and the entry of Indian laborers into South Africa was to stop totally after 1920. The Union Immigration Restriction Act also remained in force, except that as a gesture the government allowed six educated Indians to immigrate to South Africa every year. Gandhi now felt that a substantial victory had been won. Consequently, he did not insist on an enquiry into police brutality toward Indians, nor did he raise the crucial issue of the "locations" (ghettos) in which Indians were forced to live. He felt that this was not the time to press his advantages. The Satyagraha campaign was called off and among the Indians Gandhi emerged as a hero.

(Continued)

TABLE 4.3
(Continued)

Mohandas Gandhi—Socialized Leader

It was no easy task for a European to conduct negotiations with Gandhi. Lord Gladstone, the Governor-General, certainly echoed General Smuts's thoughts when, in a letter to the Secretary of State, he referred to Gandhi as "an unusual type of humanity, whose peculiarities, however inconvenient they may be to the Minister, are not devoid of attraction to the student . . . His ethical and intellectual attitude, based it appears on a curious compound of mysticism and astuteness, baffles the ordinary process of thought." Lord Hardinge's emissary Robertson felt that Gandhi "has a terrible amount of conscience and is very hard to manage."

The peaceful march had made a good impression on the public, and this was undoubtedly responsible for the compromise settlement that ensued. Despite limited gains Gandhi regarded the agreements as the "Magna Carta" of South African Indians. He asserted that the victory, however limited, certainly sought to remove the racial taint in the law and was a vindication of civil resistance.

Pol Pot—Personalized Leader

In the negotiations between the Americans and the Vietnamese in Paris, ongoing since 1968, the Vietnamese delegations now saw short-term advantages in accepting U.S. offers of a cease-fire throughout Indochina. The Americans were eager to reach an agreement before the November presidential election in the United States. For the Vietnamese, time was on their side. Most of the U.S. combat forces had been withdrawn. The remaining ones would pull out as the cease-fire took effect. At that point, the Vietnamese could prepare for an assault on Saigon without facing the threat of American intervention. Until all the Americans were gone—and it would be almost impossible for them to return—the Vietnamese could concentrate on political tactics that would undermine the South Vietnamese regime. Should they refuse a cease-fire, the Americans assured the North Vietnamese, U.S. bombardment would begin again. In January 1973 the Vietnamese agreed to American conditions.

In Cambodia the agreement meant that the Vietnamese would withdraw most of their forces. Those who remained behind, in frontier areas, supported activities in Vietnam rather than the Red Khmer. The Vietnamese urged [Pol Pot] to join them in the cease-fire. He almost certainly refused, as he said he did in the *Livre noir*. The Americans put similar pressure on Lon Nol, whose government was reeling from a series of scandals, missteps, and military defeats. Lon Nol reluctantly agreed, hoping to bring the fighting to an end. A temporary cease-fire went into effect at the end of January 1973. It was broken almost immediately.

According to the *Livre noir*, [Pol Pot] and his colleagues rejected the Vietnamese requests to honor the cease-fire for several reasons. First, they had come to believe that they could win the war themselves. Second, they were unwilling to revert to political struggle without Vietnamese military protection. Doing so would have meant coming into the open against Lon Nol, sharing power with his forces in the countryside, and reviving the fiction that Sihanouk was the leader of the front. Under such an agreement, presumably, Sihanouk would be free to negotiate with Lon Nol. None of these scenarios was palatable to the Red Khmer. The preferred civil war, American bombardment, and operating in secret to reviving a genuine united front.

Note. Gandhi is from *Gandhi: A Life*, by Y. Chadha (1997, pp. 188–189). Copyright © 1997 by Wiley. Reprinted by permission. Pol Pot is from *Brother Number One*, by D. Chandler (1999, pp. 94–95). Copyright © 1999 by Westview Press. Reprinted by permission of Westview Press, a member of Perseus Books, L.L.C.

Not only do the findings obtained in our examination of performance confirm the existence of performance differences among socialized and personalized leaders, they suggest that the socialized and personalized distinction can be extended to pragmatic leaders as well as charismatic and ideological leaders. The more central findings to emerge with respect to leader type, however, is that charismatic, ideological, and pragmatic leadership are not associated with marked differences in performance when appropriate controls are applied in contrasting these leaders with regard to performance differences. This finding, or more correctly nonfinding, holds across a range of measures—all measures evidencing adequate reliability and validity. It is a noteworthy result in the sense that it suggests that charismatic, ideological, and pragmatic leadership, at least when the socialized and personalized orientation is taken into account, represent equally viable pathways to outstanding leadership.

SPECIFIC CRITERIA

The notable exception to this rule of thumb occurred for the initiation of mass movements. Consistent with the earlier observations of Mumford and Van Doorn (2001) and Strange and Mumford (2002), we found that charismatic and ideological leaders were more likely to initiate mass movements than were pragmatic leaders. This finding, however, may reflect less a difference in general performance capability than the tendency of pragmatic leaders to work through elites. This finding is of some interest because it suggests that although charismatic, ideological, and pragmatic leadership represent equally viable pathways to outstanding leadership, charismatic, ideological, and pragmatic leaders may differ on more specific outcome measures linked to the strategies through which they exercise influence. Accordingly, in this section we examine the similarities and differences observed among charismatic, ideological, and pragmatic leaders with respect to outcomes, or performance measures, bearing on leader–follower relationships, communication strategies, political tactics, and problem-solving strategies.

Leader–Follower Relationships

Two measures examining the quality of exchange relationships could be abstracted from the material presented in the prologue or epilogue chapters. These measures examined whether (a) the leader maintained contact with close followers after they left power and (b) if they remained close to their followers after they left power. Psychologists made these 5-point ratings after a review of the material presented in the prologue or epilogue chapters. Ratings on these scales produced an average interrater agreement coefficient of .91. Moreover, these ratings evidenced a pattern of relationships indicative of adequate construct validity. Thus, the measures of closeness and contact produced a positive correlation of .73 while yielding a correlation of .26 with the number of people affected and a correlation of .51 with the biographer's appraisal of the leader.

Given this reliability and validity evidence, it is feasible to examine differences among leaders with respect to their performance on these measures. The results obtained in this multivariate analysis of covariance are presented in Table 4.4. As may be seen, a significant main effect [$F(2, 113) = 43.95; p \leq .001$] was obtained for orientation. As might be expected, socialized, as opposed to personalized, leaders were more likely to maintain contact ($\overline{X} = 4.26, SE = .14$ vs. $\overline{X} = 2.37, SE = .14$) and maintain a close relationship ($\overline{X} = 4.28, SE = .16$ vs. $\overline{X} = 2.96, SE = .16$) after they left power. Apparently, a socialized orientation contributes not only to performance but to the creation and maintenance of strong positive ties between the leader and followers.

A marginally significant [$F(2, 114) = 2.53; p \leq .10$] interaction was obtained between type and orientation with respect to these measures of relational outcomes in the multivariate analysis of covariance. Examination of associated cell means indicated that personalized ideological ($\overline{X} = 2.75, SE = .28$) leaders were less likely to maintain positive relationships with followers than were socialized ideologues ($\overline{X} = 3.80, SE = .28$), charismatic leaders (both socialized and personalized), and pragmatic leaders (both socialized and personalized). Along similar lines, personalized ideologues ($\overline{X} = 1.88, SE = .24$) were less likely to remain in contact with followers after they left power than were socialized ideologues ($\overline{X} = 3.59, SE = .24$), charismatic leaders (both socialized and personalized), and pragmatic leaders (both socialized and personalized). Apparently, personalized ideologues by virtue of the self-centered focus on ideals, and the tendency to see others as objects, find it difficult to maintain relationships with others as individuals. An illustration of this point may be found in Table 4.5, which presents the relationships of a socialized and personalized leader with their old colleagues.

TABLE 4.4
Multivariate Analysis of Covariance Results Contrasting Leaders With Respect to Relational Outcomes

Covariates	F	df	p	η^2
Main Effects				
Orientation (socialized or personalized)	43.95	2, 113	0.001	0.438
Type (charismatic, ideological, pragmatic)	0.87	2, 114	0.410	0.015
Interaction				
Orientation * Type	2.53	2, 114	0.080	0.043

Note. F = F-ratio; df = degrees of freedom; p = significance level using Roy's Largest Root; η^2 = effect size.

TABLE 4.5
Illustration of Relationship Maintenance
for a Socialized Leader and a Personalized Leader

Sam Walton—Socialized Leader

Not only did Sam seek Centurions in the enemy camps, he also closely inspected his own ranks for lively soldiers who looked like future corporals, captains—even generals. He took an interest in Ron Loveless, the eight-year-old son of the Walton housekeeper, and kept tabs on him. Ron was a good high school baseball player and Sam offered to help him go to college. Instead Ron went into the Air Force and came out in 1964 to take a job in a garage.

Sam offered him a chance to learn retailing—from the bottom up. Ron went off to St. Robert, Missouri, to work as a stock boy in the Ben Franklin there. He moved up fast. By the time Loveless was forty-two he was senior vice-president and general manager of Sam's Wholesale Club division of Wal-Mart, with a six-figure salary.

It is a wonder Loveless survived his first promotion—from stock boy to head of the pet department at the St. Robert variety store. Two pet orders he filled were incredible, perhaps unbelievable. But, in a long feature on his career, the *Arkansas Gazette* said August 24, 1986:

> In his youthful enthusiasm, Loveless, then in his early twenties, said "Why not?" when a customer from nearby Fort Leonard Wood asked for an elephant. Loveless cheerfully placed the order.
>
> He found out why not. The elephant arrived dead.
>
> "Some of the ideas I had were costly," Loveless said. "It took a few years to laugh about it."
>
> But it was a different story for the baby leopard. It arrived alive—far too alive, as it turned out. The customer took it home, only to return it after his home had been shredded.
>
> While those efforts may have been expensive, they demonstrated two qualities that Walton wanted—imagination and aggressiveness—while he was building his Wal-Mart discount retailing empire.

Ron was promoted to manager of the Wal-Mart in Mountain Home, Arkansas. His magic touch failed him. He kept running out of stock over the weekends. Sam threw a fit.

"It got awfully touchy," said Ron Loveless. "If you don't produce, you'll be gone. Mr. Sam is a very demanding individual."

The Mountain Home problem was solved, and Ron Loveless went on to be district manager, regional operations manager, and assistant to the president and general merchandise manager before Sam picked him to head the new Sam's Wholesale Club Division, which by 1990 has grown to 123 stores with annual sales of over $5 billion.

When he retired at age 42 in 1986, Loveless blamed burnout: "I was feeling the stress. Mr. Sam hated to see me go. But he pointed out whenever anyone took their money and ran, it had the beneficial effect of creating more opportunity for other ambitious executives to move up."

Deng Xiaoping—Personalized Leader

When Deng heard this declaration of war at the Politburo meeting of March 28, he convened his Secretariat to an emergency session on the ninth of April. From within his trusted circle, he thought once and for all to ferret out the game Mao was playing. Trust—what an illusion! His opponents had long since isolated Deng's Secretariat. To everyone's astonishment, Mao's secretary, Chen Boda, and the head of the Secret Service, Kang Sheng, appeared at the meeting, explaining that as candidates for the Politburo they had the right to participate. Deng let them have their way, not contradicting them, even though as General Secretary he could have interrupted the two left-wingers when they began attacking his deputy with harsh criticism in Mao's name.

(Continued)

TABLE 4.5
(Continued)

Deng Xiaoping—Personalized Leader

Deng, known for his political instincts, sensed meanwhile what game was being played. In a flash, he went over to the side of the Maoists, joining the dance of the critics. In a few words, he distanced himself from his most able colleagues, and delivered a close family friend up to the radicals.

Peng Zhen had been a frequent visitor in the Deng house. The two wives, Zhuo Lin and Zhang Jieqing, had known each other since the Yan'an days. There they had worked together in the Women's Federation of the Northern Office of the CCP. What then, had driven Deng to this lightning change of front? Fear, conviction, and hope! As a flexible politician, Deng recognized quickly the extent of the Maoist Cultural Revolution. He sensed that this was mortal combat. At the same time, he saw himself as a loyal, if critical, follower of his superior. Deng was much too disciplined a party worker to join a conspiracy against the head of the party. In sacrificing Peng Zhen, he hoped to appease Mao and to contain the extent of his radical enterprise. How mistaken he was!

Note. Walton is from Trimble (1990, pp. 116–117). Copyright © 1990 by V. H. Trimble. Used by permission of Dutton, a division of Penguin Group (USA) Inc. Deng is from *Deng Xiaoping*, by U. Franz (1988, p. 184), Boston: Harcourt Brace Jovanovich, Publishers.

Communication Strategies

Seven measures examining outcomes of the leader's speeches or mass-communication strategies could be obtained from the material presented in the prologue or epilogue chapters. These measures examined (a) whether people continue to quote speeches, (b) whether the speeches are considered landmark events, (c) whether the speeches continue to influence others, (d) whether the speeches are still considered relevant, (e) how many of the speeches led to institutional change, (f) whether the speeches are still read today, and (g) whether the ideas in the speeches are still discussed today. These evaluations, made on a 5-point scale with the exception of the count measure, produced interrater agreement coefficients in the .80s.

These performance measures typically produced positive correlations in the .30 to .60 range. These positive correlations, of course, provide some convergent validity evidenced for these specific outcome measures. Somewhat more compelling evidence along these lines was provided by the specific pattern of correlations observed among these measures. Thus, if a speech was still considered relevant, it was likely to still be quoted ($r = .65$). The fact that a speech was still quoted, however, was only weakly related ($r = .22$) to whether the speech resulted in organizational change. Some further evidence pointing to the validity, or meaningfulness, of these evaluations may be obtained by considering the correlations of these communication evaluations with the general criteria. As expected, evaluations of the outcomes of leader communications were positively related to the indices of overall performance—typically producing correlations in the .20 to .40 range. Thus, it appears that effective communication by outstanding leaders is, in fact, related to performance.

Table 4.6 presents the results obtained in contrasting outstanding leaders with respect to the measures of communication effectiveness. In this analysis, three covariates, audience size [$F(7, 105) = 5.24; p \leq .001$], frequency of speeches [$F(7, 105) = 2.90; p \leq .001$], and total number of speeches [$F(7, 105) = 40.83; p \leq .001$], all speech-specific covariate controls, produced significant effects. Even when the effects of these controls were taken into account, however, differences were observed among the various kinds of outstanding leaders under consideration.

Again, the orientation variable contrasting socialized and personalized leaders produced a significant main effect [$F(7, 105) = 13.94; p \leq .001$]. Inspection of the associated univariate tests indicated that socialized leaders produced more effective communications than did personalized leaders in that (a) their speeches were still quoted [$F(1, 111) = 31.55; p \leq .001; \overline{X} = .82, SE = .05$ vs. $\overline{X} = .38, SE = .06$], (b) their speeches continued to influence others [$F(1,111) = 52.00; p \leq .001; \overline{X} = 3.38, SE = .13$ vs. $\overline{X} = 1.97, SE = .14$], (c) their speeches were still considered relevant [$F(1, 111) = 57.92; p \leq .001; \overline{X} = 3.35, SE = .14$ vs. $\overline{X} = 1.87, SE = .13$], (d) their speeches resulted in institutional changes [$F(1, 111) = 19.42; p \leq .001; \overline{X} = 5.22, SE = .58$ vs. $\overline{X} = 3.02, SE = .41$], (e) their speeches are still read on specific occasions [$F(1, 111) = 29.74; p \leq .001; \overline{X} = 3.08, SE = .14$ vs. $\overline{X} = 2.12, SE = .13$], and (f) their speeches are still discussed [$F(1, 111) = 22.22; p \leq .001; \overline{X} = 3.37, SE = .14$ vs. $\overline{X} = 2.43, SE = .15$]. Apparently, socialized leaders, at least over the long haul, are more effective communicators than are personalized leaders. In fact, more effective communication may, in part, account for the marked performance differences observed between socialized and personalized leaders.

A significant interaction [$F(7, 106) = 2.29; p \leq .05$], however, was also obtained between orientation and leader type. The univariate analyses indicated that this effort could be traced to two criteria. First, the significant differences

TABLE 4.6
Multivariate Analysis of Covariance Results Contrasting
Leaders With Respect to Communication Outcomes

	F	df	p	η^2
Covariates				
Audience size	5.24	7, 105	.001	.25
Frequency of speeches	2.90	7, 105	.008	.16
Total number of speeches	40.93	7, 105	.001	.73
Main Effects				
Orientation (socialized or personalized)	13.94	7, 105	.001	.48
Type (charismatic, ideological, pragmatic)	1.64	7, 105	.130	.09
Interaction				
Orientation * Type	2.29	7, 105	.032	.13

Note. F = F-ratio; *df* = degrees of freedom; *p* = significance level using Roy's Largest Root; η^2 = effect size.

observed with respect to whether the leader's speeches were considered landmark events [$F(2, 111) = 4.60; p \leq .05$] indicated that socialized pragmatics ($\overline{X} = 2.52, SE = .17$) were less likely to produce landmark speeches than all other leader types ($\overline{X} = 3.09, SE = .16$) including personalized pragmatics. Apparently, socialized pragmatics, by virtue of their ability to work through elites, do not need to produce exceptional speeches to influence others.

Second, significant univariate effects were obtained for the question examining whether the leader's speeches induced institutional change in the orientation by type interaction [$F(2, 111) = 3.39, p \leq .05$]. The relevant cell means indicated that socialized ideologue's ($\overline{X} = 8.05, SE = 5.2$) speeches were more likely to involve institutional change than those of all other leader types ($\overline{X} = 3.33, SE = .71$) including personalized ideologues. This pattern of differences is noteworthy because it suggests that socialized ideologues may, by effectively articulating shared beliefs, prove to be powerful change agents. This point is illustrated by the speech drawn from the socialized ideologue presented in Table 4.7.

Problem Solving

Because biographers do not generally discuss the nature and success of the leader's problem-solving efforts as part of the career summaries provided in the prologue, or epilogue, chapter, a different approach was used to assess problem-solving performance than that applied for leader–follower relationships, communication strategies, and political tactics. Here judges, four graduate students in industrial and organizational psychology, were asked to evaluate the quality and originality of the solutions produced in response to each incident of leader problem-solving activities using a set of quality and originality markers appropriate for the material presented in biographies.

More specifically, quality was assessed through three questions where judges were asked to indicate (a) whether the solution was effective in solving the problem, (b) whether the solution proved useful over time, and (c) whether the solution led to noteworthy changes in society. Originality was assessed through four questions where judges were asked to indicate (a) whether the solution was considered novel, (b) whether others were surprised by the leader's actions, (c) whether the leader's solution differed from those posed by others, and (d) whether the leader's solution induced critical reactions. These questions were evaluated on a 5-point behavioral outcome scale for each of the three incidents drawn from the rise-to-power and pinnacle-of-power chapters. The average of judges' evaluations across the three incidents drawn from the rise-to-power and pinnacle-of-power chapters provided the four performance measures examining quality and originality during the rise-to-power and pinnacle-of-power periods. The average interrater agreement coefficients obtained for these quality and originality evaluations was .84.

TABLE 4.7
Illustration of Articulation of Shared Beliefs
by a Speech Drawn From a Socialized Ideologue

Mohandas Gandhi

It is a matter of deep humiliation and shame for us that I am compelled this evening, under the shadow of this great college in this sacred city, to address my countrymen in a language that is foreign to me . . . our language is the reflection of ourselves, and if you tell me that our languages are too poor to express the best thoughts, then I say that the sooner we are wiped out of existence the better for us. . . . The charge against us is that we have no initiative. How can we have any if we are to devote the precious years of our lives to the mastery of a foreign tongue? We fail in this attempt also. Was it possible for any speaker yesterday and today to impress his audience as was possible for Mr. Higginbotham?

But suppose that we have been receiving, during the past fifty years, education through our vernaculars, what should we have today? We should have today a free India, we should have our educated men, not as if they were foreigners in their own land but speaking to the heart of the nation, they would be working among the poorest of the poor, and whatever they would have gained during the past fifty years would be a heritage for the nation.

If a stranger dropped from above on to this great temple and he had to consider what we as Hindus were, would he not be justified in condemning us? Is not this great temple a reflection of our own character? I speak feelingly as a Hindu. Is it right that the lanes of our sacred temple should be as dirty as they are? The houses round about are built anyhow. The lanes are tortuous and narrow. If even our temples are not models of cleanliness, what can our self-government be? Shall our temples be abodes of holiness, cleanliness and peace as soon as the English have retired from India, either of their own pleasure or by compulsion, bag and baggage? . . .

. . . We may foam, we may fret, we may resent, but let us not forget that India of today in her impatience has produced an army of anarchists. I am myself an anarchist, but of another type. But there is a class of anarchists amongst us, and if I was able to reach this class, I would say to them that their anarchism has no room in India if India is to conquer the conqueror. It is a sign of fear. If we trust and fear God, we shall have to fear no one, not Maharajahs, not Viceroys, not the detectives, not even King George . . .

. . . Yes, many members of the Indian Civil Service are most decidedly overbearing, they are tyrannical, at times thoughtless. Many other adjectives may be used, but what does that signify? They were gentlemen before they came here, and if they have lost some of their moral fiber, it is a reflection upon ourselves. Just think out for yourselves, if a man who was good yesterday has become bad after having come in contact with me, is he responsible that he has deteriorated or am I? The atmosphere of sycophancy and falsity that surrounds them on their coming to India demoralizes them, as it would many of us. The Indians by not taking power in their own hands have become the willing victims of oppression. If we are to receive self-government, we shall have to take it. We shall never be granted self-government."

Note. From *Gandhi: A Life*, by Y. Chadha (1997, pp. 212–215). Copyright © 1997 by Wiley. Reprinted with permission of John Wiley & Sons, Inc.

Some evidence for the meaningfulness of these evaluations was obtained by examining the correlations among these scales and their correlations with the 12 general outcome measures derived from the epilogue, or prologue, chapters. The quality and originality ratings evidenced the moderate positive correlations ($\bar{r} = .37$) commonly observed in studies of complex problem solving (e.g.,

Baughman & Mumford, 1995). Moreover, the cross-time stability of problem-solving skills was evident in the positive correlations of quality ($r = .24$) and originality ($r = .27$) ratings of incidents drawn from the "rise to power" and "pinnacle of power" chapters.

Because historic evaluations are typically based on leaders' actions when they are in power, it was expected that quality and originality evaluations of problem solving in the pinnacle-of-power period would be more strongly related to historic-outcome measures than quality and originality evaluations of problem solving in the rise-to-power period. In keeping with this hypothesis, quality ($\bar{r} = .09$) and originality ($\bar{r} = .04$) ratings derived from the rise-to-power chapters were less strongly related to the 12 historic-outcome measures than quality ($\bar{r} = .19$) and originality ($\bar{r} = .15$) ratings derived from the pinnacle-of-power chapters. More specifically, quality and originality ratings of incidents abstracted from the "pinnacle of power" chapters were particularly strongly related to how long the leader's contributions lasted ($\bar{r} = .26$), whether institutions established by the leader still exist ($\bar{r} = .23$), and whether the leader's vision was maintained after they left power ($\bar{r} = .23$). Apparently, effective problem solving during the period when the leader is at the pinnacle of their career is related to enduring historic impact.

Table 4.8 presents the results obtained in the multivariate analysis of covariance contrasting outstanding leaders on these measures of problem-solving performance. In this analysis, three covariates, the effectiveness of the problem-solving effort apart from the leader's efforts [$F(2, 110) = 46.67$; $p \leq .001$], the time required to solve the problem [$F(2, 110) = 9.00$; $p \leq .001$], and whether the problem-solving occurred in an individual or group setting [$F(2,$

TABLE 4.8
Multivariate Analysis of Covariance Results Contrasting
Leaders With Respect to Problem-Solving Creativity

	F	df	p	η^2
Covariates				
Effectiveness	46.75	2, 110	.001	.459
Time to solve	9.00	2, 110	.001	.141
Individual vs. group	4.36	2, 110	.015	.073
Main Effects				
Orientation (socialized or personalized)	1.42	2, 110	.247	.025
Type (charismatic, ideological, pragmatic)	3.44	2, 111	.035	.058
Time ("rise to power" or "pinnacle of power")	0.16	2, 110	.849	.003
Interactions				
Orientation * Type	2.16	2, 111	.120	.037
Orientation * Time	.316	2, 110	.730	.006
Type * Time	6.07	2, 111	.003	.099
Type * Time * Orientation	3.04	2, 111	.052	.052

Note. F = F-ratio; df = degrees of freedom; p = significance level using Roy's Largest Root; η^2 = effect size.

110) = 4.35; $p \leq .05$], all produced significant effects. Nonetheless, even when these controls were taken into account, significant differences were observed in the problem-solving performance of the leaders under consideration.

More specifically, in the multivariate analysis, type yielded a significant [$F(2, 110) = 3.44$; $p \leq .05$] main effect. Inspection of the associated univariate tests indicated that the effect was attributable to significant [$F(2, 111) = 3.40$; $p \leq .05$] differences among charismatic, ideological, and pragmatic leaders on the quality measures. Here it was found that ideological leaders ($\overline{X} = 9.34$, $SE = .18$) tended to produce higher quality problem solutions than did charismatic ($\overline{X} = 8.76$, $SE = .18$) and pragmatic ($\overline{X} = 8.88$, $SE = .18$) leaders. Although at first glance the finding may appear surprising, it appears attributable to the particular pattern of problem-solving skills applied by ideological leaders—skills that emphasize evaluation.

A significant interaction [$F(2, 110) = 6.06$; $p \leq .01$] was also obtained between the type and time variables in the multivariate analysis. The univariate analysis indicated that the effect was attributable to change over time in the quality of leaders' problem solutions [$F(2, 110) = 2.88$; $p \leq .10$]. Inspection of the associated cell means indicated that the quality of the problem solutions produced by ideological leaders improved as they moved from the rise-to-power period ($\overline{X} = 9.17$, $SE = .23$) to the pinnacle-of-power period ($\overline{X} = 9.61$, $SE = .30$) whereas the quality of the solutions produced by pragmatic leaders decreased as they move from the rise-to-power period ($\overline{X} = 9.68$, $SE = .30$) to the pinnacle-of-power period ($\overline{X} = 8.36$, $SE = .23$). Charismatic leaders, in contrast, produced solutions of comparable quality during the rise-to-power ($\overline{X} = 8.78$, $SE = .23$) and pinnacle-of-power ($\overline{X} = 8.74$, $SE = .30$) periods.

Apparently, ideological leaders, particularly when they are in power, are capable of producing solutions of unusually high quality. Although we do not think of ideological leaders as especially skilled problem solvers, their intense involvement in select issues may make it possible for them to craft especially effective solutions. An illustration of this point may be found in the ideological problem-solving incident presented in Table 4.9.

Political Tactics

Unlike problem solving, the prologue and epilogue chapters of the biographers did discuss the outcomes of leaders' political behaviors. The material presented in the prologue or epilogue chapters provided four criteria that might be used to assess the outcomes of political behaviors: (a) degree of divisiveness arising from the leader's actions, (b) maintenance, over time, of arrangements brought about by the leader's political behavior, (c) institutionalization of the leader's base of influence, and (d) positive relationships of groups to the leader. Ratings of these variables, made on a 5-point scale, produced interrater agreement coefficients in the .70s.

TABLE 4.9
Illustration of Problem-Solving Quality by Ideological Leaders

Ronald Reagan

Reagan was soon presented with a new opportunity to exercise his leadership when on August 3, 13,000 members of the Professional Air Traffic Controllers Organization (PATCO)—one of the few labor unions which had backed Reagan in the 1980 campaign—walked off their jobs when the federal government refused them a salary increase. The walkout left the airport control towers and radar centers responsible for the safety of the nation's skies unattended.

Another President might have hesitated. In February 1981, Reagan's pollster, Richard Wirthlin, had conducted a poll on how people felt about public employees and specifically their right to strike. "What I found in that study was that people favored giving public employees the right to strike in a ratio of about two to one. Now the President was aware of that when the air traffic controllers went on strike."

But polls never mattered much to Ronald Reagan, who objected to the strike as a matter of principle. He gave the air strike controllers forty-eight hours to return to their posts. The ones who didn't, he simply fired. As he later wrote, "No President could tolerate an illegal strike by federal employees . . . and every union member had signed a sworn affidavit agreeing not to strike . . . I agreed with Calvin Coolidge, who said, 'There is no right to strike against the public safety by anybody, anywhere, at anytime.' "

Although it would take two years to train and replace all the controllers Reagan fired that day, the decision would be looked upon as a turning point in the Reagan presidency.

> All of a sudden, a kind of shock therapy had been administered to the American electorate, that—wait a second—this guy isn't necessarily what we thought he was. Here's someone who is willing to take a stand.

Much as the American electorate, Reagan's domestic and foreign adversaries also took notice of Reagan's toughness and determination.

> That was the moment when Tip O'Neill and the world learned that this guy was different—that he wasn't [just] a nice guy. He could be very, very tough. He didn't have a meeting. He didn't have a cooling off period. He didn't negotiate like Jimmy Carter or like Gerald Ford [would have]. He broke them. Tip had contacts in the Soviet Union. I think [it was] Dwayne Andreas, a business guy who had been going back and forth there, who heard that the Russians were very impressed, that [this] American President was like a Czar.

Note. From *Reagan: An American Story*, by A. Bosch (1988, pp. 172–174), New York: TV Books.

These measures of overall political success typically produced positive correlations in the .30 to .50 range. More centrally, the pattern of the correlations observed among these outcome measures provided some evidence for construct validity. For example, institutionalization of the leader's base of influence produced the expected positive correlation ($r = .45$) with maintenance over time of arrangements brought about by the leader's political behavior. Institutionalization of the influence base and maintenance of arrangements were both positively related to other groups having positive reactions ($r = .39$). In contrast, residual divisiveness was not strongly related to positive reactions by other groups ($r = .12$).

Of somewhat greater interest, however, was the finding that residual divisiveness was positively related to institutionalization of the influence base ($r = .58$) and maintenance of arrangements ($r = .51$). This pattern of relationships reflects the fact that when leaders establish political support structures, it will tend to maintain, over time, any controversy surrounding the leader's politics. This finding, of course, provides some further evidence for the validity of our measures examining the outcomes of the political tactics employed by outstanding leaders.

Table 4.10 presents the results obtained in contrasting outstanding leaders with respect to their performance on the measures examining the outcomes of the leader's political behavior. Only one significant [$F(8, 102) = 2.43; p \leq .05$] covariate emerged in this analysis—the amount of risk associated with the incidents of political behavior in which the leader was involved. As might be expected, high-risk political activities were positively related to higher scores on all of the political-outcome measures.

More centrally, the orientation variable contrasting socialized and personalized leaders, again, produced a significant main effect [$F(8, 102) = 2.74; p \leq .01$]. Inspection of the relevant univariate effects indicated that socialized, as opposed to personalized, leaders were more likely to create political arrangements that were maintained over time [$F(1, 109) = 4.95; p \leq .05; \overline{X} = 3.40, SE = .10$ vs. $\overline{X} = 3.08, SE = .10$], institutionalize their base of influence [$F(1,109) = 3.01; p \leq .10; \overline{X} = 3.94, SE = .11$ vs. $\overline{X} = 3.65, SE = .11$], and establish lasting positive relationships [$F(1, 109) = 17.92, p \leq .001; \overline{X} = 3.76, SE = .12$ vs. $\overline{X} = 2.93, SE = .12$).

Notably, however, the amount of divisiveness arising from the leaders' actions, as reflected in prologue or epilogue chapters, yielded a marginally significant effect [$F(1, 109) = 3.49; p \leq .10$] where greater long-term divisiveness was observed for socialized ($\overline{X} = 3.42, SE = .14$) than personalized ($\overline{X} = 3.01, SE = .14$) leaders. Although the finding may, at first glance, appear surprising, it should be recognized that organizations often become united in their distaste

TABLE 4.10
Multivariate Analysis of Covariance Results Contrasting
Leaders With Respect to Political Behaviors Creativity

	F	df	p	η^2
Covariates				
Amount of risk	2.43	8, 102	.019	.16
Main Effects				
Orientation (socialized or personalized)	2.74	8, 102	.009	.17
Type (charismatic, ideological, pragmatic)	1.54	8, 102	.149	.10
Interactions				
Orientation * Type	2.05	8, 102	.052	.13

Note. F = F-ratio; df = degrees of freedom; p = significance level using Roy's Largest Root; η^2 = effect size.

TABLE 4.11
Illustration of Political Consensus Rising
From Negative Relations to a Personalized Leader

Leona Helmsley

Did Helmsley float the line drawings out in public to divert his critics, so he could then corral them by agreeing to preserve something he intended to save all along? McGrath wouldn't say. His critics think that unlikely. "It just couldn't have been," said Lewis. But the same sort of thought came up during the Tudor City park fight. Stein's former aide, McLaughlin, had just a suspicion—nothing provable by any means—that Helmsley never really wanted to build on the Tudor City parks. Or at the least, that he changed his mind about wanting the parks when he realized the alternative city-owned site had that nice full river view his attorney Lindenbaum spoke of. Some involved in that fight even thought the Memorial Day bulldozers were a mere ploy to stir up public anger and thus push the city to make the swap.

   Those line drawings showing a demolished Gold Room would have been Harry's bulldozer in the Villard fight.

Note. From *Palace Coup: The Inside Story of Harry and Leona Helmsley*, by M. Moss (1989, p. 172), New York: Doubleday.

for personalized leaders once they have left power. This point is illustrated in Table 4.11, which provides summaries describing the negative consensus arising from reactions to a personalized leader.

A marginally significant [$F(8,102) = 2.05; p < .10$] interaction was obtained between the orientation and type variables in the multivariate analyses. However, in the univariate analyses significant effects of the interaction of orientation and type were not especially compelling. Apparently, orientation (socialized vs. personalized) is a more powerful influence on leader political performance than type (charismatic, ideological, pragmatic)—a pattern of findings consistent with those obtained in examining leader–follower relationships and communication strategies.

Summary

Taken as a whole, the findings obtained for the various domain-specific criteria seem consistent with the findings obtained for the general performance criteria. More specifically, socialized leaders again displayed better performance than personalized leaders with differences being observed on measures examining leader–follower relationships and communications strategies. However, some significant effects were observed for leader type (charismatic, ideological, and pragmatic), with respect to problem solving. Moreover, orientation (socialized vs. personalized) did interact with leader type (charismatic, ideological, and pragmatic), suggesting that cross-type differences in proscriptive mental models may lead to shifts in the kind of performance emphasized as a way to exercise influence.

CONCLUSIONS

In this chapter, we have examined the performance of outstanding leaders. A central premise underlying this chapter is that although outstanding leaders are, by definition, effective leaders with respect to the exercise of influence, they will differ with respect to the social outcomes associated with the exercise of influence. Thus we have, in the present endeavor, an effort concerned with describing the similarities and differences among outstanding leaders, focused on contrasting different leaders, socialized and personalized, charismatic, ideological, and pragmatic, with respect to the social outcomes emerging from their exercise of influence. This point is of some importance because other criteria for outstanding leadership, such as follower motivation, were not examined.

Along similar lines, it should be recognized that all of the outcomes under consideration, with the exception of problem solving, were drawn from the prologue and epilogue chapters of biographies where authors summarized the accomplishments of the leaders under consideration. Though evidence is available for the consistency of these evaluations across different biographies examining the lives of a given leader, it is also true that the social outcomes that could be examined were those typically addressed by biographers in summarizing the outcomes of a leader's career. In this regard, however, it should be borne in mind that it did prove possible to obtain a robust set of general performance measures (e.g., how many institutions did the leader establish, how many positive contributions did they make). Moreover, in all of the behavioral domains under consideration, it proved possible to obtain at least one, and in some cases five or six, domain-specific performance measures.

The question that arises at this juncture is rather straightforward: Put directly, were these measures any good? The bulk of the available evidence, in fact, indicates that these outcome measures provided a viable strategy for assessing the performance of outstanding leaders. At a basic level, it is clear not only that biographers agreed in their assessments of leader performance, but also that judges agreed in their appraisals of a leader's status on these outcome measures after reviewing the material presented in the prologue or epilogue chapter. This point is of some importance because it indicates that it is possible to apply a historiometric, outcome-oriented approach to obtain reliable measures of leader performance—measures on which outstanding leaders, in fact, display differences.

Although this outcome-oriented approach produced reliable measures of the performance differences among outstanding leaders, the question remains, a question of validity, as to whether these measures provided a meaningful description of performance differences among outstanding leaders. The findings obtained in this present study, in fact, indicate that this approach can yield valid, meaningful, measures of leader performance. On the general criteria, the pattern of relationships observed evidenced the convergent and divergent validity indicative of truly meaningful measures. The convergence of the general performance with evaluations focusing on more specific domains, of course, provides some further evidence along these lines, as does the fact that convergence was observed across measurement formats (counts vs. ratings). This later point is of some importance because it suggests that performance evaluations derived from these outcome measures were not subject to undue method bias.

If it is granted that the outcome-oriented approach applied herein provided a plausible, reasonably reliable and valid, method for assessing the performance of outstanding leaders, then two new questions come to fore. First, are there differences among socialized and personalized leaders with regard to performance? Second, are there differences in the performance of charismatic, ideological, and pragmatic leaders?

With regard to our first question, do socialized and personalized leaders differ in performance, it seems clear that at least on social-historical-outcome measures performance differences do exist. In fact, marked differences were observed between socialized and personalized leaders on both the general criteria and many of the domain-specific criteria. In fact, this pattern of findings is so strong, and so consistent, one must ask: Why does orientation make such a difference in the performance of outstanding leaders?

Traditionally, the distinction we have drawn between socialized and personalized leaders has been considered more a matter of integrity than performance (House & Howell, 1992; O'Connor et al., 1995). Apparently, however, integrity, at least as it is reflected in the socialized-versus-personalized distinction, is a critical determinant of performance with respect to the social outcomes associated with the actions of outstanding leaders. A rather compelling explanation for this pattern of effects may be found in Bass and Steidelmier (1999).

Outstanding leaders operate in roles where they are granted substantial discretion to deal with crises—crises that often have multiple effects on society and social institutions. When decisions with regard to these crises are framed in terms of the *leaders'* well-being and the maintenance of his or her power, the resulting decisions may not, and often will not, prove beneficial to society and the institutions under consideration. Though socialized leadership does not always ensure good decisions and good outcomes, it does make it more likely that the leader's actions will result in the enhancement of the institutions. The difference between socialized and personalized leaders is that they look at different crises and pursue different goals in their decision making with socialized leaders applying a longer time frame and more accurately identifying socially critical issues—both attributes of orientation likely to contribute to the performance of socialized leaders.

Although this model of performance differences among socialized and personalized leaders seems plausible given the findings presented in this chapter, other, more subtle, effects appear to be operating. Personalized leaders do not establish close lasting relationships with lieutenants and this lack of support among lieutenants may undermine their impact on society and social institutions. Personalized leaders, moreover, were apparently less effective communicators and so were less able to convey and build acceptance, lasting acceptance, for their prescriptive models. Finally, it appears that political behavior and divisive political tactics may also act to limit the ability of personalized leaders to make lasting contributions.

The differences observed between socialized and personalized leaders with regard to performance were not observed in contrasting charismatic, ideological, and pragmatic leaders. In fact, main effects attributable to leader type were not obtained, except in the case of problem solving where some weak effects were observed favoring ideological leaders with respect to solution quality. This nonfinding, as noted earlier, suggests that charismatic, ideological, and pragmatic leadership may represent different, albeit equally viable, pathways to outstanding leadership, with leader performance depending on the conditions and issues at hand (Mumford & Van Doorn, 2001).

Nonetheless, it should also be recognized that differences were observed among charismatic, ideological, and pragmatic leaders when the interaction with orientation (socialized vs. personalized) was taken into account. This pattern of effects is intriguing because it suggests that stylistic differences may exist between charismatic, ideological, and pragmatic leaders in how they bring about change and exercise influence—differences that may result in a unique pattern of strengths and weaknesses with respect to various aspects or domains of behavior. In the following chapters, we examine the nature of these behavioral differences and their implications for performance.

5

Problem Solving—Turning Crises Into Opportunities: How Charismatic, Ideological, and Pragmatic Leaders Solve Problems

Michael D. Mumford
Katrina E. Bedell
Samuel T. Hunter
Jazmine Espejo
Paul R. Boatman
The University of Oklahoma

When one mentions the names of outstanding leaders, for example, Ronald Reagan, Emma Goldman, and Mikhail Gorbachev, our thoughts turn to a particular issue. We think about how these leaders changed the world through their exercise of influence—we think about their speeches, we think about the political issues of the day, and we think about the debates in which they were involved. By framing our understanding of outstanding leadership in terms of the exercise of influence, however, we often lose sight of a more basic point. The effective exercise of influence, particularly under crisis conditions, calls for a rather complex form of social problem solving (Jacques, 1976; Mumford, Zaccaro, Harding, et al., 2000).

Even the most cursory review of the lives of outstanding leaders demonstrates the importance of problem-solving activities in shaping the nature and success of a leader's efforts. Jenkins (2001), in his biography of Churchill, illustrated this point in his description of Churchill's work style: "Once a week or oftener, Mr. Churchill came into the office bringing with him some adventurous or impossible projects; but after half an hour's discussion something evolved which was still adventurous but not impossible" (p. 32). Apparently, Churchill was not just a great communicator, he was actively engaged in thinking about and working through the problems of his day. The biographies of Theodore Roosevelt (Morris, 1979) and J.P. Morgan (Strouse, 1999) also underscore the importance of problem solving in the efforts of outstanding leaders. Apparently, outstanding leaders do not just talk, they think.

In this chapter, we examine the kinds of problem-solving strategies employed by outstanding leaders. We begin by describing the role of problem solving, specifically creative problem solving, in incidents of outstanding leadership. Subsequently, we contrast charismatic, ideological, and pragmatic leaders with respect to the strategies they use in creative problem solving considering how these differences in problem solving strategies are related to subsequent leader performance.

PROBLEM SOLVING

Cognition

Although problem solving, or cognition, has received less attention than other topics, few scholars contest the point that problem solving is likely a critical determinant of leader performance. Bass (1990), for example, in his review of the traits related to leadership found that intelligence, general cognitive ability, has consistently proven to be one of the most powerful predictors of leader emergence and performance. Some support for this conclusion may be found in Lord, de Vader, and Alliger (1986). Their meta-analytical study of the traits related to leader emergence and performance indicated that general cognitive ability was strongly ($r = .30$ to $.40$) related to these leadership criteria.

If it is granted that cognitive ability is related to leader emergence and performance, one must ask why cognition and problem solving have tended to be discounted as explanations of leader behavior and performance. One explanation for this trend may be found in the work of Mintzberg and his colleagues (Finkelstein, 2002; Mintzberg, 1990). They argued that the pressure placed on leaders, vis-à-vis role demands, is such that it effectively prohibits analytical thought, the active conscious processing of information that is commonly held to be the basis for problem solving. Instead, they argue that leaders "get by" applying an intuitive, rather reactive, decision-making strategy. Although it is true that leaders may at times eschew active analytical thought as they deal with the pressures of the day, it is also true that studies by Isenberg (1986), Komaki, Desselles, and Bowman (1989), and Thomas and McDaniel (1990) all have indicated that the acquisition and effective analysis of information bearing on organizational problems may, in fact, be critical to leader performance.

This debate about the role of cognition, however, may reflect a broader and somewhat more complex phenomenon. More specifically, leaders may not go about understanding and solving problems in exactly the same way as others. This point is aptly illustrated in the Isenberg (1986) and Thomas and McDaniel (1990) studies cited earlier. The findings obtained in these studies indicated that leaders may be especially effective at boiling down complex multifaceted organizational issues to a small set of critical core causes. Along similar lines, Mumford et al. (2004) argued that leaders' problem-solving efforts often are embedded in opportunistic plans. In other words, leaders invest their cognitive analysis in the construction and adaptation of plans—plans involving the analysis of resources, restrictions, contingencies, and social expectations in relation to the leader's appraisal, or forecasts, of the effects of plan execution in a dynamic environment.

In contrast to the view that cognition and problem solving among leaders may be manifest in unique ways, other scholars have argued that cognition, in leadership, may shift as a function of role requirements. Jacques (1976) argued that as leaders move into progressively more influential positions, they are granted greater discretion in defining and structuring organizational problems—problems that typically increase in complexity and time frame as a function of level. As a result, changes may be observed over the course of leaders' careers in both requisite problem-solving skills and the impact of these skills on performance.

Mumford and his colleagues (Connelly et al., 2000; Mumford, Marks, et al., 2000; Mumford, Zaccaro, Harding, et al., 2000; Zaccaro, Mumford, Connelly, Marks, & Gilbert, 2000) conducted a study to investigate these two propositions. One aspect of this study examined unique cognitive capacities—specifically creative problem-solving skills, expertise, and wisdom, or social judgment, skills. The other aspect of this study examined changes in these skills as leaders moved into progressively more complex and influential roles.

In this study, measures of problem-solving skills (e.g., problem construction, information gathering, idea generation, and idea evaluation) were administered, along with measures of wisdom and expertise, to 1,818 Army officers serving in organizational leadership roles. These roles differed in level of complexity such that the sample in use contained officers ranging in grade from second lieutenants (20-year-olds responsible for units containing roughly 30 soldiers) to colonels (40- to 50-year-olds responsible for units containing roughly 2,000 soldiers).

Analysis of the resulting measures indicated that changes in these cognitive capacities were observed as leaders moved through their careers and into more complex roles. With time leaders acquired better organized knowledge structures and were more likely to appraise the fit of ideas and potential problem solutions to the demands imposed by organizational operations, organizational history, and organizational culture. Moreover, measures of expertise and wisdom, along with measures of creative problem-solving skills, were found to be effective predictions of leader performance on criteria ranging from awards won (e.g., medals) to critical-incident descriptions. Notably, creative problem-solving skills (e.g., problem construction or problem identification, information gathering, idea generation, idea evaluation) were found to be particularly powerful predictors of leader performance producing multiple correlations in the .40 to .50 range.

There is also reason to suspect that creative problem-solving skills will prove of some importance in accounting for the performance of *outstanding leaders*. Earlier, we argued that outstanding leaders emerge under conditions of crisis where crises are broadly defined as change events causing decrements in the performance of an organization or social system (Hunt et al., 1999). What should be recognized here, however, is that crises reflect change—changes that obviate the value of extant routine solutions (Tushman & O'Reilly, 1997). This point is of some importance because it implies that crises present organizations, and potential leaders within these organizations, with novel, ill-defined problems. Novel, ill-defined problems, moreover, are the type of problems known to call for creative thought and the application of creative problem-solving processes such as problem construction and idea generation (Finke et al., 1992; Mumford et al., 1991; Mumford, Whetzel, & Reiter-Palmon, 1997; Reiter-Palmon & Illies, 2004). In fact, it appears that creative problem solving and the application of requisite creative problem-solving skills, influences the performance of outstanding leaders in at least four ways.

First, as noted earlier, outstanding leadership ultimately depends on sensemaking. Sensemaking in response to crises, however, requires leaders to construct, or find, alternatives to extant descriptive models. Combining and reorganizing extant descriptive models through exposure to and reflection on alternative models and the analysis of critical causes and goals gives rise to the new prescriptive mental models applied in sensemaking (Strange & Mumford, 2002, 2005). This restructuring of extant understandings to create new understandings, however, can be expected to depend on the kind of skills, or cognitive processing activities, held to underlie creative thought—in particular, conceptual combination skills (Estes & Ward, 2002; Scott et al., 2005).

Second, once a prescriptive mental model has been formulated, leaders must be able to begin application and execution of this model. What should be noted here, however, is that execution of a prescriptive mental model occurs in a dynamic social context—typically a highly dynamic context as a result of the ambiguity and disruption that surrounds crises in social systems. This ambiguity and disruption implies that it is not enough for leaders to formulate plans for making their models a reality. In addition, leaders must reconfigure and rearrange these plans to adapt plans to emerging opportunities and changes in the requirements for plan execution (Boal & Hooijberg, 2000). This ongoing construction, and reconstruction, of plans will, of course, place a premium on creative problem-solving skills (Mumford et al., 2004).

Third, it should be recognized that plan formation, as well as plan execution, will require the application of creative problem-solving skills. For example, plan construction is known to depend on forecasting where mental simulations of plan execution are used to identify relevant considerations, refine initial plans, and formulate backup plans (Doerner & Schaub, 1994; Mumford, Shultz, & Van Doorn, 2001; Xiao et al., 1997). Effective forecasting and plan construction, however, are known to require creative problem-solving skills such as idea generation and information gathering (Berger, Guilford, & Christensen, 1957; Mumford, 2001).

Fourth, and finally, plans for action, along with the prescriptive mental models applied in sensemaking, must be communicated to followers. Not only is this communication necessarily selective but communications must be constructed and presented in such a way that they will maximize impact on follower behavior. Thus a leader engaging in sensemaking and planning ultimately must become something of an actor. Although acting is a topic of some interest in its own right (Noice, 1991), what should be noted here is that effective acting on the part of outstanding leaders will require creative thought (Feldhusen & Pleiss, 1994).

Creative Problem Solving

Taken as a whole, there appears substantial reason to expect that creative problem-solving skills will be necessary for outstanding leadership. This conclusion, however, begs another question: Exactly what capacities must people posses to engage in creative problem solving? Prior studies by Ericsson and Charness (1994), Vincent, Decker, and Mumford (2002), and Weisberg (1999) have indicated that creative problem solving requires expertise. Thus without substantial exposure to, and experience working in, the social system at hand, the creative thought needed for outstanding leadership is unlikely to be observed. Thus it is not surprising that outstanding leadership is, more often than not, a phenomenon of mid-to-late life. It takes time to acquire the requisite experience.

By the same token, however, if we only had existing expertise to work with, it would be impossible for people to create something new. This rather straightforward observation has led most students of creativity to stress the importance of creative problem-solving skills on the process by which people work with extant knowledge to create new ideas and new understandings (Finke et al., 1992; Lubart, 2001; Sternberg, 1988b). In a comprehensive review of the various models of the processes held to be involved in creative thought, Mumford et al. (1991) identified eight core processes: (a) problem construction or problem identification, (b) information gathering, (c) concept selection, (d) conceptual combination, (e) idea generation, (f) idea evaluation, (g) implementation planning, and (h) monitoring.

Over the course of the last 10 years, a number of studies have been conducted that provide some rather compelling evidence for this model of the processes involved in creative thought (Lubart, 2001; Ward, Patterson, & Sifonis, 2004). In one series of studies along these lines, Mumford and his colleagues (Mumford, Baughman, Supinski, & Anderson, 1998; Mumford, Baughman, Supinski, & Maher, 1996; Mumford, Supinski, Baughman, Costanza, & Threlfall, 1997; Mumford, Supinski, Threlfall, & Baughman, 1996) developed a set of measures, performance measures, intended to assess individual differences in the effectiveness with which people executed processes such as problem construction, information gathering, concept selection, and conceptual combination. They found that process execution measures were effective predictors of the quality and originality of the solutions obtained as people worked on a set of complex, ill-defined problems.

In another study along these lines Scott et al. (2005) examined the influence of one of these processes, conceptual combination, on performance in organizational leadership roles. In this study, undergraduates were asked to assume the role of a principal designing a curriculum for a new experimental school. The quality and originality of the resulting curriculum plans was evaluated. As students worked on these plans they were provided with prompts encouraging the application of heuristics, or strategies, needed for effective execution of the conceptual combination process. It was found that effective application of these heuristics, heuristics contributing to effective conceptual combination, led to the production of higher quality and more-original plans by people in leadership roles.

More direct, albeit less precise, evidence bearing on the need for application of these processes in leadership roles was provided by Mumford et al. (1999). They asked managers drawn from a variety of organizations to rate the extent to which these processes were required on their jobs. In comparison to people working in other types of jobs (e.g., police officers, teachers), managers indicated that these processing capacities were particularly important to job performance.

Leader Types

Though some available evidence indicated that effective execution of creative problem-solving processes may be important to leadership, it is less clear exactly how application of these processes will vary across leader types. Because creative problem solving, and the associated processing activities, contribute to multiple activities required for outstanding leadership, it is not implausible to argue that outstanding leaders, regardless of type and orientation, will display substantial similarity in this regard. In other words, one can argue that the fundamental nature of these processes is such that, to lead, one must be effective in applying all these processes.

By the same token, however, an argument can be put forth that there will be differences across outstanding leaders with regard to the application of these processes in problem solving. Mumford et al. (1991), along with Russ (2003), argued that different types of problems stress the need for effective execution of different processes. Thus some problems are easily solved once the problem has been defined whereas other problems are easily solved once one has identified the right concepts.

These cross-problem differences in processing requirements suggest that differences may be observed among charismatic, ideological, and pragmatic leaders. For example, charismatic leaders by articulating a future-oriented vision, and using this vision as a basis for problem solving, can be expected to rely on idea generation skills. Ideological leaders, in contrast, reference problem solutions against a fixed set of beliefs and values. The tendency to approach problems through evaluation, in turn, suggests that idea evaluation may be particularly important in shaping the performance of ideological leaders. Along similar lines, Mumford (2001) and Mumford and Van Doorn (2002) argued that pragmatic leaders, due to their reliance on solution effectiveness as a basis for the exercise of influence, tend to stress information gathering in their problem-solving efforts. Thus differences in approach to problems and issues may lead to shifts across the charismatic, ideological, and pragmatic types in the kind of process applied.

In addition to cross-type differences in approach, differences in the application of various problem-solving processes may arise as a result of the tactics, or strategies, outstanding leaders prefer to apply in crisis resolution. As noted earlier, charismatic leaders exercise influence by motivating people to work toward a better future. Thus, for charismatic leaders, the issue at hand is less evaluation of ideas than stimulating idea generation—an observation that suggests that idea generation may be emphasized by charismatic leaders. Pragmatic leaders, in contrast, exercise influence by building acceptance among knowledgeable elites—an observation that suggests concept selection and information gathering may be emphasized by pragmatic leaders.

Not only may differences exist across charismatic, ideological, and pragmatic leaders in the kind of processes applied, it is possible that differences will exist in overall investment in problem solving. More specifically, because pragmatic leaders exercise influence by crafting viable problem solutions, it seems plausible to argue that more intense and extensive application of various problem-solving processes will be evident in the careers of pragmatic, as opposed to charismatic and ideological leaders. Not only is there reason to suspect that differences might be observed across charismatic, ideological, and pragmatic leaders, it is possible that differences might be observed among socialized and personalized leaders. The uncertainty and fear evident in personalized leaders (O'Connor et al., 1995) will tend to draw resources away from problem-focused cognition to self-focused cognition. This pattern of effects, in turn, suggests less investment in problem solving and poorer execution of the various processes needed for effective problem solving. Along related lines, the control orientation and power motives of personalized leaders (House & Howell, 1992) may tend to inhibit generative activities in problem solving, suggesting that problem construction, conceptual combination, and idea generation may play a less important role in personalized leaders' problem-solving efforts than is the case for socialized leaders.

Summary

Problem solving appears to be a critical component of performance in leadership positions; and, by virtue of the nature of the crises, outstanding leadership may require substantial creative problem-solving skills. Prior studies of creative problem solving, including creative problem solving in leadership roles, have indicated that effective execution of eight basic processes determine performance on creative problem-solving tasks: (a) problem construction or problem identification, (b) information gathering, (c) concept selection, (d) conceptual combination, (e) idea generation, (f) idea evaluation, (g) implementation planning, and (h) monitoring. Due to the way leaders approach problems and the strategies used in the exercise of influence, it appears, moreover, that differences in the emphasis placed on, and effective application of, these processes may be observed in contrasting the actions taken by outstanding leaders in their attempts to resolve crises and solve significant organizational problems.

METHOD

Study Method

Material Selection. To examine differences across leaders in their problem-solving processes, the leader biographies were reviewed by three psychologists to identify material describing the leaders' activities in solving historically noteworthy problems. These psychologists reviewed the relevant biographical material to identify issues, or crises, that reflected complex, multifaceted organizational issues, or problems, where there was no clear path to issue resolution. Because the focus of the present effort was on leader problem solving, identified incidents were retained only if the leader was a key actor in the problem-solving effort and had some discretion concerning the kind of actions that might be taken to resolve the problem situation.

As noted earlier, prior studies have indicated changes as leaders move through their careers in the application of requisite problem-solving skills (Mumford, Marks, et al., 2000). To take these potential changes into account, incidents were drawn from two distinct career periods. More specifically, problem-solving incidents were drawn from the rise-to-power and pinnacle-of-power chapters included in the biographies. Within these chapters, three problem-solving incidents were identified. The selected incidents, in cases where more than three incidents appeared in the relevant chapters, were those that (a) presented the most complex problem, (b) described the leader's actions in the greatest detail, and (c) in the view of the biographer, proved to be historically important incidents. Application of these criteria resulted in 90% agreement in the problem-solving incidents retained. Across the 120 biographies, the 720 incidents identified based on these criteria were typically two to four pages in length. These incident descriptions provided not only a description of the problem and the leader's behavior, but also relevant contextual information and outcomes, thereby providing a reasonably comprehensive description of the problem-solving incident.

Rating Procedure. To examine these incidents with respect to problem-solving skills four judges were asked to evaluate these incidents using a set of benchmark rating scales. It is of note that judges were asked to evaluate only incidents, not the whole biography, with the incidents identified for a given leader being presented in a random order. The benchmark rating scales applied in evaluating (a) problem construction or problem identification, (b) information gathering, (c) concept selection, (d) conceptual combination, (e) idea generation, (f) idea evaluation, (g) implementation planning, and (h) monitoring are presented in Fig. 5.1.

As may be seen, these benchmark rating scales presented the processing skills and an operational definition of each skill. Following this material, these rating scales presented example behaviors indicative of effective skill application. The behavioral benchmarks were developed in a two-step process. Initially, a psychologist reviewed the literature on each of the eight problem-solving processes under consideration to identify the heuristics, or strategies, involved in effective process application (e.g., Finke et al., 1992; Mumford et al., 1998; Scott et al., 2005). After the heuristics, or strategies, involved in effective process execution had been specified, the biographies of 10 charismatic, 10 ideological, and 10 pragmatic leaders were reviewed to identify behaviors indicative of application of these heuristics. This behavioral contextualization of benchmark behaviors was used to tie evaluations to the kind of material presented in the biographies, taking into account the potential for differential expression of the heuristics, or strategies, given the pathway being pursued by a given leader.

The four judges who evaluated the various problem-solving incidents were graduate students in industrial and organizational psychology. These judges were given a 16-hour training program. This training program began by describing the nature of the problem-solving skills and their role in solving novel, ill-defined problems. Subsequently, judges were familiarized with the operational definition of these skills and the strategies, or heuristics, required for effective process execution. After judges had been familiarized with the material, they were presented with the benchmark rating scales and asked to apply these rating scales in evaluating six practice incidents. Judges were then reconvened in a panel to discuss their ratings. At this time, feedback was provided to clarify rating scales, dimensional definitions, and application of the benchmarks in appraising the problem-solving incidents.

In applying these rating scales to evaluate each problem-solving incident, judges were informed as to the particular sort of rating scales—charismatic,

CHARISMATIC LEADER

1. PROBLEM IDENTIFICATION: *Identifying the nature of problem*	2. INFORMATION GATHERING: *Knowing how to find information and identifying essential information*	3. CONCEPT SELECTION: *Finding ways to structure or classify multiple pieces of information*	4. CONCEPTUAL COMBINATION: *Reorganizing information to get a better approach to problems or tasks*
• Identifies weaknesses with status quo • Pays little attention to specific details • Focuses on macrolevel problems • Defines problems based on vision • Defines more distal or long-range problems • Examines characteristics of majority of potential or actual followers	• Searches for information to support vision only • Searches for information from potential followers (consensus) • Searches for radically different information from status quo • Searches for discrepant information • Low amount of information gathering	• Uses emotionally evocative heuristics to order information (e.g., most sensational to least) • Uses symbols to chunk information • Uses imagery to order information • Prioritizes information that is congruent with personal vision	• Defines features of two radically different ideas • Does not rely heavily on past cases • Combines two radically different ideas to form unique idea • Examines affective-based differences between ideas • Examines similarities of ideas in terms of their common emotional content (e.g., both will evoke fear, etc.) • Searches for optimal match between unlike features of ideas • Examines strengths and weaknesses of ideas based on how they will shape the future • Combines ideas that have relatively strong emotions attached with ideas of lesser emotional content (e.g., less emotionally evocative ideas ride on coat-tails of more powerful ideas—leader links them) • Combines ideas that are easily understood with more difficult ideas

5. IDEA GENERATION: *Generating a number of different approaches to problems*	6. IDEA EVALUATION: *Evaluating the likely success of an idea in relation to the demands of the situation*	7. IMPLEMENTATION PLANNING: *Developing approaches for implementing an idea*	8. SOLUTION APPRAISAL: *Observing and evaluating the outcomes of a problem solution to identify lessons learned or redirect efforts*
• Generates ideas that address future goals • Produces ideas that are have high performance expectations attached • Generates ideas radically different from status quo (i.e., require followers to do something totally different) • Generates ideas that promise a better life in distal future for followers • Generates ideas that are loosely linked to specific goals • Generates ideas that evoke strong affective response from followers	• Evaluates ideas based on likelihood of acceptance by majority of followers • Evaluates ideas based on adherence to vision • Evaluates ideas based on degree of emotional content of each idea • Evaluates ideas based on amount of difference from status quo (i.e., more different ideas will be evaluated as better) • Judges ideas based on communicability (ideas that are easier to understand will be selected) • Examines ideas for appeal to majority of followers • Assesses whether ideas address weaknesses in status quo • Overweights social reactions when evaluating ideas • Uses acceptance from masses in place of performance standards • Revises ideas to gain more support from followers	• Identifies vision-based key causes that the plan should address • Generates backup plans that are in line with vision, just modifications of original plan • Forecasts likely acceptance of backup plans • Forecasts downstream consequences that might affect acceptance of plan • Plans markers to give feedback about acceptance of the plan • Identifies aspects in the environment that may influence acceptance of the plan • Identifies restrictions of acceptance • Plans for different ways to communicate/sell idea to followers	• Samples some followers to gauge success of plan • Looks for evidence of self-sacrifice of followers • Monitors progress toward distal goals • Scans plan for weaknesses to be addressed in future ideas • Abstracts key success and failure elements of plan acceptance for use in future planning

FIG. 5.1. *(Continued)*

117

IDEOLOGICAL LEADER

1. PROBLEM IDENTIFICATION: *Identifying the nature of problem*	2. INFORMATION GATHERING: *Knowing how to find information and identifying essential information*	3. CONCEPT SELECTION: *Finding ways to structure or classify multiple pieces of information*	4. CONCEPTUAL COMBINATION: *Reorganizing information to get a better approach to problems or tasks*
• Identifies violations of standards or morals to define problems • Uses personal values to find problems with other groups • Uses a priori defined standards to find problems • Defines problems based on black-and-white distinctions of right and wrong values • *Pays little attention to performance requirements*	• Searches extant standards or values for information • Searches for support for personal values from powerful sources • Searches for evidence of adverse consequences for other values or ideas • Searches for evidence of rewards of others who adhered to ideas • Searches for ways to transmit values • Searches for others who share values	• Uses personal values to order information in terms of importance • Uses extant ideas or standards to prioritize discrepant information • Makes clear distinctions between "good" and "bad" information • Chunks information according to standards to be maintained	• Uses past cases or situations as analogies • Examines ideas based on similarities and differences from belief system • Examines strengths and weaknesses of ideas based on how they worked in the past • Elaborates features of newly combined ideas to incorporate standards of belief system (e.g., amends ideas that are not 100% congruent with beliefs) • Examines ideas based on morals; makes judgments based on what is right and wrong with ideas • Reorganizes extant ideas to incorporate other standards of behavior • Combines features of ideas that are congruent with belief system of leader • Combines concepts from belief systems that are only somewhat divergent from personal beliefs • Combines older ideas with newer situation to draw parallels between old and new values

5. IDEA GENERATION: *Generating a number of different approaches to problems*	6. IDEA EVALUATION: *Evaluating the likely success of an idea in relation to the demands of the situation*	7. IMPLEMENTATION PLANNING: *Developing approaches for implementing an idea*	8. SOLUTION APPRAISAL: *Observing and evaluating the outcomes of a problem solution to identify lessons learned or redirect efforts*
• Generates ideas to uphold past standards • Produces ideas that manifest or display beliefs of leader • Generates ideas that are based on ideological principles of right and wrong • Generates ideas that prescribe clear, black-and-white actions • Generates ideas that mirror past solutions • Generates ideas that require strict adherence; no derivations • Generates ideas that evoke strong affective response from followers	• Evaluates ideas based on congruence to standards • Judges ideas based on degree of moralistic correctness (i.e., more "morally right" ideas will get selected) • Examines right and wrong actions of each idea (e.g., "if idea a is accepted, then behavior 1 will be wrong") • Evaluates ideas based on similarity to past solutions (ideas more similar to past will be more accepted) • Assesses extant ideas reflect leader's belief system • Judges ideas based on personal beliefs and values, not performance of organization • Revises ideas to make them more congruent with ideological goals • Discounts negative consequences of past problem solutions of ideologically congruent ideas • Uses ideological beliefs in place of performance standards • Revises ideas to incorporate more personal beliefs, not based on performance considerations	• Identifies ideological or abstract key causes that the plan should address (no concrete causes) • Does not generate backup plans (self-serving bias) • Overweights likelihood of good consequences of plan that mirrors personal beliefs • Forecasts downstream consequences that might alter nature of plan • Plans markers to monitor the adherence of the plan to belief system • Attends to specifics of standard adherence versus big picture	• Monitors standard adherence versus performance markers to guide monitoring • Scans environment for dissenting ideas or violators of solution • Scans environment for others who share beliefs and values • Discounts disconfirming evidence

PRAGMATIC LEADER

1. PROBLEM IDENTIFICATION: *Identifying the nature of problem*	2. INFORMATION GATHERING: *Knowing how to find information and identifying essential information*	3. CONCEPT SELECTION: *Finding ways to structure or classify multiple pieces of information*	4. CONCEPTUAL COMBINATION: *Reorganizing information to get a better approach to problems or tasks*
• Identifies functional concerns of objective situation • Examines rational problems with socio-technical status quo • Identifies local needs in specific situations • Defines problems based on practical needs within social context • Scans environment to find problems with people's everyday lives • *Defines more proximate problems*	• Searches for restrictions and causes of problem • Analyzes people and social system involved to identify needs • Searches for key intervention points • Searches for people with high levels of expertise in problem area • Gathers information based on extant values of social system (in face of own values) • High amount of information gathering	• Uses a cost-and-benefit analysis to order information • Chunks information according to restrictions and causes • Prioritizes information in terms of practicality and performance concerns • Outlines logical steps described in information gathered • Arranges information according to situational contingencies • Orders information based on requirements and constraints of organization	• Uses past cases or situations • Uses analogies of more simple problem solutions to solve current problem • Examines strengths and weaknesses of ideas in terms of their practicality or utility for proximate goals • Examines features of ideas based on similarities and differences of analogous problem solutions that were either successful or unsuccessful • Elaborates or extends extant concepts with minor changes • Adjusts ideas to be more efficient and/or economical • Reorganizes existing ideas or concepts incrementally • Adjusts ideas based on functional needs • Combines strategies or tactics of action • Combines unique skills of people with activities that suit them • Combines ideas that meet multiple needs

5. IDEA GENERATION: *Generating a number of different approaches to problems*	6. IDEA EVALUATION: *Evaluating the likely success of an idea in relation to the demands of the situation*	7. IMPLEMENTATION PLANNING: *Developing approaches for implementing an idea*	8. SOLUTION APPRAISAL: *Observing and evaluating the outcomes of a problem solution to identify lessons learned or redirect efforts*
• Generates ideas that address present needs • Produces ideas that entail only minor adjustments to status quo • Generates viable solutions that work within current socio-technical context • Generates ideas that have more proximate goals • Generates ideas that are flexible to situational contingencies • Generates ideas that are subtle to followers (e.g., ideas that do not require drastic changes will sometimes go unnoticed) • Generates practical ideas • Tailors idea to extant situation	• Evaluates ideas based on likelihood of objective success • Compares costs and benefits of ideas • Examines possible changes in situation to look at adaptability of ideas • Analyzes organizational requirements for each idea • Evaluates organizational constraints for each idea • Objectively analyzes situation to identify key restrictions and intervention points • Evaluates ideas for most added practical value with least effort or change in status quo (i.e., compare ideas based on most bang for the buck) • Evaluates ideas based on utility/effectiveness concerns (e.g., how likely will followers be able to perform requisite tasks of ideas) • Revises ideas multiple times to improve ideas' chances of success • Considers multiple goals of ideas • Revises ideas based on restrictions operating in situation • Does not evaluate plan based on personal beliefs/values	• Projects realistic consequences of ideas in socio-technical setting • Identifies manipulatable causes • Develops backup plans in case of situational event changes • Acquires resources needed for backup plans • Plans objective monitor markers to gauge success of solution • Forecasts downstream consequences to plan as well as backup plans • Identifies practical key causes or issues the plan should address • Identifies aspects of the environment that may influence the effectiveness of the plan • Identifies key personnel and resources needed to execute the plan	• Builds evaluative, concrete marker events into idea to guide monitoring • Abstracts key success and failure elements of effectiveness for use in future planning • Scans environment for changing conditions that might affect the utility of the solution • Adjusts and transforms solution incrementally to cope with event changes • Scans environment for multiple perspectives on idea success

FIG. 5.1.   Benchmark rating scales for evaluating problem-solving skills.

ideological, or pragmatic—to be applied. The judges were then asked to read through the incident and, considering the benchmarks provided for each skill, rate, on a 5-point scale, the extent to which behaviors similar to these benchmark items appeared in the incident. After evaluating the frequency, or extent to which, behaviors indicative of each of the eight processing activities appeared in an incident, they were asked to rate on a 5-point scale the overall effectiveness of the leader's problem-solving efforts. Scores on the overall and process scales were aggregated over the three problem-solving incidents abstracted from the biographical material presented in the rise-to-power and pinnacle-of-power chapters.

Study-Specific Controls.   In addition to these ratings of problem-solving skills, judges were asked to appraise a study-specific set of controls to be applied along with the general biographical control measures described earlier. The first control, intended to take into account the amount of material available, was a simple word count reflecting the length of the incident description. The remaining study-specific controls focused on attributes of the social setting that might moderate leaders' problem-solving behavior. Here judges were asked to indicate whether the problem was social or nonsocial in nature, whether the problem solving was individual or occurred in a group setting, and whether the problem solving occurred in a public or private setting. Additionally, the judges were asked to rate the number of people involved in problem solving (5-point scale), the effectiveness of the problem solution apart from the leader's efforts (5-point scale), the relative amount of time needed to solve the problem (5-point scale), the number of people affected by the problem (5-point scale), and the number of institutions affected by the problem (4-point scale). The average interrater agreement coefficients (Shrout & Fleiss, 1979) obtained for these control variable ratings lay above .80.

Study-Specific Criteria.   Because the prologue, or epilogue, chapters included in the biographies included little information bearing on the success of leaders' problem-solving efforts, an alternative strategy was used to obtain evaluations of solution originality and quality. Here three judges, again graduate students in psychology, were asked to review all problem incidents identified for a leader. After reviewing the incidents obtained for a leader, they were asked to rate, on a 5-point scale, four questions bearing on solution originality and three questions bearing on solution quality. The originality questions asked judges to indicate (a) whether the solution was considered novel, (b) whether others were surprised by the leaders actions, (c) whether the solution differed from those proposed by other leaders, and (d) whether the solution involved critical reactions. The quality questions asked judges to indicate (a) whether the solution led to noteworthy changes in society, (b) whether the solution was effective in solving the problem, and (c) whether the solution proved useful over time. The average interrater agreement coefficient obtained for the originality ratings was .79, whereas the average interrater agreement coefficients obtained for the quality ratings was .81. Judges' average scores across questions for the "rise to power" and "pinnacle of power" incidents provided the quality and originality criteria used to supplement the general criterion measures described earlier.

Descriptive Findings

Table 5.1 presents the means, standard deviations, interrater agreement coefficients, and correlation coefficients obtained for the ratings of process application. The average interrater agreement coefficient obtained for judges' evaluations of process application was .55. Although these interrater agreement coefficients are somewhat lower than those obtained for evaluations of overt behavior, they are adequate when the concern at hand is evaluation of behavioral manifestations of underlying cognitive processes—evaluations that are more difficult for judges to reach agreement on due to the complexity of the inferences to be made. It is of note that these ratings, made using four judges, ranged between .50 and .69, indicating that all cases met minimally acceptable levels of reliability for this kind of evaluation. The correlations presented in Table 5.1 also provide some initial evidence for the construct validity of these ratings. To begin, the rating scales evidenced the moderate positive correlations that would be expected among a substantially integrated set of processing operations used in solving complex novel problems (Mumford et al., 1991). Moreover, processes focusing on the acquisition, integration, and reorganization of information displayed strong positive relationships ($r = .52$) but weaker relationships with processes, such as implementation planning and solution monitoring, involved in this real-world execution of ideas ($r = .33$). This pattern of findings is consistent with the findings obtained by Vincent et al. (2002) in a study examining the application of these processes using data obtained in a modified think-aloud protocol.

Given the availability of this evidence for the meaningfulness, or construct validity, of the ratings of process application, a new question comes to fore: More specifically, how did leaders differ with respect to application of the various processes under consideration? The means presented in Table 5.1 indicate that leaders, in general, tended to obtain especially high scores with respect to problem identification ($\overline{X} = 3.61$) and idea generation ($\overline{X} = 3.50$) and especially low scores with respect to conceptual combination ($\overline{X} = 2.85$) and solution monitoring ($\overline{X} = 2.55$). Apparently in historically notable incidents of problem solving, leaders are likely to engage in behavior that defines the problem and allow for the generation of ideas for solving the problem. In other words, leaders act as generators.

In this regard, however, two further points should be borne in mind. First, virtually all of the scales produced mean ratings above the scale midpoint on a 5-point scale. Thus, there is reason to believe that all of these processing activi-

TABLE 5.1
Means, Standard Deviations, Agreement Coefficients, and Correlations for Problem-Solving Processes

	$\overline{X}$	SD	r_{tt}	1	2	3	4	5	6	7	8
1. Problem Identification	3.61	.47	.52	1.00	.30	.22	.05	.41	.45	.23	-.02
2. Information Gathering	3.21	.59	.69		1.00	.56	.33	-.16	.31	.30	.39
3. Concept Selection	3.18	.62	.65			1.00	.69	-.10	.37	.38	.35
4. Conceptual Combination	2.85	.61	.60				1.00	-.01	.20	.50	.53
5. Idea Generation	3.59	.50	.58					1.00	.41	.41	.08
6. Idea Evaluation	3.31	.40	.55						1.00	.34	.25
7. Implementation Planning	3.13	.46	.50							1.00	.48
8. Solution Monitoring	2.55	.46	.51								1.00

Note. $r \geq .17$ significant at .05 level.

ties are, in one way or another, relevant to understanding the problem-solving activities of leaders. Second, the processes involved in gathering information, evaluating ideas, and planning solution implementation were evident in leader behavior, suggesting that the leader is not just generating but instead generating solutions based on his or her analysis of the problem at hand.

RESULTS

Comparison of Leader Types

Table 5.2 presents the results obtained in the multivariate analysis of covariance examining leader type (charismatic, ideological, pragmatic), leader orientation (socialized and personalized), and time of incident ("rise to power" or "pinnacle of power"). As may be seen, a number of covariates yielded significant effects in this analysis. The significant effects obtained for number of systems affected [$F(8, 102) = 4.78$; $p \leq .001$], time required to solve the problem [$F(8, 102) = 2.79$; $p \leq .001$], and length of incidents [$F(8, 102) = 4.72$; $p \leq .001$], indicated that as the problem at hand became more complex, more manifestations of problem-solving activities were likely to be observed. The significant effects obtained for the effectiveness variable [$F(8, 102) = 6.17$; $p \leq .001$] reflect the fact that more attention was given to the problem-solving activities of leaders in incidents of effective as opposed to ineffective performance—a bias endemic to many biographies. Finally, the significant effect [$F(8, 102) = 2.76$; p

TABLE 5.2
Summary of Results of Multivariate Analysis of Covariance

	F	df	p	η^2
Covariates				
Number of systems affected	4.78	8, 102	.001	.271
Length of incidents	4.72	8, 102	.001	.270
Pre– or post–World War II	2.76	8, 102	.001	.128
Effectiveness	6.17	8, 102	.001	.326
Time to solve	2.79	8, 102	.001	.180
Main effects				
Orientation (socialized or personalized)	1.87	8, 102	.072	.128
Type (charismatic, ideological, or pragmatic)	33.63	8, 102	.001	.723
Time ("rise to power" or "pinnacle of power")	1.69	8, 102	.110	.117
Interactions				
Orientation * Type	.54	8, 102	.819	.041
Orientation * Time	1.11	8, 102	.359	.080
Type * Time	2.16	8, 102	.036	.144
Type * Time * Orientation	1.33	8, 102	.237	.094

Note. F = F-ratio, df = degrees of freedom, p = significance level using Roy's Largest Root, η^2 = effect size (partial eta squared).

≤ .001] for the time the biography was written (pre– or post–World War II) reflects the tendency of biographers writing in the post–World War II era to devote more space to discussion of the leaders' problem-solving activities.

Even when these requisite controls were taken into account, significant differences [$F(8, 102) = 33.63; p ≤ .001$] were observed in comparing charismatic, ideological, and pragmatic leaders with respect to expression of behaviors indicative of the eight processing activities under consideration. Examination of the associated univariate effects indicated that problem identification [$F(2, 109) = 3.49; p ≤ .001$], information gathering [$F(2, 109) = 108.15; p < .001$], concept selection [$F(2, 109) = 20.17; p ≤ .001$], and conceptual combination [$F(2, 109) = 7.75; p ≤ .001$] all produced significant differences among charismatic, ideological, and pragmatic leaders.

Given the observation of Mumford and Van Doorn (2001), indicating that pragmatic leadership depends on the careful analysis of critical problems, it was not surprising that pragmatic leaders obtained higher scores than did charismatic leaders on problem identification ($\overline{X} = 3.73, SE = .06$ vs. $\overline{X} = 3.48, SE = .06$), information gathering ($\overline{X} = 3.69, SE = .05$ vs. $\overline{X} = 2.59, SE = .05$), concept selection ($\overline{X} = 3.50, SE = .08$ vs. $\overline{X} = 2.76, SE = .08$), and conceptual combination ($\overline{X} = 2.86, SE = .06$ vs. $\overline{X} = 2.62, SE = .08$). Apparently, pragmatic leaders succeed through problem solving, especially problem analysis, whereas charismatic leaders succeed through other strategies.

In this regard, however, it is important to note that ideological leaders also outperformed charismatic leaders with regard to these dimensions, displaying more similarity to pragmatic leaders than charismatic leaders. More specifically, ideological leaders received higher scores than did charismatic leaders with respect to problem identification ($\overline{X} = 3.60, SE = .05$ vs. $\overline{X} = 3.48, SE = .06$), information gathering ($\overline{X} = 3.37, SE = .05$ vs. $\overline{X} = 2.59, SE = .05$), concept selection ($\overline{X} = 3.29, SE = .08$ vs. $\overline{X} = 2.76, SE = .08$), and conceptual combination ($\overline{X} = 3.07, SE = .08$ vs. $\overline{X} = 2.62, SE = .08$). This pattern of findings suggests that ideological leaders, like pragmatic leaders, engage in intensive problem analysis—although the domain of analysis may be circumscribed in terms of certain select beliefs and values.

Charismatic leaders, however, did produce higher scores than pragmatic leaders and ideological leaders on one dimension. The significant [$F(2, 109) = 14.40; p ≤ .001$] difference observed with regard to the idea generation ratings indicated that charismatic leaders ($\overline{X} = 3.87, SE = .07$) evidenced more idea generation activities than either pragmatic ($\overline{X} = 3.34, SE = .07$) or ideological ($\overline{X} = 3.58, SE = .07$) leaders. This finding suggests that charismatic leaders rely on the generation of ideas to move organizations toward the future-oriented vision being advocated.

Earlier, we noted that by virtue of their focus on certain extant standards, ideological leaders would tend to be more evaluative than charismatic and pragmatic leaders. In keeping with this proposition, the significant effects obtained for the idea evaluation [$F(2, 109) = 7.70; p \leq .001$] and solution monitoring [$F(2, 109) = 3.23; p \leq .05$] were attributable to the higher scores obtained by ideological leaders over charismatic leaders on the idea evaluation ($\overline{X} = 3.49, SE = .06$ vs. $\overline{X} = 3.09, SE = .07$) and solution-monitoring ($\overline{X} = 2.69, SE = .06$ vs. $\overline{X} = 2.48, SE = .07$) scales.

The first discriminant function obtained when ratings on these problem-solving scales were used to distinguish charismatic, ideological, and pragmatic leaders produced a canonical correlation of .80 ($p \leq .001$). The dimensions yielding sizable loadings on this function included information gathering, ($r = .75$), concept selection ($r = .42$), and idea generation ($r = -.35$). Because the two dimensions yielding the largest positive loadings on this function focused on acquisition and organization of information for use in problem solving, this function was labeled *expertise*. As might be expected, pragmatic leaders ($\overline{X} = 1.57$) obtained higher scores on this function than did both charismatic ($\overline{X} = -1.73$) and ideological leaders ($\overline{X} = .15$)—although ideological leaders engaged in more expertise acquisition activities than charismatic leaders.

The second discriminant function obtained in contrasting charismatic, ideological, and pragmatic leaders produced a canonical correlation of .39 ($p \leq .001$). The dimensions yielding sizable loadings on this function included conceptual combination ($r = .79$), solution monitoring ($r = .46$), and problem identification ($r = -.31$). Conceptual combination and solution monitoring, of course, require linking information and reappraising information in the context of other ongoing activities. Based on the sizable loadings obtained for conceptual combination, this dimension was labeled *conceptual integration*. The tendency of ideological leaders ($\overline{X} = .60$) to obtain higher scores on this function than charismatic ($\overline{X} = -.25$) and pragmatic ($\overline{X} = -.34$) leaders may be attributed to the need for ideological leaders to integrate strongly held beliefs and values with ongoing patterns of current social activity.

In the multivariate analysis of covariance, orientation, socialized versus personalized, also produced a marginally significant [$F(8, 102) = 1.87; p \leq .10$] main effect. Examination of the associated univariate effects indicated that socialized leaders obtained higher scores than personalized leaders on two of the eight problem-solving dimensions: (a) conceptual combination [$F(1, 109) = 7.59; p \leq .01; \overline{X} = 2.97, SE = .06$ vs. $\overline{X} = 2.73, SE = .06$] and (b) solution monitoring [$F(1, 109) = 5.86; p \leq .05; \overline{X} = 2.64, SE = .05$ vs. $\overline{X} = 2.46, SE = .05$]. The discriminant analysis obtained in contrasting socialized and personalized leaders produced a significant canonical correlation of .25 ($p \leq .05$) with conceptual combination ($r = .82$) and solution monitoring ($r = .82$) producing the only sizable loadings. This pattern of loadings suggests that integration may distinguish the problem-solving activities of socialized and personalized leaders—albeit integration vis-à-vis the monitoring of external events. Given the narcissism characteristic of personalized leaders—narcissism is associated with a strong self-focus—it was not surprising that socialized leaders ($\overline{X} = .26$) obtained higher scores on this *external integration* function than did personalized leaders ($\overline{X} = -.26$).

The time variable, "rise to power" versus "pinnacle of power," did not produce significant main effects, suggesting that, at least in the case of outstanding leaders, strong developmental effects on problem solving are not observed— perhaps because even in the rise-to-power period outstanding leaders have already achieved positions of some eminence. A significant interaction [$F(8, 102) = 5.86; p \le .05$] was obtained, however, between time and type, indicating the existence of some type-specific developmental effects.

Examination of the associated univariate effects indicated that this multivariate effect could be traced to three of the eight dimensions of problem solving under consideration. More specifically, pragmatic leaders were less likely to evidence activities indicative of concept selection ($\overline{X} = 3.35$, $SE = .08$ vs. $\overline{X} = 3.66$, $SE = .11$) and implementation planning ($\overline{X} = 2.95$, $SE = .08$ vs. $\overline{X} = 3.28$, $SE = .10$) later as opposed to earlier in their careers—a pattern of findings suggesting that with experience pragmatic leaders may come to place less faith in abstract plans.

In addition to the effects obtained for concept selection and implementation planning, the univariate analyses produced a significant effect [$F(2, 109) = 3.54; p < .05$] for idea generation. Examination of the associated group means indicated that this effect was due to a shift in the idea generation activities of ideological leaders with ideological leaders evidencing more idea generation later ($\overline{X} = 3.72$, $SE = .08$) rather than earlier ($\overline{X} = 3.44$, $SE = .08$) in their careers. Apparently, the realities of power require ideological leaders to move beyond initial preconceptions thereby giving rise to more idea generation activity.

Although some significant differences were obtained in the univariate analyses with respect to the Type × Time interaction, the discriminant analysis examining the groups involved in this interaction produced a somewhat different pattern of effects. Although two functions were significant, they reflected little more than general type effects noted earlier. Because the remaining functions, the functions indicative of interactive effects, were insignificant, no function scores derived from this interaction were applied in examining performance relationships.

Performance Relationships

Table 5.3 presents the correlations of the discriminant function scores derived from the type and orientation variables with the general and study-specific performance criteria. As might be expected, expertise was positively related ($r = .26$) to the quality of the problem solutions obtained during the leaders' rise to power. Solution quality, however, during both the rise-to-power and pinnacle-

TABLE 5.3
Correlations of Performance Criteria with Discriminant Functions

General Criteria	Expertise	Conceptual Integration	External Integration
1. How much did the leader contribute to society?	−.19	.16	.15
2. How long did the leader's contributions last?	.01	.18	.18
3. How many people did the leader affect?	−.02	.04	.15
4. How favorably did the biographer view the leader?	.01	.03	.10
5. How many positive contributions did the leader make?	−.12	.19	.26
6. How many negative contributions did the leader make?	−.11	−.09	−.15
7. How many different types of positive contributions?	−.03	.06	.25
8. How many different types of negative contributions?	−.13	−.11	−.12
9. Do institutions established by the leader still exist?	.12	.03	.07
10. How many institutions were established by the leader?	.07	.03	.16
11. Was the leader's vision maintained after they left power?	−.01	.23	.29
12. Did the leader initiate mass movements?	−.27	.12	.17
Problem-Solving Criteria			
1. Quality of solutions during "rise to power" period	.26	.01	.15
2. Quality of solutions during "pinnacle of power" period	.07	.17	.28
3. Originality of solutions during "rise to power" period	.10	.20	.34
4. Originality of solutions during "pinnacle of power" period	.12	.22	.35

Note. $r \geq .18$ significant at .05 level.

of-power periods, was found to be more strongly related to external integration ($r = .21$). Both external integration ($r = .21$) and conceptual integration ($r = .34$) were related to the originality of the solutions obtained to the kind of problems outstanding leaders confront in the real world. Apparently, the success of leaders' problem-solving efforts is contingent on bringing ideas together in relation to the requirements imposed by external demands.

As might be expected based on these observations, when examining the various outcome criteria derived from the prologue, or epilogue, chapter, expertise was not found to be strongly related to the various performance measures. Conceptual integration, however, was found to be related to whether the leader's vision was maintained ($r = .23$), how long their contributions lasted ($r = .18$), and the number of positive contributions made ($r = .19$). Thus new ideas for linking or restructuring relationships and institutions appear to be critical if leaders are to make lasting contributions.

The success of efforts along these lines, however, depends on whether external social feedback is considered. Accordingly, the external-integration function was found to be related to the number of positive contributions ($r = .26$), the number of different types of positive contributions ($r = .25$), maintenance of the leader's vision after leaving power ($r = .29$), and how long the leader's contributions lasted ($r = .18$). This pattern of findings suggests that the critical component of leader performance in organizational problem solving may involve bringing problem solutions in line with the demands of the external environment. Moreover, when it is recognized that this environment is, more often than not, a distinctly social environment, then it becomes apparent why socialized leaders outperform personalized leaders—they may be better able to take into account the needs and expectations of others.

Of course, the question that arises at this juncture is whether these effects were maintained when other variables are taken into account. Table 5.4 presents the results obtained in the regression analyses when the general and study-specific criteria were regressed on the discriminant function scores after first entering the covariate controls that proved significant in the multivariate analysis of covariance. The discriminant functions produced significant ($p \leq .05$) regression weights, even after taking requisite controls into account, on 7 out of the 12 general criteria and all of the study-specific criteria.

In keeping with our foregoing observations, external integration was found to be the best predictor of leader performance with respect to both historic outcomes and the quality and originality of the problem solutions proposed. Across the relevant problem-solving criteria, external integration produced an average regression weight of .32, indicating that external integration influenced the generation of viable solutions to leadership problems. Moreover, the generation of viable problem solutions appeared to be related to subsequent historic outcomes—specifically the number of positive contributions ($\beta = .28$), the number of different types of positive contributions ($\beta = .34$), how long the leader's contributions lasted ($\beta = .22$), maintenance of the leader's vision ($\beta = .34$) and initiation of mass movements ($\beta = .34$).

In this regard, however, it should be noted that expertise, although not always a significant influence on historic performance, tended to produce negative regression weights. This finding should not be taken to imply that expertise is of no importance to the performance of outstanding leaders. In fact, expertise did contribute to production of high-quality solutions during the leader's rise to power ($\beta = .20$). Rather, given a necessary level of expertise to permit external and conceptual integration, further gains in expertise are simply less important to leader performance than the integration of activities and ideas.

Summary

The findings obtained in the present effort indicate that charismatic, ideological, and pragmatic leaders display some noteworthy differences in how they go about solving organizational problems. Pragmatic leaders emphasize analysis. Charismatic leaders emphasize idea generation. And, ideological leaders emphasize idea evaluation. Regardless of these stylistic differences, however, the critical determinant of performance was the leader's ability to integrate ideas, potential problem solutions, with the demands imposed by the external environment.

TABLE 5.4
Summary of Regression Results

Criteria	R	R^2	p	Significant Functions ($p \leq .05$)	Beta	High Group	Low Group
General Criteria							
How much did the leader contribute to society?	.48	.23	.001	Conceptual integration Expertise	.22 -.21	Ideological Pragmatics	Charismatics/pragmatics Charismatics
How long did the leader's contributions last?	.38	.14	.007	Conceptual integration	-.21	Ideological	Charismatic/pragmatics
How many people did the leader affect?	.37	.13	.009	External integration	.22	Socialized	Personalized
How favorably did the biographer view the leader?	.19	.03	.603				
How many positive contributions did the leader make?	.36	.13	.010	External integration	.28	Socialized	Personalized
How many negative contributions did the leader make?	.21	.04	.49				
How many different types of positive contributions?	.33	.11	.029	External integration	.34	Socialized	Personalized
How many different types of negative contributions?	.27	.07	.161				
Do institutions established by the leader still exist?	.39	.15	.004				
How many institutions established by the leader?	.22	.05	.424				
Was the leader's vision maintained after they left power	.43	.18	.001	External integration	.34	Socialized	Personalized
Did the leader initiate mass movements?	.38	.15	.004	External integration Expertise	.30 -.33	Socialized Pragmatics	Personalized Charismatics
Problem-Solving Criteria							
Quality of solutions during "rise to power" period	.35	.12	.020	Expertise	.20	Pragmatics	Charismatic
Quality of solutions during "pinnacle of power" period	.41	.17	.002	External integration	.32	Socialized	Personalized
Originality of solutions during "rise to power" period	.39	.13	.010	External integration	.29	Socialized	Personalized
Originality of solutions during "pinnacle of power" period	.50	.25	.001	External integration	.35	Socialized	Personalized

Note. R = multiple correlation; R^2 = percentage of variance accounted for; p = significance level; Beta = standardized regression weight. Significant covariates are not presented in this table, only significant functions.

129

CONCLUSIONS

In considering the results obtained in the present study, certain limitations should be borne in mind. To begin, the findings obtained herein were based on a particular model of the cognitive processes involved in solving the kind of complex novel problems presented to people in the upper-level roles occupied by outstanding leaders (Jacques, 1976; Mumford, Zaccaro, Harding, et al., 2000). More specifically, we examined problem solving with respect to the general model of requisite processing activities proposed by Mumford et al. (1991). Although application of this model seems justified by virtue of both its generality and the available validation evidence (Lubart, 2001), it is also true that a number of other processes, particularly processes specific to managerial problem solving such as scanning and forecasting (Doerner & Schaub, 1994; Thomas & McDaniel, 1990) exist that were not examined in the present study. Accordingly, the findings obtained herein should be viewed as a first, rather than a last, word on the nature of problem-solving activities on the part of outstanding leaders.

Along similar lines, it should also be recognized that problem-solving activities were assessed using a particular approach. In the present effort, application of these processes was assessed in terms of the leaders' engagement in behaviors indicative of application of the heuristics, or strategies, associated with effective process application (e.g., Scott et al., 2005). Although application of this approach seemed appropriate given what we know about the nature of process execution, and the nature of the material presented in leader biographies, it is also true that different results might have been obtained if a different approach had been used to assess process application.

Of course, one attractive feature of the approach applied in assessing process execution is that it provided specific contextual behavioral benchmarks for assessing processes with respect to the heuristics involved in process execution. Application of this approach seemed necessary given the difficulties involved in appraising underlying processes based on overt behaviors. Although application of this approach proved successful in that minimally acceptable interrater agreement coefficients were obtained for all of the processes under consideration, it is also true that somewhat more powerful effects would have been obtained if a larger sample of judges had been applied to increase the reliability of our assessments.

Even bearing these limitations in mind, however, we believe that the results obtained in the present effort have some important implications for understanding the nature of outstanding leadership and the differences observed among charismatic, ideological, and pragmatic leaders. Perhaps the most clear-cut finding to emerge from the present effort is that charismatic, ideological, and pragmatic leaders appear to apply rather different skills and different approaches in solving complex novel organizational problems of the sort captured by the incidents abstracted from the biographies.

In accordance with the observations of Mumford and Van Doorn (2001), pragmatic leaders appeared to emphasize problem identification, information gathering, and information organization in their problem-solving efforts. Put more directly, pragmatic leaders appear to rely on expertise and careful detailed analysis of the problem to resolve the issue at hand. Although this abstract analytical bent was mitigated to some extent by the demands of their ultimate leadership role, this trend was evident throughout their careers.

This analytical problem-solving style contrasts with the generative style employed by charismatic leaders. It is not the case that charismatic leaders don't think. Rather, they think in terms of possibilities, or a future-oriented vision, relying on idea generation, presumably vision-relevant idea generation, as a preferred approach to problem solving. This statement, however, should not be taken to imply that charismatic leaders are necessarily more creative than pragmatic leaders because problem identification and analysis is often a basis for creative thought (Russ, 2003). Instead, pragmatic and charismatic leaders appear to differ with respect to application of an analytic versus a generative style. Table 5.5 illustrates the application of these stylistic differences using historically noteworthy problem-solving incidents derived from the biographical material obtained for one charismatic and one pragmatic leader.

The existence of this stylistic difference between pragmatic and charismatic leaders has a number of noteworthy implications. First, one might expect to see charismatic and pragmatic leaders emerge and prove successful in settings consistent with their preferred problem-solving style. In fact, given the fact that complex systems require analysis, it is not surprising that pragmatic leaders are often found in business organizations. In contrast, the need to move people to a better future with new ideas, or programs, may account for the tendency of charismatic leaders to be found in politics. Second, these stylistic differences may make pragmatic and charismatic leaders subject to rather different kinds of errors (Finkelstein, 2002)—pragmatic leaders will be subject to error due to overanalysis just as charismatic leaders will be subject to errors of optimism. Third, it can be expected that the tactics used to bring about problem solutions will differ as a function of these styles. Thus, whereas arguments based on expertise will appeal to pragmatics, charismatics' arguments will stress more evocative images and ideas.

Although these differences in the problem-solving styles of pragmatic and charismatic leaders are not especially surprising, a somewhat more surprising pattern of findings emerged for the ideological leaders. As expected, given the focus of ideological leaders on the maintenance of certain values and standards, ideological leaders differed from charismatic and pragmatic leaders in that they stressed evaluative aspects of problem solving such as idea evaluation and solution monitoring. Despite our stereotypes of the ideologues as a rather rigid dogmatic person, however, ideological leaders were found to engage in active analysis of problems, often obtaining scores close to those of pragmatic leaders on dimensions such as problem identification, information gathering, and concept

TABLE 5.5
Illustrative Incidents of Analytic and Generative Problem Solving by Charismatic and Pragmatic Leaders

---

Thomas Watson—Analytic/Pragmatic

The crash rattled the nation and left businessmen with a hollow ache in their guts. Stocks kept falling. Companies quickly cut workforces. Financial institutions struggled to stay afloat. The economy seemed instantly, shockingly, crippled. For those 20 days, when this group of men needed Watson to stand tall and assure them, he disappeared. Had he given up? Was IBM sunk? Was he busy planning a way out of the mess?

"I have been thinking this over very carefully over the weekend, and that is why I have called you all together this morning, so we can get to thinking along sane and sound lines," Watson told them. "I have not done anything in the interests of this business for the last three weeks."

The executives must have gasped. That didn't sound like good news.

"You know I have not talked with any of you about sales, money, collections, et cetera," he continued. "I have run a stock broker's office for three weeks."

It dawned on them: Probably every one of those men individually had gone to see Watson since the crash. They had built their lives and finances on IBM stock, which so far had almost exclusively gone up. As it hit new highs in the summer of 1929, some executives used their holdings as collateral for margin loans to buy other stocks. But not the value of their IBM holdings had been cut in half, and the share price kept falling. Margin calls might have wiped out some of the men, leaving them in need of loans or salary advances. Other executives might have only wanted to hear that the company was sound and the stock would recover. They paraded into Watson's office seeking help or comfort or both. He took the time to give it to them, in a gesture that said that his men were the business. He had to steady his executives before he could steady his company.

He'd had enough of that, though. The Watson stock brokerage office was closed, he told the group. "I have now opened up on the IBM company with a vengeance, and I want all of you to get your heads up and tails over the dashboard," he said. "We have a big job to do, a hard job to do, and the only way is thinking and working constructively, and we must start it immediately."

He put the situation on the table. IBM's business was going to dip, Watson admitted. Every U.S. business was about to experience, as he put it, "a temporary slowing up." But IBM would not sit still and await its fate. It would find new ways to keep business growing. IBM had to open new markets for its machines, selling to businesses and entities that might never have thought they needed data processing. The company had to push harder in foreign countries. "We are not going to wait for something to happen—we are going to make something happen, Watson said.

He went around the room handing out assignments. Drawing on his belief that engineering could drive sales, Watson ordered the research department to come up with marketable inventions. It was a remarkably different reaction than that of CEOs, throughout history, who often slash research and development budgets to try and save money during down times. Watson then told the manufacturing executives to tighten costs and boost productivity. The finance group had to beef up its ability to collect on bills because the economy was going to leave a lot of companies in arrears. Purchasing, sales, service—boom, boom, boom—he hit every department. It was time to get serious, and they were going to have to do it together.

"I hope that every man in this room feels that he can start doing a bigger job than he has done before," he said as he was winding down. "And if there is any man in this meeting who doesn't feel that way and will come to me alone, I will be glad to talk with him and help him, because now is the time to make the most of everything."

It wasn't a threat. It was a call to rely on each other and not tear the organization apart.

(Continued)

TABLE 5.5
(Continued)

David Ben-Gurion—Generative/Charismatic

On 13 February, United States diplomats in the Middle East had sent President Truman a secret report stating that Arabs were preparing a major offensive against the Jews for the end of March. The American President appealed to the Arabs to hold back, while at the same time he refused to see Zionist leaders. The State Department was considerably alarmed just then by Communist take-over in Czechoslovakia. In Washington, London and Paris there was talk of the possibility of another world war. And Palestine was one more danger-spot which could spark off the conflict. An armistice had to be arranged there at all cost, even if it meant sacrificing the plan of partition. The Jewish State was about to become the first victim of the Cold War. In the greatest secrecy, State Department specialists began to prepare an urgent plan so that the mechanism which the United Nations had set in motion the previous November. The chief American delegate at the United Nations, Senator Warren Austen, lodged a resolution by which the United States renounced the plan of partition and proposed that Palestine be placed under the aegis of the United Nations. The Jewish State looked like being stillborn.

The defeats inflicted on the Jews during the last week of March caused something of a panic among friends of Zionism. When General Marshall heard of the convoy which had been almost wiped out on the way to Jerusalem he foresaw the Jews being massacred like flies. He lost all faith in Haganah. A scheme was hurriedly drawn up in Washington to send a delegation of experts to Palestine to convince the Jews of the folly of proclaiming an independent State at this time. The Americans were prepared to send the delegation in President Truman's personal airplane. Several American Zionist leaders came in on the project.

They had no conception of the character of the men fighting in Palestine, especially of Ben-Gurion. When, on 20 March, he heard of the American resolution to place Palestine under the protection of the United Nations, he could not restrain himself. "The American proposal is more injurious to the United Nations," he declared angrily. "It does not change the situation in Palestine nor can it prevent the establishment of the Jewish State, which does not in fact depend on the decision taken by the United Nations on 29 November, although that decision has immense moral and political value. It depends upon us winning the trial of strength in this country. The State will be created by our own strength. It is we who will decide the destiny of this country. We form the basis of the Jewish State and we are going to create it. . . . We will not accept any 'protection,' either temporary or permanent. We will not agree to any form of foreign government in the future, whatever happens. We insist upon the rapid removal of British domination and the withdrawal of their troops. . . . Our political programme is the same as a month ago, as six months ago. It can be summarized in three points—security, the Jewish State, Judaeo-Arab peace."

These forcible phrases were only a part of Ben-Gurion's response. An even more energetic reaction came ten days later. On 25 March he asked for the setting up of a supreme authority to deal with military matters, and the same day a mobilization order was issued. Then, on 30 March, when the Americans were placing their armistice proposal before the United Nations, Ben-Gurion defiantly announced the formation of a "Council of Thirteen", the provisional government of the State due to come into being forty-five days later.

But his real and most effective reply was directed at Arab bands which had almost paralyzed the Jewish communications, cutting the roads to the Negev and to Galilee, to the Etzion group of villages and to Jerusalem. It was a reply aimed, too, at the numerous defeats in Palestine as well as in New York. On the evening of 31 March, Ben-Gurion held a meeting of the army command and demanded that all available forces be mobilized to open the road into Jerusalem. Yigal Sukenik, the Chief of Operations, proposed sending four hundred men. "Fifteen hundred" replied Ben-Gurion. The others were stunned at this, but it had no effect on Ben-Gurion's decision. That night, units

---

(Continued)

TABLE 5.5
(Continued)

David Ben-Gurion—Generative/Charismatic

---

were withdrawn from several fronts to carry out the largest military operation ever mounted by the Jews. That night, too, a Skymaster landed at a secret airfield after a direct flight from Czechoslovakia. It was carrying the first consignment of weapons and ammunition under an agreement recently signed in Prague. The two hundred rifles and forty machine-guns, together with thousands of rounds of ammunition, were issued to the soldiers there and then.

Operation Nakhshon began the following morning, 1 April 1948. Ten days later, El Husseini's forces had been crushed, the strategic points around Jerusalem had been captured and the road to the Holy City was open. In the Arab town, a lamenting crowd followed the funeral of El Husseini, who had been killed in the fighting on Mount Kastel.

This was the turning point. From then on, until the proclamation of their State, the Jews went from victory to victory. Ben-Gurion had struck his great blow from the initiative passed on the Jewish forces.

Note. Watson is from Maney (2003, pp. 129–131). Copyright © 2003 by Wiley. Reprinted by permission. Ben-Gurion is from Bar-Zohar (1966, pp. 111–113), London: Arthur Barker Limited.

---

selection or information organization. Table 5.6 provides an illustration of this point using material drawn from the biographies of two ideological leaders.

The unexpected, but apparently pronounced analytical bent of ideological leaders may arise from their tendency to seek and appraise information bearing on key issues of concern. Thus ideological leaders, in contrast to pragmatic leaders, may display a rather focused, albeit potentially highly effective, form of analysis. This point is of some importance because it suggests, given the evaluative orientation evident in the problem-solving activities of ideological leaders, that ideological leaders may be capable of exceptional planning (Mumford, Schultz, & Van Doorn, 2001). In other words, we should not view the activities of ideological leaders as madness but rather we should recognize the method underlying this "madness."

Although charismatic, ideological, and pragmatic leaders displayed marked differences in problem solving, the differences observed between socialized and personalized leaders were less pronounced. However, these differences did give rise to a significant discriminant function concerned with external integration. Differentiation of the problem-solving activities of socialized and personalized leaders in terms of external integration is consistent with the finding (O'Connor et al., 1995) that personalized leaders tend to be narcissistic. The self-focus characteristic of narcissists will make it more difficult to consider the views of others in problem solving.

External integration along with conceptual integration are of interest not just with respect to understanding the differences between socialized and personalized leaders. External integration along with conceptual integration were found to be positively related to indices examining both historic performance and the quality and originality of leaders' problem solutions. This finding is of

TABLE 5.6
Illustration of Analytic Activities by Two Ideological Leaders

Incident 1—Jane Addams

One of her principle [sic] tasks as an interpreter was to get the parents and the children of the ward to understand each other. Thousands of the parents, by far the majority, were immigrants. As children, they had been Bohemian, Italian, Russian, and Greek. But their children, born in this country, or with English as their first language, regarded themselves as Americans. Their view was obviously one to be encouraged, and yet it inevitably brought about clashes in the family life. The parents were often resentful of the different ideas of their children, the children often contemptuous of their parents, stuck in the rut of old European habits, customs, opinions. At worst, the fathers whipped their daughters for being different, and the sons sneered at their mothers' dress and ignorance, or at their fathers' maudlin babble of old days. Even at best, the pleasures of the parent and child were seldom in common, and they seldom went anywhere together:

> One thing seemed clear in our associations with immigrants: we must preserve and keep whatever of value their past life contained and bring them in contact with a better type of Americans ... at the same time however we were forced to recognize that the faithful child is sometimes ruthlessly imposed upon by immigrant parents who, eager for money and accustomed to the patriarchal authority of peasant households, held their children in stern bondage. .... I meditated that perhaps the power to see life as a whole is more needed in the immigrant quarter of a large city than anywhere else, and that the lack of this power is the most fruitful source of misunderstanding between European immigrants and their children.

Out of this meditation grew first an effort to bring parents and their children together at Hull House, to give them facilities to amuse one another as families. This effort worked with some groups, like the Germans; it did not work with others, like the Italians. It was however persisted in. Yet there seemed more to be done somehow. It seemed that "Hull House ought to be able to devise some sort of *educational* enterprise, which should build a bridge between European and American experiences in such ways as to give them both more meaning and a sense of relation."

And finally the idea she had longed for came to her. The sight which stirred her imagination to it may be fairly compared in influence on her life drama with that glimpse of the Whitechapel food auction in 1882, which ever afterward clutched at her heart; or with the picture of the Belgian mothers in the hall at The Hague in 1915, embracing the German women who had come as representatives of Germany to the first woman's peace conference in wartime. Only that Mile End Road vision had been horrible, the meeting of "enemies" had been dramatic, this sight in Chicago was simple and sweet:

> Walking down Polk Street one early spring day I saw an old Italian woman I knew, her distaff against her homesick face, patiently spinning a thread by the stick spindle so reminiscent of all Southern Europe ... She was sitting in the sun on the steps of a tenement house. She might have served as a model for one of Michel Angelo's Fates, but her face brightened as I passed, and holding up her spindle for me to see, she called out that when she had spun a little more yarn, she would knit a pair of stockings for her granddaughter.

Jane Addams never forgot that incident either. "When you write about Hull House," she said only a little while before she died, "don't leave out my old woman spinning." It determined her to make a place in which the older people could practice their known, traditional crafts, which should parallel the studios and the music school for the younger ones who inherited aptitude for the arts. What the children did in drawing and music and playacting drew the admiration of their parents; and so in what their parents did, in spinning, weaving, sewing, carving, metal-working, the dramatic

(Continued)

TABLE 5.6
(Continued)

Incident 1—Jane Addams

---

representation of the abilities of the parents would rouse the admiration of the children. Such a place was found and fitted up—one room at first, very simply equipped. That one room has grown into many, the equipment has become elaborate and historically interesting. Indeed, the room for old-craft practice grew into a real exhibition place of industry—the Labor Museum, it came finally to be called.

Incident 2—Woodrow T. Wilson

When on March 5, 1912, Wilson awoke for the first time in the White House, a primary concern was to assure that the man he was would not be submerged by new circumstance of his life. He was intent on remaining himself, on keeping what was within alive. A first move is highly suggestive. He announced that office-seekers would not be welcome at the White House unless specifically invited. To many it seemed that their worst suspicions had been confirmed and that Wilson's arrogance, as well as his political experience, had been proved. Disgruntled, a great horde of the hungry shifted their venue to the doors of the new cabinet members, or lay in wait at a distance outside the Executive Offices. But the new President had in mind a purpose deeper than they knew. By this gesture he was affirming his determination to have freedom to see and to think, sometimes to be alone; to keep a cool space between the person who was Woodrow Wilson and the annihilating pressures of the public scene. This first step was as much symbolic as it was practical, but the need for reflection was real. Throughout his Presidency, and especially in moments of crisis, Wilson would disappear into his study and remain isolated. Once his mind had been cleared and basic truths had been clarified he would consult with others and accept open-mindedly advice on the timing or the details of a given course. In these periods of withdrawal he did not feel the need to be told what other people were saying; but he deeply cared to know what was being thought by people who said nothing, and yet whose judgment, he believed would prove valid in the end. "He sought above everything," wrote a contemporary, "to catch the trend of inarticulate rather than vociferous opinion." For this he needed composure, and he needed to be completely himself.

Wilson's method of leadership depended heavily on being able to interpret national will. In his early description of the leader he had made allowance for the historic moments when "a *Cause*" arises, when a man becomes the champion of "a political or moral principle." Such a moment came for Wilson when he was defending the League of Nations; then his own judgment superseded a nice adjustment to the popular mind. But for most occasions he saw leadership as being actions taken in conformity to opinions which, though they might not be expressed, were nevertheless widely held. To ascertain these opinions was a prime gift of statesmanship. Lacking modern polling techniques, he felt compelled to rely on political instinct and an almost mystical identification with the people. When it appeared that a true public opinion had not been formed on an issue he would procrastinate, avoiding action even when his personal views and preferences were clear.

In a revealing speech to the national press early in his administration Wilson confessed to a "passionate sense of being connected with my fellow men in a peculiar relationship of responsibility." It made him tremble, he said, not only with a feeling of his own inadequacy and weakness, "but as if I were shaken by the very things that have shaken them." This self-image was very different from the impression held at the time by most observers, who had judged the President to be cold and to be governed entirely by intellectual processes. A feeling of identity with the people could mislead Wilson, but at its best it could give him a Lincolnesque quality, often noted at the time. In any case it was a feeling he valued and guarded. It caused him to organize his life as a President in such a way as to preserve a central calm and to create a White House that was more of a sanctuary than a sounding board.

Note. Addams is from *Jane Addams: A Biography*, by J. W. Linn (1935, pp. 179–181), New York: Appleton-Century. Wilson is from *Woodrow Wilson*, by A. Heckscher (1991, pp. 275–277). Copyright © 1991 by August Heckscher. Reprinted with the permission of Scribner, an imprint of Simon & Schuster Adult Publishing Co.

some importance because it suggests that the key role outstanding leaders play in organizational problem solving is to bring solutions into line with the demands of the external environment and the expectations of different constituencies. This external integration, in fact, appears more important in shaping the success of leaders' problem-solving efforts than expertise—although it is true that integrative efforts of this sort will require some minimum level of systems expertise.

The importance of this integrative activity has also been stressed in recent discussions of strategic leadership (Boal & Hooijberg, 2000). What is important to recognize in this regard, however, is that integration of ideas, perspectives, and expectations is an unusually demanding, resource-intensive cognitive activity. In the case of outstanding leaders where organizational history and capabilities, environmental change, and the interests of different stakeholder groups must be taken into account (a synthesis of the past, the present, and the future), integration may prove to be a particularly demanding undertaking.

This observation, in turn, broaches a new question: Exactly how do outstanding leaders bring about integration? Although unusual intellectual capacity is clearly part of the answer to this question, another part of the answer may be found in the fundamental nature of outstanding leadership. More specifically, the prescriptive mental models constructed by outstanding leaders may provide the framework around which integrative problem-solving efforts are built.

6

Leader–Follower Interactions— Heroes, Leaders, and Tyrants: How Do They Relate?

Michael D. Mumford
Jill M. Strange
Ginamarie Scott
Lesley Dailey
Cassie Blair
The University of Oklahoma

People have a rather romantic view of outstanding leaders. We see outstanding leaders as heroes. They are people who have changed the world through the dint of their efforts—often working against impossible odds as they attempt to bring about change. As attractive as this image may be, it is not consistent with much of what we know about outstanding leaders from the historical record. Scholars commonly attribute the success of J.P. Morgan to his ability to attract and motivate an unusually talented group of partners (Chernow, 1990). Indeed, Morgan's partners played a key role in virtually all of his ventures, often literally working themselves to death to insure the success of the enterprise. Henry Chauncey in creating the Educational Testing Services (ETS) certainly articulated a powerful vision, yet he lacked the technical background needed for successful implementation of this vision. As a result, the success of ETS owes as much to William Turnbull, the organization's technical director, as Henry Chauncey (Lemann, 2000). John Kennedy relied on his brother Robert not only to implement key policy but also to provide advice with regard to broader policy decisions (Perret, 2001).

Although numerous other examples might be cited, the foregoing seem sufficient to make our basic point. Outstanding leaders depend on close followers or lieutenants. The key roles that these lieutenants play in the careers of outstanding leaders broach two questions. First, how do outstanding leaders create and maintain such strong relationships with their lieutenants? Second, are there differences among charismatic, ideological, and pragmatic leaders in the nature or character of the leaders' relationships with their key lieutenants? In the present chapter, we hope to provide some initial answers to both of these questions.

THEORY

Leaders and Followers

Any attempt to answer these questions, however, requires some understanding of the role of followers in incidents of outstanding leadership. As noted earlier, outstanding leadership occurs in response to broad, complex crises where the key role of the leader in crisis resolution is sensemaking (Drazin et al., 1999). What should be recognized in this regard, however, is that any single individual will not typically have available all the information needed to understand a crisis, nor all of the expertise that will be required to grasp the implications of this information. One way leaders deal with the complexity and ambiguity of the information bearing on a crisis (Ireland & Hitt, 1999) is to rely on capable, trusted lieutenants. These lieutenants, furthermore, serve as sounding boards, providing leaders with feedback concerning their interpretation of events and the likely success of subsequent action plans (Kedia, Nordtvedt, & Perez, 2002; Schwenk, 1995).

Not only do close followers contribute to the eventual success of leaders' sensemaking, they play a key role in the articulation of the leader's understanding of the crisis and eventual implementation of the leader's plans for crisis resolution. Frequently, followers are better able to represent a leader's understanding of the crisis situation to key constituencies than the leader by virtue of their connections to, and representation of, these key constituencies. Not only do lieutenants represent the leader, and by virtue of their efforts build support for the leader's understanding of the situation, they are also integral to effective crisis resolution. The complexity of the crises being addressed by outstanding leaders is such that multiple leaders affecting multiple subsystems, or groups, will be required over a period of years (Jacobs & Jaques, 1987). Because no single individual, however energetic, can possibly take all the actions necessary in resolving complex system crises, lieutenant(s) are typically required for crisis resolution. These lieutenants, or close followers, appear to be critical to the success of outstanding leaders.

Although the role of lieutenants has not traditionally received as much attention in studies of outstanding leadership, the role of lieutenants has received somewhat more attention in studies of strategic leadership (Boal & Hooijberg, 2000; Hambrick & Finkelstein, 1987; Hambrick & Mason, 1984). In studies of strategic leadership, a line of research concerned with the ways corporate executives shape the strategy of a firm, it has been common to focus on the top-management teams (TMTs) composed of the chief executive officer (CEO) and other major officers of the corporation. Scholars have sought to understand how the composition of TMTs influence strategy and firm performance (Hale-blain & Finkelstein, 1993; Hoskisson, Hitt, Wan, & Yiu, 1999).

For the most part, studies of TMTs have employed a demographic approach examining how manifest demographic characteristics of the TMT are related to indicators of firm performance such as profitability and adaptation to change (Bluedorn, Johnson, Cartwright, & Barringer, 1994). The findings obtained in these studies indicated that the heterogeneity of TMTs with respect to educational background, age, and gender is positively related to adaptation to change but not necessarily to performance in more stable environments (Murray, 1989). The strategy pursued by organizations, moreover, seems to depend on the functional background (e.g., sales, manufacturing, finance) of members of the TMT (Song, 1982). Finally, the characteristics of the TMT make a unique, and surprisingly large, contribution to the prediction of organizational outcomes vis-à-vis a simple examination of the characteristics of the CEO (Tushman & Anderson, 1986).

Taken as a whole, these studies of TMTs suggest that the nature and capabilities of lieutenants will have an impact on the performance and success of outstanding leaders. Although these findings dovetail nicely with our earlier observations about the importance of close followers to outstanding leaders, demographic studies have little to say about how outstanding leaders select, establish relationships with, and interact with close followers or lieutenants.

Leader–Member Exchange

In contrast to demographic studies of top management teams, studies of leader–member exchange (LMX) have expressly sought to understand characteristics of the relationships leaders form with followers and the consequences of relationships evidencing different characteristics. Initially, LMX studies focused on one critical issue: Do leaders form unique relationships, relationships of varying quality or closeness, with different followers (Dansereau et al., 1975; Dienesch & Liden, 1986)? Broadly speaking, the results obtained in these studies indicate that leaders, especially high-performance leaders, do form different kinds of relationships with different followers. These differential dyadic relationships, moreover, appear to form relatively rapidly and to be maintained over time once they have been formed due to self-propagating expectations on the part of the parties involved, escalating commitment, and the effects of positive and negative interactions on actual performance (Dockery & Steiner, 1990; Duarte, Goodson, & Klich, 1994; Liden, Wayne, & Stillwell, 1993). In fact, Gerstner and Day (1997), in a meta-analytic study, found that the formation of positive, close, exchange relationships was positively related to evaluations of leader performance, evaluations of follower performance, follower satisfaction, organizational commitment on the part of the followers, perceptions of role clarity, and feelings of competence on the part of the followers.

The findings of Gerstner and Day (1997) are noteworthy in the context of the present discussion because they suggest that positive exchange relationships make it possible for leaders to build a cadre of committed, motivated, high-performing followers—the kind of close followers that outstanding leaders need to support development and execution of their plans. In keeping with this observation, Howell and Hall-Merenda (1999) found that behaviors of transformational leaders contributed to the formation of positive exchange relationships.

The question that arises at this juncture, however, is what attributes, or dimensions, of interaction characterize, or define, close positive relationships with followers. In fact, a number of dimensions have been proposed that might be used to characterize positive exchange relationships (Schriesheim et al., 1999). For example, Graen and Uhl-Bien (1998) stressed the importance of perceptions of competence (ability to do the work), loyalty, and trust in their analysis of the interactional dimensions causing leaders to form and maintain close relationships with lieutenants. Similarly, Dienesch and Liden (1986) stressed the importance of contributions, loyalty, and positive affect. Other dimensions held to underlie the formation of positive exchange relationships include effort (Maslyn & Uhl-Bien, 2001), interpersonal attraction (Graen & Cashman, 1975), successful delegation (Bauer & Green, 1996), contingent rewards (Howell & Hall-Merenda, 1999), information exchange, effective communication (Graen & Schiemann, 1978), autonomy, work role negotiation (McClane, 1991), and high manifest performance (Gerstner & Day, 1997).

When one examines the dimensions linked to the formation of positive exchange relationships, a distinct pattern emerges. More specifically, as contributions to the work, loyalty, and trust increase, the leader more effectively interacts with followers in the decision-making process. This pattern of findings is consistent with the notion that leaders are in a position of authority where they have control over rewards and punishments and are willing to loosen control, and provide rewards, based on follower competence, loyalty, and trustworthiness.

Outstanding Leaders' Exchange Relationships

Although the overall pattern of findings emerging from LMX studies appears reasonable, the relevance of these dimensions may vary as a function of the "level" of leaders and their followers. Most LMX studies have focused on first-line supervisors and middle managers (Schriesheim et al., 1999) using dimensions appropriate for describing exchange relationships in lower- or midlevel positions. As a result, the question arises as to whether these dimensions can be used to describe the exchange relationships occurring in upper-level positions of the sort held by outstanding leaders. In other words, it is open to question whether these dimensions can be used to characterize a leader's interactions with members of their top-management team.

The close followers of outstanding leaders are typically successful leaders in their own right. Because close followers tend to be leaders, it is open to question whether individual-level or dyadic variables will provide a comprehensive description of positive exchange. Instead, close relationships, and positive exchange, may be manifest in the leaders support for, and recognition of, the group the follower represents. The leader, moreover, must manage power relationships with close followers, many of whom have responsibility for autonomous, or semiautonomous, organizations where they are not dependent on the leader for rewards and recognition. These observations suggest that dimensions such as recognition of follower representational requirements, respect for follower power bases, autonomy granted followers in the leadership of their group, and negotiation vis-à-vis the needs of follower constituencies, may prove useful in describing the exchange relationships among outstanding leaders and their close followers.

Along similar lines, Jacobs and Jaques (1987) argued that effective exchange relationships in the upper levels of an organization follow a collegial pattern. In these collegial interactions, peers or near peers build alliances around a common set of objectives providing support for *select* efforts based on shared objectives and mutual interest. This kind of selective alliance formation implies that dimensions such as collaborative definition of issues and priorities, collegial exchange, maintenance of relationships with peers, public recognition and dissemination of the groups views, adherence to norms of the group, and commitment to the entire alliance or group, will also influence the kind of relationships outstanding leaders form, and the emergence of positive exchange relationships.

Although there is reason to suspect that somewhat different dimensions may characterize the exchange relationships formed by outstanding leaders, as opposed to more run-of-the-mill leaders, the potential relevance of these dimensions broaches a new question: Do outstanding leaders stress just these "upper-level" dimensions in forming positive exchange relationships, or do they also consider the kind of dimensions identified in traditional LMX studies? Because leaders must deal with close followers as *both* individuals and leaders in their own right, it seems that both sets of dimensions might be used to characterize the formation of positive exchange relationships among outstanding leaders and their lieutenants. For example, it is difficult to see why competence, trust, and positive affect would not operate in top-management teams even though other considerations might come to fore.

Not only is there a need to consider multiple types of dimensions in describing how outstanding leaders form positive exchange relationships, the nature of these exchange relationships may vary across leader types. Earlier, we noted that personalized leaders evidence power motives, negative life themes, object beliefs, outcome uncertainty, fear, and narcissism (O'Connor et al., 1995). Attributes such as narcissism, fear, and uncertainty will make it difficult for personalized leaders to form positive exchange relationships with any individual.

Negative life themes, power motives, and object beliefs will, moreover, make collaborative exchanges difficult. Thus, there is reason to suspect that socialized and personalized leaders will differ on both normative and upper-level dimensions of exchange, with socialized leaders forming more positive exchange relationships. In fact, the failing of personalized leaders to form positive exchange relationships might, in part, account for their poor performance.

There is also reason to suspect that charismatic, ideological, and pragmatic leaders will differ with respect to the kind of dimensions that shape positive exchange relationships. For example, ideological leaders, by virtue of the similarity of values and beliefs, may find it easier to engage in collaborative exchanges with followers than with either charismatic or pragmatic leaders. Charismatic and pragmatic leaders, however, will see alliances as more flexible, resulting in a lower investment in positive exchange relationships with close followers.

Summary

Although we tend to think of outstanding leaders as heroes operating on their own, it seems clear that outstanding leaders rely on lieutenants or select close followers in framing and implementing their agendas. Prior research on LMX suggests that these relationships will be characterized by recognition of competence, trust, and loyalty, among other dimensions. However, the unique demands made on outstanding leaders as the occupants of upper-level leadership roles suggests that other dimensions might also be evident in these relationships. Moreover, there is reason to suspect that different types of outstanding leaders will differ with respect to the kind of dimensions that shape the formation of positive exchange relationships.

METHOD

Study Method

Material Selection. The design applied to examine the character of the exchange relationships of outstanding leaders involved identifying three close followers, or lieutenants, of the leader based on the index provided in the biography. Subsequently, the sections in the pinnacle-of-power chapters that described the leader's interactions with these followers were identified. Four judges, all doctoral students in industrial/organizational psychology, were presented with this material expressly selected to describe significant interactions, and were asked to evaluate each interaction with respect to expression of dimensions underlying the formation of positive exchange relationships. These interactional ratings were made on a 5-point scale. The leader's characteristic pattern of interaction with close followers or lieutenants was assessed by obtaining their average score on these dimensions across all followers.

Rating Procedure. The first set of ratings was intended to examine attributes of positive exchange relationships that had been identified in earlier LMX studies (Dienesch & Liden, 1986; Graen & Uhl-Bien, 1998; Schriesheim et al., 1999). Specifically, the judges were asked to evaluate the extent to which the interactions presented were characterized by behaviors, or reactions, indicative of dimensions such as loyalty, trust, competence (performance), and rewards. The 17 dimensions on which these 5-point ratings were to be made are presented in Table 6.1. These ratings were made using behaviorally anchored rating scales. Illustrations of these rating scales may be found in Table 6.2.

In addition, these judges were asked to evaluate the interactions with respect to the dimensions held to influence relationship formation in upper-level leadership positions such as respect for "subordinate" power base, collegial interac-

TABLE 6.1
Exchange Dimensions and Operational Definitions

Normative Exchange Dimensions

1 **Attitudinal Similarity:** How similar are the ideas and attitudes concerning key organizational issues between the leader and the follower?
2 **Loyalty:** How important is follower loyalty to the leader?
3 **Level of Trust:** What is the degree of trust that the leader has in the follower to carry out everyday organizational activities?
4 **Rewards:** How much does the leader rely on monetary bonuses or praise to reward followers?
5 **Communication Quality:** What is the quality (i.e., clarity, quantity, degree of follower input) of the communications between the leader and the follower?
6 **Relationship Stability:** How stable is the relationship between the leader and the follower?
7 **Level of Contact:** How much does the leader stay in contact with his or her followers?
8 **Level of Collaboration:** How much does the leader collaborate with his or her followers?
9 **Decision-Making Participation:** How much does the leader involve the follower in organizational decision making?
10 **Mutual Influence:** How much do the leader and follower influence each other in everyday organizational and suborganizational decision making?
11 **Work Autonomy:** To what degree does the leader allow the followers to determine their own day-to-day work and goals?
12 **Work Negotiation:** To what degree does the leader negotiate the nature of work with the follower?
13 **Professional Effort:** How much effort does the leader put into maintaining the follower relationship on a professional level?
14 **Personal Effort:** How much effort does the leader put into maintaining the follower relationship on a personal level?
15 **Follower Innovation and Usefulness:** To what degree do the followers come up with new and useful ideas that help the leader to attain organizational goals?
16 **Follower Performance:** How successful is the follower in attaining organizational goals?
17 **Contractual Obligation:** To what degree is the follower obligated by contract (legal or psychological) or some other agreement to work with the leader?

(Continued)

TABLE 6.1
(Continued)

Upper-Level Exchange Dimensions

1 **Functional Autonomy:** How much autonomy does the leader allow the follower to have when dealing with their suborganization?
2 **Collegial Interaction:** To what degree do the leader and the follower treat each other as equals?
3 **Conflict Resolution:** Does the leader help the follower work out conflicts with other followers?
4 **Competition Management:** How competitive are the followers with each other and with the leader?
5 **Suborganization Maintenance:** To what degree does the leader allow close followers to control suborganizations within the organization and support their decisions with regard to the suborganization?
6 **Respect for Subordinate Power Base:** How much does the leader show respect for the follower's suborganization?
7 **Recognition of Representation Requirements:** To what degree does the leader expect and allow the follower to publicly represent their suborganization?
8 **Advisory Influence:** To what degree do the followers act as an adviser to the leader?
9 **Dissemination of Leader Views:** How much are the followers used to disseminate leader's vision/ policies?
10 **Negotiation Within System Structure:** To what degree do the leader and follower engage in deal-making and negotiation activities regarding systems issues such as resources and direction to further the suborganization?
11 **Maintenance of Group Working Relationship:** To what degree does the leader encourage collaborative efforts among followers?
12 **Demonstration of System Commitment Requirements:** To what degree does the leader require public displays of organizational and leader alliance from his or her close followers?
13 **Adherence to the Normative Process:** To what degree is the follower expected to respect the bounds of authority placed upon him or her by the leader?
14 **Consensual Growth Creation:** To what degree does the leader expect the followers to place emphasis on the overall growth of the organization rather than their own and their organization's needs?
15 **Collaborative Issues Structure:** To what degree does the leader collaborate with the follower when determining key priorities and issues?
16 **Overall Follower Influence:** To what degree does the follower influence the leader in overall organizational matters?
17 **Overall Leader Influence:** To what degree does the leader influence the follower in suborganizational matters?

LMX-7 Items

1 Do the followers know where they stand with their leader; do they usually know how satisfied their leader is with what they do?
2 How well does the leader understand the followers' job problems and needs?
3 How well does the leader recognize the followers' potential?
4 Regardless of how much formal authority he or she has built into his or her position, what are the chances that the leader would use his or her power to help the followers solve problems in their work?
5 Again, regardless of the amount of formal authority the leader has, what are the chances that he or she would "bail the followers out" at his or her expense?
6 The followers have enough confidence in their leader that they would defend and justify the leader's decision if he or she were not present to do so.
7 How would you characterize the followers' working relationships with the leader?

TABLE 6.2
Example Rating Scales for Two Normative Dimensions

1) Attitudinal Similarity

How similar are the ideas and attitudes concerning key organizational issues between the leader and the follower?

1-The beliefs of the leader and the follower completely oppose each other. Follower acts in such a way that this opposition is demonstrated.

3-Follower may sometimes disagree with the attitudes and beliefs of the leader. Leader will listen to follower point of view but will ultimately make own decision.

5-Attitudes of leader and follower are completely the same. Follower does not question the beliefs of the leader.

3) Communication Quality

What is the quality (i.e., clarity, quantity, degree of follower input) of the communications between the leader and the follower?

1-Quality of communications is very low. Leader will be ambiguous when communicating and followers will have no input into communications.

3-Quality of communications varies. At times the leader will be ambiguous but at other times communications will be direct and understandable. Followers have some input during communications.

5-Leader and follower have high-quality communications where orders are direct and understandable. Followers have a great deal of input during communications.

tion, and competition management. The 17 dimensions used in evaluating interactions based on the requirements for effective exchange in top-management teams are also presented in Table 6.1. Again, these ratings were made using 5-point behaviorally anchored rating scales. These rating scales are illustrated in Table 6.3.

The third, and final, set of ratings judges were asked to make in describing these interactions involved a somewhat different assessment method. Here, judges were asked to complete a standard behavior description inventory, the LMX-7 (Schriesheim et al., 1999), commonly used to appraise the quality of leader–follower relationships. These seven behavioral description items are also presented in Table 6.1. In evaluating exchanges based on these items, judges were asked to indicate the extent to which these behaviors were evident in, or indicated by, the interaction descriptions abstracted from the leader biography.

Descriptive Findings

Table 6.4 presents the mean, standard deviation, interrater agreement coefficients, and correlation coefficients obtained for the various rating scales under consideration. As may be seen, these ratings of the character of leader–follower interactions evidenced adequate reliability given the number of judges under consideration. The average interrater agreement coefficient obtained for the

TABLE 6.3
Example Rating Scales for Two Upper-Level Dimensions

1) Functional Autonomy

How much autonomy does the leader allow the follower to have when dealing with their sub-organization?

1- The leader keeps tight control over the suborganization and allows the follower to have very little autonomy. All decisions must be cleared by the leader before implementation.

3- The leader allows the follower autonomy, but stays informed of all follower actions with regard to the suborganization. At times, the leader may take over operations or make decisions for the suborganization in times of great conflict or need.

5- The leader allows the follower complete autonomy in dealing with the suborganization. He or she will never take any kind of control over the suborganization.

2) Respect for Subordinate Power Base

How much does the leader show respect for the follower's suborganization?

1- The leader shows no respect for the follower's suborganization. He or she never talks about it publicly or acts as if it is an important part of the organization.

3- The leader shows a moderate amount of respect for the follower's suborganization. He or she will talk about it in public at times, but will never seem to view it as a very important part of the organization.

5- The leader shows a great deal of respect for the follower's suborganization. He or she often references it in speeches and in everyday work and talks about it as if it were a very important part of the organization.

normative (traditional LMX) dimensions was .67, whereas the average inter-rater agreement coefficient obtained for the outstanding (upper-level) dimensions was .63. Adequate interrater agreement was not obtained for two of the LMX-7 items ($\bar{r} \leq .50$). Hence, these items were dropped from all subsequent analyses. The remaining five items produced an average interrater agreement coefficient of .61.

Because the various normative dimensions were held to reflect attributes of positive exchange relationships, it was not surprising that these dimensions produced, on average, positive correlations in the .30 to .50 range. What is of note here, however, is that these correlations were not so large that they indicated that the dimensions could be collapsed or that a general rating bias factor was operating. Along similar lines, positive correlations were also observed among the dimensions describing exchange relationships in upper-level positions. These correlations were, however, larger than those obtained for the normative dimensions with correlations in the .40 to .60 range being obtained. This result, however, may reflect the effects of a team or group, as opposed to a dyadic focus, in the dimensions under consideration. Positive correlations, typically lying in the .20 to .40 range, were also obtained between the normative and outstanding dimensions—a finding suggesting that dyadic and group relationships are, at least to some extent, independent in cases of outstanding leadership.

TABLE 6.4
Means, Standard Deviation, Interrater Agreement Coefficients, and Correlations for Interactional Dimensional Ratings

	R	R²	p	1	2	3	4	5	6	7	8	9	10	11	12	13	14	15	16	17	18	19
Normative																						
1 Attitudinal Similarity	3.48	.71	.66		.86	.69	.38	.49	.52	.49	.44	.30	.30	.42	.54	.48	.55	.57	.56	.49	.46	.33
2 Loyalty	3.68	.65	.63			.82	.55	.50	.53	.46	.41	.30	.30	.42	.53	.51	.56	.55	.54	.51	.50	.38
3 Level of Trust	3.79	.62	.69				.85	.73	.49	.33	.37	.34	.34	.33	.33	.26	.34	.36	.35	.34	.33	.25
4 Rewards	3.97	.62	.66					.78	.43	.08	.16	.26	.32	.26	.14	.07	.10	.09	.07	.11	.19	.18
5 Communication Quality	3.81	.59	.68						.77	.46	.35	.36	.36	.33	.24	.17	.23	.24	.20	.20	.25	.25
6 Relationship Stability	3.85	.54	.71							.81	.60	.34	.29	.39	.45	.44	.47	.45	.39	.34	.36	.32
7 Level of Contact	3.79	.70	.62								.74	.38	.16	.30	.49	.53	.58	.58	.53	.42	.33	.24
8 Level of Collaboration	3.52	.63	.73									.74	.53	.30	.46	.40	.45	.46	.49	.40	.36	.22
9 Decision-Making Participation	3.13	.68	.63										.85	.61	.27	.10	.13	.14	.19	.19	.21	.13
10 Mutual Influence	2.93	.83	.61											.79	.41	.04	.06	.08	.13	.17	.25	.21
11 Work Autonomy	3.26	.68	.74												.75	.43	.26	.24	.26	.34	.39	.33
12 Work Negotiation	3.55	.70	.75													.82	.65	.58	.56	.59	.59	.45
13 Professional Effort	3.80	.71	.61														.84	.74	.65	.66	.62	.41
14 Personal Effort	3.68	.74	.70															.94	.86	.71	.62	.36
15 Follower Innovation and Usefulness	3.72	.78	.74																.94	.81	.64	.40
16 Follower Performance	3.73	.79	.68																	.87	.69	.36
17 Contractual Obligation	3.78	.64	.63																		.86	.63
Upper-Level																						
18 Functional Autonomy	3.80	.55	.62																			.82
19 Collegial Interaction	3.81	.52	.74																			
20 Conflict Resolution	3.69	.53	.62																			

21	Competition Management	3.65	.61	.64
22	Suborganization Maintenance	3.58	.71	.62
23	Respect for Subordinate Power Base	3.41	.72	.67
24	Recognition of Representation Requirements	3.38	.78	.51
25	Advisory Influence	3.36	.80	.75
26	Dissemination of Leader Views	3.36	.82	.65
27	Negotiation Within System Structure	3.35	.78	.59
28	Maintenance of Group Working Relationship	3.27	.78	.66
29	Demonstration of System Commitment Requirements	3.58	.75	.65
30	Adherence to the Normative Process	3.70	.74	.48
31	Consensual Growth Creation	3.82	.72	.65
32	Collaborative Issues Structure	3.35	.75	.64
33	Overall Follower Influence	3.12	.78	.64
34	Overall Leader Influence	2.94	.88	.63
LMX-7				
35	Item 1	3.35	.75	.34
36	Item 2	3.39	.67	.59
37	Item 3	3.50	.66	.49
38	Item 4	3.34	.73	.59
39	Item 5	3.30	.84	.57
40	Item 6	3.20	.98	.65
41	Item 7	3.37	.97	.68

(Continued)

TABLE 6.4
(Continued)

	20	21	22	23	24	25	26	27	28	29	30	31	32	33	34	35	36	37	38	39	40	41
Normative																						
1 Attitudinal Similarity	.40	.37	.42	.42	.38	.35	.30	.33	.36	.41	.32	.20	.11	.11	.13	.29	.36	.42	.49	.46	.47	.41
2 Loyalty	.40	.39	.44	.45	.40	.38	.33	.35	.37	.42	.34	.18	.08	.06	.10	.30	.38	.48	.49	.44	.43	.36
3 Level of Trust	.19	.20	.24	.27	.21	.17	.14	.18	.21	.27	.19	.05	-.13	-.17	-.15	.08	.19	.33	.27	.24	.24	.23
4 Rewards	.04	.04	.08	.13	.06	.02	.03	.07	.10	.10	.03	-.12	-.30	-.34	-.33	-.15	-.04	.14	.03	.01	.01	.09
5 Communication Quality	.19	.18	.18	.27	.21	.19	.11	.14	.18	.28	.22	.11	-.08	-.13	-.10	.04	.12	.23	.16	.16	.15	.18
6 Relationship Stability	.41	.46	.46	.51	.47	.46	.35	.35	.37	.54	.50	.41	.28	.21	.23	.29	.32	.34	.35	.33	.32	.28
7 Level of Contact	.42	.50	.54	.56	.56	.57	.44	.43	.44	.64	.63	.64	.55	.48	.47	.54	.55	.45	.43	.41	.36	.30
8 Level of Collaboration	.33	.37	.41	.41	.41	.40	.30	.28	.30	.54	.52	.54	.39	.35	.32	.48	.49	.46	.44	.44	.40	.31
9 Decision-Making Participation	.09	.07	.09	.13	.13	.13	.05	.04	.06	.26	.25	.25	.05	.07	.06	.30	.32	.36	.25	.23	.16	.20
10 Mutual Influence	.11	.02	.00	.04	.04	.02	-.01	-.01	.01	.16	.15	.09	-.09	-.06	-.03	.16	.20	.35	.31	.25	.20	.20
11 Work Autonomy	.29	.24	.26	.27	.26	.25	.27	.25	.26	.30	.29	.17	.08	.08	.14	.27	.33	.49	.46	.35	.27	.32
12 Work Negotiation	.54	.48	.54	.51	.50	.50	.51	.48	.48	.49	.50	.39	.38	.35	.40	.50	.56	.65	.66	.56	.48	.45
13 Professional Effort	.56	.60	.69	.65	.64	.67	.66	.62	.60	.58	.56	.47	.53	.51	.53	.60	.62	.61	.63	.59	.56	.53
14 Personal Effort	.51	.57	.64	.64	.63	.65	.57	.56	.55	.58	.56	.51	.55	.54	.56	.66	.66	.64	.70	.68	.67	.53
15 Follower Innovation and Usefulness	.51	.56	.60	.61	.60	.61	.51	.50	.50	.57	.53	.47	.52	.51	.53	.63	.67	.65	.74	.75	.74	.52
16 Follower Performance	.48	.53	.55	.55	.52	.52	.43	.43	.44	.54	.52	.44	.46	.44	.48	.59	.63	.62	.72	.75	.75	.52
17 Contractual Obligation	.57	.59	.58	.58	.55	.54	.48	.47	.50	.52	.47	.35	.41	.39	.45	.52	.59	.58	.65	.66	.68	.50
Upper-Level																						
18 Functional Autonomy	.74	.62	.60	.59	.53	.50	.48	.46	.49	.46	.41	.25	.29	.28	.35	.42	.46	.53	.60	.59	.60	.53
19 Collegial Interaction	.81	.63	.51	.52	.46	.41	.42	.39	.41	.31	.22	.05	.12	.13	.22	.28	.34	.41	.41	.39	.36	.34
20 Conflict Resolution		.85	.78	.71	.64	.60	.58	.55	.56	.49	.42	.26	.36	.36	.41	.43	.43	.45	.51	.52	.50	.44
21 Competition Management			.92	.84	.75	.75	.72	.69	.70	.63	.53	.39	.52	.51	.54	.50	.47	.43	.47	.47	.49	.46

	22	23	24	25	26	27	28	29	30	31	32	33	34	35	36	37	38	39	40
22 Suborganization Maintenance	.92																		
23 Respect for Subordinate Power Base	.86	.95																	
24 Recognition of Representation Requirements	.83	.92	.97																
25 Advisory Influence	.80	.81	.84	.89															
26 Dissemination of Leader Views	.78	.78	.84	.89	.97														
27 Negotiation Within System Structure	.77	.78	.79	.81	.94	.96													
28 Maintenance of Group Working Relationship	.71	.74	.76	.77	.68	.70	.96												
29 Demonstration of System Commitment Requirements	.63	.64	.65	.66	.58	.55	.62	.75											
30 Adherence to the Normative Process	.48	.49	.53	.55	.43	.40	.41	.76	.91										
31 Consensual Growth Creation	.58	.60	.64	.68	.62	.58	.56	.72	.87	.83									
32 Collaborative Issues Structure	.56	.58	.65	.70	.63	.59	.56	.64	.75	.68	.94								
33 Overall Follower Influence	.57	.57	.61	.66	.61	.58	.57	.65	.68	.71	.87	.93							
34 Overall Leader Influence	.56	.55	.59	.62	.55	.51	.50	.61	.66	.78	.84								
LMX-7																			
35 Item 1	.53	.55	.56	.56	.47	.46	.45	.56	.59	.61	.69		.90						
36 Item 2	.50	.56	.54	.54	.46	.56	.46	.52	.48	.50	.52		.68	.81					
37 Item 3	.51	.54	.55	.49	.43	.43	.43	.49	.50	.39	.43	.43	.46	.57	.65	.83			
38 Item 4	.50	.49	.50	.47	.40	.39	.43	.48	.50	.38	.41	.41	.47	.56	.56	.67	.92		
39 Item 5	.50	.50	.50	.43	.42	.37	.41	.44	.47	.35	.40	.41	.47	.52	.53	.54	.83	.94	
40 Item 6	.50	.50	.50	.43	.42	.39	.41	.44	.47	.30	.32	.40	.47	.44	.46	.49	.54	.83	.94
41 Item 7	.50	.47	.49	.42	.39	.41	.35	.30	.32	.32	.35			.44	.46	.49	.54	.61	.66

Note. r > .18 significant at .05 level.

151

Some additional evidence for the validity or meaningfulness of these ratings may be obtained by considering the relationships among the various dimensions. For example, evaluations of trust were highly related to appraisals of loyalty and attitudinal similarity ($\bar{r} = .75$) but were less strongly related to effort, contact, and decision-making participation ($\bar{r} = .31$). Similarly, conflict resolution and conflict management, two of the outstanding dimensions, produced the expected sizable positive correlation ($\bar{r} = .85$), but conflict resolution was less strongly related to adherence to normative processes, consensual growth creation, and collaborative issue structuring ($\bar{r} = .34$). Thus, some evidence is available for the convergent and divergent validity of these dimensional ratings.

Some additional evidence in this regard is provided by the correlation of the normative and outstanding dimensions, with the behavioral description items drawn from the LMX-7. Again, strong positive correlations were observed between these behavioral appraisals and ratings of relationship characteristics based on the normative dimensions. These positive correlations typically ranged between .20 and .50, with somewhat stronger correlations being obtained for the outstanding, as opposed to the normative, dimensions.

The mean ratings obtained for both the normative and outstanding dimensions were typically above the scale midpoint. This finding suggests that the relationships of outstanding leaders are characterized by both sets of dimensions. Interestingly, however, not much variation was observed in the relating importance of these dimensions. Apparently, outstanding leaders may, to some extent, exhibit all the attributes in relation formation.

RESULTS

Comparison of Leader Types

Normative Exchange. Table 6.5 presents the results obtained in the multivariate analysis of covariance examining differences across leader types (charismatic, ideological, and pragmatic) and leader orientation (socialized and personalized) with respect to the normative, outstanding, and LMX-7 measures. In the case of the normative variables, only one control, demographic similarity of leaders and followers, proved marginally significant [$F(17, 97) = 1.58$; $p \le .09$] with, as expected, greater similarity between leaders and followers being positively related to higher scores on the exchange measures. More centrally, however, orientation yielded a highly significant main effect [$F(17, 97) = 2.71$; $p \le .001$]. Inspection of the associated univariate relationships indicated that 9 out of the 17 dimensions displayed significant differences across socialized and personalized leaders.

On six of these nine dimensions socialized leaders received higher average ratings than did personalized leaders. More specifically, these differences were

TABLE 6.5
Summary Results of Multivariate Analysis of Covariance

	Normative				Upper-Level				LMX-7			
	F	df	p	η	F	df	p	η	F	df	p	η
Covariates												
Close Follower Demographic Similarity	1.586	17, 97	.083	.218	—	—	—	—	1.353	5, 108	.248	.059
Geographic Region	—	—	—	—	—	—	—	—	6.112	5, 108	.001	.221
Biography Translation	—	—	—	—	—	—	—	—				
Main Effects												
Orientation (Socialized vs. Personalized)	2.710	17, 97	.001	.322	1.695	17, 98	.056	.246	2.371	5, 108	.044	.099
Style (Charismatic, Ideological, Pragmatic)	1.524	17, 98	.102	.209	3.034	17, 99	.001	.355	3.902	5, 109	.003	.152
Interaction												
Orientation × Style	.879	17, 98	.559	.132	1.058	17, 99	.405	.159	2.094	5, 109	.072	.088

Note. F = F ratio, *df* = degrees of freedom, *p* = significance level (determined by using Roy's Largest Root), η = effect size.

observed on measures examining level of contact [$F(1, 113) = 4.86; p \leq .02, \overline{X}$ = 3.92, SE = .07 vs. $\overline{X}$ = 3.64, SE = .07], professional effort [$F(1, 113) = 7.70$; $p \leq .01, \overline{X} = 3.97, SE = .09$ vs. $\overline{X} = 3.62, SE = .09$], personal effort [$F(1, 113) = 8.36; p \leq .01, \overline{X} = 3.86, SE = .09$ vs. $\overline{X} = 3.48, SE = .09$], follower innovation and usefulness [$F(1, 113) = 9.11; p \leq .01, \overline{X} = 3.92, SE = .10$ vs. $\overline{X} = 3.50, SE = .10$], follower performance [$F(1, 113) = 6.42; p \leq .05, \overline{X} = 3.91, SE = .09$ vs. $\overline{X} = 3.55, SE = .10$], and contractual obligation [$F(1, 113) = 5.83; p \leq .05, \overline{X} = 3.92, SE = .08$ vs. $\overline{X} = 3.64, SE = .08$]. Taken as a whole, it appears that socialized leaders stress motivation and contribution in forming relationships with followers more so than do personalized leaders.

In contrast, personalized leaders appeared to form relationships with followers on a somewhat different basis. More specifically, personalized leaders as opposed to socialized leaders stressed extrinsic rewards [$F(1, 113) = 6.95; p \leq .01$, $\overline{X} = 4.11, SE = .08$ vs. $\overline{X} = 3.81, SE = .08$], mutual influence [$F(1, 113) = 5.96; p \leq .05, \overline{X} = 3.94, SE = .08$ vs. $\overline{X} = 3.68, SE = .080$], and communication [$F(1, 113) = 5.54; p \leq .05, \overline{X} = 3.10, SE = .10$ vs. $\overline{X} = 2.74, SE = .10$]. Apparently, personalized leaders form relationships based on joint external rewards, or shared extrinsic outcomes, where intense communication provides a basis for oversight and negotiation.

Taken at face value, these findings would seem to suggest that socialized and personalized leaders define relationships on rather different bases. In this regard, however, it should be noted that mean scores on all these dimensions were high relative to the scale midpoint of 3. Thus, all leaders, either socialized or personalized, appear to stress normative LMX dimensions in relational formation. What differs across socialized and personalized leaders is the emphasis placed on certain dimensions. Thus, socialized leaders weighed competence and motivation more heavily whereas personalized leaders weighed mutual extrinsic interests more highly.

Some support for this interpretation was obtained in the discriminant analysis contrasting socialized and personalized leaders based on the normative dimensions. The single function emerging in this analysis produced a canonical correlation of .55 ($p \leq .001$) with socialized ($\overline{X} = .66$) leaders receiving higher scores than personalized ($\overline{X} = -.66$) leaders. Ratings of professional effort ($\overline{r} = .39$), follower innovation ($\overline{r} = .39$), personal effort ($\overline{r} = .37$), and follower performance ($\overline{r} = .31$) produced positive loadings on this function whereas ratings of rewards ($\overline{r} = -.36$), communication ($\overline{r} = -.32$), mutual influence ($\overline{r} = -.29$), and participative decision making ($\overline{r} = -.20$) produced negative loadings. Although, at first glance, these loadings appear complex, they suggest that the differing emphases of socialized and personalized leaders may reflect the value placed on *intrinsic versus extrinsic* considerations in establishing exchange relationships with followers. In other words, socialized leaders stress the worth of the work in forming relationships whereas personalized leaders stress the worth of the outcomes.

Outstanding Exchange.   Table 6.3 also presents the multivariate analysis of covariance results obtained for the outstanding, or upper-level, dimensions of exchange. No significant covariates were obtained in this analysis. More centrally, although again it was found that outstanding leaders evidenced these relational attributes, as indicated by average scale scores, only a marginally significant [$F(17, 98) = 1.69; p \le .10$] effect was obtained for leader orientation. However, the univariate analyses produced significant, or marginally significant, effects for all 17 of the dimensions of outstanding leadership where all observed differences favored socialized as opposed to personalized leaders: (a) functional autonomy [$F(1, 114) = 3.54; p \le .10; \overline{X} = 3.88$, $SE = .07$ vs. $\overline{X} = 3.71, SE = .07$], (b) collegial interaction [$F(1, 114) = 4.23; p \le .05; \overline{X} = 3.90, SE = .06$ vs. $\overline{X} = 3.71, SE = .06$], (c) conflict resolution [$F(1, 114) = 7.22; p \le .01; \overline{X} = 3.81, SE = .06$ vs. $\overline{X} = 3.56, SE = .06$], (d) competition management [$F(1, 114) = 10.15; p \le .01; \overline{X} = 3.81, SE = .07$ vs. $\overline{X} = 3.47, SE = .07$], (e) suborganization maintenance [$F(1, 114) = 12.82; p \le .001; \overline{X} = 3.78, SE = .08$ vs. $\overline{X} = 3.36, SE = .08$], (f) respect for subordinate power base [$F(1, 114) = 9.02; p \le .01; \overline{X} = 3.60, SE = .08$ vs. $\overline{X} = 3.22, SE = .08$], (g) recognition of representation requirements [$F(1, 114) = 8.86; p \le .01; \overline{X} = 3.58, SE = .09$ vs. $\overline{X} = 3.17, SE = .09$], (h) advisory influence [$F(1, 114) = 8.88; p \le .01; \overline{X} = 3.56, SE = .10$ vs. $\overline{X} = 3.15, SE = .10$], (i) dissemination of leader's views [$F(1, 114) = 6.69; p \le .01; \overline{X} = 3.55, SE = .10$ vs. $\overline{X} = 3.17, SE = .10$], (j) negotiation within system structure [$F(1, 114) = 6.03; p \le .05; \overline{X} = 3.51, SE = .09$ vs. $\overline{X} = 3.17, SE = .09$], (k) maintenance of group working relationship [$F(1, 114) = 4.30; p \le .05; \overline{X} = 3.41, SE = .09$ vs. $\overline{X} = 3.12, SE = .09$], (l) demonstration of system commitment [$F(1, 114) = 3.83; p \le .10; \overline{X} = 3.71, SE = .09$ vs. $\overline{X} = 3.44, SE = .09$], (m) adherence to normative processes [$F(1, 114) = 3.87; p \le .05; \overline{X} = 3.82, SE = .09$ vs. $\overline{X} = 3.56, SE = .09$], (n) consensual growth creation [$F(1, 114) = 4.85; p \le .05; \overline{X} = 3.96, SE = .09$ vs. $\overline{X} = 3.67, SE = .09$], (o) collaborative issues structure [$F(1, 114) = 12.27; p \le .001; \overline{X} = 3.57, SE = .08$ vs. $\overline{X} = 3.13, SE = .08$], (p) overall follower influence [$F(1, 114) = 11.91; p \le .001; \overline{X} = 3.34, SE = .09$ vs. $\overline{X} = 2.89, SE = .09$], and (q) overall leader influence [$F(1, 114) = 11.40; p \le .01; \overline{X} = 3.19, SE = .10$ vs. $\overline{X} = 2.68, SE = .10$]. Apparently, socialized leaders are more likely than personalized leaders to collaborate in a collegial fashion with followers, respecting followers as leaders in their own right participating in a management team. Although the discriminant function associated with these differences was not significant, in part due to the relatively high correlations among the outstanding leadership dimensions (multicolinearity), a sizable canonical correlation was obtained ($\overline{r} = .43$). The sizable loadings of suborganization maintenance ($\overline{r} = .66$), collaborative issues structuring ($\overline{r} = .64$), overall follower influence ($\overline{r} = .63$), overall leader influence ($\overline{r} = .62$), competition management ($\overline{r} = .60$), and respect for subordinate power bases ($\overline{r} = .57$) are consistent with this interpretation. More specifically, socialized ($\overline{X} = .47$)

leaders are more likely than personalized ($\overline{X} = -.47$) leaders to apply a *team leadership* style in interacting with close followers.

Table 6.3 also indicates that a significant main effect was obtained for leader type [$F(17, 99) = 3.03$; $p \leq .001$] in contrasting charismatic, ideological, and pragmatic leaders with respect to the outstanding, or upper-level, relational formation dimensions. In the univariate analyses, 7 of the 17 dimensions produced significant relationships where ideological leaders obtained higher scores than either charismatic or pragmatic leaders: (a) suborganization maintenance [$F(2, 114) = 4.54$; $p \leq .05$; $\overline{X} = 3.82$, $SE = .10$ vs. $\overline{X} = 3.44$, $SE = .10$], (b) dissemination of leader views [$F(2, 114) = 3.75$; $p \leq .05$; $\overline{X} = 3.63$, $SE = .12$ vs. $\overline{X} = 3.24$, $SE = .12$], (c) negotiation within system structure [$F(2, 114) = 3.45$; $p \leq .05$; $\overline{X} = 3.60$, $SE = .12$ vs. $\overline{X} = 3.21$, $SE = .012$], (d) maintenance of group working relationship [$F(2, 114) = 3.07$; $p \leq .05$; $\overline{X} = 3.50$, $SE = .12$ vs. $\overline{X} = 3.14$, $SE = .12$], (e) collaborative issues structuring [$F(2, 114) = 7.20$; $p \leq .101$; $\overline{X} = 3.67$, $SE = .10$ vs. $\overline{X} = 3.19$, $SE = .10$], (f) overall follower influence [$F(2, 114) = 7.08$; $p \leq .01$; $\overline{X} = 3.45$, $SE = .11$ vs. $\overline{X} = 2.4$, $SE = .11$], and (g) overall leader influence [$F(2, 114) = 5.90$; $p \leq .01$; $\overline{X} = 3.30$, $SE = .13$ vs. $\overline{X} = 2.76$, $SE = .13$].

Taken as a whole, these effects indicate that ideological leaders apparently are rather different from charismatic and pragmatic leaders with respect to their characteristic pattern of interactions with followers. Despite our common stereotypes of ideological leaders as cold and aloof idealists, ideological leaders not only are close to their followers but give followers substantial influence, allowing them autonomy in carrying out their responsibilities and representing the leader's views. One reason ideological leaders may allow such freedom of action is that the followers of ideological leaders share a set of strongly held core beliefs—core beliefs that permit the followers to exercise influence based on their commitment to the position of the leader and the group.

In the discriminant analyses, only one of the two potential functions that might be used to distinguish between charismatic, ideological, and pragmatic leaders proved significant. This discriminant function produced a canonical correlation of .55 ($p \leq .01$) with collaborative structuring of issues ($\overline{r} = .48$), overall follower influence ($\overline{r} = .47$), overall leader influence ($\overline{r} = .41$), suborganization maintenance ($\overline{r} = .36$), and dissemination of leader views ($\overline{r} = .35$) yielding sizable loadings. Apparently, *shared direction* of the organization underlies these effects—shared direction based on shared beliefs and values among the close followers. Ideological leaders ($\overline{X} = .77$) tended to obtain high scores on this dimension whereas charismatic leaders ($\overline{X} = -.83$) obtained low scores. Pragmatic leaders lay between those extremes ($\overline{X} = .01$). Although the high scores of ideological leaders on this dimension are not especially surprising given our foregoing observations, the scores obtained for charismatic and pragmatic leaders are somewhat more surprising. However, in this regard it should be borne in mind that charismatic leaders are pursuing a vision stressing change from the status quo—typically a vision unique to the leader. As a result, the leader, and his or her vision, provides direction rather than a group that shares basic beliefs and values. Pragmatic leaders may not have followers who share basic beliefs and values but by virtue of their reliance on elites, typically elites of which they are a member, they fall between these two extremes.

LMX-7. The multivariate analysis of covariance examining differences across leaders with respect to the five LMX-7 variables yielding adequate agreement coefficients are also presented in Table 6.3. The only significant $[F(5, 108) = 6.11; p \leq .001]$ covariate to emerge in this analysis was whether or not the biography was translated with lower LMX ratings being obtained for translated biographies as opposed to biographies that had not been translated. Again, as was the case in all prior analyses, leader orientation produced a significant main effect $[F(5, 108) = 2.37; p \leq .05]$. With regard to orientation, two of these five ratings produced significant effects in the univariate analyses with socialized as opposed to personalized leaders evidencing higher scores: how well the leader understands follower problems $[F(1, 112) = 10.78, p \leq .001; \overline{X} = 3.58, SE = .08$ vs. $\overline{X} = 3.18, SE = .08]$ and whether the leader will use power to help followers $[F(1, 112) = 5.07; p < .05; \overline{X} = 3.48, SE = .09$ vs. $\overline{X} = 3.19, SE = .09]$. Apparently, socialized as opposed to personalized leaders are more likely to support followers. The discriminant function obtained when the LMX-7 items were used to distinguish these groups produced a canonical correlation of .31 $(p \leq .05)$ where socialized $(\overline{X} = .32)$ leaders obtained higher scores than personalized $(\overline{X} = -.32)$ leaders. Understanding followers' problems $(r = .94)$, using power to help followers $(r = .62)$, and willingness to bail out followers $(r = .47)$ all produced sizable loadings on a function that might be labeled *follower support*.

A significant main effect for type was also obtained $[F(5, 109) = 3.90; p < .01]$ in examining the LMX-7 items. Inspection of the associated univariate effects indicated that ideological and charismatic leaders produced significantly higher scores than pragmatic leaders on three items: whether the leader will use power to help followers $[F(2, 112) = 4.30; p \leq .05; \overline{X} = 3.46, SE = .11$ vs. $\overline{X} = 3.0, SE = .11]$, willingness to bail out followers $[F(2, 112) = 4.01; p \leq .05; \overline{X} = 3.45, SE = .13$ vs. $\overline{X} = 2.94, SE = .13]$, and followers will defend the leader's decisions $[F(2, 112) = 3.88; p \leq .05; \overline{X} = 3.36, SE = .15$ vs. $\overline{X} = 2.87, SE = .15]$.

The one function that proved significant $(p \leq .05)$ when these groups were contrasted in the discriminant analyses produced a canonical correlation of .33 with follower defense of the leader $(\overline{r} = .59)$, leader use of power to help followers $(\overline{r} = .55)$, and favorability of working relationships $(\overline{r} = .17)$ producing positive loadings. Apparently, this dimension reflects *mutual exchange of support*. Charismatic $(\overline{X} = .48)$ leaders produced high scores whereas pragmatic $(\overline{X} = -.34)$ produced low scores on this dimension. The scores of ideological $(\overline{X} = -.13)$ leaders on this dimension fell between those two extremes. In a sense, this pattern of findings with regard to mutual exchange of support is not surprising given charismatic leaders' focus on people as opposed to the focus of ideological leaders and pragmatic leaders on ideas and problems, respectively.

A marginally significant [$F(5, 109) = 2.09, p \leq .10$] interaction was also obtained between the type and orientation variables. In the univariate analyses, however, significant differences were not obtained. Hence, no attempt was made to assess the nature and implications of this interaction.

Performance Relationships

Taken as a whole, it appears that outstanding leaders do differ in their characteristic pattern of interactions with followers. The question that arises at this juncture, however, is whether these differences in characteristic interaction patterns are related to the various indices of leader performance. To address this question the 12 core performance items, and the 2 relation-specific items were correlated and regressed on the discriminant-function scores summarizing the differences observed among the various leaders.

Table 6.6 presents the results obtained in the correlational analysis. As may be seen, the three variables capturing the differences between socialized and personalized leaders, intrinsic versus extrinsic control (normative measures), team leadership (outstanding measures), and leaders' follower support (LMX-7 measures) produced a number of significant ($p \leq .05$) correlations with the various performance measures. More specifically, basing relationships on intrinsic as opposed to extrinsic considerations, using a team leadership approach, and support of followers were positively related to the number of positive contributions made ($\bar{r} = .21$), the number of different types of positive contributions ($\bar{r} = .20$), and the biographer's view of the leader ($\bar{r} = .37$) while being negatively related to the number of negative contributions ($\bar{r} = -.28$) and the number of different types of negative contributions ($\bar{r} = -.22$). Apparently, effective exchange with close followers makes it possible for leaders to make positive contributions.

Moreover, the creation of positive relationships with followers through a supportive, intrinsically oriented team approach makes it possible for leaders to make a lasting contribution. Thus, these dimensions produced positive correlations with how long the leader's contributions lasted ($\bar{r} = .21$), the continued existence of institutions established by the leader ($\bar{r} = .21$), and maintenance of the leader's vision ($\bar{r} = .37$). As might be expected based on these findings, the supportive, intrinsically oriented team approach characterizing socialized leaders was also related to maintenance of contact and relationships with followers ($\bar{r} = .35$).

Although the creation of prosocial intrinsic relationships with a dedicated team is critical to the success of outstanding leaders, at least one of the discriminant functions discriminating among leader types (charismatic, ideological, and pragmatic) was also found to be related to leader performance. Specifically, the shared-direction variable that emerged in contrasting charismatic, ideological, and pragmatic leaders on the upper-level exchange dimensions was found to be positively related to indices of the maintenance of impact [how long

TABLE 6.6
Correlations of Performance Criteria With Discriminant Functions Summarizing Differences Among Leaders

Criteria	Intrinsic vs. Extrinsic Relationships	Team Leadership	Shared Direction	Leaders' Follower Support	Mutual Exchange of Support
How much did the leader contribute to society?	.09	.11	.16	-.07	-.05
How long did these contributions last?	.14	.26	.18	.23	.01
How many people did this leader affect?	.03	.17	.09	-.02	-.05
How favorably did the author view the leader?	.44	.40	.30	.29	-.03
How many positive contributions did the leader make?	.29	.22	.13	.12	.06
How many negative contributions did the leader make?	-.35	-.26	-.23	-.25	.04
How many different types of positive contributions did the leader make?	.21	.24	.24	.15	-.01
How many different types of negative contributions did the leader make?	-.31	-.21	-.18	-.17	.08
To what degree do the institutions established still exist?	.20	.24	.15	.19	-.05
How many institutions were established by the leader?	.11	.24	.19	.06	-.04
Did the leader have a vision that was maintained after they were out of power?	.19	.33	.23	.26	-.02
Did the leader effect mass movements?	.01	.01	.02	-.03	.18
Did the leader maintain a positive relationship with the followers?	.35	.30	.03	.25	-.04
Did they remain in contact after term of power was over?	.47	.40	.17	.33	-.03

did contributions last ($\bar{r} = .18$), how many institutions were established ($\bar{r} = .19$), was the leader's vision maintained ($\bar{r} = .23$)], and performance [how favorably did the biographer view the leader ($\bar{r} = .30$), how many different types of positive contributions ($\bar{r} = .24$), how many negative contributions ($\bar{r} = -.23$), and how many different types of negative contributions ($\bar{r} = -.18$)]. Apparently, the willingness of ideological leaders, the leaders scoring high on this dimension, to share direction of the group makes it possible for them to prove unusually effective.

Table 6.7 presents the results obtained in the regression analyses examining the joint effects of these discriminating variables on performance. It is of note that prior to examining effects for the discriminating variables for relationships, all significant ($p \leq .05$) controls identified as relevant predictors of each criteria in earlier analyses were entered as the first block of predictors. Thus, in the present set of analyses, conclusions about relational variables are made only after taking relevant controls into account.

Perhaps the most clear-cut conclusion that can be drawn from Table 6.7 is that relational variables do make a difference in accounting for the performance of outstanding leaders. Of these variables, the formation of relationships appears especially important with this variable contributing to prediction ($\beta = .31$) for 9 out of the 14 performance criteria under consideration. Thus, outstanding leadership appears to depend on the leader's ability to create a cadre of followers committed to the work rather than the rewards. Indeed, the performance of socialized leaders may, to a large extent, be contingent on their ability to establish relationships with followers on an intrinsic as opposed to extrinsic basis.

In this regard, however, two further points should be borne in mind. First, other dimensions of exchange, in particular team leadership, were found at times, for certain criteria, to contribute to the prediction of leader performance even when the intrinsic-versus-extrinsic relational orientation was taken into account. This finding is of some importance because it points to the need to take upper-level as well as normative exchange dimensions into account in discussions of outstanding leadership. Second, relational differences linked to leader type, specifically shared direction, also at times made a unique contribution to performance prediction.

Summary

The findings obtained in the present study indicate that outstanding leaders, in their formation of close relationships with followers, evidence a variety of behaviors, both normative exchange behaviors and exchange behaviors unique to the upper-level positions held by outstanding leaders. Personalized and socialized leaders display differences on both these sets of relational behaviors as well as standard markers of LMX. Although different types of leaders, charismatic, ideological, and pragmatic, do not differ with respect to normative relational

TABLE 6.7
Summary of Regression Results

	R	R²	p	Significant Functions (p ≤ .05)	Beta Weight	High Group	Low Group	R
How much did the leader contribute to society?	—	—	—	None	—	—	—	—
How long did these contributions last?	.23	.05	.01	Intrinsic vs. Extrinsic	.23	Socialized	Personalized	.23
How many people did this leader affect?	.26	.07	.01	Team Leadership	.20	Socialized	Personalized	.26
How favorably did the author view the leader?	.98	.23	.001	Intrinsic vs. Extrinsic	.39	Socialized	Personalized	.98
				Shared Direction	.18	Ideological	Charismatic	
How many positive contributions did the leader make?	.29	.08	.001	Intrinsic vs. Extrinsic	.29	Socialized	Personalized	.29
How many negative contributions did the leader make?	.35	.12	.001	Intrinsic vs. Extrinsic	-.34	Socialized	Personalized	.35
How many different types of positive contributions did the leader make?	.24	.05	.008	Team Leadership	.24	Socialized	Personalized	.24
How many different types of negative contributions did the leader make?	.31	.10	.001	Intrinsic vs. Extrinsic	-.30	Socialized	Personalized	.31
To what degree do the institutions established still exist?	.37	.13	.002	Intrinsic vs. Extrinsic	.22	Socialized	Personalized	.37
How many institutions were established by the leader?	—	—	—	None	—	—	—	—
Did the leader have a vision that was maintained after they were out of power?	.32	.10	.001	Intrinsic vs. Extrinsic	.23	Socialized	Personalized	.32
				Shared Direction	.19	Ideological	Charismatic	
Did the leader effect mass movements?	.26	.06	.016	Mutual Exchange of Support	.21	Charismatic	Pragmatic	.26
Did the leader maintain a positive relationship with the followers?	.35	.12	.001	Intrinsic vs. Extrinsic	.35	Socialized	Personalized	.35
Did they remain in contact after term of power was over?	.50	.25	.001	Intrinsic vs. Extrinsic	.41	Socialized	Personalized	.50
				Leader's Follower Support	.19	Socialized	Personalized	

behaviors, they do differ on the relational behaviors called for in upper-level leadership positions. More specifically, ideological leaders differ from charismatic and pragmatic leaders with respect to shared direction. These differences across leaders in the relational formation strategies were found to be related to performance, with an intrinsic, supportive, team-based approach where direction is shared with close followers proving particularly important in shaping leader performance.

CONCLUSIONS

When considering these results, and their broader implications, certain limitations of the present study should be borne in mind. First, we have focused on the dimensions of interaction that characterize leaders' relationships with close followers or lieutenants. Thus, the results obtained herein do not speak to differences in the interactions of leaders with more distant followers. Instead, we have, following Graen and Uhl-Bien (1995), focused on a more narrow issue of how outstanding leaders interact with close followers.

Along somewhat different lines, Schriesheim et al. (1999) noted that within the LMX literature, a variety of different dimensions have been used to characterize leader–follower relationships. Though we have in the present study examined a number of the *key* dimensions identified in prior studies, it is also true that not *all* dimensions that have appeared in the literature were considered herein.

In fact, the present study is unique in that we have examined not only traditional LMX dimensions but also dimensions of exchange believed to be involved in the upper-level positions held by outstanding leaders and their close followers. Studies of LMX have for the most part focused on dyadic relationships among lower-level and midlevel leaders where the leader exercises substantial control (Yukl, 2002). In the present study, we found that the dimensions identified in this research can also be extended to outstanding leaders and their followers as evidenced by both typical scores on the normative LMX dimensions (loyalty, trust, rewards, performance, etc.) and the differences observed between socialized and personalized leaders with respect to manifestation of these dimensions in their interactions with close followers.

The formation of positive exchange relationships with followers, however, does appear somewhat more complex for outstanding leaders than more run-of-the-mill leaders. Outstanding leaders typically have close followers, or lieutenants, who are noteworthy leaders in their own right. As a result, relational formation must take into account the autonomy and responsibility of followers to their constituencies. Furthermore, outstanding leaders tend to interact with lieutenants on a collegial basis, stressing alliance formation. The dimensions flowing from this proposition, recognition of follower representation requirements, consensual growth creation, and collegial interaction, were found to be evident in outstanding leaders' interactions with key lieutenants. Moreover, these dimensions were found to differentiate both socialized and personalized leaders as well as charismatic, ideological, and pragmatic leaders. This later finding, of course, is of some importance from a validation perspective because one would expect the upper-level dimensions to be particularly important in discriminating among different types of outstanding leaders.

These observations are noteworthy in part, however, because they suggest that relational formation may be an unusually complex activity for outstanding leaders. In forming relationships, outstanding leaders must consider the individual follower—their competence, loyalty, and trustworthiness (Graen & Uhl-Bien, 1995). However, individual-level appraisals will not, for outstanding leaders, prove fully sufficient as a basis for relational formation. Outstanding leaders must also consider who and what the individual is representing, their willingness to commit to an alliance that includes not only the leader but other lieutenants, and their willingness and capability to work with what is effectively a top-management team (Hambrick & Mason, 1984). Of course, the question that arises at this juncture, a question that needs to be addressed in future research, is how these two aspects of relational formation operate together in shaping outstanding leaders' relationships with their close followers.

Studies along these lines may prove particularly important because it appears that the performance of outstanding leaders is, in fact, dependent on the formation of strong effective ties between the leader and his or her lieutenants. Perhaps the most compelling support for this conclusion emerged in our comparisons of socialized and personalized leaders. Socialized leaders formed relationships based on intrinsic concerns, providing followers with support and stressing a team-oriented approach when working with close followers. In contrast, personalized leaders seem to use a divide-and-conquer strategy where the follower was tied to the leader, not the team, vis-à-vis extrinsic rewards.

An intrinsically motivated team not only provides leaders with better input and better work in support of the leader's agenda, but also provides more effective integration of organizational efforts and stronger articulation of the leader's views. Consistent with these observations, the observed differences between socialized and personalized leaders with respect to relational formation were found to be strongly related to performance. High-performing outstanding leaders were those who built high-performance top-management teams. A concrete illustration of this conclusion may be found in Table 6.8, describing one socialized and one personalized leader's relationships with key lieutenants and their consequences of performance.

The importance of followers to the performance of outstanding leaders, however, broaches a number of questions—both theoretical and practical. With regard to research, we need to know more about how outstanding leaders recruit and manage teams during crises. We need to know more about how the leader's sensemaking influences, and is influenced by, followers' understanding of the situation. And, we need to know more about how leaders create and manage al-

TABLE 6.8
Summary of Case Material for Orientation Effects on Performance

Rudolf Hess—Personalized

Hess's chief of staff was a thirty-three-year-old man, heavyset and somewhat bull-like, who had been a party member since 1927. He proved to be a good bookkeeper, rude in handling subordinates but completely honest in money matters and a veritable workhorse with an astonishingly precise memory. He was assigned to the deputy's staff in July 1933 and Hess was happy to have him as his chief of staff, the "deputy's deputy." Hess trusted him because he never forced his way into the limelight, and gradually he gave the man more power.

Margaret Thatcher—Socialized

Whitelaw and Parkinson, however, had something else in common: a particularly personal relationship with their leader. During both the preparations and the war itself, they could offer her a special kind of solace. They felt a desire to protect her. . . . Whitelaw, with his Military Cross as proof of sometime gallantry in the Scots Guards, saw it as part of his job to remind this inexperienced lady, who had no first-hand knowledge of gunfire, that she must steel herself for casualties, prepare for bloodiness, not imagine that it could be a painless victory.

Note. Hess is from Schwarzwaller (1988, p. 138). Copyright © 1988 by National Press. Thatcher is from Young (1989, p. 269). Copyright © 1989 by Macmillan UK. Reprinted by permission.

liances. With regard to practical performance issues, we need studies examining the effects of team building on leader performance. We also need studies examining how leaders should manage intrinsic and extrinsic rewards in top-management teams, especially, given the potential detrimental effects of excessive extrinsic rewards.

The importance of followers to the performance of outstanding leaders brings to fore the question as to whether different types of outstanding leaders differ in their characteristic interactions with followers. The results obtained in the present study, in fact, indicate that differences do exist among charismatic, ideological, and pragmatic leaders in this regard. More specifically, charismatic leaders evidence a mutual exchange of support—an exchange that does not appear to characterize the relationships of ideological and pragmatic leaders. This finding, however, is not surprising given the focus of charismatic leaders on people rather than problems and ideas. Of somewhat greater importance was the finding emerging from our examination of upper-level exchange dimensions indicating that ideological leaders, in contrast to charismatic and pragmatic leaders, were more likely to share direction with key lieutenants.

Although this finding may at first glance appear surprising, it is not inconsistent with historic studies of ideological leaders. For example, Chernow (1998) in his study of J. D. Rockefeller stressed the importance of his shared direction in the management of Standard Oil. Table 6.9 provides a description of how this shared direction was manifest in Rockefeller's interactions with his top-management team.

TABLE 6.9
Shared Direction as Evident in the Case of J. D. Rockefeller

In these new quarters, the Standard Oil mandarins preserved a tradition launched years before. Each day at noon, the executive committee gathered for lunch in a top-floor room decorated with hunting and fishing trophies and with a port view that suited their global empire. There was no surer proof of favor in the Standard Oil empyrean than to receive an invitation to dine at the long table. Arriving in silk hats, frock coats, and gloves, the directors always took the same assigned seats. In this deceptively self-effacing style, Rockefeller yielded the head of the table to his most frequent adversary, Charles Pratt, who was the group's oldest member; Flagler sat to Pratt's right, then Rockefeller, then Archbold. It says much about his managerial approach that Rockefeller sat indistinguishably among his colleagues, though the leveling arrangement scarcely disguised his unique status. . . .

Few outsiders knew that one of Rockefeller's greatest talents was to manage and motivate his diverse associates. As he said, "It is chiefly to my confidence in men and my ability to inspire their confidence in me that I owe my success in life." He liked to note that Napoleon could not have succeeded without his marshals. Free of an autocratic temperament, Rockefeller was quick to delegate authority and presided lightly, genially, over his empire, exerting his will in unseen ways. At meetings, Rockefeller had a negative capability: The quieter he was, the more forceful his presence seemed, and he played on his mystique as the resident genius immune to petty concerns. As one director recalled, "I have seen board meetings, when excited men shouted profanity and made menacing gestures, but Mr. Rockefeller, maintaining the utmost courtesy, continued to dominate the room." Sometimes, he dozed on a couch after lunch. "I can see him now," one executive recalled, "lying back on a lounge at a directors' meeting, eyes closed taking it all in. Now and then he'd open his eyes and make a suggestion."

Rockefeller placed a premium on internal harmony and tried to reconcile his contending chieftains. A laconic man, he liked to canvass everyone's opinion before expressing his own and then often crafted a compromise to maintain cohesion. He was always careful to couch his decisions as suggestions or questions. Even in the early days, he had lunched daily with brother William, Harkness, Flagler, and Payne to thrash out problems. As the organization grew, he continued to operate by consensus, taking no major initiative opposed by board members. Because all ideas had to meet the supreme test of unanimous approval among strong-minded men, Standard Oil made few major missteps. As Rockefeller said, "We made sure that we were right and had planned for every contingency before we went ahead."

Note. From *Titan*, by R. Chernow (1998, pp. 221–222). Copyright © 1998 by Ron Chernow. Used by permission of Random House, Inc.

Not only does the historic literature support the notion that ideological leaders are especially willing to share direction with other members of the top-management team, there are sound substantive reasons for their behavior. Ideological leaders, and their followers, share a common set of core beliefs and values where movement into upper-level leadership positions typically involves not only extensive vetting in this regard but ongoing monitoring by other group members with respect to adherence to these ideals. As a result of this shared worldview, ideological leaders are in a position where it becomes especially feasible to share direction with closer followers by virtue of their "like-mindedness."

The tendency of ideological leaders to stress shared direction to a greater extent than charismatic and pragmatic leaders is noteworthy for another reason.

More specifically, shared direction between a leader and his or her lieutenants is related to performance, at times making a unique contribution to the prediction of performance above and beyond the formation of relationships based on intrinsic versus extrinsic considerations. These performance effects may, in part, reflect the value of autonomous contributions from members of a top-management team—contributions that become more likely when the leader allows shared direction. In part, however, these performance effects may reflect the value, over the long term, of embedding leadership in a group where direction is not dependent on a single individual. In fact, the careers of J. D. Rockefeller, Ronald Reagan, Vladimir Lenin, and Osama bin Laden all illustrate this point and the potential impact of ideology in building strong bonds between leaders and their lieutenants.

These observations about the differences observed between ideological, charismatic, and pragmatic leaders point to a broader conclusion. Our stereotypic view of outstanding leadership, a rather romantic view, where the focus is on the leader, has led us to discount the importance of close followers, or lieutenants, in shaping the nature and success of the leader's efforts. Hopefully, the present effort by demonstrating the importance of leader–follower relationships in studies of outstanding leadership will serve as an impetus for a new wave of research examining the role of lieutenants, or close followers, in creating the conditions needed for outstanding leadership.

7

Communication Strategies— Persuasion or Logic: How Do Outstanding Leaders Connect With Their Followers?

Michael D. Mumford
Blaine Gaddis
Brian Licuanan
Brooke Ersland
Katie Siekel
The University of Oklahoma

It is difficult to see how one can lead, and influence people, without communicating with followers or potential followers. Accordingly, communication and persuasion are commonly considered critical aspects of leader performance (Fleishman et al., 1991; Yukl, 2001). Although communication is a necessary part of every leadership role, the nature of, and requirements for, communication can, and do, differ across roles. The roles occupied by outstanding leaders, by virtue of the number of followers and the leader's distance from most followers, stresses the importance of mass communication—the communications we see in speeches, debates, interviews, and public commentaries.

We recognize the impact of mass communication by leaders whenever we discuss and react to their speeches. And, even the most cursory analysis indicates that speeches are indeed critical to outstanding leadership. The annual state of the union address, given by American presidents, has come, with the passage of time, to represent a high-stakes event that both defines the political agenda and determines perceptions of the success of the presidency. In fact, we often remember outstanding leaders as much for their speeches as what they actually accomplished. We may not know much about what Winston Churchill did during the battle of Britain, but we remember the pronouncement he made at the end of this battle. "Never have so few done so much for so many" is a statement that aptly summarizes both what had been accomplished and the challenges facing Britain in the coming years.

Although we remember leaders for the tag lines of their great speeches—"I have a dream" (Martin Luther King), "Ich bein ein Berliner" (John Kennedy), and "The evil empire" (Ronald Reagan)—the true significance of leaders' speeches lies in the effects they have on people and organizations. One illustration of the impact of speeches on leader performance may be found in Emrich, Brower, Feldman, and Garland (2001). In this study the concern at hand was how speeches influenced appraisals of presidential greatness. Evaluations of presidential greatness were obtained from historians who took into account actual presidential accomplishments. Presidential speeches were evaluated for use of words involving imagery (e.g., explore, growth) versus concepts (e.g., unique, produce). It was found that the use of imagery as opposed to concepts in speeches was related to evaluations of greatness. In other words, the nature and style of leader communications apparently impacts performance.

Some further evidence bearing on the impact of communication strategies on leader performance was provided by Baum et al. (1998). They examined the performance of architectural woodworking firms. Descriptions of leaders' (e.g., CEO's) visions, vision content, and vision communication were obtained. It was found that effective communication of the leader's vision was positively related to growth, the measure of firm performance, along with vision and vision content, even when past growth, organizational size, and organizational age were taken into account. Other work by Calantone and Schatzel (2000) indicates that CEO communications may have rather complex effects on organizational performance, affecting not just motivation and direction of effort within the organization, but also the firm's ability to acquire requisite financial resources.

COMMUNICATION AND OUTSTANDING LEADERSHIP

Communication Impacts

Our foregoing examples seem sufficient to make our base point. How leaders structure and convey their message influences leader performance, particularly in the kind of upper-level roles occupied by outstanding leaders. This observation, in turn, brings to fore a new question: Exactly what do outstanding leaders do in communicating that allows them to have such an impact on people and organizations?

A framework to begin answering this question may be found in the general theory of outstanding leadership presented in chapter 2. Essentially, this theory holds that outstanding leaders emerge in response to crises—ambiguous changes affecting the functioning and performance of social systems. The critical role of leaders in guiding responses to crises is sensemaking. These sensemaking activities are based on a prescriptive mental model constructed by the leader. What should be recognized here, however, is that mass communications—speeches, debates, interviews, letters, and so on—provide leaders with the opportunity for conveying their understanding of the crisis and the way people in general should respond to this crisis (Crowell, 1936). In other words, outstanding leaders are not simply communicating information. Instead, they are attempting to communicate their understanding of the issues at hand vis-à-vis the prescriptive mental model they have constructed.

A similar point was made by Fiol et al. (1999). They argued that the goal of leader communication is frame alignment, or the establishment of an interpretive structure that encourages people to attend to certain events, which allows people to place these events in a broader framework that serves to organize experience and guide the actions of both individuals and groups. Because crises imply change, the leader in communicating with followers must often break extant frames and bring people to accept the frame, or prescriptive mental model, being articulated by the leader.

Fiol et al. (1999) sought to provide evidence supporting this theory of communication by outstanding leaders. More specifically, they conducted a content analysis of the speeches made by U.S. presidents who were held to be either charismatic (e.g., Franklin Roosevelt, John Kennedy) or noncharismatic (e.g., Jimmy Carter, Lyndon Johnson). Speeches were content coded for the expression of three attributes: (a) negation statements (not), (b) inclusive statements (we), and (c) abstractions. The first hypothesis underlying examination of these speech attributes was that frame breaking would require negation statements whereas abstractions would be required to convey the leader's prescriptive model. The second hypothesis held that inclusive statements following frame breaking and abstraction would serve to build a foundation for collective action based on the new frame being provided. Consistent with these hypotheses, Fiol et al. found that the use of negation and inclusive words changed over time in the speeches of charismatic leaders as they moved from frame breaking to calls for the need for collective action. More centrally, charismatic leaders differed from noncharismatic, less outstanding leaders in that they were more likely to use negation statements and articulate abstractions in their speeches.

The Fiol et al. (1999) study is noteworthy, in part, because it reminds us that the communications of outstanding leaders must serve at least two purposes: (a) frame breaking and (b) articulation of new models that might be used to understand the issues, or crises, at hand. This point is of some importance because it underscores the fact that outstanding leaders' articulation of new frames may contribute to performance in a number of ways—breaking maladaptive response patterns and providing a framework for action. Leaders' communication of frames, or prescriptive mental models, however, may serve a number of other purposes. It may clarify goals and paths to goal attainment thereby reducing anxiety and enhancing performance (House, 1971), contribute to creation of the shared mental models that provide a basis for coordination and effective action by teams or groups (Zaccaro et al., 1995), and may serve to build a sense of involvement and self-referential commitment to addressing the crisis at hand (Shamir et al., 1993).

For leader communications to have these many valued effects, however, leaders cannot simply communicate facts or the sheer substance of their prescriptive models (Kihlstrom & Israel, 2002). Instead, leaders must shape communications to call attention to key causes and outcomes in the context of audience members' lives. They must provide illustrations of key points, concrete emotionally evocative illustrations, that make their models real for people. They must also be able to articulate the logic of their argument indicating why the crisis is significant and how the causes and goals being articulated provide a sound basis for responding to the situation at hand. In other words, leaders must make their models "real" to people, even if this means they tell only part of the story.

Leader Types

The selective articulation of prescriptive mental models in leader communication suggests, in turn, that differences will emerge among different types of outstanding leaders due to differences in the nature of the prescriptive mental models being applied in sensemaking. Perhaps the most clear-cut difference likely to emerge in this regard arises from the way pragmatic leaders understand and respond to crises. Pragmatic leaders, in contrast to charismatic and ideological leaders, stress the analysis and manipulation of key causes in responding to crises (Mumford & Van Doorn, 2001). Thus the crisis, or issue, is understood in an objective fashion.

This tendency of pragmatic leaders suggests that, in comparison to charismatic and ideological leaders, they will be more likely to apply rational arguments while de-emphasizing affect, personally involving stories, and appeals to followers' personal needs in their communications. Their emphasis on rational presentation of arguments should, moreover, lead pragmatics, vis-à-vis charismatics and ideologues, to de-emphasize propaganda in their communications.

In contrast, charismatic and ideological leaders will seek, in their communications, to articulate the value-laden visions that arise from their prescriptive mental models. Moreover, given the criticality of goals and values to the sensemaking activities of charismatic and ideological leaders, effective communication requires building acceptance for the goals and values being articulated. These observations, in turn, suggest that charismatic and ideological leaders, in comparison to pragmatic leaders, will place a greater emphasis on marketing or direction of public opinion with respect to acceptance of these desired end states.

Not only is there reason to expect differences in the communication strategies used by charismatic, ideological, and pragmatic leaders, there is reason to expect that socialized and personalized leaders will also differ in this regard. As noted earlier, personalized leaders, in contrast to socialized leaders, tend to have negative views of people and their motives (O'Connor et al., 1995). These differences in conceptual models would lead one to expect that socialized and personalized leaders' communications will differ with respect to the expression of positive and negative affect. Along related lines, use of imagery, logic, and stories should be more common in the communications of socialized leaders whereas the use of propaganda should be more common in the communications of personalized leaders.

Summary

Mass communications are a critical mechanism through which leaders influence followers. Although communication serves many functions, among outstanding leaders it appears to serve a unique and critical function. More specifically, it allows outstanding leaders to convey their prescriptive mental models, the models used to understand and guide responses to crises, to followers. As a result, differences among different types of outstanding leaders with respect to the prescriptive mental models being applied are also expected to result in differences in leaders' communication strategies.

METHOD

Study Method

Material Selection.   The design used to examine differences among outstanding leaders in their communication strategies was based on the speeches they gave when they were at the "pinnacle of power." Pinnacle-of-power chapters were used to sample communications based on the proposition that speeches given during this period would best represent the prototypic communication strategies used by outstanding leaders. Typically 6 to 10 historically noteworthy speeches or mass communications were identified in the pinnacle-of-power chapters presented in the biography with the associated material describing the context of the communication, the content and delivery of the communication, and reactions to the communication. Typically, this material averaged three to four pages in length.

Rating Procedure.   Following training, five judges were asked to review each speech or mass communication, and evaluate the material provided using rating scales. These 24 rating dimensions were drawn from prior studies intended to cover three critical areas of communication performance identified in prior studies (Hosman, Huebner, & Sictanen, 2002; Samaras, 1980): (a) style, (b) content, and (c) strategy. The 8 rating scales examining style included (a) expression of positive affect, (b) expression of negative affect, (c) use of nonverbals, (d) humor, (e) directive style, (f) participative style, (g) eloquence, and (h) audience confrontation (e.g., O'Hair, Friedrich, Wiemann, & Wiemann, 1995; Priest & Swain, 2002; Sagie, 1996). The 10 rating scales examining content included (a) use of stories or analogies, (b) position debate, (c) emotional persuasion, (d) use of propaganda, (e) rational persuasion, (f) use of imagery, (g) definition of goals, (h) definition of paths to goal attainment, (i) appeals to social needs, and (j) appeals to personal needs (e.g., Collison & MacKenzie, 1999; Fiol et al., 1999; Sproule, 1989). The 7 strategy rating scales included (a) consensus building, (b) consolidation of different perspectives, (c) management or direction of public opinion, (d) vision articulation, (e) definition of role relationships, (f) application of logic, and (g) impression management (e.g., Baum et al., 1995; Emrich et al., 2001; Kihlstrom & Israel, 2002).

The five judges made ratings of each speech using 5-point Likert scales intended to reflect the extent to which a given attribute or rating dimension was present in the speech. Table 7.1 presents examples of these rating scales—the rating scales applied for positive affect, use of stories or analogies, and appeal to social needs. Judges' average ratings on these dimensions across the speeches abstracted for the leader provided the scores applied in the present study.

TABLE 7.1
Example Rating Scales for Positive Affect,
Stories, and Appeal to Social Needs

Expression of Positive Affect—*To what extent does the leader express positive emotions (e.g., happiness, joy) in his or her speeches and communications with the mass public?*

1—The leader never expresses positive emotions in his or her speeches and communications with the mass public.
3—The leader occasionally expresses positive emotions in his or her speeches and communications with the mass public.
5—The leader frequently expresses positive emotions in his or her speeches and communications with the mass public.

Use of Stories and Analogies—*To what extent does the leader communicate his or her points through the use of stories and analogies in his or her speeches and communications with the mass public?*

1—The leader never uses stories and analogies to communicate his or her points in speeches and communications with the mass public.
3—The leader occasionally uses stories and analogies to communicate his or her points in speeches and communications with the mass public.
5—The leader frequently uses stories and analogies to communicate his or her points in speeches and communications with the mass public.

Appeal to Social Needs—*To what extent does the leader articulate social needs (e.g., education, developmental programs) of their country or organization?*

1—The leader never describes the social needs of their country or organization.
3—The leader occasionally describes the social needs of their country or organization.
5—The leader frequently describes the social needs of their country or organization.

Study-Specific Controls.   In addition to rating the style, content, and strategy of the speech, judges were asked to appraise a study-specific set of controls to be applied along with the general control variables described earlier. These study-specific controls focused on controls relevant to evaluation of communication strategies and included: (a) total number of communications identified, (b) frequency of major communications during the period the leader was in power, (c) the amount of material quoted in the biography, (d) need for translation of speeches, (e) amount of input others had into preparation of speeches, and (f) size of the leader's audience. Some of these controls (e.g., the total number of communications and speech translation) were coded by only one judge due to their objective nature. The remaining control measures were obtained through 5-point ratings made by judges after they had read through the relevant material. These ratings provided interrater agreement coefficients in the .70s.

Study-Specific Criteria.   Not only were judges asked to appraise study-specific controls, they were also asked to appraise a set of study-specific criteria. These evaluations, typically made on a 5-point Likert scale, included:

1. To what extent do people continue to quote the leader's communications or speeches?
2. Are the leader's speeches considered landmark events?
3. Do the leader's speeches continue to influence others?
4. To what extent are the ideas presented in these speeches still considered relevant?
5. Did the leader's speeches lead to institutional change?
6. Are the leader's communications or speeches still read today on special occasions?
7. Do people still discuss the ideas presented in the leader's communications?

Again, judges' average ratings on these dimensions provided the scores applied. Table 7.2 illustrates the nature of two of these rating scales—scales that produced interrater agreement coefficients in the .80s.

Descriptive Findings

Table 7.3 presents the mean, standard deviation, and interrater agreement coefficients for the speech ratings of style, content, and strategy. As may be seen, the ratings of the speeches generally proved of adequate reliability. The average interrater agreement coefficient obtained across the 25 dimensions

TABLE 7.2
Example of Domain-Specific Rating Scales

Control Rating Scale

Excerpts or Interpretations of Speeches Used in Biography—*Did the biographer incorporate actual portions and quotes of the leader's speeches in their biography, or did they use their own interpretation of the leader's speeches?*

1—Only excerpts and/or quotes of speeches used.
3—Equal balance of excerpts, quotes, and interpretations of speeches used.
5—Only interpretation (no excerpts and/or quotes) of speeches used.

Criterion Rating Scale

Are the Leader's Speeches Still Read Today on Special Occasions?—*To what extent are the leader's speeches read on special occasions (e.g., holidays, birthdays)?*

1—The leader's speeches are never read today on special occasions.
3—The leader's speeches are occasionally read today on special occasions.
5—The leader's speeches are frequently read today on special occasions.

was .71. Some evidence bearing on the meaningfulness of construct validity of these ratings may be obtained by considering the correlations observed among these ratings.

As may be seen, the correlations among these rating scales did not produce the uniformly high positive correlations that would be indicative of general biasing factors. However, the correlations observed among the content and strategy variables were systematically higher than those obtained for the style variables.

More centrally, the correlations observed among these variables are consistent with the nature of the constructs under consideration. The evaluations of positive affect were negatively related to evaluations of negative affect ($r = -.69$) whereas the use of rational persuasion was positively related to the logic of argumentation ($r = .68$). More centrally, content and strategy dimensions commonly linked to leadership such as the use of imagery, goal and goal path definition, and vision articulation produced the expected positive correlations ($r = .46$). These content and strategy dimensions, moreover, were positively related to direction and audience engagement ($r = .48$) but not to the expression of negative affect ($r = .03$).

Given that the speech ratings produced an interpretable pattern of relationships, the next question that comes to fore concerns the common use of the various style, content, and strategy dimensions by outstanding leaders in general. Notably, directive activities ($\overline{X} = 3.6$), goal definition ($\overline{X} = 3.6$), role definition ($\overline{X} = 3.5$), opinion management ($\overline{X} = 3.5$), and vision articulation ($\overline{X} = 3.8$) were commonly observed in the communications of outstanding leaders. Apparently, outstanding leaders provide structure and direction to followers

TABLE 7.3
Means, Standard Deviations, Agreement Coefficients, and Correlations for Style, Content, and Strategy Ratings of Speeches

	$\bar{X}$	SD	r_{tt}	1	2	3	4	5	6	7	8	9	10	11
1. Positive Affect	3.1	.69	.83	1.0	-.69	-.04	.21	-.15	.37	.49	-.10	.22	-.18	.38
2. Negative Affect	2.8	.54	.74		1.0	.26	-.12	.33	-.01	-.22	.31	.03	.35	.02
3. Nonverbals	2.0	.48	.66			1.0	.28	.20	.12	.09	.35	.28	.24	.32
4. Humor	1.6	.45	.73				1.0	-.02	.02	.01	.01	.37	-.01	.03
5. Directive Style	3.6	.48	.63					1.0	.43	.04	.43	.01	.39	.17
6. Participative Style	3.4	.56	.75						1.0	.38	.49	.26	.25	.49
7. Eloquence	3.1	.63	.81							1.0	.08	.29	.17	.48
8. Audience Confrontation	3.1	.65	.72								1.0	.30	.47	.33
9. Use of Stories	2.4	.56	.68									1.0	.16	.33
10. Position Debate	3.4	.67	.77										1.0	.32
11. Emotional Persuasion	3.2	.65	.74											1.0
12. Propaganda	2.8	.49	.48											
13. Rational Persuasion	3.1	.56	.65											
14. Use of Imagery	2.8	.62	.75											
15. Definition of Goals	3.6	.55	.74											
16. Definition of Goal Paths	3.3	.60	.76											
17. Social Appeals	3.3	.72	.82											
18. Personal Appeals	3.5	.70	.74											
19. Consensus Building	3.3	.58	.69											
20. Perspective Consolidation	2.7	.54	.68											
21. Opinion Management	3.5	.43	.53											
22. Vision Articulation	3.8	1.3	.74											
23. Definition of Roles	3.5	.56	.71											
24. Logical Argumentation	3.4	.57	.77											
25. Impression Management	3.3	.41	.49											

(Continued)

TABLE 7.3
(Continued)

	12	13	14	15	16	17	18	19	20	21	22	23	24	25
1. Positive Affect	-.11	.41	.37	.22	.28	.37	.42	-.01	.53	.13	.13	-.25	.56	.26
2. Negative Affect	.23	-.19	.01	.03	-.03	.01	.02	.19	-.33	.10	-.03	.27	-.31	-.05
3. Nonverbals	.10	.06	.24	.18	.13	.16	.19	.33	-.01	.28	.05	.32	-.01	.32
4. Humor	.12	.14	.11	-.12	-.12	.01	-.01	.00	.06	.10	.08	-.08	.05	.13
5. Directive Style	.29	.03	.25	.48	.55	.32	.33	.40	-.12	.45	.11	.45	-.11	.33
6. Participative Style	.06	.38	.51	.61	.66	.54	.69	.45	.24	.38	.10	-.04	.40	.20
7. Eloquence	-.04	.54	.61	.26	.33	.45	.40	.22	.56	.22	.12	-.16	.68	.24
8. Audience Confrontation	.35	.07	.33	.39	.38	.37	.41	.55	-.01	.36	.02	.30	-.12	.34
9. Use of Stories	.09	.34	.45	.03	.07	.12	.25	.13	.14	.11	-.01	-.03	.25	.14
10. Position Debate	.36	.22	.27	.47	.33	.45	.32	.53	-.03	.49	.07	.33	.04	.34
11. Emotional Persuasion	.14	.36	.68	.44	.48	.53	.60	.35	.34	.39	.09	-.08	.34	.26
12. Propaganda	1.0	.09	.14	.08	.06	.22	.17	.21	-.08	.38	.09	.40	-.13	.36
13. Rational Persuasion		1.0	.47	.37	.41	.40	.42	.23	.49	.32	.16	-.10	.68	.28
14. Use of Imagery			1.0	.46	.57	.50	.58	.34	.33	.36	.14	-.02	.44	.30
15. Definition of Goals				1.0	.80	.64	.60	.54	.18	.50	.27	.16	.26	.26
16. Definition of Goal Paths					1.0	.61	.65	.47	.22	.47	.24	.13	.30	.31
17. Social Appeals						1.0	.76	.48	.43	.46	.16	.08	.42	.36
18. Personal Appeals							1.0	.51	.34	.44	.08	.10	.43	.33
19. Consensus Building								1.0	.09	.44	.12	.38	.14	.39
20. Perspective Consolidation									1.0	.26	.17	-.24	.62	.19
21. Opinion Management										1.0	.10	.34	.14	.46
22. Vision Articulation											1.0	-.02	.13	.04
23. Definition of Roles												1.0	-.29	.42
24. Logical Argumentation													1.0	.10
25. Impression Management														1.0

through their communications. In keeping with this observation, humor ($\overline{X}$ = 1.6), use of stories ($\overline{X}$ = 2.4), and use of nonverbals ($\overline{X}$ = 2.0) were relatively uncommon. This pattern of findings suggests that the directive communications of outstanding leaders tend, more often than not, to be relatively formal.

RESULTS

Comparison of Leader Types

Table 7.4 presents the results obtained in the multivariate analysis of covariance examining differences across leader types (charismatic, ideological, and pragmatic) and leader orientation (socialized and personalized) with respect to the various communication dimensions. As may be seen, a number of covariates produced significant effects ($p \leq .05$) in this analysis. Only one of the general covariates, type of position, produced a significant effect [$F(25, 85)$ = 2.02; $p \leq .01$]. Examination of the effects associated with this variable indicated that politicians tended to build consensus and try to consolidate positions by articulating a vision that appealed to followers' social and personal needs.

The remaining covariates producing significant relationships all focused on specific attributes of the leader's communication. Audience size produced significant effects [$F(25, 85)$ = 2.05; $p \leq .001$]. The effects of audience size with respect to the speech ratings indicated that, with larger audiences, leaders used a more affective communication strategy that evidenced both positive and negative affect, humor, propaganda, and an emphasis on goals and needs. Apparently leaders, in addressing large audiences, communicate through emotion,

TABLE 7.4
Summary of Results of Multivariate Analysis of Covariance

	F	df	p	η^2
Covariates				
Audience Size	2.05	25, 85	.008	.37
Frequency of Speeches	2.78	25, 85	.001	.45
Total Number of Speeches	2.09	25, 85	.007	.38
Degree of Political Conflict	2.28	25, 85	.003	.40
Type of Position	2.02	25, 85	.009	.37
Main Effects				
Orientation (socialized or personalized)	2.11	25, 85	.006	.38
Type (charismatic, ideological, or pragmatic)	1.52	25, 85	.078	.31
Interactions				
Orientation * Type	1.78	25, 85	.026	.34

Note. F = F ratio; df = degrees of freedom; p = significance level using Roy's Largest Root; η^2 = effect size.

perhaps as a way of engaging followers, building engagement by linking their arguments to followers' needs and goals.

Significant effects were also obtained for the frequency of speeches [$F(25, 85) = 2.78; p \leq .001$] and the total number of speeches [$F(25, 85) = 2.09; p \leq .01$]. The total number of speeches given was related to less expression of negative affect and more emphasis on logic. The frequency of speeches given by leaders was related to greater use of audience engagement techniques such as storytelling, confrontation, participation, and position debate. Apparently experience allows leaders to become better able to actively engage the audience in the creation of the message.

The final covariate that produced significant effects [$F(25, 85) = 2.28; p \leq .01$] was the degree of political conflict. Political conflict was related to more expression of negative affect, less expression of positive affect, more audience confrontation, and less consensus building, but a clearer articulation of the leader's vision. Apparently, conflict sharpens positions but results in a more negative tone in leaders' communications.

As was the case in prior analyses, leader orientation produced a highly significant [$F(25, 85) = 2.11; p \leq .001$] main effect. Examination of the associated univariate effects indicated that personalized leaders displayed a more directive controlling style in their communications, obtaining higher scores than socialized leaders with respect to use of propaganda [$F(1, 109) = 7.53; p \leq .01; \overline{X} = 2.99, SE = .06$ vs. $\overline{X} = 2.77, SE = .07$], specification of roles and role relationships [$F(1, 109) = 7.88; p \leq .01; \overline{X} = 3.75, SE = .07$ vs. $\overline{X} = 3.42, SE = .07$], and use of a directive communication style [$F(1, 109) = 3.37; p \leq .01; \overline{X} = 3.68, SE = .07$ vs. $\overline{X} = 3.52, SE = .05$].

In contrast, socialized leaders' communications displayed a more positive logical character. Socialized leaders, in contrast to personalized leaders, were more likely to apply logic [$F(1, 109) = 34.01; p \leq .001; \overline{X} = 3.66, SE = .06$ vs. $\overline{X} = 3.14, SE = .07$], present rational arguments [$F(1, 109) = 10.46; p \leq .01; \overline{X} = 3.34, SE = .06$ vs. $\overline{X} = 3.04, SE = .07$], and display positive affect [$F(1, 109) = 4.08; p \leq .05; \overline{X} = 3.34, SE = .08$ vs. $\overline{X} = 2.99, SE = .10$]. In keeping with the positive prosocial orientation of socialized leaders, socialized as opposed to personalized leaders, were more likely to try to consolidate different perspectives in their communications [$F(1, 109) = 12.58; p \leq .001; \overline{X} = 2.90, SE = .06$ vs. $\overline{X} = 2.53, SE = .07$]. Notably, socialized leaders also differed from personalized leaders in that they appeared better able to reach out to followers and connect to their lives through the use of stories [$F(1, 109) = 4.68; p \leq .05; \overline{X} = 2.58, SE = .07$ vs. $\overline{X} = 2.39, SE = .07$], imagery [$F(1, 109) = 3.35; p \leq .10; \overline{X} = 2.98, SE = .08$ vs. $\overline{X} = 2.76, SE = .08$], appeals to personal needs [$F(1, 109) = 5.20; p \leq .05; \overline{X} = 3.62, SE = .09$ vs. $\overline{X} = 3.39, SE = .09$], and greater eloquence [$F(1, 109) = 14.07; p \leq .001; \overline{X} = 3.39, SE = .07$ vs. $\overline{X} = 2.97, SE = .08$]. These effects, moreover, are not surprising given the focus of socialized leaders on others rather than on their own personal needs.

The discriminant function obtained when ratings on these dimensions were used to distinguish socialized and personalized leaders produced a canonical correlation of .62 ($p \leq .01$). The dimensions yielding sizable loadings on this function included (a) use of logic in argumentation ($r = .64$), (b) consolidation of different perspectives ($r = .46$), (c) eloquence of argumentation ($r = .45$), and (d) use of rational persuasion ($r = .34$). This pattern of loadings suggests that socialized leaders ($\overline{X} = .78$) differed from personalized leaders ($\overline{X} = -.78$) in their use of *prosocial argumentation*.

A marginally significant main effect [$F(25, 85) = 1.52; p \leq .10$] was obtained for the type variable. Because significant univariate effects were not obtained, this effect was considered trivial. The Type × Orientation interaction, however, did produce a significant effect [$F(25, 85) = 1.78; p \leq .05$]. Inspection of the relevant univariate tests indicated that socialized pragmatics, in contrast to all other leaders, were less likely to engage in opinion management [$F(2, 109) = 4.15; p \leq .05; \overline{X} = 3.23, SE = .08$ vs. $\overline{X} = 3.57, SE = .10$] and use of nonverbal behaviors [$F(2, 109) = 3.04; p \leq .05; \overline{X} = 1.86, SE = .10$ vs. $\overline{X} = 2.02, SE = .10$]. Apparently, socialized pragmatic leaders who are focused on the problem and its solution feel no need to attempt to manipulate their audience's perceptions of them as a leader. In keeping with their emphasis on solving problems, the use of logical argumentation was found to differ across leader types [$F(2, 109) = 4.58; p \leq .01$] with socialized and personalized pragmatics ($\overline{X} = 3.42, SE = .11$ and $\overline{X} = 3.22, SE = .13$) displaying less difference in this regard than socialized and personalized charismatic and ideological leaders ($\overline{X} = 3.78, SE = .09$ and $\overline{X} = 3.10, SE = .12$). Similarly, with regard to the use of stories [$F(2, 109) = 2.44; p \leq .10$], pragmatics ($\overline{X} = 2.40, SE = .14$), due to their focus on the problem, were less likely to persuade through stories than socialized charismatic and ideological leaders ($\overline{X} = 2.68, SE = .12$).

Prior studies indicate that charismatic leadership depends on attraction (Conger & Kanungo, 1998). In keeping with this observation, charismatic leaders, both socialized ($\overline{X} = 3.35, SE = .07$) and personalized ($\overline{X} = 3.24, SE = .10$), evidenced comparable levels of impression management [$F(2, 109) = 3.36; p \leq .05$]. However, for ideological and pragmatic leaders, impression management was more common among personalized ($\overline{X} = 3.44, SE = .09$) than socialized ($\overline{X} = 3.23, SE = .09$) leaders.

The degree to which followers' personal needs were emphasized in leader communications also produced a marginally significant [$F(2, 109) = 2.53; p \leq .10$] interaction between type and orientation. This interaction appears attributable to the tendency of socialized ideologues to produce particularly high scores on this dimension vis-à-vis other groups ($\overline{X} = 3.93, SE = .13$ vs. $\overline{X} = 3.42, SE = .15$) whereas pragmatics, regardless of orientation, produced particularly low scores ($\overline{X} = 3.26, SE = .14$ vs. $\overline{X} = 3.63, SE = .15$). The tendency of socialized ideologues to focus on follower needs may be attributed to a concern for others sharing their core beliefs whereas the tendency of pragmatics to discount these needs may be traced to their focus on the problem rather than people.

In the discriminant analyses contrasting the groups being examined in this Type × Orientation interaction, two functions produced significant ($p \leq .05$) canonical correlations. The first function produced a canonical correlation of .68 ($p \leq .001$) with ratings of emotional persuasion ($r = .54$), eloquence ($r = .47$), focus on the personal needs of followers ($r = .37$), and focus on the social needs of followers ($r = .35$) producing sizable loadings. This function, labeled *follower based appeals*, produced high scores for socialized ideologues ($\overline{X} = 1.51$) and socialized charismatics ($\overline{X} = .46$), but low scores for socialized and personalized pragmatics ($\overline{X} = -1.07$). The second function produced a canonical correlation of .64 ($p \leq .10$). The two rating dimensions yielding the highest loadings on this function were the degree of logic in argumentation ($r = .54$) and the use of rational persuasion techniques ($r = .37$). Not surprisingly, personalized charismatics ($\overline{X} = -1.01$) and personalized ideologues ($\overline{X} = -1.22$) tended to obtain low scores on this dimension vis-à-vis socialized charismatics ($\overline{X} = .85$), socialized ideologues ($\overline{X} = .44$), socialized pragmatics ($\overline{X} = .66$) and personalized pragmatics ($\overline{X} = .27$). Accordingly, this dimension was labeled *logical appeals*.

Performance Relationships

Table 7.5 presents the correlations of scores on the three discriminant-function scores derived from the speech ratings with scores on 12 general performance criteria. As may be seen, prosocial argumentation ($r = .26$), follower-based appeals ($r = .20$), and logical appeals ($r = .17$) tended to be positively related to the various indices of leader performance such as contributions to society, positive contributions, establishment of institutions, and so on. Similarly, prosocial argumentation ($r = -.30$), follower-based appeals ($r = -.01$), and logical appeals ($r = -.29$) tended to be negatively related to the overall number, as well as number of different types of negative contributions. Thus, differences among outstanding leaders in their communication strategies are related to indices of overall leader performance.

Overall, prosocial argumentation, follower-based appeals, and logical appeals displayed a rather consistent pattern of relationships with the general performance criteria. However, a few noteworthy variations on this general trend were observed. Unsurprisingly, follower-based appeals tended to be strongly related to initiation of mass movements ($r = .41$). Logical appeals, in contrast, were more strongly related to biographers' appraisals of the leader ($r = .37$). It appeared, moreover, that the use of logical appeals ($r = -.29$) was less likely to result in negative contributions and different types of negative contributions than follower-based appeals ($r = -.01$) by outstanding leaders.

TABLE 7.5
Correlations of Performance Criteria With Discriminant Functions

	Prosocial Argumentation	Follower-Based Appeals	Logical Appeals
General Criteria			
1. How much did the leader contribute to society?	.25	.32	.07
2. How long did the leader's contributions last?	.34	.13	.30
3. How many people did the leader affect?	.11	.23	−.04
4. How favorably did the biographer view the leader?	.45	.24	.37
5. How many positive contributions did the leader make?	.41	.24	.32
6. How many negative contributions did the leader make?	−.32	−.08	−.27
7. How many different types of positive contributions?	.34	.20	.26
8. How many different types of negative contributions?	−.29	.05	−.32
9. Do institutions established by the leader still exist?	.37	.06	.39
10. How many institutions were established by the leader?	−.11	−.05	−.03
11. Was the leader's vision maintained after they left power?	.32	.20	.24
12. Did the leader initiate mass movements?	.04	.41	−.18
Speech Criteria			
13. Do people still quote the leader's speeches?	.23	.16	.17
14. Are the leader's speeches considered landmark events?	.13	.42	−.01
15. Do the leader's speeches continue to influence others?	.45	.19	.39
16. Is material from the leader's speeches still considered relevant?	.45	.17	.41
17. Did the leader's speeches lead to institutional change?	.19	.35	.10
18. Are the leader's speeches still read today on special occasions?	.31	.24	.24
19. Do people still discuss ideas presented in the leader's speeches?	.27	.19	.21

Note. $r \geq .19$ significant at .05 level.

The communication criteria produced a better differentiated, albeit some-what weaker, pattern of relationships with the discriminant-function scores. The continued relevance and influence of leaders' speeches was more strongly related to logical appeals ($r = .40$) than follower-based appeals ($r = .18$)—a finding that reflects the fact that logical appeals may, to some extent, transcend the immediate social context. Follower-based appeals, however, were more likely than logical appeals to lead to institutional change ($r = .35$ vs. $r = .10$) and continue to be considered landmark events ($r = .42$ vs. $r = −.01$). Prosocial argumentation produced a pattern of relationships similar to those obtained for follower-based appeals—a finding reflecting the tendency of socialized leaders to take others into account. Notably, however, all three communication strategies—prosocial argumentation (r = .29), follower-based appeals (r = .22), and logical appeals (r = .22)—appeared useful for outstanding leaders in that they all lead to the leader's speeches continuing to be read and discussed.

Table 7.6 presents the results obtained when the general and study-specific criteria were regressed on the discriminant function scores. Again, these analyses were based on a blocked strategy where the discriminant function was added to the regression equation only after the relevant controls (e.g., audience size, number of speeches, frequency of speeches) had been entered. Thus, conclusions drawn about the relationship of the discriminant-function scores to performance are made after taking into account requisite controls.

In examining the general criteria, it is clear that the function scores, reflecting alternative communication strategies, contributed to the prediction of leader performance on the general criteria even when requisite controls were taken into account. In virtually all these analyses, 9 out of 12, at least one function produced a sizable regression weight after being added to the controls. More centrally, of the three functions under consideration, prosocial argumentation consistently produced the largest regression weights. Moreover, these effects were sizable, producing an average regression weight of .42 for the seven criteria where this function contributed to prediction of the general performance criteria. Apparently, prosocial argumentation is integral to the performance of outstanding leaders—a communication strategy characteristic of socialized leaders.

A similar pattern of findings emerged in examining the speech-specific criteria. More specifically, prosocial argumentation was related (β = .31) to the leader's speeches continuing to be considered relevant and influential. However, the tendency of people to continue to discuss and read the leaders' speeches seemed to be linked to logical appeals—a finding suggesting that pragmatic leaders, along with socialized charismatics and ideologues, exert a lasting influence through the power of their ideas.

Summary

The findings obtained in the present study indicate that outstanding leaders differ in the communication strategies used to influence followers and convey the leader's prescriptive mental models. Socialized and personalized leaders differed in terms of socialized leaders' tendency to present a positive prosocial image cast in terms likely to connect to the lives of followers. Personalized leaders tended to be more directive and rely on propaganda. It was also found that these differences attributable to orientation varied as a function of leader type. Socialized charismatics and ideologues, in contrast to pragmatics, were likely to make arguments based on followers' needs. Socialized charismatics, and socialized ideologues, like pragmatic leaders, also tended to rely on logical appeals—a communication strategy not used by personalized charismatics and personalized ideologues.

TABLE 7.6
Summary of Regression Results

Criteria	R	R^2	p	Significant Functions ($p \leq .05$)	Beta	High Group	Low Group
General Criteria							
1. How much did the leader contribute to society?	.51	.26	.001	Prosocial argumentation	.77	Socialized	Personalized
2. How long did the leader's contributions last?	.39	.15	.001	Prosocial argumentation	.30	Socialized	Personalized
3. How many people did the leader affect?	.46	.21	.001	None	—	—	—
4. How favorably did the biographer view the leader?	.47	.22	.001	Prosocial argumentation	.36	Socialized	Personalized
5. How many positive contributions did the leader make?	.43	.19	.001	Prosocial argumentation	.31	Socialized	Personalized
6. How many negative contributions did the leader make?	.46	.21	.001	Prosocial argumentation	-.43	Socialized	Personalized
7. How many different types of positive contributions?	.48	.23	.001	Prosocial argumentation	.57	Socialized	Personalized
8. How many different types of negative contributions?	.52	.27	.001	None	—	—	—
9. Do institutions established by the leader still exist?	.45	.20	.001	Logical appeals	.23	Pragmatics	Personalized ideologues & Charismatics
10. How many institutions were established by the leader?	.23	.05	.090	None	—	—	—
11. Was the leader's vision maintained after they left power?	.36	.13	.003	Prosocial argumentation	.20	Socialized	Personalized
12. Did the leader initiate mass movements?	.51	.26	.001	Follower-based appeals Logical appeals	.20 -.22	Socialized ideologues & Charismatics Pragmatics	Pragmatics Personalized ideologues & Charismatics

(Continued)

TABLE 7.6
(Continued)

Criteria	R	R^2	p	Significant Functions (p ≤ .05)	Beta	High Group	Low Group
Speech Criteria							
13. Do people still quote the leader's speeches?	.47	.22	.001	None	—	—	—
14. Are the leader's speeches considered landmark events?	.76	.58	.001	None	—	—	—
15. Do the leader's speeches continue to influence others?	.56	.31	.001	Prosocial argumentation	.38	Socialized	Personalized
16. Is material from the leader's speeches still considered relevant?	.52	.27	.001	Prosocial argumentation	.23	Socialized	Personalized
17. Did the leader's speeches lead to institutional change?	.90	.80	.001	None	—	—	—
18. Are the leader's speeches still read today on special occasions?	.45	.21	.001	Logical appeals Follower-based appeals	.25 .24	Pragmatics Socialized ideologues & Charismatics	Personalized ideologues & Charismatics Pragmatics
19. Do people still discuss ideas presented in the leader's speeches?	.34	.12	.01	Logical appeals	.16	Pragmatics	Personalized ideologues & Charismatics Pragmatics

Note. R = multiple correlation; R^2 = percent of variance accounted for; p = Significance level; Beta = standardized regression weight. Significant covariates are not presented in this table, only significant functions.

CONCLUSIONS

In considering these observations bearing on the communication strategies used by outstanding leaders, certain issues bearing on the methods applied herein should be noted. To begin, the present study was not based on direct observation of leaders as they communicated with followers. Instead, biographers' summary accounts of the communication, its content, and its effects were applied as the basis for appraising leader communication strategies. Although this historiometric approach is commonly applied in studies of leader communications (e.g., Deluga, 2001; Fiol et al., 1999), and may prove advantageous in that a more balanced view of content and context is provided, it is also true that some aspects of leader communication, for example, followers' affective reactions or leader wording emphasis, could not be readily assessed.

Along similar lines, it should be recognized that the focus of the present effort was on the *leaders'* communications. In fact, our focus on leader communications is integral to the application of speeches, or formal mass communications, as a basis for appraising communication strategies. By the same token, however, it should be recognized that all communications are, by definition, interactive phenomena involving multiple parties—specifically, in the case at hand, followers' perceptions of the leader's communications. Though historic summaries of the sort applied herein provide some information in this regard, it would also be desirable to examine communication effects from an audience perspective.

Finally, it should be noted that communication, especially leader communication, is a highly complex phenomenon. We tried to take this complexity into account by examining multiple dimensions of communications subsumed under the rubrics of style (e.g., expression of positive affect), content (e.g., consensus building), and strategy (e.g., rational persuasion). Although this approach to the definition of dimensions helped ensure a reasonably comprehensive description of leader communication, it is also true that not all dimensions of communication were, or indeed could be, considered.

Even bearing these limitations in mind, we would still argue that the results presented in this chapter have some noteworthy implications for understanding leader communication in general, and the similarities and differences among outstanding leaders with respect to the communication strategies being employed. To begin, the results presented earlier indicate that socialized and personalized leaders do differ with regard to communication strategies. Personalized leaders use a directive strategy that emphasizes propaganda. In contrast, socialized leaders' communications are based on a more positive prosocial approach that seeks to engage people in a cooperative enterprise. The differences between the communication strategies applied by socialized and personalized leaders are illustrated in Table 7.7, which presents speeches drawn from the biographies of a socialized and a personalized leader.

TABLE 7.7
Speech Abstracts for a Socialized Leader and a Personalized Leader

---

Winston Churchill—Socialized Leader

You ask, what is our policy? I will say: It is to wage war, by sea, land and air, with all our might and with all the strength that God can give us; to wage war against a monstrous tyranny, never surpassed in the dark, lamentable catalogue of human crime. That is our policy.

You ask, what is our aim? I can answer in one word: victory, victory at all costs, victory in spite of all terror, victory, however long and hard the road may be; for without victory there is no survival. Let that be realized; no survival for the British Empire, no survival for all that the British Empire has stood for, no survival for the urge and impulse of the ages, that mankind will move forward towards its goal.

But I take up my task with buoyancy and hope. I feel sure that our cause will not be suffered to fail among men. At this time I feel entitled to claim the aid of all, and I say, "Come then, let us go forward together with our united strength."

Adolf Hitler—Personalized Leader

Since 1914 when, as a volunteer, I made my modest contribution in the World War which was forced upon the Reich, over thirty years have passed.

In these three decades only love for my people and loyalty to my people have guided me in all my thoughts, actions, and life. They gave me the strength to make the most difficult decisions, such as no mortal has yet had to face. I have exhausted my time, my working energy, and my health in these three decades.

It is untrue that I or anybody else in Germany wanted war in 1939. It was desired and instigated exclusively by those international statesmen who were either of Jewish origin or working for Jewish interests. I have made so many offers for the reduction and limitation of armaments, which posterity cannot explain away for all eternity, that the responsibility for the outbreak of this war cannot rest on me. Furthermore, I never desired that after the first terrible World War a second war should arise against England or even against America. Centuries may pass, but out of the ruins of our cities and monuments of art there will arise anew the hatred for the people who alone are ultimately responsible: international Jewry and its helpers!

Note. Churchill is from *Churchill: A Life*, by M. Gilbert (1991, p. 646). Copyright © 1991 by Martin Gilbert. Reprinted by permission of Henry Holt and Co. Hitler is from *The Life and Death of Adolf Hitler*, by R. Payne (1973, pp. 555–556). Copyright © 1973. Reprinted by permission of Greenwood, Westport, CT.

The differences observed between socialized and personalized leaders in this regard are not especially surprising given the earlier observations of O'Connor et al. (1995). Negative life themes, object beliefs, and power motives, all characteristics of personalized leaders, would be expected to lead to a directive communication style stressing propaganda. In contrast, by virtue of their investment in and positive view of others, socialized leaders can be expected to present more positive communications that seek to engage others through rational arguments. Thus, it appears that leaders' beliefs and motives, in fact, condition the kind of communication strategies they apply.

What should be recognized here, however, is that the communication strategies employed by socialized and personalized leaders are related to performance. On both the general and the domain-specific criteria, prosocial argumentation, the variable discriminating socialized and personalized leaders, was found to be related to performance with the prosocial communication strategy employed by socialized leaders contributing to long-term performance. By building broader engagement through presentation of an attractive positive image connected to the lives of real people, socialized leaders can engage others in a broader enterprise—an engagement that allows effective influence.

In this regard, however, it is important to bear in mind a finding that emerged in the regression analysis. Though prosocial argumentation exerted strong effects on leader performance, some noteworthy effects also emerged with regard to leader type. In comparing charismatic, ideological, and pragmatic leaders, significant differences in the style, content, and strategy of leader communications were observed. The discriminant analyses indicated that these differences were captured by two variables: (a) follower-based appeals and (b) logical appeals.

As might be expected based on our foregoing observations, pragmatics tended to rely on logical, problem-centered appeals differing from personalized charismatics and ideologues, who applied more affective, personalized appeals (Mumford & Van Doorn, 2001). Pragmatics, moreover, differed from socialized charismatics and socialized ideologues who tended, instead, to rely on follower-based appeals—eloquent emotional appeals focused on the personal and social needs of followers. Apparently, visionary leaders, at least prosocial visionary leaders, due to their focus on people and social systems, frame communications to maximize their affective motivational impact on others (Conger & Kanungo, 1998; Shamir et al., 1993).

These differences among charismatic, ideological, and pragmatic leaders are noteworthy for two reasons. First, they provide some support for the theoretical model underlying the distinction we have drawn between charismatic, ideological, and pragmatic leaders. These three types of leaders apply different communication strategies, and the strategies applied are consistent with the prescriptive mental models constructed by leaders as part of their sensemaking activities. Thus, pragmatics preferred a problem-centered approach, whereas charismatic and ideological leaders applied a person/system-centered approach. In fact, the unwillingness of leaders, regardless of orientation, to depart from these preferred approaches drove many of the interactions observed between the orientation and type variables. In other words, outstanding leaders communicate what they are and what they believe. The question that arises at this juncture, of course, is how a leader's communication of his or her prescriptive mental model shapes the models applied by followers and their subsequent behavior.

Second, the differences observed among charismatic, ideological, and pragmatic leaders in this regard are apparently noteworthy influences on leader performance. Both follower-based appeals and logical appeals were related to the general and domain-specific criteria. Bearing in mind the lack of overall performance differences among charismatic, ideological, and pragmatic leaders, this pattern of findings suggests that the performance of charis-

TABLE 7.8
Speech Abstracts for a Socialized Charismatic
Leader and a Socialized Pragmatic Leader

Martin Luther King Jr.—Socialized Charismatic Leader

We believe in the American Dream of democracy, in the Jeffersonian doctrine that "all men are created equal and are endowed by their Creator with certain unalienable rights, among these being life, liberty and the pursuit of happiness."

Twice since September we have deferred our direct action thrust in order that a change in city government would not be made in the hysteria of a community crisis. We act today in full concert with our Hebraic-Christian tradition, the law of morality and the Constitution of our nation. The absence of justice and progress in Birmingham demands that we make a moral witness to give our community a chance to survive. We demonstrate our faith that we believe that the beloved community can come to Birmingham.

We appeal to the citizenry of Birmingham, Negro and white, to join us in this witness for decency, morality, self-respect and human dignity. Your individual and corporate support can hasten the day of "liberty and justice for all." This is Birmingham's moment of truth in which every citizen can play his part in her larger destiny.

Warren Buffett—Socialized Pragmatic Leader

I mentioned that in 1910 there were 1207 cities in the country with daily papers, of which 689 had two or more competing papers. In 1971, there were 1511 cities with daily papers, of which 37 had two or more competing papers. Since I wrote that letter, the Washington *Daily News*, backed by the enormously powerful Scripps-Howard chain, has folded, as has the Boston *Herald-Traveler* and the Newark *Evening News*.

Suggestions are constantly made to me—frequently by academicians who are somewhat unhappy with the editorial views of the local monopoly daily—that a wonderful future would await us if we would convert to a daily paper. This advice is well intended and sincere. The inescapable fact is that it has never been done . . . doesn't register on these theoreticians.

Note. King is from *A Biography of Martin Luther King, Jr.*, by L. Bennett (1976, pp. 133–134), Chicago: Johnson Publishing Co., Inc. Buffett is from Lowenstein (1995, pp. 146–147), New York: Random House. Reprinted by permission.

matic and ideological leaders, in contrast to pragmatic leaders, may hedge on effective follower-based communication. This point is illustrated in Table 7.8, which summarizes a speech given by a socialized charismatic and a speech given by a socialized pragmatic.

One question broached by these observations pertains to the mechanisms underlying the impact of follower-based appeals by charismatic and ideological leaders. Follower-based appeals are, of course, more motivating and involving than logical appeals. However, the impact of these appeals may be somewhat more subtle. Follower-based appeals make models apparent in graphic emotional terms to followers, thereby facilitating internalization of the vision or the prescriptive mental model being applied by the leader. This internalization, in turn, allows the leader's communication to have a broad and relatively powerful impact contributing to mass movements and institutional change.

The other question broached by these findings pertains to the overall suc-cess of pragmatic leaders despite their failure to apply follower-based appeals. What should be recognized in this regard, however, is that the logical appeals preferred by pragmatics work well with knowledgeable elites where there is no need to build consensus (Mumford & Van Doorn, 2001). Thus, pragmatics' success as communicators may lie in their appeal to, and communication with, a more limited but potentially influential audience—a point attested to by the positive relationship of logical appeals to both the creation and mainte-nance of institutions.

Of course, these observations suggest that outstanding leadership may arise through different mechanisms of influence giving rise to alternative pathways to outstanding leadership. By the same token, however, one is left with a ques-tion: When, and under what conditions, will follower-based, as opposed to logi-cal, appeals prove particularly beneficial for leaders in the exercise of influence? Moreover, it seems likely that the exceptional performance of socialized charis-matics and socialized ideologues may be traced to their ability to harness fol-lower-based appeals and logical appeals in a prosocial argument.

8

Political Tactics—Getting Ahead: How Charismatic, Ideological, and Pragmatic Leaders Use Influence Tactics

Michael D. Mumford
Brian Licuanan
Richard T. Marcy
Lesley Dailey
Cassie Blair
The University of Oklahoma

The term *politics* carries with it a negative, highly negative, connotation. We tend to disparage the office politician. We often believe that politics are an inherently corrupt, and corrupting, activity. We see politics as a source of self-serving compromise that undermines effective organizational action. Although we have a negative view of politics, it appears that the leaders we cherish, and look up to, are inherently political beings. In fact, the biographies of outstanding leaders are replete with incidents of political behavior—incidents that are critical in describing leaders' careers.

Consider, for example, the building of the Panama Canal—a singular achievement of Theodore Roosevelt's career. To get the canal built, Roosevelt had to do more than obtain the support and approval of Congress. He became involved in the politics of South America, facilitating, through various means, Panama's separation from Colombia and, ultimately, sending gunboats to ensure that the revolution succeeded (Morris, 2001).

The political behavior of outstanding leaders is observed not only in international events. One illustration of these more mundane forms of leader political behavior may be found in Hirshon's (2002) biography of George Patton. Like most junior officers, Patton needed the support of more senior officers to further his career. One way Patton garnered this support was by actively encouraging a romance between his sister and Jack Pershing, the commander of American expeditionary forces, during the First World War. Later in his career, Patton carefully built connections with elected officials—a set of connections that did much to move his career forward during the Second World War.

The pervasiveness and importance of political behavior in the careers of outstanding leaders is not simply an issue of the controversy that surrounds their ideas. Instead, the importance and pervasiveness of politics reflects a far more fundamental phenomenon. Ultimately, outstanding leaders must exercise influence. Although the exercise of influence occurs, in part, through the prescriptive mental models being articulated by outstanding leaders (Strange & Mumford, 2002), one must remember that somehow outstanding leaders must get people to go along with their model and take the actions needed to make their model real. Thus, the articulation and implementation of prescriptive models involves coalition building, the exploitation of situations, the management of information, and effective self-presentation. In other words, articulation and implementation depend on the effective exercise of influence tactics. Accordingly, in this chapter, we examine the political tactics used by outstanding leaders to influence others, considering the differences observed among charismatic, ideological, and pragmatic leaders with respect to the tactics applied and their influence on performance.

POLITICS AND OUTSTANDING LEADERSHIP

Political Behavior

In our theoretical model of outstanding leadership, we presented a rather straightforward description of the origins of outstanding leadership. We argued, more specifically, that outstanding leaders emerge in response to broad social crises, with the key to outstanding leadership lying in the construction of a prescriptive mental model that permits sensemaking in relation to the crisis at hand. These propositions, however straightforward, have an important, albeit often overlooked implication with regard to politics and political behavior on the part of outstanding leaders.

Porter, Allen, and Angle (1981) argued that political behavior is more likely to be observed in organizations under conditions of uncertainty. Crises of course, by definition, give rise to uncertainty. As a result, one can argue that the conditions giving rise to outstanding leadership will also give rise to political behavior as individuals, groups, and organizations seek to understand and cope with uncertainty.

Other factors related to the conditions giving rise to outstanding leadership, however, may also operate to create a link between political behavior and outstanding leadership. First, crises undermine the effectiveness of extant organizational structures and routines while bringing to question existing norms and cultural practices. This disruption of extant social structures, in turn, leads to political behavior as people, and organizations, attempt to define a new direction and a new basis for interaction (Ammeter et al., 2002). Second, outstanding leaders typically operate in upper-level leadership roles characterized by ambiguity and differences in the goals of various constituencies (Jaques, 1976). Ambiguity and differences of opinion will induce political behavior on the part of leaders as leaders seek to engage relevant constituencies in their long-term plans (Brass, 2001; Madison, Allen, Porter, Renwick, & Mayes, 1980).

Because the conditions giving rise to political behavior display substantial overlap with the conditions giving rise to outstanding leadership, it is not surprising that outstanding leadership and politics appear to be yoked phenomena. Moreover, the pervasiveness of political behavior under the conditions confronting outstanding leaders suggests that outstanding leaders may need to be skilled politicians. Indeed, there is reason to suspect that political skill, the ability to understand and apply power effectively (Mintzberg, 1983), may be critical to the performance of outstanding leaders (Perrewé, Ferris, Frink, & Anthony, 2000). In fact, the evidence accrued by Perrewé, Zeccans, Ferris, Rossi, Kacmar, and Ralston (2004), in a study of oil company managers, suggests that outstanding leaders may find the exercise of political skill gratifying such that political demands increase engagement and involvement in the task at hand.

The fact that outstanding leaders need political skill does not tell us what the exercise of political skills contributes to incidents of outstanding leadership. One framework for understanding the function of political behavior may be found in Sederberg (1984). He argued that political behavior not only helps leaders build acceptance for sensemaking activities, it may play a role, an important role, in construction of the prescriptive mental models that provide a basis for sensemaking and the construction of shared meaning. Political behavior, moreover, may be critical to effective articulation of the prescriptive mental models that serve to reduce the ambiguity associated with crises (Bolman & Deal, 1991).

Although at first it may be unclear why political behavior contributes to sensemaking, this point might be clarified by considering a few examples. One form of political behavior may be found in an influence tactic referred to as information management, or, more colloquially, spin control. By controlling the presentation and interpretation of information, it becomes possible for leaders to define and interpret events in terms of the prescriptive mental model being articulated. Along similar lines, W. L. Gardner and Avolio (1998) argued that outstanding leaders apply political tactics they referred to as vision promotion and organizational promotion. In vision promotion, leaders highlight desirable features of their vision while portraying alternatives in an undesirable light. In organizational promotion, leaders selectively highlight the achievements of their organization, portraying competing organizations in a negative light. These contrasts not only build support, they serve to articulate critical differentiating features of the vision being advocated by the leader.

In addition to providing a basis for sensemaking and effective articulation of prescriptive mental models, leader political behavior serves two other functions. First, execution of a prescriptive mental model requires the support, or at least the acquiescence, of various key constituencies—often, in the case of outstanding leaders, constituencies that have substantial autonomy and their own goals. Thus, outstanding leadership will require bargaining and coalition building (Ammeter et al., 2002; House, 1988). In keeping with the need to build commitment and support, W. L. Gardner and Cleavenger (1998) found, in a study of historically notable leaders, that transformational (charismatic) leaders were more likely than nontransformational leaders to use ingratiation tactics (e.g., compliments, flattery).

Second, outstanding leaders, by virtue of the crises they are addressing, must call forth exceptional effort on the part of followers. One influence tactic employed by outstanding leaders to build commitment is exemplification or overt displays of personal commitment. In keeping with this proposition, Jones and Pittman (1982) and Mumford and Van Doorn (2001), in qualitative studies of Martin Luther King, Mahatma Gandhi, and Benjamin Franklin, found that exemplification, or manifest personal commitment, is a key influence tactic used by outstanding leaders to motivate followers. In fact, the use of impression management tactics by outstanding leaders may arise from this need of leaders to create a favorable personal image that allows exemplification to prove effective (Ammeter et al., 2002).

Political Tactics

Our foregoing observations with regard to the functions of political behavior implicitly underscore the selective use of certain political tactics, or influence tactics, by outstanding leaders (W. L. Gardner & Cleavenger, 1998). This selective use of influence tactics is noteworthy because a host of influence tactics have been identified that might be used by leaders, albeit with varying levels of success (e.g., Kipnis, Schmidt, & Wilkinson, 1980; Yukl, 2002; Yukl & Tracey, 1992).

In a review of this literature, Zanzi and O'Neill (2001) classified the influence tactics used by leaders into two broad categories: (a) sanctioned tactics and (b) unsanctioned tactics. Sanctioned tactics reflect behaviors that are commonly held to be appropriate vehicles for the exercise of influence in organizational settings such as (a) coalition building, (b) rational persuasion, (c) image building, (d) use of expertise, and (e) appeals to superordinate goals. Unsanctioned tactics reflect behaviors that are commonly held to be inappropriate vehicles for the exercise of influence in organizational settings such as (a) distorting or misrepresenting the organization's position, (b) control of information, (c) blaming or attacking others, (d) co-option, and (e) the use of surrogates. Fairholm (1993), in a study of unsanctioned influence tactics, noted that influence may also be exercised in an indirect fashion by manipulating the conditions under which decision making occurs. Thus, he stressed the importance of influence tactics such as agenda control, brinkmanship, incurring obligations, defining criteria, and creating ambiguity.

With regard to these tactics, and other tactics such as appeal to authority, relationship creation, resource control, intimidation, coercion, rewards, resource exchange, and consultation (e.g., Ammeter et al., 2001; Ashforth & Lee, 1990), it is important to bear in mind a point made by Ammeter et al. They argued that what is a sanctioned or unsanctioned tactic will, in part, depend on the situation at hand. Thus, agenda control may be viewed as an acceptable influence tactic in political settings although it is frowned upon in business settings. To complicate matters further, leaders may, at times, use unsanctioned tactics to achieve legitimate goals. For example, agenda setting may be used to focus attention on high-priority issues whereas ambiguity may be created to allow leaders to juggle potentially promising, but unpopular, alternatives.

Even bearing in mind the point that influence tactics are not, in and of themselves, a universal good or a universal evil, it does appear that some tactics are more effective than others. For example, W. L. Gardner and Cleavenger (1998), in their study of historically notable leaders, found that the tendency to apply intimidation tactics, presenting oneself as a dangerous person willing to harm others, was negatively related to indices of leader effectiveness and follower satisfaction. Along similar lines, rewards and coercion appear less effective vehicles for the exercise of influence than expertise, rational persuasion, legitimating tactics, and inspirational appeals (Yukl, 2002). Apparently, influence tactics limiting others' discretion will generally prove ineffective, although such tactics may have value under conditions where simple compliance is needed rather than acceptance of the leader's position.

In any discussion of the effectiveness of influence tactics, it is important to bear in mind a point made by Yukl (2002). He argued that the effectiveness of any given influence tactic will, to some extent, depend on the position and concerns of the target of the influence attempt. Thus, tactics such as ingratiation, exchange, and inspirational appeals appear particularly effective when the leader is interacting with followers, although they may prove less effective when leaders are interacting with peers. When leaders are interacting with peers, or relatively powerful followers, rational persuasion, coalition building, collaboration, networking, and expertise appear to represent more effective influence tactics.

These shifts in the effectiveness of influence tactics across targets, however, has an important, although perhaps somewhat more subtle, implication. More specifically, as leaders move through their careers, and acquire positions of greater authority, it can be expected that the targets of influence will change. These changes in influence targets, in turn, imply changes over the course of leaders' careers in preferred influence tactics. These changes will, moreover, be associated with the shifts in relevant power bases that occur as a function of position.

Outstanding Leadership

Although it appears that situational factors, such as setting, target, and position, have noteworthy effects on the influence tactics employed by leaders, evidence is also available indicating some stability in the influence tactics employed by leaders throughout their careers. Churchill seemed to prefer inspirational appeals throughout his career, just as Stalin seemed to prefer intimidation. To account for this apparent stability in preferred influence tactics, Fiol, O'Connor, and Aguinis (2001) proposed the concept of power mental models. Power mental models can be viewed as a schema, or a cognitive representation, of the sources of one's own power and the ways in which power can be effectively exercised to influence others' behavior. As schematic knowledge structures, power mental models are subject to change as a function of experience. By the same token, however, the availability and application of these schemata will induce some stability in the kind of influence tactics applied by leaders.

One intriguing implication of this theory is that power mental models, by identifying causes of others' behavior, will influence construction of the prescriptive mental model used by outstanding leaders in sensemaking. What should be recognized here, however, is that the power mental models applied by leaders may be influenced by broader cognitive structures that people use to understand events in their lives. As a result, significant life events may play a role in defining power mental models as well as the life narratives, or life stories, people apply in understanding their lives. If people frame their understandings of how power is exercised and the effects of influence tactics in terms of their understandings of themselves, and their own lives, then one would expect to see differences, stable differences, emerge among charismatic, ideological, and pragmatic leaders with regard to preferred strategies for the exercise of influence.

For example, the importance of proactive change and turning point events in the life narratives of charismatic leaders might cause charismatics to stress affective influence tactics and apply brinkmanship strategies. In contrast, the importance of anchoring events in defining the narratives of ideological leaders should lead to an emphasis on personal commitment as a preferred influence tactic. Pragmatic leaders, by virtue of the importance of originating events in their lives (events that stress goals and plans), may find strategic tactics and expertise tactics particularly attractive vehicles for the exercise of influence.

Not only will influence tactics differ across charismatic, ideological, and pragmatic leaders as a result of life narratives, differences can also be expected as a result of the boundary conditions under which they operate and the mechanisms employed for the exercise of influence. For example, Mumford and Van Doorn (2001) argued that pragmatic leaders rely on knowledgeable elites as a basis for the exercise of influence. Accordingly, one would expect that expertise, rational persuasion, and bargaining would represent preferred tactics for the exercise of influence. Charismatic and ideological leaders, however, operate under conditions where consensus is weak by building support for a broader vision that provides a framework for collective action. These characteristics of charismatic and ideological leaders would lend one to expect that vision promotion, emotional arousal, exemplification, and impression management would prove to be preferred influence tactics.

The notion that identity and setting condition the influence tactics employed by charismatic, ideological, and pragmatic leaders also suggests that differences will be observed in the influence tactics employed by socialized and personalized leaders. The O'Connor et al. (1995) study, cited earlier, indicated that personalized leaders, in contrast to socialized leaders, are more likely to manifest negative life themes and object beliefs—characteristics of personalized leaders that may be associated with exposure to contaminating events. These narrative themes, in turn, imply that personalized leaders may be more willing to employ intimidation and disinformation tactics while being less willing to apply the relational and persuasive tactics employed by socialized leaders.

Again, however, it should be noted that setting, as well as identity, may give rise to differences in the influence tactics used by socialized and personalized leaders. Because personalized leaders will find it difficult to exert influence through interpersonal relationships, intimidation, aggression, and resource control tactics may be preferred. Socialized leaders, by virtue of their willingness and ability to work through others, may stress relationship formation and personal commitment.

Summary

Outstanding leadership requires political skill to allow leaders to engage in sensemaking and build support for implementation of the prescriptive mental models they have proposed. A variety of influence tactics have been identified that might be used by leaders with the value of these tactics varying as a function of setting, position, targets, and career stage. There is also reason to suspect, however, that different styles of leaders, specifically charismatic, ideological, and pragmatic leaders, will differ in preferred influence tactics due to differences in identity and the conditions associated with the emergence of certain leader types.

METHOD

Study Method

Material Selection. To examine potential differences among outstanding leaders with respect to preferred influence tactics, it seemed critical to take into account career stage. Accordingly, incidents of political behavior were drawn from the rise-to-power, pinnacle-of-power, and fall-from-power chapters included in the biographies of the 120 leaders under consideration. Incident identification required an explicit definition of exactly what is meant by the term *political behavior*. Accordingly, the literature was reviewed to identify alternative definitions of political behavior (e.g., Ammeter et al., 2002; Yukl, 2002). Based on prior definitions, political behavior was held to be reflected in incidents where the leader took actions intended to affect the behavior of others, or ensure compliance, to achieve some goal through the exercise of power under conditions of uncertainty or disagreement.

An incident of political behavior was considered significant if the issues at hand had potentially important positive or negative outcomes for both the leader and one or more parties involved in the incident. Four psychologists were asked to review the rise-to-power, pinnacle-of-power, and fall-from-power chapters included in the biographies to identify three to seven significant incidents of political behavior on the part of the leader. Pilot studies indicated that given this definition, and adequate practice, judges agreed more than 90% of the time with regard to the significant incidents of political behavior abstracted from the relevant chapters.

Typically five to seven significant incidents of political behavior were identified for each leader in a given chapter. Of the 1,611 incidents identified overall, 547 incidents were drawn from the rise-to-power chapters, 548 from the pinnacle-of-power chapters, and 516 from the fall-from-power chapters. Typically these incidents were two to four pages in length and involved the exercise of 9 to 11 influence tactics by the leader.

Categorizing Influence Tactics.   To assess the leader influence tactics evident in the incidents abstracted from these biographies, the following procedures were applied. Initially, the available literature on the influence tactics used by leaders was reviewed (e.g., Ammeter et al., 2002; Bass, 1990; Kipnis et al., 1980; Valle & Witt, 2001; Zanzi & O'Neill, 2001). This review was used to identify a candidate list of influence tactics, taking into account both "sanctioned" and "unsanctioned" influence tactics. Subsequently, this list of candidate influence tactics was reviewed by four psychologists. In this review, an attempt was made to eliminate obvious redundancies and merge closely related influence tactics. In all, this revised list included 149 distinct, or apparently distinct, influence tactics.

After this list of influence tactics had been constructed, four psychologists, all doctoral students in industrial and organizational psychology, were asked to review these influence tactics and group these tactics into broader categories using a modified Q-sort procedure. In this modified Q-sort, judges, five in all, were asked to group the incidents into categories and label these categories. Following this initial grouping, judges met as a panel to review their categories and category assignments. Based on the overlap observed in categories, and category assignments, a consensus list of categories was developed and influence tactics were reallocated in these categories. Application of these procedures resulted in the identification of 15 categories of influence tactics. The resulting categories contained between 4 and 20 discrete influence tactics. Table 8.1 lists these categories and the influence tactics assigned to each category.

Rating Procedures. Given the availability of these categories, and the list of influence tactics assigned to each category, scoring of the incidents could proceed in a relatively straightforward fashion. More specifically, four judges, again all doctoral candidates in industrial and organizational psychology, were asked to review each incident description abstracted from the biographies and indicate each time a given influence tactic appeared in an incident. Scoring occurred by determining the total number of times, across judges, the use of a given influence tactic was observed. These incident scores were then aggregated into category scores by summing the number of category-relevant influence tactics observed and then dividing by the number of incidents assigned to a category to control for cross-category differences in the number of relevant influence tactics.

Prior to making these evaluations, the four judges were asked to participate in a 48-hour training program extending over 4 weeks. In this training program, judges were familiarized with the definition of leader political behavior and the operational definition formulated for each of the various influence tactics under consideration. Subsequently, judges were asked to apply the list of influence tactics discussed earlier in evaluating a series of sample incidents. After making their initial evaluations, judges met as a panel to review their evaluations and discuss any observed discrepancies. This procedure was repeated until judges evidenced adequate agreement.

Study-Specific Controls. In addition to evaluating the frequency with which various influence tactics appeared in the incidents, judges were asked to appraise a set of control variables as they reviewed each incident. In addition to evaluating the length of each incident and the biographer's reactions to political tactics, judges were asked to evaluate controls concerned with the social constraints placed on influence tactics and the visibility or impact of political behavior. The social-constraint variables, rated on a 5-point scale, included: (a) the number of targets of influence, (b) the number of actors involved in the incident, (c) public or private behavior (degree of visibility), and (d) the amount of trust the parties involved put in the leader. The visibility and impact controls, again control variables rated on a 5-point scale, included: (a) the amount of risk for the leader, (b) the implications of the issues at hand for the institutions under consideration, and (c) the amount of conflict surrounding the event. These control variables produced an average interrater agreement coefficient of .52 using the procedures suggested by Shrout and Fleiss (1979).

Political Behavior	Influence Tactics
Social Relationships	Be a supporter of others' needs
	Building others' self-esteem
	Developing champions
	Expressing respect for others
	Maintain appropriate relations
	Maintain rapport
	Managing others
	Recognition of people's contributions
	Recognize others' interests
	Recognizing and acting on others' needs
	Reducing tension/friction
	Role modeling
Resources	Managing resources
	Offering inducements
	Resource control
	Utilize others' resource to achieve goals
Authority	Appealing to a higher authority
	Asserting
	Authority
	Delegate
	Disregarding rules
	Establish regulations
	Legitimating tactics
	Limiting exercise of others' power
	Remodeling regulations
	Rule citing
	Use of power
Expertise	Consultation
	Display ability to accomplish goals through actions
	Instruct
	Personalized knowledge
	Pointing out weaknesses
	Portrayal as experts
	Rationality
	Reasoning
	Recognizing success or failure
	Straightforwardness
Common Decision Strategies	Absence
	Behind-the-scenes maneuvering
	Convey one's interests
	Create compelling spectacles
	Defining situations
	Forecasting
	Framing perspectives
	Keep opponents in close view
	Keep options open

(Continued)

TABLE 8.1
(Continued)

Political Behavior	Influence Tactics
Common Decision Strategies (cont.)	Looking out for greater good
	Lower defenses
	Maintain a level of uncertainty
	Maintain reasonable options
	Obtain information discreetly
	Provide reassurance to others
	Remain flexible
	Remain involved when seeking end goal
	Retarding/delaying compromises
	Strategize a game plan
	Working the system
Managing Situations	Co-opting
	Maintain efficient planning time
	Managing sanctions
	Managing the use of others
	Managing to maximize returns
	Manipulating
	Striving for centralization
	Utilizing span of control
Information	Appraising
	Apprising
	Articulating implication of crisis
	Control the amount of factual information
	Feedback
	Focus on important issues
	Highlighting important details
	Limit the amount of information to be revealed
	Limit your message revelation
	Maintain a level of personalized information
	Maintain confidentiality
	Managing the representation of information
	Revealing of information
	Selective expression of issues
	Selective presentation
	Selectively prevent courses of action
	Selectively withhold information
Coalition	Building consensus
	Coalition building
	Collaborate with others but maintain own beliefs
	Collaboration
	Gather support groups
	Networking
	Selective association with others
	Emphasizing group ideals

(Continued)

TABLE 8.1
(Continued)

Political Behavior	Influence Tactics
Bargaining	Accommodation
	Appease difficult people
	Bargaining
	Compromise
	Display social needs
	Excessive contributions
	Exchange
	Invoke past behaviors
	Promises
	Trading of favors
	Trading off commitments
Aggression	Advise departure from responsibilities
	Aggressive acts to hurt others
	Display warnings
	Pressure
	Resistance
	Stimulate negative affect
Status	Make self known/visible
	Self-affirmation
	Self-marketing
	Self-serving behavior
	Stand firm on beliefs
Personal Commitment	Appeal to others' self-image
	Display eagerness to learn
	Display modesty
	Exhibit reliance
	Expressing commitment
	Expressing loyalty
	Ingratiation
	Making requests
	Personal appeals
	Recognize others' accomplishments
	Simple requests
	Tailor personal identity to reflect personal needs
Vision Promotion	Appeal to others' feelings and thoughts
	Humility
	Inspirational appeals
	Keep issues and thoughts in an enthusiastic manner
	Maintain a level of achievement ideals
	Persuasion
	Promoting an idea
	Rational persuasion

(Continued)

TABLE 8.1
(Continued)

Political Behavior	Influence Tactics
Disinformation	Betray confidence
	Covering up
	Distort information
	Masking emotions
	Masking intentions
	Mastering emotions
	Pretend good intentions
	Simulate lack of knowledge
Emotion	Appealing to others' emotions
	Display calmness
	Display confidence
	Display enthusiasm
	Mastering emotions (also in disinformation category)
	Recognize each other's feelings
	Stimulate others' emotions (also in aggression category)

Study-Specific Criteria. Although the impact of influence tactics on performance could be appraised using the 12 general performance criteria described earlier, it seemed desirable to examine performance attributes directly relevant to political behavior in accordance with the recommendations of Ammeter et al. (2002). Here four judges were asked to rate, on a 5-point scale, using the material presented in the prologue or epilogue chapters: (a) the degree of divisiveness arising from the leader's actions, (b) maintenance, over time, of arrangements brought about by the leader's political behavior, (c) institutionalization of the leaders' base of influence, and (d) positive relationships of groups to leaders. These evaluations of the success of leaders' influence attempts yielded interrater agreement coefficients in the .70s.

Descriptive Findings

Table 8.2 presents the mean, standard deviation, interrater agreement coefficient, and correlation coefficients for scores on the 15 dimensions of political tactics under consideration. The interrater agreement coefficients obtained in assessing the frequency with which relevant political tactics were evident in the incidents abstracted from the biographies ranged from .57 to .99. The unusually high agreement coefficients obtained for control of decision strategies and information reflects the tendency of biographers to "call out," and expressly analyze, the leader's use of tactics subsumed under these dimensions. Given this observation, it is not surprising that the average interrater agreement coefficient (r = .64) was larger than the median interrater agreement coefficient (r = .58). Regardless of the metric applied, however, the obtained agreement coefficients fall in the range considered adequate when frequency data is being employed.

TABLE 8.2
Means, Standard Deviations, Agreement Coefficients, and Correlations for Political Behavior

	$\bar{X}$	SD	r_{tt}	1	2	3	4	5	6	7	8	9	10	11	12	13	14	15
1) Social Relationships	.10	.09	.57	1.0	.09	-.40	.27	.02	.06	.05	.35	-.02	-.22	-.03	.15	.15	-.24	.02
2) Resources	.09	.15	.57		1.0	-.80	.01	.05	.29	.02	.07	.09	-.01	-.01	-.06	-.12	-.15	-.18
3) Authority	.08	.11	.61			1.0	-.14	.13	.33	-.09	-.12	-.02	.35	-.18	-.14	-.16	.24	-.05
4) Expertise	.10	.11	.58				1.0	.04	-.20	.07	-.05	-.17	-.19	-.02	-.10	.09	-.20	-.09
5) Control of Decision Strategies	.15	.07	.99					1.0	.37	.21	.23	.07	.16	.16	.01	.03	.05	-.24
6) Managing Situations	.12	.10	.51						1.0	.15	.23	-.01	.12	-.04	-.01	-.12	.09	-.17
7) Information	.06	.07	.99							1.0	.10	-.09	.02	-.05	.04	.01	.30	-.09
8) Coalition	.12	.15	.61								1.0	.07	.02	.09	.25	.15	-.21	-.15
9) Bargaining	.06	.08	.57									1.0	-.01	-.05	.03	.06	-.05	-.02
10) Aggression	.16	.16	.71										1.0	-.12	-.08	-.32	.16	-.05
11) Status	.17	.20	.60											1.0	.14	.19	-.10	.08
12) Personal Commitment	.07	.08	.58												1.0	.19	.03	-.03
13) Vision Promotion	.08	.10	.58													1.0	-.15	.30
14) Disinformation	.04	.08	.65														1.0	.04
15) Emotion	.09	.10	.57															1.0

Note. $p \geq .18$ significant at .05 level. Means adjusted by constant.

More centrally, the correlations among the dimensions provided some evidence for the meaningfulness, or construct validity, of these evaluations. For example, the frequency with which social relationships were used as a basis for the exercise of influence was positively correlated ($r = .35$) with the use of coalitions as a basis for the exercise of influence but negatively correlated with the exercise of influence through authority ($r = -.40$) and aggression ($r = -.22$)—findings that are not especially surprising given the fact that authority and aggression typically disrupt social relationships. Along similar lines, it was found that the use of political tactics involving control of decision strategies was positively related to managing situations ($r = .37$), and information ($r = .21$), to further one's agenda. Finally, given the observations of Shamir et al. (1993), it was not surprising that the tendency to exercise influence through vision promotion proved to be positively related to the exercise of influence through emotions ($r = .30$).

Given the evidence for the meaningfulness of the measures of political tactics abstracted from the biographies, a new question comes to fore: Which of these 15 tactics are most likely to be applied by outstanding leaders? The data presented in Table 8.2 indicate that outstanding leaders use a variety of political tactics. However, they appear especially likely to use control of decision strategies ($\overline{X} = .15$), aggression ($\overline{X} = .16$), and status ($\overline{X} = .17$) as tactics for influencing others. Although this observation may, at first glance, appear surprising, in conflict and crisis situations, the situations that call for outstanding leadership, it may be necessary for leaders to take strong, highly directive positions—a point illustrated in Lyndon Johnson's behavior in "pushing" through civil rights legislation. This characteristic of the political tactics used by outstanding leaders, in fact, may account for the finding that bargaining ($\overline{X} = .06$) behaviors were not frequently observed.

In addition, two other dimensions were observed relatively infrequently in the incidents abstracted from the biographies. Outstanding leaders rarely used tactics subsumed under the disinformation ($\overline{X} = .04$) dimension. And, they rarely used tactics involving control of information ($\overline{X} = .06$). Apparently, information, perhaps because it is widely available and often verifiable, does not provide outstanding leaders with an especially useful tool for the exercise of influence.

RESULTS

Comparison of Leader Types

Table 8.3 presents the results obtained in the multivariate analysis of covariance examining differences across leader types (charismatic, ideological, and pragmatic), leader orientation (socialized or personalized), and time ("rise to power," "pinnacle of power," and "fall from power") with respect to the political tactics observed. As may be seen, a number of covariates produced signifi-

TABLE 8.3
Summary of Results of Multivariate Analysis of Covariance

	F	df	p	η^2
Covariates				
Incident length	4.95	15, 95	0.001	0.43
Amount of risk	2.46	15, 95	0.004	0.28
Prior conflict	2.66	15, 95	0.002	0.29
Author reactions to tactics	2.59	15, 95	0.003	0.29
Organizational size	1.71	15, 95	0.061	0.21
Main Effects				
Orientation (socialized or personalized)	1.01	15, 95	0.443	0.13
Type (charismatic, ideological, or pragmatic)	2.26	15, 95	0.009	0.26
Time ("rise to power," "pinnacle of power," "fall from power")	0.89	30, 80	0.662	0.25
Interactions				
Orientation * Type	1.26	15, 95	0.241	0.16
Orientation * Time	0.80	30, 80	0.74	0.23
Type * Time	0.93	30, 80	0.57	0.25
Type * Time * Orientation	1.22	30, 80	0.222	0.31

Note.   F = F-ratio, df = degrees of freedom, p = significance level using Roy's Largest Root, η^2 = effect size (partial eta squared).

cant $(p \leq .05)$ effects. As expected, incident length $[F(15, 95) = 4.95; p \leq .001]$ produced a significant relationship due to the fact that longer incidents provided more opportunities to identify relevant political behaviors. Additionally, the likelihood of political behaviors being observed increased with the size of the organization $[F(15, 95) = 1.71; p \leq .10]$ and the amount of risk $[F(15, 95) = 2.46; p \leq .01]$ involved for the leader.

Whereas these relationships were quite straightforward, the remaining two covariates produced a somewhat more complex pattern of relationships. The effects for prior conflict $[F(15, 95) = 2.66; p \leq .01]$ appear to reflect the fact that hostile political tactics (or aggression) were more likely to occur when the parties involved had a history of distrust and disagreement. The effects for authors' reactions to political tactics $[F(15, 95) = 2.59; p \leq .01]$ reflect the tendency of authors to spend more time examining political behavior of which they approved.

When these controls were taken into account, only one significant effect emerged in the multivariate analysis of covariance. More specifically, leader type (charismatic, ideological, and pragmatic) produced a significant $[F(15, 95) = 2.26; p \leq .01]$ main effect. Inspection of the associated univariate effects indicated, in accordance with our foregoing observations, that pragmatic leaders were more likely than charismatic and ideological leaders to exercise influence through expertise $[F(2, 109) = 2.15; p \leq .15; \overline{X} = .12, SE = .012$ vs. $\overline{X} = .09, SE = .012]$ and control of resources $[F(2, 109) = 2.34; p \leq .10; \overline{X} = .12, SE = .017$ vs. $\overline{X} = .08, SE = .01]$. Charismatic leaders, on the other hand, were more likely than pragmatic and ideological leaders to exercise influence through political tactics intended to enhance status perceptions $[F(2, 109) = 2.14; p \leq .15; \overline{X} =$

.21, SE = .021 vs. $\overline{X}$ = .16, SE = .021]. This finding, of course, is consistent with the observation that charismatic leaders seek to convey an aura of success to encourage personal identification and acceptance of the vision being articulated. Finally, charismatic and ideological leaders, in contrast to pragmatic leaders, were more likely to use coalition building [$F(2, 109)$ = 2.75; $p \leq .10$; $\overline{X}$ = .15, SE = .016 vs. $\overline{X}$ = .09, SE = .016] as a vehicle for the exercise of influence. Given the focus of pragmatic leaders on rational self-interest, however, this pattern of findings is not especially surprising.

The discriminant function obtained when scores on the political-tactics dimension were used to account for group membership produced a canonical correlation of .53, which was significant at the .01 level. The dimensions yielding sizable positive loadings on this function included expertise (r = .33), social relationships (r = .28), and resources (r = .27). The dimensions yielding sizable negative loadings on this function included control of decision strategies (r = −.45), aggression (r = −.30), coalition building (r = −.29), and personal commitment (r = −.25). This pattern of loadings suggests that with respect to political tactics, charismatic, ideological, and pragmatic leaders differ in their emphasis on rational economic influence. As might be expected, pragmatic leaders ($\overline{X}$ = .88) obtained substantially higher scores on this *rational-influence* function than charismatic ($\overline{X}$ = .33) and ideological ($\overline{X}$ = .54) leaders.

Performance Relationships

Table 8.4 presents the correlations of this rational-influence dimension with the various performance criteria. Although scores on this rational-influence dimension were not strongly related to the 4 political criteria, they were significantly ($p \leq .10$) related to scores on 5 of the 12 general performance criteria. Use of rational-influence tactics was negatively related to the leader's ability to initiate mass movements (r = −.35). The limited utility of rational-influence tactics in mobilizing large numbers of people may account for the finding that use of rational-influence tactics was also negatively related to how much the leader contributed to society (r = −.25), and the number of people affected by the leader's actions (r = −.17).

Although the exercise of rational-influence tactics may limit the leader's impact on people, it may prove beneficial to society as a whole by limiting the damage that can be done by leaders. Thus, use of rational-influence tactics resulted in fewer negative contributions (r = −.25) and fewer different types of negative contributions (r = −.30). Because leaders applying rational-influence tactics did less harm to society, they tended to be more favorably appraised by biographers (r = .26).

The question that arises at this juncture is whether these effects were still evident when the relevant covariate controls were taken into account. The results obtained in the regression analysis where each criterion was regressed on the rational-influence dimension after first taking these controls into account are

TABLE 8.4
Correlations of Performance Criteria With Discriminant Functions

Criteria	Rational Influence
General Criteria	
1) How much did the leader contribute to society?	−0.25
2) How long did the leader's contribution last?	−0.02
3) How many people did the leader affect?	−0.17
4) How favorably did the biographer view the leader?	0.26
5) How many positive contributions did the leader make?	0.02
6) How many negative contributions did the leader make?	−0.25
7) How many different types of positive contributions?	−0.05
8) How many different types of negative contributions?	−0.30
9) Do institutions established by the leader still exist?	0.02
10) How many institutions were established by the leader?	−0.05
11) Was the leader's vision maintained after he/she left power?	−0.04
12) Did the leader initiate mass movements?	−0.35
Political Criteria	
1) Amount of divisiveness arising from the leader's positions?	−0.02
2) Maintenance over time of arrangements brought about by the leader's political behavior?	0.12
3) Institutionalization of the leader's base of influence?	0.12
4) Positive relationship of group to leader?	0.16

Note. $r \geq .18$ significant at .05 level.

presented in Table 8.5. As may be seen, the rational-influence dimension provided significant ($p \leq .05$) regression results for 4 of the 12 general criteria. In keeping with the results obtained in the correlational analyses, pragmatics' use of rational influence made it less likely ($\beta = -.27$) that they would initiate mass movements, thereby limiting their impact on society ($\beta = -.18$). By the same token, however, use of rational-influence tactics limited the number of different types of negative contributions ($\beta = -.16$) that might be made by a leader, resulting in a more favorable appraisal of the leader's performance by biographers ($\beta = .26$).

Summary

Outstanding leaders are apparently political beings who have at their disposal and use a wide variety of political tactics to influence others. In fact, the use of political tactics was not related to orientation—socialized versus personalized—and outstanding leaders, regardless of orientation, employed some rather harsh tactics such as control of decision strategies and aggression. Charismatic, ideological, and pragmatic leaders, however, were found to differ in the kind of

TABLE 8.5
Summary of Regression Results

Criteria	R	R^2	p	Significant Functions ($p \leq .10$)	Beta	High Group	Low Group
General Criteria							
1) How much did the leader contribute to society?	0.56	0.32	0.001	Rational influence	−0.18	Pragmatics	Ideologues & Charismatics
2) How long did the leader's contribution last?	0.53	0.28	0.001	None	—	—	—
3) How many people did the leader affect?	0.56	0.28	0.001	None	—	—	—
4) How favorably did the biographer view the leader?	0.49	0.24	0.001	Rational influence	0.26	Pragmatics	—
5) How many positive contributions did the leader make?	0.52	0.27	0.001	None	—	—	—
6) How many negative contributions did the leader make?	0.59	0.35	0.001	None	—	—	—
7) How many different types of positive contributions?	0.46	0.21	0.001	None	—	—	—
8) How many different types of negative contributions?	0.58	0.33	0.001	Rational influence	−0.16	Pragmatics	Ideologues & Charismatics
9) Do institutions established by the leader still exist?	0.48	0.23	0.001	None	—	—	—
10) How many institutions were established by the leader?	0.20	0.04	0.403	None	—	—	—
11) Was the leader's visions maintained after they left power?	0.58	0.34	0.001	None	—	—	—
12) Did the leader initiate mass movements?	0.56	0.39	0.001	Rational influence	−0.27	Pragmatics	Ideologues & Charismatics
Political Criteria							
1) Amount of divisiveness arising from the leader's actions?	0.28	0.08	0.089	None	—	—	—
2) Maintenance over time of arrangements brought about by the leader's political behavior?	0.35	0.12	0.010	None	—	—	—
3) Institutionalization of the leader's base of influence?	0.48	0.23	0.001	None	—	—	—
4) Positive relationships of groups to leader?	0.48	0.23	0.001	None	—	—	—

Note. R = multiple correlation; R^2 = percentage of variance accounted for; p = significance level; Beta = standardized regression weight. Significant covariates are not presented in this table, only significant functions.

208

political tactics they employed. More specifically, pragmatic leaders, in contrast to charismatic and ideological leaders, were more likely to employ the tactics of rational influence (expertise, resources, and social relationships) than the tactics of control and intimidation (control of decision strategies, coalition building, and aggression). This tendency of pragmatic leaders to employ the tactics of rational influence while limiting impact resulted in less harm to society and more favorable appraisals.

CONCLUSIONS

These findings must be evaluated, however, taking into account certain limitations of the present study. To begin, although the political tactics examined in this study were based on a systematic taxonomy of the major kinds of political behavior discussed in the leadership literature (Ammeter et al., 2002; Yukl, 2002; Zanzi & O'Neil, 2001), it is possible that other taxonomies of relevant political behavior might be developed that would perhaps result in a somewhat different pattern of findings. Along related lines, although a wide variety of political behaviors were examined as potential manifestations of the various categories of political behavior under consideration, it is also true that not all possible political behaviors relevant to these categories were, or indeed could be, examined in the present study.

In fact, in this study the focus was on the kind of political behaviors likely to be described in the biographies of outstanding leaders. This point is of some importance because political behaviors exist, often behaviors linked to ingratiation, that are not commonly considered in academic biographies due to the paucity of historical evidence. As a result, the dimensions of political tactics, and the specific political behaviors linked to these tactics, must be viewed as a select sample of the domain of relevant dimensions and behaviors.

Finally, the results obtained in the present study were based on a particular measurement strategy. More specifically, tactics were assessed in terms of the frequency with which relevant behaviors appeared in incidents of significant political activity drawn from the biographies of outstanding leaders. The use of a frequency-based assessment strategy offers some distinct advantages with regard to objectivity—a point of some concern in studies of leader political behavior (Fedor & Maslyn, 2002). By the same token, however, certain attributes of political behavior, such as impact and compliance, cannot be taken into account when a frequency approach is applied in assessment.

Even taking these considerations into account, however, we believe that the results obtained in the present study have some important implications for understanding political behavior on the part of outstanding leaders. Earlier, we hypothesized that differences would be observed in the political tactics employed by socialized and personalized leaders. Although this hypothesis, a hypothesis based on the tendency of personalized leaders to evidence negative life themes and power motives (O'Connor et al., 1995), seemed plausible, it was not borne out by the results obtained in the present study. Put more directly, significant differences were *not* observed between socialized and personalized leaders with regard to the frequency with which different political tactics were used.

A potential explanation for this "nonfinding" may be found in the overall frequency with which outstanding leaders, regardless of orientation and type, employed the various political tactics under consideration. More specifically, outstanding leaders, across the board, displayed a surprising tendency to apply tactics such as control of decision strategies and aggression. What should be recognized here, however, is that outstanding leaders emerge under conditions of crisis and conflict. The demands made by crisis and conflict, however, may, regardless of orientation, require outstanding leaders to evidence a tough-minded orientation toward politics. In other words, outstanding leaders do what is necessary to get the job done, sometimes employing rather unattractive tactics in the cause of a greater good. An illustration of this point may be found in Table 8.6, which presents an incident of political behavior drawn from the biography of Franklin Roosevelt—a socialized charismatic.

Along related lines, it should be noted that the time, or career period, variable also failed to produce significant differences in the political tactics used by outstanding leaders. The obvious implication of this finding is that preferred political tactics are apparently quite stable across the course of leaders' careers. Thus, Joseph Stalin was equally likely to rely on aggressive tactics early as well as later in his career. A more subtle implication of this observation, however, is that something fundamental and enduring in leaders leads to substantial stability in preferred political tactics once they have begun to assume significant leadership roles.

TABLE 8.6
Illustration of Tough-Minded Political Behavior

Franklin Roosevelt

In February, Ickes told FDR that everyone knew Farley was disloyal. "You only have to look at his face at Cabinet to know that," FDR replied.

In August, FDR invited Farley to Hyde Park to try to tell him that if he was nominated he had no chance of winning. "I know perfectly well that you will have enough delegates at the next national convention to hold the balance of power," he said, and then outlined Farley's record, adding: "You don't want to spoil that record. Neither of us wants to nominate a ticket next year of such a sort that as we leave the Convention Hall we will know that that ticket will be defeated. Only liberal candidates on a liberal platform can win next year. I will not support anyone but a liberal. I will not support either a conservative or straddlebug. I will not support a tweedle-dumer. . . . I not only won't support a reactionary on the Democratic ticket, I will not support anyone who apologizes for the New Deal." The message did not get through, for Farley still had visions of the unattainable.

Note. From *FDR: A Biography*, by T. Morgan (1985, p. 517), New York: Simon & Schuster, Inc.

One potential explanation for this apparent stability in preferred political tactics may be found in Fiol et al.'s (2001) concept of power mental models. These schemata about how power is acquired and the ways in which power can be exercised to influence others, may represent stable, self-perpetuating, interpretive strategies if people interpret and respond to political incidents on the basis of schemata where events are appraised and outcomes assessed in terms of certain models. In other words, power mental models may create a confirmatory bias that results in substantial stability in people's preferred political tactics over time and situations.

Some support for this notion may be found in the differences observed among charismatic, ideological, and pragmatic leaders. Mumford and Van Doorn (2001) argued that pragmatic leaders emerge, and succeed, under conditions of consensus where influence is exercised through elites. Charismatic and ideological leaders, however, emerge, and succeed, under conditions of conflict where the leader's vision serves as a basis for resolution and integration of diverse perspectives. Given the conditions of their emergence, and their tendency to work through elites, it seems likely that pragmatic leaders will construct power mental models that stress rational economic exchange (Yukl, 2002). Charismatic and ideological leaders' power mental models, however, by virtue of the conditions of leader emergence, are likely to stress themes involving conflict leading to the use of tactics such as control of decision strategies, coalition building, and aggression.

These differences in the power mental models of pragmatic leaders as opposed to charismatic and ideological leaders are, in fact, consistent with our findings bearing on the use of rational influence techniques by pragmatic leaders. This difference between pragmatic and charismatic and ideological leaders is illustrated in Table 8.7, which presents the response of a pragmatic leader and a charismatic leader to a crisis arising during their period at the "pinnacle of power." These illustrations, however, make a broader point. Although we may find the tendency of charismatic and ideological leaders to eschew rational-influence techniques for control unattractive, this control orientation may, at times, prove highly effective.

These illustrations of the political tactics used by pragmatic leaders and the political tactics used by charismatic and ideological leaders point to a fundamental paradox posed by outstanding leadership in its varied real-world manifestations. The rational-influence tactics preferred by pragmatic leaders allow followers autonomy and freedom of action—autonomy and freedom of action that charismatic and ideological leaders take from followers through control of decision strategies, coalition building, and the threat implied by the potential for aggression. Though we may value freedom and autonomy, it comes at a cost in that it limits the leader's potential impact on followers, and society, at least over the short run. Over the long run, however, as indicated by our findings contrasting leader types with regard to performance, the rational-in-

TABLE 8.7
Illustrations of Effective Political Behavior by a Pragmatic
Leader and a Charismatic Leader in a Crisis Situation

Warren Buffett—Pragmatic

By early October 12, the yield on long-term bonds had risen to nearly 10 percent—up from only 7.4 percent as recently as March. On October 6, the Dow plunged 91.55 points, a one-day record. Markets had entered the vaporous territory in which events take on a life of their own and historical accidents may occur. In short, things were becoming serious.

On about October 12, Buffett cashed out the stock portfolio of at least one of Berkshire's profit-sharing plans. It cleaned the larder of stocks, save for his permanent three. According to a Buffett associate, "It was a clear edict: 'Sell everything.' "

Buffett was not making a forecast; he was merely obeying two cherished rules. Rule No. 1: "Never lose money." Rule No. 2: "Never forget Rule No. 1." Munger said, "Warren would never claim that he could call the market." But perhaps Buffett had been glancing a bit more anxiously at the newspaper clipping on his wall—the one from 1929. In the week following, interest rates climbed above 10 percent. Japanese shares continued to rise, but now no one Wall Street cared about Japan. On Friday, October 16, the Dow plunged 108 points.

Winston Churchill—Charismatic

Three days after this meeting, the Free State Government ended its economic blockade of Ulster, and, as envisaged by the Treaty, Free Trade began at once between North and South. On January 30, as a further gesture of conciliation to the South, Churchill prevailed upon Lloyd George, against strong War Office objections, to release thirteen Irish soldiers who had mutinied in India in 1920 and been sentenced by court martial to life imprisonment.

As friction broke out over the actual line of the border between North and South, Churchill strove to calm the tempers that fared again into violence. "I am glad to have this task in my hands," he wrote to Clementine on February 4, "and hope to be able to steer a good course between all the storms and rocks." On February 15, after thirty people had been killed in Belfast in five days by Irish Republican Army extremists who rejected the Treaty, Churchill again saw Collins in London. The two men agreed to a Boundary Commission, made up of two groups, one from the North and the other from the South, to consult together and resolve, from village to village and farm to farm, the precise line of the border.

Note. Buffett is from *Buffett: The Making of an American Capitalist*, by R. Lowenstein (1995, p. 303), New York: Random House. Reprinted by permission. Churchill is from *Churchill: A Life*, by M. Gilbert (1991, p. 444). Copyright © 1991 by Martin Gilbert. Reprinted by permission of Henry Holt and Co.

fluence tactics preferred by pragmatic leaders may prove more effective with respect to the development of lasting institutions while minimizing the risk to society imposed by the need for political behavior on the part of outstanding leaders. In this sense, our findings seem to confirm the political wisdom underlying the U.S. Constitution, which, at least in some ways, was intended to sacrifice leader impact for the cause of rational influence and follower autonomy (Ellis, 2001).

III

EARLY DISTINCT PATHWAYS
TO OUTSTANDING LEADERSHIP

9

Development—What Early Life Experiences Prepare You for Outstanding Leadership?

Michael D. Mumford
Ginamarie Scott
Richard T. Marcy
Margaret J. Tutt
Jazmine Espejo
The University of Oklahoma

In reading the biographies of outstanding leaders, one often becomes preoccupied with a nagging question: Just how did the early life of the leader shape his or her subsequent career? This question, a question clearly fundamental to understanding outstanding leadership, is not easily answered. The lives of outstanding leaders, like the lives of most people, appear to be characterized by *both* continuity and change (Mumford & Manley, 2003)—a complex pattern of continuity and change that makes it difficult to say exactly how early experiences operate in determining the course of a leader's career.

This point is aptly illustrated in Chernow's (1998) biography of John D. Rockefeller. Rockefeller's father was something of a scoundrel, albeit a rather charming scoundrel. This was a man who left his family to sell "snake oil" in a traveling medicine show. In his personal life, Rockefeller, a devoted Christian and family man, could not be more different from his father. With regard to certain business practices, however, Rockefeller seemed far more similar to his father than one might expect based on his personal life. In fact, in old age, he became something of a gambler, playing the market and playing the ladies.

Our intent in the present chapter is to examine how leaders' early lives shape their subsequent careers. More specifically, we examine how early developmental experiences begin moving leaders along a charismatic, ideological, or pragmatic pathway and how these early experiences give rise to a socialized or personalized orientation. In this regard, it is necessary to bear in mind a point of departure implied by this objective. Traditionally, studies of leader development have focused on the acquisition of requisite skills (Day & O'Connor,

2003). In this chapter, our concern is not skill acquisition but rather the developmental influences that shape people's approach to leadership—a question of differential development.

Differential development, like human development in general, is a highly complex phenomenon. Accordingly, a number of models have been proposed that might be used to understand differential development, and many of these models have, in fact, been applied in attempts to understand leader development. For example, Popper, Mayseless, and Castlenovo (2000) argued that leader emergence and leaders' careers are determined, at least in part, by early attachment styles. In their model, secure attachments give rise to a prosocial orientation and a willingness to engage others and engage crises. An alternative model may be found in Fiedler and Chemers (1982). Fiedler and Chemers' model flows from earlier work by Adler (e.g., Ansbacher & Ansbacher, 1956). Essentially, this model holds that leader development is driven by an attempt on the part of the individual to compensate for deficiencies and capitalize on perceived strengths. Still another model, one proposed by Erikson (1959), holds that leader development, and the pathways people follow as leaders, are a reflection of the social identities formed in response to personal crises.

Identity, compensatory, and attachment models all have some value in accounting for certain aspects of leader development. For example, Rockefeller's father may have been instrumental in both the formation of his son's business identity and his compensatory adoption of a Christian-family orientation. Although we do not wish to dispute the potential value of these models for understanding the development of charismatic, ideological, and pragmatic leaders, in the present chapter we argue that leader development is perhaps better understood using an alternative model. More specifically, we argue that the nature of the life narrative, or life stories, constructed by leaders as a mechanism for giving meaning to their life experiences provides the driving force underlying the emergence of charismatic, ideological, and pragmatic leaders.

Sensemaking

Clearly, a number of general theoretical models are available that might be used to understand the development of charismatic, ideological, and pragmatic leadership. The availability of these alternative models, however, begs a question: Why apply a life narrative framework in accounting for the origins of charismatic, ideological, and pragmatic leadership? This question is perhaps best answered by returning to the general theory of outstanding leadership presented in chapter 2.

Essentially, this theory holds that outstanding leadership, regardless of type, is a leadership of crisis. In other words, outstanding leadership occurs, and outstanding leaders emerge, when change leads to suboptimal performance in a social system in which the leader is embedded (Hunt et al., 1999). Crises create the opportunity for, and indeed the need for, outstanding leadership because people exposed to crises seek leaders who can make sense of the crisis (Drazin et al., 1999). Sensemaking activities on the part of leaders not only reduce stress and identify goals and paths to goal attainment, they provide a framework for collective action and the maintenance of group and personal identity (Shamir et al., 1993).

The theory of outstanding leadership presented in chapter 2 holds that leaders' sensemaking is based on the formation and articulation of a prescriptive mental model. These prescriptive mental models are built upon a descriptive mental model that describes the operations and objectives of the system "as is." Crises trigger reexamination and reconfiguration of these descriptive mental models (Strange & Mumford, 2002) through an analysis of goals and of the causes of goal attainment. In this framework, what distinguishes sensemaking, and the formation of prescriptive mental models, from plans is that they involve a self-analytical or self-reflective component. In other words, sensemaking and the formation of prescriptive mental models are not simply reflections of the crisis but rather the leader's analysis of the crisis in terms of their personal history.

Some rather compelling support for this proposition may be found in Strange and Mumford (2005). In this study, undergraduates were asked to form a vision for a new experimental school after having been presented with good or poor benchmark models under conditions where a search for goal and/or causes had been activated. The positive effects of a search for goals when poor models had been presented, however, were found to be moderated by reflection on past experiences in relation to these goals and causes. Strong prescriptive models, as defined in terms of viable vision statements, were obtained when people reflected on their past lives in relation to the situation at hand. This finding is of critical importance because it indicates that leaders' understanding of themselves, and their own lives, plays a key role in shaping the kind of prescriptive mental models they construct.

Life Narratives

Life narratives, or life stories, are defined as cognitive schemata by which people understand and make sense of the events that have occurred in their lives (Bluck & Habermas, 2000). Thus, a life narrative may be seen as a cognitive, conceptual construction that people use to summarize, organize, and interpret life events. This summarization, a narrative or storylike summarization with a distinct temporal causal orientation (Sarbin, 1986), is used as an explanatory structure that allows people to maintain a sense of continuity in their lives and establish a sense of identity (McAdams, 2001; Neimeyer & Metzler, 1994). In addition to providing people with a sense of continuity and identity, life narratives serve two other key functions (Bluck, 2003).

First, they appear to provide direction to the courses of people's lives. Life narratives are schematic structures that include information about goals, causes, actions, and settings that have salient consequences for the individual.

People appear to refer to these past events, using them as case models for under-standing current events. In keeping with this proposition, Lockhart (1989) and Pillemer (2003) found that people can abstract goals and causes from past events and use this information to forecast the consequences of current events and reactions to these events. More centrally, the available evidence suggests that when people are exposed to crises, they are especially likely to apply life narratives as a mechanism for understanding and responding to events (Bluck & Staudinger, 2000; Pillemer, 1998; Taylor & Schneider, 1984). The tendency of people to rely on life narratives as a mechanism for understanding and coping with change or crises is, of course, consistent with the tendency of leaders to re-flect on their past lives in the formation of prescriptive mental models.

Second, life narratives provide a vehicle for people to communicate personal understanding of their lives and the situations in which they find themselves (Alea & Bluck, 2003; J. M. Fitzgerald, 1995). In other words, we communicate with, influence, and establish relationships with others in terms of our under-standing of our own lives. How people convey life narratives, and the parts of autobiographical experiences recalled in conveying narratives, appears to de-pend on the content of the interaction (Barclay, 1995; Miller, 1994). This social shaping of life narratives, moreover, allows people to convey, test, and refine their understanding of the situation (Barclay, 1995)—its implications for them-selves and its implications for others. These social interactional effects of life narratives may, in fact, allow leaders to construct interpersonally evocative pre-scriptive mental models and effectively convey these models to followers.

Taken as a whole, it appears that life narratives, and autobiographical rea-soning based on these narratives, provide outstanding leaders with a basis for di-rection and effective interaction. Thus, it is not surprising that reflection on these narratives is critical to construction of prescriptive mental models and the formation of viable vision statements. Given the impact of life narratives on for-mation of prescriptive mental models, it seems plausible to argue that life narra-tives, or life stories, may represent a key mechanism by which developmental experiences influence the nature of, and actions taken by, outstanding leaders.

The potential influence of life narratives on leadership points to the need to understand the content, structure, and development of narrative schemata. Bluck (2003), Bluck and Habermas (2001), and Habermas and Bluck (2000) argued that although life narratives are ultimately based on autobiographical memory, they represent a selective reconstruction (Conway, 1995, 1996). Life narratives do not contain, or reflect, all of the events that have occurred throughout the entirety of our lives. Rather, they contain information that per-mits the formation of a coherent narrative.

In Habermas and Bluck's (2000) view, coherent narratives derive, or are built, vis-à-vis four mechanisms that may be used to structure and organize life events. First, coherence arises from cultural expectations about the narratives of autobiographical material. Second, it is often brought about by imposition of a temporal sequence to include a chronological sequence of life tasks

(Havinghurst, 1953). Third, it may be based on the identification of general causes influencing life events, especially goal-relevant, or consequential, life events (Bluck, 2003; J. M. Fitzgerald, 1995). The fourth, and final source of coherence may be found in the themes, or principles, that bind causes, outcomes, and events together.

The critical implication of this coherence theory is that life narratives, and autobiographical reasoning with these narratives, will tend to emerge in late childhood and adolescence as people acquire the ability to think about themselves, and their lives, in terms of abstract causes. In keeping with this proposition, Habermas and Paha (2001), in a content analysis of autobiographical narratives obtained from 12-, 15-, and 18-year-olds, found that life narrative coherence increased with age as a function of the number and complexity of causal linkages. Some further support for this proposition was provided by Bluck and Habermas (2001) and Habermas and Bluck (2000). They found that people, in describing their lives, tend to spontaneously report more events drawn from late childhood, adolescence, and young adulthood—a pattern of recall that would be expected if formation and consolidation of narrative schemata was occurring during these developmental periods.

Although life narrative formation depends on the construction of a schematic organizing framework based on causes and thematic principles, as is the case with most knowledge structures, the overarching organization appears to be built around prototypic exemplars, ongoing episodes, and key life events (Mobley, Doares, & Mumford, 1992). The role of exemplar events in the formation of life narratives was discussed by Korte (1995), McAdams (2001), and Pillemer (2001). Broadly speaking, people tend to remember, and view as critical exemplars, unusual, unexpected, nonroutine life events that had important consequences and were emotionally evocative (Brewer, 1986). These unique consequential, emotionally laden events, particularly events encountered in late childhood, adolescence, and early adulthood, appear to provide the substantive basis, or key exemplars, around which life narrative schemata are constructed.

Leader Types

Having provided a description of life narratives and their development, the question arises as to how narratives, and narrative differences, give rise to different pathways to outstanding leadership. Broadly speaking, the nature and structure of life narratives suggests that differences will be observed among outstanding leaders in two domains. First, one might expect that outstanding leaders, charismatic, ideological, and pragmatic leaders, and the personalized and socialized variants of each, will differ in the kind of events playing a preeminent role in the definition of life narratives or life stories. Second, outstanding leaders may differ with respect to the themes evident in key life events.

In fact, given the nature of the prescriptive mental models applied by charismatic, ideological, and pragmatic leaders, there is reason to expect that differences will be observed in the kind of events used to define life narratives. For example, by virtue of their importance in defining goals and values, it can be expected that anchoring events will prove particularly important in shaping the lives of ideological leaders. In contrast, one might expect that turning point and redemption events, by virtue of their emphasis on positive, proactive change, will prove especially important in lives of charismatic leaders. Finally, one might expect that pragmatic leaders will tend to base life narratives on originating events—events providing concrete action guidelines.

Not only is there reason to suspect that charismatic, ideological, and pragmatic leaders will differ with regard to the salience, or importance, of event types in narratives, one would also expect to see differences among socialized and personalized leaders in this regard. Given the tendency of personalized leaders to express negative life themes, outcome uncertainty, and power motives (O'Connor et al., 1995), it seems reasonable to expect that contaminating events will play a particularly important role in defining the life narratives of personalized leaders. On the other hand, the life narratives of socialized leaders should tend to emphasize redemptive events.

In addition to cross-type differences in events, it seems likely that differences will also be observed in the thematic organization of these events. A case in point may be found in temporal organization. Charismatic leaders can be expected to organize events in terms of their causal implications for the future. Ideological leaders, however, will tend to stress the casual implications of the past whereas pragmatic leaders emphasize the present. What should also be recognized here, however, is that a variety of other thematic differences may arise in contrasting charismatic, ideological, and pragmatic leaders. For example, given their emphasis on proactive change based on people's actions, one would expect that personal achievements and risk taking will represent salient thematic constructs in the lives of charismatic leaders. In the case of ideological leaders, it seems reasonable to argue that spiritual themes will prove important in organizing life events. In the case of pragmatic leaders, themes stressing the importance of evidence and incremental progress should prove to play a noteworthy role in binding together relevant life events.

It can also be expected that socialized and personalized leaders will display differences in the thematic content of their life narratives. Specifically, given the characteristics of personalized leaders (e.g., negative life themes, outcome uncertainty), it can be expected that themes stressing distrust and control will be evident in the life events of personalized leaders. In contrast, themes stressing the value of interpersonal commitment should be evident in the life events of socialized leaders.

Summary

Our foregoing observations about development indicate that the kind of life narratives constructed by leaders in late childhood, adolescence, and young adulthood will represent a potentially powerful influence on the prescriptive mental models constructed by outstanding leaders. Moreover, the nature of these life narratives, or life stories, suggests that a systematic pattern of differences will be observed among charismatic, ideological, and pragmatic leaders with respect to both the kind of events found to be important in leaders' lives and the themes that tie these events together. These differences in narrative content and themes may also help account for the expression of socialized and personalized behavior on the part of outstanding leaders.

METHOD

Study Method

Event Content.   The material examining leaders' lives during late childhood, adolescence, and young adulthood, the period when life narratives are being constructed, appears in the early-career chapters of biographies—typically chapters placed prior to the rise-to-power chapters. Accordingly, a psychologist reviewed these early-career sections and identified those chapters that described the childhood, adolescence, and young-adulthood experiences of the leader. Thus, chapters examining general family background and experiences in infancy and early childhood were not considered. Typically, three to six relevant chapters were identified describing the leaders' late childhood, adolescence, and young adulthood, which, in total, were 40 to 50 pages long.

Four undergraduates unfamiliar with the intent of the present study were asked to review the material presented in these chapters and identify (a) originating events, (b) anchoring events, (c) analogous events, (d) turning point events, (e) redemptive events, and (f) contaminating events. Prior to this event identification exercise, these undergraduates participated in a 16-hour training program where they were familiarized with the nature of these events and given training. The kappa coefficients for agreement in identification and classification of these events ranged from .64 to .98 across the six event types. Thus, the training appeared to result in reliable identification of the relevant events. Typically, these events were a half to a full page in length with 15 to 30 events falling into one of the six categories being identified for the 120 leaders included in the sample. Thus, roughly 1,400 events were identified for the 120 leaders under consideration in the present study. Table 9.1 presents illustrations of each of the six event types under consideration.

Thematic Coding.   After material describing salient events had been abstracted from the biographies, a content analysis intended to capture the themes appearing in these events was conducted. Initially, a review of the available literature on charismatic (e.g., Conger & Kanungo, 1998), ideological (e.g., Strange & Mumford, 2002), and pragmatic leadership (e.g., Mumford & Van Doorn, 2001) was conducted to identify thematic dimen-

TABLE 9.1
Examples of Event Types Drawn From Leader Biographies

Event Type	Benchmark Example
Originating Event	"From an early age, the young Rupert [Murdoch] was aware of the power and the glory and the sheer fun which accrued to his father from newspapers. Keith [Rupert's father] used to take his son around the Herald's office on Flinders Street, and Rupert often said later that the smell of the ink, the noise of the presses and the highly charged atmosphere were irresistible. 'The life of a publisher is the best life in the whole world. When kids are subjected to it there's not much doubt they'll be attracted to it.' " (Shawcross, 1992, p. 27)
Turning Point Event	"The most dramatic story concerns Lewis's involvement in the 1903 disaster at the Union Pacific Railroad Company's coal mine in Hanna, WY. Passing through the area by chance, Lewis arrived in time to assist a rescue team in carrying out the torn, charred bodies of 234 miners . . . 'what ripped his emotions to shreds was the sight of the numb, mute faces of the wives now suddenly widows of the men they loved.' " (Dubofsky & Van Tine, 1986, pp. 14–15)
Anchoring Event	"In what Fidel calls, 'a decisive moment on my life,' Angel Castro decided during the boys' summer holiday after the 4th grade that they would not go back to school . . . But Fidel [Castro] was determined to return to school. As he tells the story, 'I remember going to mother and explaining to her that I wanted to go on studying; it wasn't fair not to let me go to school. I appealed to her and told her I would set fire to the house if I wasn't sent back . . . so they decided to send me back. I'm not sure if they were afraid or just sorry for me, but my mother pleaded my case.' Fidel was learning quickly that absolute and uncompromising stubbornness was a powerful weapon. This may have been the most important lesson he had drawn from his young years at the *finca*, and he never forgot it." (Szulc, 1986, p. 112)
Analogous Event	"Almost forty years later, on the occasion of a commencement address at Fisk, and perhaps under the influence of the occasion, DuBois recalled those three years of 'splendid inspiration' and nearly 'perfect happiness' with teachers whom he respected, amid surroundings which inspired him. The ten years after Fisk he chronicled as 'a sort of prolongation of my Fisk college days. I was at Harvard, but not of it. I was a student of Berlin but still a son of Fisk. I used my days there to understand my new setting. . . .' " (Broderick, 1959, p. 9)
Redemption Event	"She [Betty Friedan], who had been the ringleader and chief instigator, the one who generated all the excitement, was suddenly alone, abandoned by her friends. The creator of clubs was not chosen for the most exclusive club at all— the high school sorority. She was desolate . . . The year of loneliness that followed was the lowest point of her life. She blamed it primarily on anti-Semitism . . . The sight of the car full of friend, a vision that she yearned for, triggered something in her, and she made a promise to herself: 'They may not like me now, but [someday] they are going to look up to me.' " (Hennessee, 1999, p. 15)
Contaminating Event	"To Mao [Ze-Dong], the failure of the independence movement was a grievous disappointment. All his efforts over the past year, he told friends, had been to 'no avail.' The Huaneses had shown themselves to be 'muddle-headed, with neither ideals nor long-term plans. In political circles, they are lethargic and extremely corrupt, and we can say that there is absolutely no hope for political reform.' It was time to start afresh, he wrote, to 'carve a new path.' " (Short, 1999, p. 109)

sions apparent in the lives of each type of leader. This literature review led to the identification of 63 candidate thematic dimensions. These dimensions were then reviewed for redundancy, clarity, and criticality. This review resulted in the identification of 28 key dimensions that appeared to capture critical thematic organizing principles applied by outstanding leaders. These thematic dimensions are presented in Table 9.2 along with supporting citations and a set of two to four behavioral benchmarks intended to illustrate how these themes are manifest in people's lives.

Rating Procedure. A panel of six judges was asked to review the material presented in each life event drawn from the biographies in relation to the thematic dimensions and behavioral benchmarks. A modified Q-sort procedure was then applied where judges were asked to assign an event to these dimensions reflecting relevant thematic content (McAdams, Hoffman, Mansfield, & Day, 1996; McKeon & Thomas, 1988; Woike, 1995). Specifically, judges were asked to indicate whether a given event did or did not reflect relevant thematic content for each of the 28 dimensions under consideration. Scoring occurred by determining those dimensions to which the majority of the judges assigned an event. Dimension scores were obtained for a leader by determining the number of events identified for a leader assigned to a given dimension, and then dividing by the total number of events identified for the leader under consideration.

Prior to making these assignments the judges were provided with a 24-hour training program extended over 2 weeks. Initially, judges were familiarized with the thematic dimensions and the nature of the events abstracted from the biographies along with the procedures to be applied in appraising the thematic content of these events. Following this initial training, judges were presented with sample biographical material and asked to apply these rating procedures. After making these initial evaluations, judges met as a panel to discuss observed discrepancies. At that time, feedback was provided to clarify decision rules, dimensional definitions, and application of the rating procedure. These practice sessions continued until the judges evidenced adequate agreement. The interrater agreement coefficients resulting from application of these procedures ranged between .56 and .63 using a kappa statistic. These agreement coefficients are considered adequate when assignments are being made to a relatively large number of categories.

Study-Specific Controls. The control measures applied in the present study consisted of the general historic and role attribute measures described earlier. In addition to these general control measures, a select set of control measures was obtained to capture variables uniquely relevant to developmental influences. These study-specific controls included: (a) presence of theoretical assumptions about the nature of developmental influences (Freudian, educational, etc.), (b) amount of objective, detailed information available for devel-

TABLE 9.2
Thematic Constructs Used in Event Content Coding

	Behavioral Examples	*Justification for Inclusion*
FUTURE FOCUS	• Speaking about concern for future goals or conditions • Prioritizing future goals over present needs or past standards	Charismatic leaders communicate visions that are loosely tied to a set of future goals (House, 1977; House & Howell, 1992; Shamir, House, & Arthur, 1993)
INSPIRATIONAL COMMUNICATION	• Persuading others using emotional or affective communication • Practice in speaking techniques such as debate or drama club	Charismatic leaders use affective speech as primary means of influence (Conger, 1989; House & Podsakoff, 1994)
IMAGE MANAGEMENT	• Role modeling desired behaviors • Concern with appearance to others	Charismatic leaders tend to exert direct influence on followers by role modeling desired behaviors (House, 1977)
RISK TAKING	• Engaging in risky endeavors • Risk-taking behavior is rewarded	Charismatic leaders engage in public risk taking to convey heroic image for followers (Conger & Kanungo, 1998; House, 1977)
PERSONAL ACHIEVEMENT	• Making obvious contributions to performance or letting others know about achievements • Direct-influence tactics such as taking credit for accomplishments	Charismatic leaders tend to take credit for contributions and engage in highly visible leadership activities (House & Howell, 1992)
PERFORMANCE EXPECTATIONS	• Witnessing rewards for high expectations • Viewing accomplishments in terms of overall goal attainment versus incremental progress	Charismatic leaders convey high expectations to followers through their visions and other direct communications (House & Podsakoff, 1994)
CHANGE EFFORTS	• Witnessing dramatic change efforts to status quo • Large-scale change efforts are rewarded	Visions of charismatic leaders portray a model for the future that is markedly different from the status quo (Shamir, House, & Arthur, 1993; Weber, 1947)
EXPOSURE TO CRISES	• Experiencing some type of crisis or emergency • Witnessing control through a crisis (having a role model of how to effectively deal with crises)	Charismatic leaders often emerge in times of crisis or events marked with instability and change (Hunt, Boal, & Dodge, 1999; House & Howell, 1992)

(Continued)

TABLE 9.2
(Continued)

	Behavioral Examples	Justification for Inclusion
PAST FOCUS	• Preferring past conditions, traditions, or way of life • Focusing on history or historical events and/or people	Ideological leaders often point to past group status or traditions in communicating their visions (Strange & Mumford, 2002)
BELIEF COMMIT-MENT	• Discounting alternative views that are not congruent with belief system • Denying normal allowances (e.g., types of food, material possessions) due to belief system	Ideological leaders use their belief systems to make decisions, influence and select followers, and motivate others (Robinson, 1996; Strange & Mumford, 2002)
SPIRITUALITY	• Viewing faith, morals, and/or religion as primary directive in life • Using symbols and/or rituals to reflect religion or spirituality	Ideological leaders view spirituality as most important aspect of daily life and display this belief through use of symbols and rituals (Post, Ruby, & Shaw, 2002)
ENVIRONMENTAL CONFLICT	• Experiencing societal events that change the way that individuals live and/or interact • Witnessing war, leader assassination, and/or change in resources	Ideological leaders tend to arise from conditions of marked societal turbulence (Post, Ruby, & Shaw, 2002)
INJUSTICE	• Witnessing inequitable distribution of resources or income disparity between groups • Seeing group as indebted by society for past wrongs	Ideological leaders' visions are based on restoring past glory or rightful place in society to group members and may be based on a sensitivity to injustice or victimization (Bond, Kwan, & Li, 2003; Hogan & Dickstein, 1972)
PRESENT FOCUS	• Surveying current conditions • Gathering information about people and problems in current situation	Pragmatic leaders place an emphasis on day-to-day current problems (Mumford & Van Doorn, 2001; Qin & Simon, 1990)
ANALYSIS	• Applying a logical or step-by-step process of problem solving • Witnessing flexible or malleable decision making	Pragmatic leaders amend their problem-solving strategies based on logical analysis of incoming feedback (Bartone, Snook, & Tremble, 2002; Mumford & Van Doorn, 2001)
EVIDENTIAL PREF-ERENCE	• Exposure to factual data (e.g., numbers, statistical analyses) use in decision making • Disconfirming beliefs and values in face of conflicting facts or data	Pragmatic leaders prefer to use concrete evidence to (a) make decisions and (b) influence followers (Mumford & Van Doorn, 2001)

(Continued)

TABLE 9.2
(Continued)

	Behavioral Examples	*Justification for Inclusion*
INCREMENTAL PROGRESS	• Viewing need for gradual achievements toward a goal • Delaying gratification for end state/outcome in order to break problem down into more manageable steps	Pragmatic leaders rely on iterative problem-solving activities to define and solve complex organizational problems (Reiter-Palmon & Illies, 2004)
EXPOSURE TO DIVERSITY	• Experiencing diverse people, places, and ideas • Searching for similar and nonsimilar properties of diverse people and ideas	Pragmatic problem solving relies on an integration of discrepant concepts to form unique solutions to everyday problems (D. H. Feldman, 1999; H. Gardner, 1993b)
POSITIVE VIEW OF OTHERS	• Appraising others positively or kindly • Expressing concern for the safety, needs, and happiness of others	Socialized leaders base their problem-solving efforts on the good of others (House & Howell, 1992)
POSITIVE VIEW OF SELF	• Experiencing praise or assurance from others about personal abilities • Expressing confidence in one's own ability	Socialized leaders are able to trust others based on prior experiences of reliance and confidence (McClelland, 1975)
COMMITMENT TO OTHERS	• Expressing sense of responsibility to welfare of others • Making personal sacrifices for good of the group	Socialized leaders prioritize group needs above personal motives (J. A. O'Connor, Mumford, Clifton, Gessner, & Connelly, 1995)
EXPOSURE TO SUFFERING	• Witnessing others suffer pain or life strife • Empathizing with others' suffering	Socialized leaders demonstrate a marked concern for the well-being of others; such empathy may be developed through experiences with others' pain (Nidich, Nidich, & Alexander, 2000)
UNCERTAINTY/ POWERLESSNESS	• Experiencing powerless due to rapidly changing situation • Experiencing insecurity due to lack of control over one's own situation	Personalized leaders evidence a strong need to protect themselves over the good of the group (Goodstadt & Hjelle, 1973; Martin, Scully, & Levitt, 1990)
NEGATIVE VIEW OF OTHERS	• Expressing distrust of others, possibly due to abandonment and rejection from others in past • Viewing others as objects or means to an end with little regard for their safety or needs	Personalized leaders are willing to use others as tools or objects for personal gain (Eisenberg & Miller, 1987; House & Howell, 1992)

(Continued)

TABLE 9.2
(Continued)

	Behavioral Examples	Justification for Inclusion
NEGATIVE VIEW OF SELF	• Viewing others as superior to self, either internally or hearing such appraisals from others • Experiencing doubt in personal abilities	Narcissism, or a motivated defense of a weak-self system based on early experiences (Emmons, 1981; Fromm, 1973) is associated with personalized leadership (J. A. O'Connor et al., 1995)
POWER MOTIVES	• Subduing or overpowering others in pursuit of personal goals • Converting others to serve personal goals with use of threat, promise of reward, and/or persuasion	Personalized leaders have a high need for power and justify harm to others in pursuit of such personal needs (McClelland, 1975; J. A. O'Connor et al., 1995)
NEGATIVE LIFE THEMES	• Expressing a destructive image of the world and one's place in it • Viewing world as evil, sinister, and cruel	Personalized leaders' lack of concern for social system may be due to their negative perceptions or worldview (J. A. O'Connor et al., 1995)
FOCUS ON SELF (OVER OTHERS)	• Prioritizing protection of oneself over welfare of others • Exaggerating one's own abilities and skills in presence of a group	Self-protection and self-aggrandizement are positively associated with personalized leadership (House & Howell, 1992)

opmental events, (c) number of developmental events, (d) length of developmental events, (e) number of pages devoted to the development, (f) age at rise to power, (g) amount of external documentation provided for developmental events, (h) source of information about developmental events (teachers, siblings, friends, etc.), and (i) the number of leader recollections used as a basis for describing developmental events. The counts and rating scales used to appraise these control variables produced an average interrater agreement coefficient of .94 using the procedures suggested by Shrout and Fleiss (1979).

Study-Specific Criteria. To examine the influence of thematic content on performance, the 12 general criteria derived from the prologue, or epilogue, chapter were applied (e.g., how many positive contributions? how many people did the leader affect?). Because the primary concern in the study at hand was the influence of thematic event content on overall performance, no study-specific criteria were applied. In the following chapter, however, we examine the influence of these thematic dimensions on leader behavior in the areas of problem solving, leader–follower relationships, communication strategies, and political tactics.

Summary

The present study was based on a two-stage methodological approach. Initially, critical life events relevant to the construction of life narratives were abstracted from biographies and these events were classified into one of six event types: (a) originating, (b) anchoring, (c) analogous, (d) turning point, (e) redemptive, and (f) contamination. The frequency with which these events were identified as significant influences on leaders' careers was then used to examine the similarities and differences among outstanding leaders with respect to event exposure. Next, the thematic content evident in the events identified for a given leader was assessed using a modified Q-sort procedure. Leaders were to be compared with respect to the themes evident in events occurring during the period of life narrative construction. The implication of these differences in thematic content for leader performance was to be assessed.

RESULTS

Life Events

Table 9.3 presents the results obtained in the chi-square analyses contrasting socialized and personalized leaders with respect to the frequency with which different types of life events appeared in the early-career chapters of leader biographies. Before comparing leaders in this regard, it might be useful to consider the frequency with which different types of events were identified. Originating and anchoring events, the key events used in constructing life narratives, were frequently identified in biographies. As expected, turning point, redemptive, and contamination events appeared less frequently than originating and anchoring events. Relatively few analogous events were identified, however, perhaps reflecting the fact that the focus of the present study was early development of life narratives—a period where relatively few analogous events are typically observed. Given the frequency of analogous events, we focus on differ-

TABLE 9.3
Frequency of Event Types by Orientation

	Originating	Anchoring	Analogous	Turning Point	Redemption	Contaminating
Socialized						
Frequency	150	236	14	93	127	117
Percent[a]	49.3	54.8	73.7	53.4	61.7	44.3
Personalized						
Frequency	154	195	5	81	79	147
Percent[a]	50.7	45.2	26.3	46.6	38.3	55.7

[a]Percent within type of event.

ences among leaders with respect to originating, anchoring, turning point, contamination, and redemptive events.

In contrasting socialized and personalized leaders with regard to the frequency with which these event types appeared in leader biographies, a significant $[\chi^2(5) = 19.56, p \leq .01]$ chi-square was obtained. As expected, contaminating events were observed more frequently in the biographies of personalized leaders ($n = 147$ vs. $n = 117$) whereas redemptive events were observed more frequently in the biographies of socialized leaders ($n = 127$ vs. $n = 77$). Apparently, loss and disappointment result in the construction of negative life narratives whereas unexpected progress, often progress attributable to the aid of others, results in a more positive prosocial worldview (Gessner et al., 1993; Oyserman & Markus, 1990).

In this regard, however, it should be noted that socialized and personalized leaders also differed with respect to another kind of life events. More specifically, anchoring events were identified more frequently in the biographies of socialized leaders ($n = 236$) than personalized leaders ($n = 195$). This pattern of findings suggests that events leading to the development of strong personal-value systems are integral to the emergence of a socialized orientation in later life perhaps because these values buffer leaders against contaminating influences.

Table 9.4 presents the results obtained in contrasting charismatic, ideological, and pragmatic leaders with respect to these events. Again, a significant $[\chi^2(10) = 51.58, p \leq .001]$ was obtained indicating that charismatic, ideological, and pragmatic leaders differ in the kind of events they encounter during the period when they are forming life narratives. More specifically, charismatic, ideological, and pragmatic leaders differ in the frequency with which redemptive events, anchoring events, turning point events, and originating events are reported in biographies.

Ideological leaders, consistent with their emphasis on beliefs and values, were substantially more likely to be exposed to anchoring events during the pe-

TABLE 9.4
Frequency of Event Types by Leader Type

	Originating	Anchoring	Analogous	Turning Point	Redemption	Contaminating
Charismatic						
Frequency	102	116	7	71	71	93
Percent[a]	33.6	26.9	36.8	40.8	34.5	35.2
Ideological						
Frequency	88	206	4	47	58	83
Percent[a]	28.9	47.8	21.1	27.0	28.2	31.4
Charismatic						
Frequency	114	109	8	56	77	88
Percent[a]	37.5	25.3	42.1	32.2	37.4	33.3

[a]Percent within type of event.

riod of life narrative formation than either charismatic or pragmatic leaders (n = 206 vs. n = 113). This effect of value anchoring was such that turning point events were less likely to be evident in the lives of ideological leaders than the lives of charismatic and pragmatic leaders (n = 47 vs. n = 63). Similarly, ideological leaders were less likely to evidence exposure to redemptive events than charismatic and pragmatic leaders (n = 56 vs. n = 74). Thus, as a whole, it appears that ideological leaders, in contrast to charismatic and pragmatic leaders, remain on a steady course—a course established by anchoring events that provides a basis for defining core beliefs and values.

In contrast, charismatic leaders were more likely than ideological and pragmatic leaders to evidence exposure to turning point events (n = 71 vs. n = 52). Turning point events, of course, play a particularly important role in shaping the lives of charismatic leaders because they illustrate the value of proactive change—an experience that may encourage charismatic leaders to act as change agents in their later lives. Pragmatic leaders differed from charismatic and ideological leaders (n = 114 vs. n = 95) in that they were more likely to evidence exposure to originating events. This difference, however, is not especially surprising when one remembers that originating events frame the plans and goals—central components in complex social problem solving (Mumford & Van Doorn, 2001).

In considering these general trends, however, it is important to bear in mind the significant $[\chi^2(25) = 93.02, p \leq .001]$ chi-square obtained in examining the interaction between the type and orientation variables. This interaction, illustrated in Table 9.5, appeared to be linked to four major effects. First, as might be expected based on our foregoing observations, socialized ideologues were especially likely to evidence exposure to anchoring events (n = 114 vs. n = 63.4). Personalized pragmatic leaders, however, were especially *unlikely* to evidence exposure to anchoring events (n = 41 vs. n = 78)—a finding suggesting that opportunism resulting from the lack of value anchors may help account for destructiveness on the part of pragmatic leaders.

Second, in keeping with our foregoing observations, socialized pragmatics were especially likely to evidence exposure to redemptive events (n = 45 vs. n = 32.2) whereas personalized pragmatics were especially likely to evidence exposure to contamination events (n = 60 vs. n = 40). Apparently, pragmatic leaders, perhaps by virtue of their willingness to adopt the position that they must "look out for number one," are particularly sensitive to the negative effects of contamination events.

Third, personalized ideologues were substantially less likely than other leaders to evidence exposure to redemptive events (n = 21 vs. n = 37) during the period of narrative formation. The lack of exposure to redemptive events may make it difficult for ideological leaders to see good in the world, resulting in the adoption of a rigid, repressive, ideological orientation where the emphasis is on change by any means.

TABLE 9.5
Frequency of Event Type by Leader Orientation and Leader Type

	Originating	Anchoring	Analogous	Turning Point	Redemption	Contaminating
Socialized Charismatic						
Frequency	52	54	6	29	45	48
Percent[a]	17.1	12.5	31.6	16.7	21.8	18.2
Personalized Charismatic						
Frequency	50	62	1	42	26	45
Percent[a]	16.4	14.4	5.3	24.1	12.6	17.0
Socialized Ideological						
Frequency	41	114	3	29	37	41
Percent[a]	13.5	26.5	15.8	16.7	18.0	15.5
Personalized Ideological						
Frequency	47	92	1	18	21	42
Percent[a]	15.5	21.3	5.3	10.3	10.2	15.9
Socialized Pragmatic						
Frequency	57	68	5	35	45	28
Percent[a]	18.8	15.8	26.3	20.1	21.8	10.6
Personalized Pragmatic						
Frequency	57	41	3	21	32	60
Percent[a]	18.8	9.5	15.8	12.1	15.5	22.7

[a]Percent within type of event.

Fourth, consistent with this interpretation, personalized ideologues were less likely than other leaders to evidence exposure to turning point events ($n = 18$ vs. $n = 31.2$). More centrally, however, personalized charismatics were more likely to evidence exposure to a number of turning point events than other leaders ($n = 42$ vs. $n = 26.2$). Apparently, very high levels of life instability lead charismatics to adopt a personalized orientation—a point illustrated in the life of Adolph Hitler.

Summary

The findings obtained in examining key events used to define life narratives indicated that differential event exposure in late childhood, adolescence, and young adulthood is related to the emergence of different pathways to outstanding leadership. Socialized leaders were likely to be exposed to redemptive events whereas personalized leaders were likely to be exposed to contamination events with contaminating events proving particularly likely to be evident in the lives of personalized pragmatics. Charismatic, ideological, and pragmatic leaders also differed in events held to shape life narratives. Ideological leaders tended to be exposed to anchoring and redemptive events. Pragmatic leaders were more likely to be exposed to originating events. Charismatic leaders' lives were characterized by exposure to turning point events.

Correlations

Having examined differences in exposure to the various events involved in life narrative formation, we now turn to the results obtained in thematic analysis of these events. Table 9.6 presents the mean and standard deviation of scores on the 28 thematic dimensions along with the correlations observed among these dimensions. As might be expected in a sample of outstanding leaders, life events were found to evidence themes involving power ($\overline{X} = 10.91, SD = 18.53$). The prevalence of events involving themes related to conflict ($\overline{X} = 13.96, SD = 18.50$), uncertainty ($\overline{X} = 10.01, SD = 13.96$), and injustice ($\overline{X} = 13.16, SD = 16.70$) suggests that outstanding leaders begin their development in a turbulent, conflict-laden environment where the leader forms strong belief commitments ($\overline{X} = 13.56, SD = 17.70$) about events. Given the tendency of outstanding leaders to emerge from turbulent, conflict-laden environments (Erikson, 1957), the relevance of these themes is not especially surprising.

Of somewhat greater interest is the pattern of correlations observed among the various thematic dimensions. Again, the magnitude of the correlations observed among these dimensions was not sufficient to indicate operation of a general biasing factor. More important, however, was the finding that dimensions linked to a given type (e.g., thematic dimensions derived from an analysis of pragmatic or socialized leaders) tended to display the expected positive correlations. For example, themes stressing analytic problem solving, a preference for objective evidence, incremental progress, and exposure to diverse people and diverse ideas, all thematic dimensions associated with pragmatic leadership, displayed the expected positive correlations ($\overline{r} = .48$). Similarly, thematic dimensions linked to ideological leadership, such as belief commitment, spirituality, conflict, and injustice, produced sizable positive correlations ($\overline{r} = .28$). Notably, these thematic dimensions linked to ideological leadership showed no relationship with the thematic dimensions linked to pragmatic leadership ($\overline{r} = .00$). In the case of charismatic leadership themes, such as future focus, inspirational communication, and image management, the expected positive correlations ($\overline{r} = .22$) were again obtained. These themes, however, were less strongly related to thematic dimensions linked to pragmatic and ideological leadership. Thus, at least some evidence is available for the convergent and divergent validity of the scores reflected thematic content of the life events abstracted from the leader biographies.

In keeping with this observation, the various thematic dimensions linked to a personalized orientation, for example, a negative view of self and others, uncertainty, and negative life themes, produced the expected positive correlation ($\overline{r} = .50$). These thematic dimensions, however, were not strongly related to thematic dimensions associated with charismatic, ideological, and pragmatic leadership ($\overline{r} = .02$). Along similar lines, exposure to suffering, spirituality, and commitment to others, thematic dimensions linked to socialized leadership, produced the expected positive correlations ($\overline{r} = .39$). The existence of these coherent, substan-

TABLE 9.6
Means, Standard Deviations, and Correlations for Thematic Dimensions

Dimensions	$\bar{X}$	SD	1	2	3	4	5	6	7	8	9	10	11	12	13
1 Future Focus	5.07	8.37	1.0	.24	.24	.11	.29	.11	.05	.06	.01	-.05	-.10	-.20	-.03
2 Inspirational Communication	8.31	10.58		1.0	.31	.07	.17	.21	.03	.13	.04	.00	.01	.05	.15
3 Image Management	8.82	13.12			1.0	.11	.56	.18	.06	.02	-.08	-.19	-.02	.04	-.05
4 Risk Taking	5.59	8.50				1.0	.14	.34	.14	.13	-.03	-.12	.02	.10	.05
5 Personal Achievement	5.42	8.56					1.0	.29	.24	.10	-.04	-.13	-.15	-.15	-.14
6 Performance Expectations	6.26	9.56						1.0	-.08	-.11	-.12	-.13	-.07	-.17	-.20
7 Dramatic Change Efforts	5.39	8.68							1.0	.15	.05	.22	.01	.18	.09
8 Exposure to Crises	7.55	10.94								1.0	.26	-.09	-.06	.25	.17
9 Past Focus	6.54	12.25									1.0	.26	.38	.33	.24
10 Belief Commitment	13.56	17.70										1.0	.40	.11	.26
11 Spirituality	7.05	14.37											1.0	.19	.17
12 Conflict	13.96	18.50												1.0	.55
13 Injustice	13.16	16.70													1.0
14 Present Focus	5.69	11.08													
15 Analysis	12.68	17.34													
16 Evidential Preference	9.96	16.55													
17 Incremental Progress	6.16	11.65													
18 Exposure to Diversity	9.67	13.20													
19 Positive View of Others	8.59	13.10													
20 Positive View of Self	8.99	14.26													
21 Commitment to Others	10.68	15.05													
22 Exposure to Suffering	7.36	13.07													
23 Uncertainty/Powerlessness	10.03	13.96													
24 Negative View of Others	15.02	17.37													
25 Negative View of Self	6.20	10.03													
26 Power Motives	10.91	18.53													
27 Negative Life Themes	6.36	11.56													
28 Focus on Self	8.52	14.73													

(Continued)

TABLE 9.6
(Continued)

Dimensions	14	15	16	17	18	19	20	21	22	23	24	25	26	27	28
1 Future Focus	-.13	.07	.06	.06	-.18	.09	.19	-.03	-.03	.07	.04	.17	.06	.05	.21
2 Inspirational Communication	-.23	-.12	-.14	-.12	-.18	.07	.01	.09	.16	-.14	-.26	-.09	-.17	-.17	-.10
3 Image Management	-.25	-.24	-.24	-.15	-.17	.00	-.03	-.02	-.03	-.11	-.10	-.12	.04	-.20	.02
4 Risk Taking	.27	.32	.33	.06	.17	.32	.11	.36	.24	.07	.00	.06	.08	.04	.17
5 Personal Achievement	-.23	-.12	-.16	-.10	-.15	.07	.14	-.08	-.02	-.02	.00	-.02	.04	-.10	.06
6 Performance Expectations	.04	.12	.05	.02	.03	.25	.17	.02	-.01	-.06	.00	.12	.01	.10	.10
7 Dramatic Change Efforts	-.14	-.06	-.05	.28	-.14	-.04	-.11	.00	.05	.05	-.05	-.11	.01	-.04	-.02
8 Exposure to Crises	-.03	.05	.02	-.08	-.14	-.05	-.18	.07	.32	.20	-.06	.04	-.10	-.07	-.07
9 Past Focus	-.17	-.19	-.20	-.19	-.08	.03	-.02	.07	.06	.11	.10	-.05	-.10	-.06	-.06
10 Belief Commitment	-.04	-.15	-.07	-.20	.03	.24	.23	.19	.06	-.02	-.15	-.13	.27	-.09	-.21
11 Spirituality	-.08	-.15	-.16	-.14	.14	.08	-.09	.09	.05	.03	-.02	-.15	-.16	-.10	-.20
12 Conflict	-.03	-.06	-.06	-.13	-.07	.02	-.12	.28	.44	.17	.02	-.05	.03	.02	-.05
13 Injustice	-.14	-.21	-.16	.09	-.14	.05	.04	.29	.48	.23	.08	.04	-.14	.11	-.08
14 Present Focus	1.0	.63	.72	.35	.49	.15	.09	.13	-.05	.05	-.18	.02	.04	.09	.07
15 Analysis		1.0	.83	.35	.45	.17	.06	.21	-.06	.05	-.02	.11	.06	.06	.15
16 Evidential Preference			1.0	.30	.49	.22	.09	.19	.06	.08	-.06	.07	.08	.05	.12
17 Incremental Progress				1.0	.13	-.02	.12	.04	-.05	.01	-.11	-.08	-.05	-.01	.10
18 Exposure to Diversity					1.0	.33	.06	.25	-.11	.00	-.10	-.13	-.04	.05	.05
19 Positive View of Others						1.0	.47	.53	.27	-.16	.14	-.11	-.18	-.10	-.10
20 Positive View of Self							1.0	.09	-.04	-.14	-.15	.07	-.17	-.12	.02
21 Commitment to Others								1.0	.47	-.04	-.19	-.08	-.24	-.11	-.25
22 Exposure to Suffering									1.0	.16	.00	.05	-.17	-.02	-.14
23 Uncertainty/Powerlessness										1.0	.43	.48	.29	.59	.38
24 Negative View of Others											1.0	.38	.55	.60	.58
25 Negative View of Self												1.0	.35	.51	.53
26 Power Motives													1.0	.53	.74
27 Negative Life Themes														1.0	.60
28 Focus on Self															1.0

tively meaningful, dimensional relationships, in turn, brings to fore an important question: How did the various leader types differ on these dimensions?

Comparison of Leader Types

Table 9.7 presents the results obtained in the multivariate analysis of covariance examining differences across leader types (charismatic, ideological, and pragmatic) and leader orientation (socialized and personalized) with respect to the expression of the various thematic dimensions evident in significant life events occurring during childhood, adolescence, and young adulthood. None of the various covariate controls under consideration produced significant ($p \leq .05$) effects. This finding is noteworthy in that it indicates that conclusions drawn with respect to type and orientation were not influenced by potential confounds such as cross-biography differences in sources and theoretical orientation.

More centrally, in the multivariate analysis of covariance, the orientation variable provided a significant [$F(28, 114) = 3.43$; $p \leq .001$] main effect. Inspection of the associated univariate effects indicated that socialized leaders tended, early in their lives, to be exposed to life events that would build moral commitment to others. Thus, the commitment to others [$F(1, 114) = 15.40$; $p \leq .001$; $\overline{X} = 15.80$, $SE = 1.84$ vs. $\overline{X} = 5.55$, $SE = 1.84$], positive view of others [$F(1, 114) = 6.64$, $p \leq .01$; $\overline{X} = 11.58$, $SE = 1.64$ vs. $\overline{X} = 5.59$, $SE = 1.64$], spirituality [$F(1, 114) = 3.49$; $p \leq .10$; $\overline{X} = 9.39$, $SE = 1.77$ vs. $\overline{X} = 4.69$, $SE = 1.77$], and inspirational communication [$F(1, 114) = 4.65$; $p \leq .05$; $\overline{X} = 10.39$, $SE = 1.36$ vs. $\overline{X} = 6.23$, $SE = 1.36$] dimensions were more likely to be evident in events occurring in the lives of socialized leaders than in the lives of personalized leaders.

Although exposure to events reinforcing the value of prosocial behavior appear critical to the development of a socialized orientation among outstanding leaders, the development of a socialized orientation may be somewhat more complex than would be indicated by our foregoing observations. Socialized

TABLE 9.7
Multivariate Analysis of Covariance Results Contrasting
Leaders With Respect to Developmental Dimensions

	F	df	p	η
Covariates				
None[a]	—	—	—	—
Main Effects				
Orientation (socialized vs. personalized)	3.43	28, 114	.001	.52
Type (charismatic, ideological, pragmatic)	2.52	28, 114	.001	.44
Interactions				
Orientation * Type	1.16	28, 114	.289	.27

Note. $F = F$ ratio, $df = $ degrees of freedom, $p = $ significance level (determined by using Roy's Largest Root), $\eta = $ effect size.

[a]No significant covariates were identified in this analysis.

leaders, as opposed to personalized leaders, are more likely to be exposed to events indicative of an exposure to injustice [$F(1, 114) = 7.72; p \leq .01; \overline{X} = 17.31, SE = 2.11$ vs. $\overline{X} = 9.00, SE = 2.11$] and exposure to others' suffering [$F(1, 114) = 14.34; p \leq .001; \overline{X} = 11.68, SE = 1.61$ vs. $\overline{X} = 3.02, SE = 1.61$]. Apparently, socialized leadership arises not only from a commitment to others but also from exposure to events indicating that actions must be taken to change the current state of affairs in order to benefit others' lives. In keeping with this observation, socialized as opposed to personalized leaders were more likely to be exposed to events indicating the value of risk taking [$F(1, 114) = 9.35; p \leq .01; \overline{X} = 7.85, SE = 1.04$ vs. $\overline{X} = 3.31, SE = 1.04$]. Socialized leadership, moreover, appears to depend on an active attempt to understand sources of injustice and suffering and find an effective basis for action. Thus, socialized leaders, as opposed to personalized leaders, evidenced more life events indicative of analytical problem solving [$F(1, 114) = 7.29; p \leq .01; \overline{X} = 13.67, SE = 1.94$ vs. $\overline{X} = 6.25, SE = 1.94$].

Whereas socialized leaders appear to develop when committed individuals are exposed to injustice and suffering, leading them to try to understand and solve problems, personalized leaders appear to emerge from a different background. More specifically, the events evident in the lives of personalized, as opposed to socialized leaders, were indicative of themes bearing on a focus on the self [$F(1, 114) = 9.79; p \leq .01; \overline{X} = 12.31, SE = 1.71$ vs. $\overline{X} = 4.71, SE = 1.71$], negative views of others [$F(1, 114) = 31.08; p \leq .001; \overline{X} = 22.86, SE = 1.99$ vs. $\overline{X} = 7.16, SE = 1.99$], negative life themes [$F(1, 114) = 14.82; p \leq .001; \overline{X} = 10.08, SE = 1.36$ vs. $\overline{X} = 2.63, SE = 1.36$], and power motives [$F(1, 114) = 24.46; p \leq .01; \overline{X} = 18.28, SE = 2.10$ vs. $\overline{X} = 3.55, SE = 2.10$]. These findings, broadly consistent with the earlier observations of O'Connor et al. (1995), indicate that narcissistic self-absorption, coupled with events that lead people to believe that power is a way to get what one wants (the exercise of which is justified based on negative views of others) results in the development of a personalized orientation.

The discriminant function contrasting socialized and personalized leaders with respect to scores on these thematic dimensions was significant ($p \leq .001$), producing a canonical correlation of .71. Thus, socialized and personalized leaders could be readily distinguished based on the themes evident in early-career events—a finding suggesting that life narratives and autobiographical experiences play an important role in shaping leader orientation. The thematic dimensions yielding the highest loadings on this function were negative view of others ($r = -.50$), power motives ($r = -.42$), commitment to others ($r = .35$), exposure to others' suffering ($r = .34$), and negative life themes ($r = -.33$). This pattern of loadings, involving dimensions stressing beliefs about, and reactions to, others, led us to label this function *interpersonal concern*. As might be expected based on our foregoing observations, socialized leaders ($\overline{X} = 1.0$) obtained higher scores on this function than personalized ($\overline{X} = -1.0$) leaders.

A significant [$F(28, 114) = 2.52; p \leq .001$] main effect was also obtained in contrasting charismatic, ideological, and pragmatic leaders with respect to their scores on these thematic dimensions. Consistent with the notion that ideological leadership is based on the formation of life narratives organized around strongly held beliefs and values, ideological leaders were more likely than charismatic and pragmatic leaders to be exposed to events that would build belief commitment [$F(2, 114) = 5.74; p \leq .01; \overline{X} = 20.68, SE = 2.70$ vs. $\overline{X} = 9.99, SE = 2.70$] and spirituality [$F(2, 114) = 4.19; p \leq .01; \overline{X} = 11.55, SE = 2.17$ vs. $\overline{X} = 4.79, SE = 2.17$]. This focus on a "higher calling" was also associated with a tendency on the part of ideological leaders not to evidence exposure to events illustrating the value of incremental change [$F(2, 114) = 5.86; p \leq .01; \overline{X} = 1.94, SE = 1.77$ vs. $\overline{X} = 8.23, SE = 1.77$].

As might be expected based on prior studies examining pragmatic leadership, pragmatic leaders [$F(2, 114) = 5.86; p \leq .01; \overline{X} = 10.48, SE = 1.77$] were more likely to evidence exposure to events illustrating the value of incremental change than charismatic and ideological leaders ($\overline{X} = 3.94, SE = 1.77$). Consistent with their focus on solving immediate practical problems, pragmatic leaders were more likely than charismatic and ideological leaders to evidence exposure to events indicative of a focus on the present [$F(2, 114) = 5.69; p \leq .01; \overline{X} = 10.28, SE = 1.66$ vs. $\overline{X} = 3.39, SE = 1.66$] and events indicative of the value of analytical problem solving [$F(2, 114) = 13.74; p \leq .001; \overline{X} = 23.19, SE = 2.54$ vs. $\overline{X} = 7.42, SE = 2.54$], and a focus on factual information [$F(2, 114) = 9.60; p \leq .001; \overline{X} = 18.47, SE = 2.38$ vs. $\overline{X} = 5.70, SE = 2.38$].

The focus of pragmatic leaders on practical problem solving in the present, however, seemed to be accompanied by, and perhaps in part arise from, a distrust of people and their intentions. Thus, pragmatic leaders, in contrast to charismatic and ideological leaders, were more likely to evidence exposure to events indicating a negative view of self [$F(2, 114) = 2.05; p \leq .05; \overline{X} = 9.23, SE = 1.54$ vs. $\overline{X} = 4.67, SE = 1.54$] and negative life themes [$F(2, 114) = 5.87; p \leq .01; \overline{X} = 10.78, SE = 1.67$ vs. $\overline{X} = 3.84, SE = 1.67$]. Apparently, pragmatic leaders, lacking faith in others, rely on analytical effort, often personal analytic effort. Thus, pragmatic leaders were found to obtain higher scores than charismatic and ideological leaders on the dimension examining events indicative of a focus on self [$F(2, 114) = 9.92; p \leq .001; \overline{X} = 15.57, SE = 2.10$ vs. $\overline{X} = 4.98, SE = 2.10$].

Pragmatic and charismatic leaders both seemed to differ from ideological leaders with respect to the prevalence of power in significant life events [$F(2, 114) = 5.87; p \leq .01; \overline{X} = 14.35, SE = 2.58$ vs. $\overline{X} = 4.05, SE = 2.58$]. Apparently, ideological leaders, in contrast to charismatic and pragmatic leaders, frame their lives more around a mission than control. In keeping with this proposition, events illustrating the importance of change were more likely to be observed in the life events of ideological leaders than pragmatic leaders [$F(2, 114) = 3.30; p \leq .05; \overline{X} = 7.54, SE = 1.35$ vs. $\overline{X} = 2.71, SE = 1.35$].

In contrasting these groups in the discriminant analysis, only one function produced a sizable ($r = .66$), and significant ($p \leq .01$), canonical correlation.

The thematic dimensions yielding sizable loadings on this function included analytical problem solving ($r = .48$), focus on self ($r = .44$), preference for evidence ($r = .39$), incremental progress ($r = .35$), belief commitment ($r = -.34$), and a focus on the present ($r = .31$). This pattern of loadings is indicative of a pragmatic orientation. As might be expected, pragmatic leaders ($\overline{X} = 1.11$) obtained substantially higher scores than ideological leaders ($\overline{X} = -1.02$) on this *pragmatism* function. Charismatic leaders' scores ($\overline{X} = .00$) fell between these two extremes.

Performance Relationships

Table 9.8 presents the correlations of scores on these discriminant functions with the general performance criteria. As may be seen, the interpersonal concern function, reflecting exposure to life events likely to develop a concern for the well-being of others, was positively related ($\overline{r} = .28$) to markers of leader performance obtained from the prologue or epilogue chapters. Apparently, successful leaders are those who form a life narrative and attempt to address complex crises with the betterment of others in mind.

Although early developmental experiences linked to interpersonal concern shape orientation, and subsequent performance, experiences linked to pragmatism tended to exert weaker effects on performance. Leaders evidencing pragmatic themes in significant life events, however, were less likely to initiate mass movements ($r = -.39$)—a tendency that may have limited their overall impact on society ($r = -.24$). Nonetheless, pragmatism was related to establishing institutions that continue to exist ($r = .22$) and maintenance of a long-term agenda ($r = .22$). Apparently, pragmatism limits social/interpersonal impact al-

TABLE 9.8
Correlations of Performance Criteria With Discriminant Functions

General Criteria	Interpersonal Concern	Pragmatism
1) How much did the leader contribute to society?	.24	−.24
2) How long did the leader's contributions last?	.29	.06
3) How many people did the leader affect?	.11	−.15
4) How favorably did the biographer view the leader?	.45	−.08
5) How many positive contributions did the leader make?	.34	−.04
6) How many negative contributions did the leader make?	−.28	−.15
7) How many different types of positive contributions?	.36	−.02
8) How many different types of negative contributions?	−.26	−.26
9) Do institutions established by the leader still exist?	.33	.22
10) How many institutions were established by the leader?	.09	.09
11) Was the leader's vision maintained after they left power?	.25	.22
12) Did the leader initiate mass movements?	.43	−.39

Note. $r \geq .18$ significant at .05 level.

though pragmatism may allow leaders to exercise ongoing influence through their impact on institutions (Jacobsen & House, 2001).

Table 9.9 presents the results obtained when the discriminant functions were used to predict performance after first taking controls into account. After adding the interpersonal concern and pragmatism scores to these controls (e.g., organizational size), it was found that these functions provided sizable and significant ($p \leq .05$) regression weights for 10 of the 12 general performance criteria. As might be expected based on our foregoing observations, across analyses, interpersonal concern exerted the strongest effects ($\overline{\beta} = .38$). Apparently, successful leaders think of themselves and their lives in terms of others.

Summary

In examining the themes tying together the events characterizing the significant experiences of outstanding leaders in childhood, adolescence, and young adulthood, it was found that thematic differences in events were related to the subsequent emergence of both socialized and personalized leaders as well as leaders' adoption of a charismatic, ideological, or pragmatic approach. Socialized leaders evidenced a concern for others—a concern that led to an attempt to take action addressing injustice and suffering. The themes evident in the lives of personalized leaders indicated a concern with self and the exercise of power over devalued others.

In addition to these differences in the thematic content evident in the significant life events of socialized and personalized leaders, differences were observed in the themes evident in the life events of charismatic, ideological, and pragmatic leaders. Ideological leaders' lives were shaped by events defining their beliefs and values. Pragmatic leaders, perhaps due to a lack of faith in themselves and in others, stressed analytical problem solving. Charismatic leaders were less easily characterized in terms of the themes apparent in significant life events, suggesting, potentially, less coherence in the early lives of charismatic leaders.

CONCLUSIONS

In considering the results obtained in our analysis of event types and event content, with regard to the development of outstanding leaders, certain characteristics of the methodology applied herein should be noted. Perhaps the most obvious, and critical, concern along these lines bears on the nature of the source material applied in the present study. Most studies of life narratives, or life stories, have examined the developmental impact of narratives based on stories obtained from the individual (Habermas & Bluck, 2000; Habermas & Paha, 2001). In the present study, narrative material was drawn from secondhand reports—specifically, from biographers' descriptions of critical life events. Although the use of biographers' description of key life events offers some ad-

TABLE 9.9
Summary of Regression Results

	R	R^2	p	Significant Functions ($p \leq .05$)	Beta	High Group	Low Group
General Criteria							
1) How much did the leader contribute to society?	.50	.25	.001	Interpersonal Concern	.28	Socialized	Personalized
2) How long did the leader's contributions last?	.29	.08	.001	Interpersonal Concern	.29	Socialized	Personalized
3) How many people did the leader affect?	.43	.19	.001	None	—	—	—
4) How favorably did the biographer view the leader?	.56	.32	.001	Interpersonal Concern	.49	Socialized	Personalized
5) How many positive contributions did the leader make?	.40	.16		Interpersonal Concern	.36	Socialized	Personalized
6) How many negative contributions did the leader make?	.31	.09	.001	Interpersonal Concern	-.27	Socialized	Personalized
7) How many different types of positive contributions?	.45	.21	.001	Interpersonal Concern	.38	Socialized	Personalized
8) How many different types of negative contributions?	.49	.24	.001	Interpersonal Concern	-.23	Socialized	Personalized
9) Do institutions established by the leader still exist?	.47	.22	.001	Interpersonal Concern	.29	Socialized	Personalized
10) How many institutions were established by the leader?	.34	.12	.01	None	—	—	—
11) Was the leader's vision maintained after they left power?	.31	.10	.01	Interpersonal Concern	.27	Socialized	Personalized
12) Did the leader initiate mass movements?	.53	.28	.001	Pragmatism	-.24	Pragmatic	Ideological

Note. R = multiple correlation; R^2 = percentage of variance accounted for; p = significance level; Beta = standardized regression weight.

vantages with regard to historic identification of relevant event descriptors, it is also true that the individual's subjective interpretation of these events was not, and indeed could not be, examined.

It should also be recognized that the life events under consideration herein were drawn from an a priori taxonomy of key life events (e.g., originating events, anchoring events) developed by Pillemer (2001). Though application of an a priori taxonomy in event identification is desirable for many reasons, particularly when biographical sources are being applied, it is, of course, possible that other events relevant to the definition of life narratives exist that were not covered in this taxonomy.

Finally, in considering the results obtained in the present effort, it is important to bear in mind the point that events were examined within a particular developmental period. More specifically, in the present study, we examined only life events occurring during late childhood, adolescence, and young adulthood—the period of life narrative formation (Habermas & Bluck, 2000). This point is of some importance because events reflecting later influences on narrative construction and application, for example, analogous events, could not be examined in the herein. Along similar lines, it should be borne in mind that the procedures applied in identification of these events made it difficult to draw conclusions about the effects of differential event timing during the period of life narrative formation. This point is of some importance because it is possible that the effects of different types of events are contingent on the timing of events in individuals' formation of their life narratives (Mumford et al., 1987).

Although there is a need to take these limitations into account in drawing conclusions, the findings obtained in the present study do point to some notable conclusions about the nature and origins of outstanding leadership. Mumford and Strange (2002) and Strange and Mumford (2005) have argued that formation of the prescriptive mental models, the models used in crisis resolution and sensemaking, is not solely a matter of analysis of goals and causes. Instead, people, in forming prescriptive mental models, reflect on their own lives in identifying goals and causes. Indeed, because crises spur reflection on past life events and application of life narratives in planning and direction, this reflection on life narratives may be integral to the construction of viable prescriptive mental models and effective sensemaking (Bluck, 2003).

Of course, the influence of life narratives and reflection on the formation of prescriptive mental models suggests that life events, and the themes evident in these life events, will influence the pathways people follow to outstanding leadership. Moreover, due to the salience, or centrality, of events encountered in childhood, adolescence, and young adulthood with respect to the definition of these life narratives (Bluck & Habermas, 2000), one could expect that events encountered during this period would be a particularly powerful influence on the pathways followed by outstanding leaders.

Overall, the results obtained in the present study provided some compelling support for this proposition. Differences were observed among personalized and socialized charismatic, ideological, and pragmatic leaders with respect to the kind of events appearing in leader biographies during the period of narrative formation. Moreover, differences were observed among outstanding leaders with respect to the thematic content of the life events biographers held to be noteworthy influences on leaders' careers.

These differences across outstanding leaders in the content and structure of life events, of course, provide some critical support for the theory of outstanding leadership underlying the present effort. More centrally, however, they suggest that attempts to understand the nature and origins of outstanding leadership may need to apply a developmental framework that moves beyond behavioral change to incorporate the narrative structures outstanding leaders apply to understand themselves and their world (Mumford & Manley, 2003). Thus, there would seem to be a need for research examining how leaders apply narrative structures in identifying the causes of system problems and how they understand operative goals and causes in terms of events drawn from their past life events. For example, do leaders use critical life events as case models for understanding problems? And are the causes applied consistent with the themes evident in their past life events?

Not only do the findings obtained in the present effort point to some potentially important directions for future research, they also allow us to draw at least some preliminary conclusions about the development of various types of outstanding leaders. Perhaps the most clear-cut conclusions that can be drawn in this regard involve the origins of socialized and personalized leaders.

When one examines the events and themes evidencing differences across socialized and personalized leaders, a coherent picture of leader development emerges. Personalized leaders are exposed to a disproportionately large number of contaminating events (apparently, positive events that had negative downstream consequences). These contaminating events, perhaps due to a sense of loss, disappointment, and exploitation, result in the construction of life narratives involving negative life themes, negative views of others, a belief that one needs to look out for oneself, and a belief in the value power as a source of protection. These themes, in turn, result in a destructive, counterproductive form of leadership that can, in the case of outstanding leaders, result in substantial harm to society.

In contrast, socialized leaders are exposed to more redemptive and anchoring events during the period of narrative formation. Exposure to redemptive events (negative events with positive outcomes), coupled with anchoring events defining strongly held beliefs and values, gives rise to themes characterized by a positive view of others and spirituality. These themes apparently sensitize socialized leaders to injustice and suffering leading to an effort on their part to understand the sources of mistreatment so as to bring about positive social change. More succinctly, socialized leaders try to redeem others just as they have been redeemed. Table 9.10 provides an illustration of these differences between socialized and personalized leaders.

TABLE 9.10
Illustration of the Influence of Developmental Events
on Socialized and Personalized Leaders

F. H. La Guardia—Socialized

The sensitive teenager [F. H. La Guardia] also noticed the exploitation of low-paid immigrant workers as he caught sight of railroad gangs working on the spur to connect Ashfork, Phoenix, and Prescott—men and draft animals side by side accorded the same rough treatment . . . labor and capital clashed violently over the conditions and rights of workers, but the laborers Fiorella [sic] saw, in the main impoverished Italian and Mexican immigrants, were unable to band together to demand higher pay and rights on their own. When the 1893 depression threw many out of work, thousands of these displaced men lined the roads or joined pools of migrant workers. Fiorella [sic] witnessed their suffering firsthand.

Andrew Carnegie—Personalized

The monitoring of the boiler's temperature and pressure struck terror in Andy [Carnegie], however. Nightmares denied him sleep and peace of mind, "It was too much for me. I found myself night after night sitting up in bed trying the steam gauges, fearing at one time that the steam was too low and that the workers above would complain they did not have enough power, and the steam then got too high and the boiler might burst." Although himself ready to explode in fear, Andy never told his parents.

Note. La Guardia is from *Fiorello H. La Guardia and the Making of Modern New York*, by T. Kessner (1989, p. 13), New York: McGraw-Hill. Carnegie is from *Carnegie*, by P. Krass (2002, p. 29). Copyright © 2002 by John Wiley & Sons, Inc. Reprinted by permission.

Not only do these differences in events and thematic content tell us something about the origins of socialized and personalized leaders, they also provide us with some important clues about the development of charismatic, ideological, and pragmatic leaders. Ideological leadership appears to be linked not only to exposure to anchoring events that define strongly held beliefs and values but also to a life in which these beliefs and values are confirmed rather than invalidated by others. Thus, turning point and redemptive events are observed less frequently in the biographies of ideological leaders. These strongly held beliefs and values lead to life themes where meaning is manifest in a higher calling. Table 9.11 provides an illustration of how these beliefs and values shaped the career of two ideological leaders.

Pragmatic leaders, in contrast to ideological leaders, are more likely to evidence exposure to originating events—events involving definitions of goals and plans. To achieve these goals and effectively execute their plans, pragmatic leaders live in the present, stressing the values of incremental change, evidence, and analytical problem solving in the themes tying these events together. This focus on practical achievement in the present, however, appears to be linked to a skepticism about the worthiness of their own efforts and those of others—a skepticism that makes pragmatic leaders especially sensitive to anchoring, contaminating, and redemptive events in shaping their expression of a socialized or personalized orientation. Table 9.12 illustrates this point considering the careers of two pragmatic leaders.

TABLE 9.11
Illustration of the Influence of Beliefs and Values on Two Ideological Leaders

Michael Collins

While at school in Edinburgh, she [Mary Collins] developed a sympathy with the Boers and on her return for the holidays to Woodfield would tell Michael [Collins] of her fights at school with "pro-jingoists." It was from Mary that Michael heard "how gallant Boer farmers used to leave their work, take part in an ambush and return perhaps to milk the cows the next morning. . . ." In its own unsophisticated way, the ballad [sung by Mary to Michael] left a lasting impression on Michael's mind. It summed up the Santry and Lyons arguments and policy he advocated throughout his short, turbulent life: The condition of Ireland could only be improved by the use of force.

Fidel Castro

Castro was fascinated by the Bible: the story of Moses, the crossing of the Red Sea, the Promised Land, and "all the wars and battles." He remembers, "I was in sacred history class when I first learned about war . . . I began to acquire a certain interest in martial arts . . . it all interested me fabulously, from the destruction of the walls of Jericho by Joshua to Samson and his Herculean strength capable of tearing down a temple with his own bare hands . . . then came the New Testament, where the whole process of death and crucifixion produced an impact."

Note. Collins is from *Michael Collins: A Biography*, by T. P. Coogan (1990, p. 13), published by Hutchinson. Reprinted by permission of The Random House Group Ltd. Castro is from *Fidel: A Critical Portrait*, by T. Szulc (1986, p. 124), New York: William Morrow.

TABLE 9.12
Illustration of the Influence of Developmental Events on Two Pragmatic Leaders

Andrew Carnegie

Self-reliance and independence: These were traits bred in young Andra's [Carnegie] bone and because he was small in physical stature, reaching only 5'3" in adulthood, he had no choice but to rely on a quit wit to solve problems. As a boy, he showed this acumen when he started keeping rabbits. His father was good enough to build a rabbit hutch, but when it came to feeding the rabbits Andra was on his own. To manage the task, the boy gathered his chums and made his first business deal: if they gathered dandelions and clover to feed the rabbits, he would name a rabbit after each of them. Playing upon vanity, the manipulative Andra learned at a young age, was a clever means to motivate others to profit. It was a technique he used time and time again to secure his desires.

Alfried Krupp

While Gustav [Krupp] was just beginning to weigh the advantages of putting the family's resources behind Hitler, his son [Alfried Krupp] was already contributing to the Nazi Party from his allowance. He had also identified himself with its darkest fringe. In exchange for his monthly dues and oath of allegiance to the SS he received a subscription to the Schutzstaffel magazine, a numbered swastika armband with the circular inscription on it perimeter (Thanks to the SS for faithful assistance in time of battle); and a membership book bearing a rousing poem by Himmler . . . Alfried's Nazi Party number was high. He remained aloof from the parent body until 1938, when the Fuhrer had consolidated his power . . . his faithful assistance to the embattled SS in 1931 clearly puts him in the vanguard of the movement . . . Alfried [began his career and] chose a party squadron. He was good, too; in six years rose from a second lieutenant to colonel.

Note. Carnegie is from *Carnegie*, by P. Krass (2002, pp. 13–14). Copyright © 2002 by John Wiley & Sons, Inc. Reprinted by permission. Krupp is from *The Arms of Krupp: 1587–1968*, by W. Manchester (1968, pp. 377–378). Reprinted by permission of Don Congdon Associates, Inc. © 1968, renewed 1996 by William Manchester.

Ideological and pragmatic leaders were sharply, and clearly, distinguished with respect to event exposure and thematic content—a point underscored by the findings obtained in the discriminant analysis. Charismatic leaders, however, were not clearly distinguished based on the thematic content evident in narrative-defining life events. Instead, charismatic leaders were characterized by event exposure—more specifically, exposure to turning point events. Though definition of life narratives in terms of turning points is consistent with the notion that charismatic leadership involves a tendency to focus on proactive future-oriented change, it should also be recognized that these turning point events make it more difficult to identify stable thematic content characterizing the lives of charismatic leaders. This point is of some importance because it suggests that charismatic leaders' developmental trajectories may be more chaotic and more situationally contingent than those of pragmatic and ideological leaders—with excessive change often giving rise to personalized orientations in charismatic leaders (Mumford et al., 1987).

Not only did outstanding leaders display an interpretable, substantially meaningful, pattern of differences in terms of the events, and event themes, relevant to life narrative formation, the thematic differences observed were found to be related to subsequent performance. As might be expected, based on our findings in comparing these leaders on the various performance criteria, the interpersonal concern function, obtained in contrasting socialized and personalized leaders, was a more powerful predictor of performance than the pragmatism function obtained in contrasting charismatic, ideological, and pragmatic leaders.

Even bearing in mind this caveat, the predictive power of the themes apparent in the significant life events abstracted from the leader biographies points to a broader conclusion. More specifically, at least in the case of outstanding leaders, broader life experiences, particularly early developmental experiences, apparently represent a significant influence not only on the pathways people pursue to outstanding leadership but also on their performance in positions of influence. This conclusion is of some importance because it suggests that more attention needs to be given to developmental influences in an attempt to understand both the nature of leader performance and the kind of actions that are likely to prove effective in enhancing leader performance (Mumford & Manley, 2003).

10

Developmental Influences—
What Kind of Leader
Are You Destined to Be?

Michael D. Mumford
Katrina E. Bedell
Ginamarie Scott
The University of Oklahoma

When one studies the lives of outstanding leaders, we are often left to reflect on a nagging question. Exactly how do early career experiences, and early life experiences, shape the behavior of leaders when they reach a position of power? Did Ronald Reagan's experience as a lifeguard lead him to believe that the Soviet threat must be countered to save human life (Bosch, 1988)? Did Theodore Roosevelt's early struggles with his health lead him to become an advocate of American power abroad (Brands, 1997)? Did the violence in Fidel Castro's early life lead him to become a proponent of international revolution (Szulc, 1986)?

When we read biographies of leaders, we find it virtually impossible to avoid these speculative questions. Despite their fascinating implications, one rarely, if ever, finds answers to these questions in well-done academic biographies. The reason biographers are loath to address these questions is quite straightforward. The kind of qualitative data presented in academic biographies effectively makes it impossible to provide sound, well-founded answers to these questions bearing on the influence of life events on subsequent leader behavior.

The approach used in the present set of studies, however, does make it possible to answer these questions, at least in a preliminary fashion. In the preceding chapter on development, we formulated a system for assessing the thematic content evident in the early career experiences of outstanding leaders—a thematic scoring system that evidenced adequate reliability and good construct validity. Moreover, the approach applied in the present set of studies, a meta-analytic approach where data are cumulated across biographies, allows us to demonstrate the generalizability, or replicability, of relationships observed between early career experiences and subsequent leader behavior. Accordingly, our intent in the present chapter is to examine how the thematic content of significant life events occurring early in leaders' careers shapes subsequent behavior. More specifically, we examine how thematic content is related to the behavioral dimensions found to distinguish both socialized and personalized leaders and charismatic, ideological, and pragmatic leaders.

Dimensions

In considering the relationship between developmental themes and subsequent leader behavior, one immediately confronts a problem. Even the most cursory review of the literature indicates that leadership involves a wide variety of different behaviors (Bass, 1990; Fleishman et al., 1991; Yukl, 2002). Thus the question arises as to the kinds of behaviors that are of critical concern in attempts to elucidate developmental relationships. A partial solution to this problem may be found in the various domains of behavior under consideration in the present effort. Although outstanding leadership might be described and understood in terms of many different kinds of behavior, there is also reason to suspect that problem-solving processes, leader–follower relationships, communication strategies, and political tactics represent critical behavioral domains likely to be of concern in any study of outstanding leadership. Beyond the empirical evidence provided in the preceding chapters, bearing on the relationship of these behaviors to leader performance, there is, in fact, a sound substantive justification for focusing on these domains in studies examining developmental influences on outstanding leadership.

Outstanding leadership, as noted earlier, is a leadership of crises—leadership that requires sensemaking activities on the part of leaders (Drazin et al., 1999; Weick, 1995). Without adequate problem-solving skills, it is unlikely that leaders can make sense of crisis situations and formulate an effective response. These crises, moreover, represent broad, ill-defined problems, often novel problems, of the kind known to call for creative problem-solving skills (Mumford & Gustafson, 1988). Thus, Strange and Mumford (2005) found that combination and reorganization of goals and causes, coupled with reflection on one's personal life, was essential for vision formation.

For outstanding leadership, however, it is not sufficient just to formulate a prescriptive mental model for use in sensemaking. Outstanding leaders must be able to communicate this model, or their vision, to followers—providing followers with a framework that guides collective action (Fiol et al., 1999). In other words, leaders must be effective communicators. Outstanding leaders must, moreover, be able to exercise control or influence over multiple groups—often multiple groups with different and competing interests. As a result, one would expect that the political tactics through which leaders exercise influence would be a critical component of outstanding leadership (Ammeter et al., 2002).

Finally, the nature and scope of the issues confronting outstanding leaders in their attempts to resolve crises indicate that outstanding leaders must have colleagues, close followers, or lieutenants who are willing to work with the leader in crisis resolution (Jaques, 1976).

If it is granted that problem-solving processes, leader–follower relationships, communication strategies, and political tactics represent critical behavioral domains that must be considered in any discussion of outstanding leadership, then a new question comes to fore: Exactly, what aspects, or attributes, of the many behaviors lying in these four domains should be used as referent points for appraising the influence of life events on subsequent behavior? One way this question might be addressed is by examining how various life themes are related to the behaviors involved in problem solving, communication, leader–follower relationships, and political tactics. The problem with this approach, however, is that the number of rating dimensions under consideration makes it difficult to formulate general conclusions about experiential influences on subsequent leader behavior.

Of course, a variety of analytic techniques are available that might be used to summarize the various behaviors, or observational dimensions, lying in each of these four domains. A particularly attractive approach to this summarization problem, however, may be found in the various discriminant analyses, used to capture the key behavioral dimensions accounting for the differences observed among charismatic, ideological, and pragmatic leaders and socialized and personalized leaders. One reason this approach is attractive is because these dimensions reflect attributes known to be critical in accounting for the differences evident in the behavior of leaders following different pathways to outstanding leadership. Another reason is because the nature of the dimensions identified in the discriminant analyses tells us something about the behavioral requirements associated with outstanding leadership.

The dimensions identified in the various discriminant analyses, in fact, paint a rather compelling picture of these behavioral requirements. As indicated in our study of problem-solving processes, outstanding leadership requires some expertise in, and understanding of the social system at hand. Expertise, however, is not fully sufficient to ensure outstanding leadership. Instead, outstanding leaders need to bring together ideas for understanding the problem (conceptual integration), and, more centrally, they need to be able to integrate these ideas with the demands imposed by the external environment (external integration).

Expertise, conceptual integration, and external integration provide a basis for problem solving, sensemaking, and crisis resolution. If one grants this point, the next question that comes to fore is: How is the leader to go about building a committed cadre of lieutenants who are willing to work with the leader in crisis resolution? The need for a committed cadre of followers flows from the fact that no individual, no matter how gifted, can fully resolve the kind of complex system problems entailed in the crises that give rise to outstanding leadership. In fact, the discriminant analyses conducted in contrasting outstanding leaders with respect to leader–follower relationships indicated that outstanding leaders must build a team (team leadership), motivating members of this team through intrinsic incentives, shared direction, follower support, and mutual exchange of support. In other words, outstanding leaders build motivation in close followers by engaging followers as partners in a broader effort of real significance where the leader actively and visibly supports others' efforts.

Of course, outstanding leaders, and their followers, must influence others. Our study of leader political behavior indicates that the effective exercise of influence was based on use of rational influence tactics—influence tactics that involved expertise and resource allocation. Consistent with this observation, in communicating with followers, outstanding leaders tended to rely on prosocial argumentation, logical appeals, and follower-based appeals. Thus, outstanding leaders, at least outstanding leaders who have a positive impact on society, do not tell people what to do or force them to do it. Instead, they explain why it is in people's interest to follow the course of action being advocated by the leader and his or her lieutenants.

Leader Types and Experiential Influences

The fact that the dimensions emerging in the discriminant analyses provided a coherent description of the behavioral requirements for outstanding leadership suggests that these dimensions might provide a useful framework for examining the relationship of early career experiences to subsequent behavior. What should be recognized here, however, is that different types of leaders were distinguished by different patterns of scores on these dimensions. This observation is of some importance because it suggests that different experiential themes evident in leaders' early careers may give rise to different pathways to outstanding leadership and thus different behaviors as leaders moved into, or attained, positions of power.

In contrasting leader types with regard to the thematic content manifest in significant life events, the discriminant analyses produced two dimensions that appeared to summarize early developmental influences: (a) pragmatism and (b) interpersonal concern. Socialized and personalized leaders were distinguished with respect to thematic content manifest in early career experiences, by virtue of their scores on the interpersonal-concern dimension. As might be expected, socialized leaders obtained higher scores on the interpersonal-concern dimension than personalized leaders (House & Howell, 1992; O'Conner et al., 1995). The specific themes defining this dimension indicated that socialized leaders were more likely than personalized leaders to be exposed to life events reinforcing the value of prosocial behavior, events engendering a sense of injustice, and events providing models for effective social change acts. In contrast, personalized leaders as opposed to socialized leaders were characterized by events giving rise to narcissistic self-absorption and a belief that power is the way to get what one wants.

In the context of the present discussion, these observations have some important implications for understanding the relationship between early career events and subsequent leader behavior. It is difficult to see how a narcissistic, power-oriented individual can share leadership. And, it seems unlikely that such individuals will support others. In contrast, life events emphasizing a prosocial worldview can be expected to allow leaders to build a cadre of close followers who are motivated to solve problems for the sake of others—a powerful form of intrinsic motivation. These observations, in turn, suggest that themes characterizing interpersonal concern will be positively related to intrinsic motivation, and shared direction.

A prosocial orientation has another, perhaps somewhat more subtle effect. A prosocial orientation encourages people to become engaged with the lives of others and to think about the problems they are encountering in their lives. This engagement with, and analysis of, others' lives should, in turn, make it possible for leaders to develop prosocial arguments and effective appeals to followers. In other words, it seems reasonable to expect that life experiences giving rise to a prosocial orientation will contribute to leader communication skills through prosocial argumentation and the effectiveness of follower-based appeals.

Unlike social behavior (e.g., leader–follower relationships and communications), problem solving and political-influence tactics represent more cognitive or analytical forms of behavior. Accordingly, one might expect that life themes giving rise to interpersonal concern would not be strongly related to cognitive analytical behaviors such as rational influence, expertise, and conceptual integration. The exception to this rule of thumb, however, may be found in external integration. External integration, of course, implies an integration of problem solutions with the concerns of others. Because a prosocial orientation promotes a concern with and analysis of others' lives, it seems reasonable to expect that life themes contributing to the development of prosocial concerns would be related, positively related, to external integration.

The second dimension obtained in contrasting leaders with respect to the themes evident in their early lives was pragmatism. This pragmatism dimension was defined by events concerned with a focus on the present, along with events stressing the importance of factual information, analytical problem solving, and incremental change. In addition, this pragmatic dimension was associated with events linked to the development of a skeptical worldview and an awareness of others' limitations. Those attributes of the pragmatism dimension are, of course, consistent with Mumford and Van Doorn's (2001) description of pragmatic leadership. Given Mumford and Van Doorn's arguments, and the nature of the life events associated with this dimension, one would expect that life events linked to pragmatism would be positively related to the use of rational-influence techniques in political interaction and a tendency to rely on expertise in problem solving.

Summary

The various dimensions obtained in contrasting charismatic, ideological, and pragmatic leaders along with socialized and personalized leaders in terms of problem-solving activities, leader–follower relationships, communication strategies, and political tactics appear to provide a plausible basis for describing the behavioral requirements for outstanding leadership. There is reason to suspect, moreover, that leaders' expression of these behaviors is related to the nature of events occurring in late childhood, adolescence, and young adulthood.

METHOD

To examine the relationship between life events and leader behavior, scores on the discriminant functions obtained in contrasting leaders with respect to problem-solving activities, leader–follower relationships, communication strategies, and political tactics, were correlated with and regressed on the 28 developmental themes identified in the analysis of significant life events. Due to the number of thematic variables, no attempt was made to include the various control variables in the regression analyses.

The method used to define these discriminant functions has been described in the earlier chapters of this book. For the sake of clarity, however, we briefly review the procedures used to define these functions. Initially, rise-to-power, pinnacle-of-power, and/or fall-from-power chapters were used to assess leader behavior with regard to problem-solving activities, leader–follower relationships, communication strategies, and political tactics. A multivariate analysis of covariance was then conducted where relevant controls served as potential covariates. If type (charismatic, ideological, or pragmatic), orientation (socialized or personalized), or the type × orientation interaction produced significant effects in the multivariate analysis of covariance, then a discriminant-function analysis was conducted to identify the dimensions summarizing the cross-group differences observed in (a) problem-solving activities, (b) leader–follower relationships, (c) communication strategies, and (d) political tactics. A discriminant function was retained only if it produced a significant ($p \leq .05$) canonical correlation. This function was then labeled based on the behavioral variables yielding sizable loadings.

Across the analyses conducted for problem-solving activities, leader–follower relationships, communication strategies, and political tactics, 11 significant discriminant functions were obtained. Table 10.1 presents the labels as-

TABLE 10.1
Summary of Significant Discriminant Functions

Problem Solving	Leader–Follower Relationships	Communication Strategies	Political Tactics
1) Expertise Hi = Pragmatic Lo = Charismatic	1) Intrinsic vs. Extrinsic Hi = Socialized Lo = Personalized	1) Prosocial Argumentation Hi = Socialized Lo = Personalized	1) Rational Influence Hi = Pragmatics Lo = Ideologues and Charismatics
2) Conceptual Integration Hi = Ideological Lo = Charismatic/Pragmatic	2) Team Leadership Hi = Socialized Lo = Personalized	2) Follower-Based Appeals Hi = Socialized Ideologues and Socialized Charismatics Lo = Pragmatics	
3) External Integration Hi = Socialized Lo = Personalized	3) Shared Direction Hi = Ideological Lo = Charismatic	3) Logical Appeals Hi = Pragmatics Lo = Personalized Ideologues and Personalized Charismatics	
	4) Leader–Follower Support Hi = Socialized Lo = Personalized		
	5) Mutual Exchange of Support Hi = Charismatic Lo = Pragmatic		

signed to these functions and describes the groups receiving high and low scores on these functions. The problem-solving analyses produced three significant discriminant functions: (a) an expertise function that distinguished pragmatic leaders (high) from charismatic leaders (low), (b) a conceptual integration function that distinguished ideological leaders (high) from charismatic and pragmatic leaders (low), and (c) an external integration function that distinguished socialized leaders (high) from personalized leaders (low). The analyses examining leader–follower relationships produced five significant functions: (a) a shared-direction function, related to upper-level role relationships, that distinguished ideological leaders (high) from charismatic leaders (low), (b) a team leadership function, related to upper-level role relationships, that distinguished socialized leaders (high) from personalized leaders (low), (c) an intrinsic versus extrinsic function, related to lower-level role relationships, that distinguished socialized leaders (high) from personalized leaders (low), (d) a leader–follower support function that distinguished socialized leaders (high) from personalized leaders (low), and (e) a mutual exchange of support function that distinguished charismatic leaders (high) from pragmatic leaders (low). The communication analyses produced three significant discriminant functions: (a) a prosocial-argumentation function that distinguished socialized leaders (high) from personalized leaders (low), (b) a follower-based appeals function that distinguished socialized ideologues and charismatics (high) from pragmatics (low), and (c) a logical-appeals function that distinguished pragmatics (high) from personalized ideologues and charismatics (low). Only one significant discriminant function was obtained in the analysis examining political tactics. The rational-influence function obtained in this analysis distinguished pragmatic leaders (high) from ideological and charismatic leaders (low).

The predictors of scores on these discriminant functions were the thematic-content dimensions. These thematic dimensions were derived from an analysis of the early-career chapters examining the leader's life during late childhood, adolescence, and young adulthood—all material examining leaders' lives prior to their "rise to power." These chapters were reviewed to identify significant life events (Pillemer, 2001) falling into one of six categories: (a) originating events, (b) anchoring events, (c) analogous events, (d) turning point events, (e) redemptive events, and (f) contaminating events. Roughly, 1,400 events falling into these six categories were identified in the biographies obtained for the 120 leaders under consideration—with 15 to 30 events being identified for a given leader.

Subsequently, a panel of judges was asked to review the content of these events. Judges, using a modified Q-sort procedure, were asked to assign these events, based on event content, to one, or more, of 28 thematic dimensions drawn from the literature on outstanding leadership. The nature and origin of these thematic dimensions are described in greater detail in the chapter on leader development. The number of events assigned to a given thematic dimension divided by the total number of events identified for the leader provided the scores used to assess frequency of exposure to relevant life events. These exposure scores provided the basis for assessment of the predominance of a given theme in the lives of outstanding leaders.

RESULTS

Problem Solving

Table 10.2 presents the correlations and regression weights obtained in examining the relationships between life themes and subsequent problem-solving activities on the part of outstanding leaders. The multiple correlations obtained when expertise, conceptual integration, and external integration were regressed on the life themes ranged from .44 to .59. Thus, it appears that early life experiences are related to leaders' problem-solving activities. However, the relationships obtained for expertise were weaker than those obtained for conceptual integration and external integration. This pattern of findings is not especially surprising when one remembers that expertise is primarily a matter of learning and experience. Nonetheless, positive view of self was found to be related to expertise in the correlational ($r = .20$) and regression ($\beta = .29$) analyses—a finding that may reflect the effects of feelings of self-efficacy on people's ability to learn from experience.

Conceptual integration, however, produced a stronger pattern of relationships with early life themes. The correlational analysis indicated that conceptual integration was less likely to occur when people evidenced experiences linked to a negative view of others ($r = -.21$), a negative view of self ($r = .20$), and negative life themes ($r = -.23$). Apparently, if leaders do not learn to value their own and others' ideas, they are less likely to engage in conceptual integration. In this regard, however, it should be noted that a somewhat different pattern of results was obtained in the regression analysis. Although negative life themes were again found to be negatively related to conceptual integration ($\beta = -.28$), experiences that would lead people to adopt a preordained worldview, spirituality ($\beta = -.32$) and performance expectations ($\beta = -.33$), were also found to be negatively related to conceptual integration. In contrast, experiences that would engender intellectual investment in an issue, specifically belief commitment ($\beta = .20$) and risk taking ($\beta = .39$), were found to be positively related to conceptual integration.

Like conceptual integration, a leader's willingness to engage in activities linked to external integration also appeared to be related to early life experiences. As might be expected, the correlational analysis indicated that life themes emphasizing analysis ($r = -.25$) and an evidential preference ($r = -.21$) were negatively related to external integration. This pattern of findings suggests that a bias toward objective problem analysis may inhibit the social contact needed for external integration. Although the findings that exposure to diver-

TABLE 10.2
Correlations and Standardized Regression Weights Obtained
in Regression Problem-Solving Functions on Early Life Themes

Themes	Expertise		Conceptual Integration		External Integration	
	r	β	r	β	r	β
1) Belief Commitment	.01		.04	.20	.04	
2) Spirituality	−.02		−.15	−.32	−.17	−.26
3) Injustice	−.01		−.16		−.04	.24
4) Environmental Conflict	.05		−.08		.03	
5) Past Focus	−.03		.02		.08	
6) Uncertainty/Powerlessness	.03		−.15		−.06	
7) Negative View of Others	−.04		−.21		−.08	
8) Negative View of Self	.05		−.20		.08	.22
9) Power Motives	.02		−.13		−.01	
10) Negative Life Themes	−.02		−.23	−.28	−.07	
11) Focus on Self	.03		−.16		−.03	
12) Analysis	−.11		−.09		−.25	
13) Evidential Preference	−.12		−.08		−.21	
14) Present Focus	−.02		−.01		−.13	
15) Incremental Progress	.08		.02		−.02	
16) Exposure to Diversity	−.08		−.14		−.25	
17) Positive View of Others	.03		−.09		.05	−.24
18) Positive View of Self	.20	.29	−.04		.19	.28
19) Commitment to Others	−.14	−.24	−.18		−.08	
20) Exposure to Suffering	.04		−.15	−.32	−.17	
21) Exposure to Crises	.01		.05		.06	
22) Future Focus	.02		.02		.05	
23) Inspirational Communication	−.02		.02		.05	
24) Performance Expectations	.03		−.16	−.33	−.04	
25) Personal Achievement	.02		.02		.01	
26) Change Efforts	.07		.12		−.03	
27) Risk Taking	−.03		.03	.39	−.05	
28) Image Management	.07		.01		.01	
Multiple Correlation		.44		.59		.57

Note. $r \geq .18$ significant at .05 level. β = standardized regression weight reported only if significant past .10 level.

sity was negatively related to external integration ($r = -.25$) may at first glance seem surprising, this relationship may reflect the tendency of people exposed to high levels of diversity to adopt the belief that external integration is too uncertain to be useful. In keeping with the interpretation, and the effects of self-esteem on social engagement, events linked to a positive view of the self were positively related ($r = .19$) to external integration.

Although a positive view of the self was related to external integration (β = .28) in the regression analysis, the regression analysis produced a somewhat different pattern of relationships. More specifically, experiences linked to injustice ($\beta = .24$), negative view of self ($\beta = .22$), a negative view of others ($\beta = .22$), and a failure to experience events linked to a positive view of others ($\beta = -.24$) were found to be related to external integration. Apparently, experiences leading to lack of trust in self or others may cause leaders to engage in external integration as a defensive strategy. This interpretation, of course, is consistent with the finding that spirituality is ($\beta = -.26$) negatively related to external integration.

Leader–Follower Relationships

Table 10.3 presents the correlations and regression weights obtained when the relationship between life themes and leader–follower relationships were examined. Across the five discriminant functions obtained in this domain, multiple correlations ranged between .49 and .69. Thus, it appears that events encountered earlier in leaders' lives do influence subsequent interaction with followers. As might be expected, exposure to life events linked to a negative view of others ($r = -.39$), power motives ($r = -.39$), negative life themes ($r = -.27$), and a focus on the self ($r = -.26$) were all negatively related to the tendency of leaders to motivate followers through intrinsic motives. In the regression analysis, a negative view of others ($\beta = -.38$) and power motives ($\beta = -.24$) were found to exert particularly strong effects in this regard along with environmental conflict ($\beta = -.33$). In contrast, commitment to others ($r = .29$), exposure to suffering ($r = .24$), and risk taking ($r = .20$) were found to be positively related to the tendency to motivate followers through intrinsic rewards in the correlational analysis. In the regression analysis, only exposure to suffering ($\beta = .29$) and image management ($\beta = .19$) were found to be related to the leader's tendency to motivate followers through intrinsic rewards.

A similar pattern of relationships emerged in considering the team leadership functions. In the correlational analysis, it was found that themes indicative of a negative view of others ($r = -.34$), power motives ($r = -.34$), and a focus on self ($r = -.21$) all made it difficult for leaders to work with followers as a team. In the regression analysis, similar findings were obtained for negative view of others ($\beta = -.26$) and power motives ($\beta = -.35$). However, the willingness of leaders to work with followers was, in the regression analysis, found to be positively related to exposure to diversity ($\beta = .22$) and a negative view of self ($\beta = .21$). Apparently, more humble leaders who are used to working with people from a range of backgrounds are more likely to build effective leadership teams.

In accordance with these findings, findings indicating that a controlling narcissistic orientation inhibits effective interactions with followers, the correlational analysis indicated that a negative view of others ($r = -.24$) and power motives ($r = -.24$) were negatively related to shared direction of the group by leaders and followers. In the regression analysis, however, power motives ($\beta = -.45$) were found to be a particularly powerful influence inhibiting shared di-

TABLE 10.3
Correlations and Standard Regression Weights Obtained in Regressing Leader–Follower Relationship Functions

Themes	Intrinsic vs. Extrinsic		Team Leadership		Shared Direction		Leader–Follower Support		Mutual Exchange of Support	
	r	β	r	β	r	β	r	β	r	β
1) Belief Commitment	.06		.04		.20		.05		.07	
2) Spirituality	.10		.08		.18	.27	.03		.01	
3) Injustice	.07		-.04		-.14		-.05		.04	.23
4) Environmental Conflict	-.11	-.33	-.07		-.17		-.01		-.07	
5) Past Focus	-.01		.04		-.01		.10		.02	
6) Uncertainty/Powerlessness	-.09		-.10		-.17	-.23	-.02		.06	.26
7) Negative View of Others	-.39	-.38	-.34	-.26	-.24		-.31	-.50	.04	
8) Negative View of Self	-.09		-.01	.21	-.04		.01		-.05	
9) Power Motives	-.39	-.24	-.34	-.35	-.32	-.45	-.07		.05	
10) Negative Life Themes	-.27		-.17		-.04	.37	-.16		-.08	-.27
11) Focus on Self	-.26		-.21		-.15		-.11		-.03	
12) Analysis	.01		.09		.09		.01		-.19	
13) Evidential Preference	.08		.09		.08		.06		-.18	
14) Present Focus	.07		.11		.14		.02		-.25	
15) Incremental Progress	-.05		-.01		-.04		-.01		-.06	
16) Exposure to Diversity	.15		.16	.22	.07		.07		-.01	

(Continued)

TABLE 10.3
(Continued)

Themes	Intrinsic vs. Extrinsic		Team Leadership		Shared Direction		Leader–Follower Support		Mutual Exchange of Support	
	r	β	r	β	r	β	r	β	r	β
17) Positive View of Others	.19		.06		.12		-.02		.06	.30
18) Positive View of Self	.15		-.05		.08		-.01		-.11	-.27
19) Commitment to Others	.29	.29	.14		.09		-.08	-.28	.05	
20) Exposure to Suffering	.24		.06		-.04		.02		-.08	
21) Exposure to Crises	.13		.14		.01		.07		-.03	
22) Future Focus	.12		.02		-.06		-.03		-.02	
23) Inspirational Communication	.09		.18		.09		.09		-.03	
24) Performance Expectations	.13		.03		.01		-.01		.08	
25) Personal Achievement	.03		.04		-.32		.01		.12	
26) Change Efforts	-.10		.03		.02		-.05		.01	
27) Risk Taking	.20		.08		-.02		-.02		-.12	
28) Image Management	.14	.19	-.07		-.07		.01		.18	
Multiple Correlation	.69		.55		.59		.49		.54	

Note. r ≥ .18 significant at .05 level. β = standardized regression weight reported only if significant past .10 level.

258

rection. Shared direction, moreover, was inhibited by uncertainty/powerlessness ($\beta = -.23$)—a finding suggesting that power and control may serve as a means of reducing uncertainty (O'Conner et al., 1995).

Shared direction, however, was positively related to negative life themes ($\beta = .37$). Apparently, bonding occurs among individuals who share exposure to negative life experiences. And, this bonding may encourage outstanding leaders to share direction. Bonding, however, may also be brought about by spirituality ($\beta = .27$), as indicated by the regression results, or belief commitment ($r = .20$), as indicated by the correlational results. Thus, it appears that ideological commitments, and the resulting contact with like-minded individuals, may contribute to the willingness of leaders to share direction of the group.

Leader–follower support was found to be negatively related to negative views of others in both the correlational ($r = -.31$) and regression ($\beta = -.50$) analyses. Apparently, we are less likely to offer support to people we dislike. In this regard, however, it should be noted that commitment to others was found to be negatively related to leader–follower support ($\beta = -.28$) in the regression analysis. Although this finding may, at first glance, seem surprising, it is possible it reflects a tendency on the part of outstanding leaders to sacrifice followers in the service of broader social commitments.

Mutual exchange of support produced significant negative relationships with analysis ($r = -.19$), evidential preference ($r = -.18$), and present focus ($r = -.25$). This pattern of findings suggests that a pragmatic orientation may inhibit exchange of support among leaders and followers, perhaps because a pragmatic orientation results in depersonalized relationships. However, as indicated by the findings obtained for image management ($r = .18$), even in depersonalized relationships people may be willing to exchange support if they believe it is a normative expectation.

In the regression analysis, however, a somewhat different pattern of relationships emerged. Here it was found that mutual support was positively related to earlier life events involving injustice ($\beta = .23$) and powerlessness/uncertainty ($\beta = .26$). Apparently, equity concerns may encourage mutual exchange of support. In keeping with this observation, mutual exchange of support was negatively related to exposure to events linked to negative life themes ($\beta = -.27$). Moreover, it appeared that mutual exchange of support was also linked to development of a servant orientation in that mutual exchange of support was found to be positively related to a positive view of others ($\beta = .30$) and negatively related to a positive view of self ($\beta = -.27$).

Communication Strategies

The findings obtained for the communication strategies functions again indicated that earlier life experiences influenced later leader behavior. The results obtained in the correlation and regression analyses examining the relationships between communication strategies and themes evident in leaders' earlier life experiences are presented in Table 10.4. As may be seen, the regression analysis produced sizable multiple correlations ranging between .56 and .62.

The results obtained for prosocial argumentation indicated that life experiences likely to develop a concern for others, specifically, spirituality ($r = .20$) and exposure to others' suffering ($r = .22$), were positively related to prosocial argumentation. Although development of concern contributes to prosocial argumentation, it appears that negative life experiences represent an inhibitor, a relatively powerful inhibitor, of prosocial argumentation. Thus, in the corre-

TABLE 10.4
Correlations and Standardized Regression Weights Obtained
in Regressing Communication Strategy Functions

Themes	Prosocial Argumentation		Follower-Based Appeals		Logical Appeals	
	r	β	r	β	r	β
1) Belief Commitment	.15		.25		−.02	
2) Spirituality	.20		.24		.08	
3) Injustice	.16	.24	.09		.07	
4) Environmental Conflict	.01		.13		−.04	
5) Past Focus	−.01		.06		−.01	
6) Uncertainty/Powerlessness	−.07		−.21		.04	
7) Negative View of Others	−.34	−.28	−.27		−.16	
8) Negative View of Self	−.12		−.18		−.01	
9) Power Motives	−.26		−.32		−.07	
10) Negative Life Themes	−.26		−.24		−.12	
11) Focus on Self	−.24		−.35		−.02	
12) Analysis	.13	.37	−.21		.25	.35
13) Evidential Preference	.08	−.32	−.22		.19	
14) Present Focus	.13		−.21		.24	.24
15) Incremental Progress	.01		−.23		.11	
16) Exposure to Diversity	.14		−.08		.18	
17) Positive View of Others	.12		.03		.09	
18) Positive View of Self	.05		−.04		.01	
19) Commitment to Others	.12	−.22	.03	−.25	.10	
20) Exposure to Suffering	.22	.25	.23		.14	
21) Exposure to Crises	.09		.02		.09	
22) Future Focus	.04		−.09		.12	
23) Inspirational Communication	.19		.18		.17	
24) Performance Expectations	.07		−.15		.20	
25) Personal Achievement	−.05		−.08		.01	
26) Change Efforts	−.01		.13		−.15	
27) Risk Taking	.18		−.07		.23	
28) Image Management	.04		.03		.08	
Multiple Correlation		.59		.62		.56

Note. $r \geq .18$ significant at .05 level. β = standardized regression weight reported only if significant past .10 level.

lational analysis, negative view of others ($r = -.34$), power motives ($r = -.26$), negative life themes ($r = -.26$), and a focus on the self ($r = -.24$) were all negatively related to prosocial argumentation. Apparently, a negative narcissistic orientation resulting from earlier life events makes it difficult for people to frame arguments with respect to the needs of others.

In the regression analysis, negative views of others were again found to inhibit prosocial argumentation ($\beta = -.28$). However, exposure to events linked to injustice ($\beta = .24$) and analysis ($\beta = .37$) were found to be positively related to prosocial argumentation. This pattern of findings suggests that a willingness to analyze social problems may also be necessary for prosocial argumentation. This observation, moreover, is consistent with the finding that strong commitments to others ($\beta = -.22$) and a focus on the evidence per se ($\beta = -.32$) were negatively related to prosocial argumentation—both a strong commitment to others and an undue focus on the facts may inhibit effective *social* analysis.

Follower-based appeals produced a pattern of relationships with the life theme scores similar to those obtained for prosocial argumentation. Again, in the correlational analysis, it was found that spirituality ($r = .24$) and exposure to others' suffering ($r = .23$), along with belief commitment ($r = .25$) and inspirational communication ($r = .18$), were positively related to the tendency of leaders to make appeals to their followers' needs and values. The ability of leaders to make these appeals was also found to be diminished by exposure to events linked to development of a negative narcissistic orientation—specifically uncertainty/powerlessness ($r = -.21$), negative view of others ($r = -.27$), negative view of self ($r = -.18$), power motives ($r = -.32$), negative life themes ($r = -.24$), and a focus on the self ($r = -.35$). In addition, follower-based appeals were inhibited by events causing leaders to adopt a strongly analytical mind-set such as events reflecting themes bearing on the value of analysis ($r = -.21$), evidence ($r = -.22$), present focus ($r = -.21$), and incremental progress ($r = -.23$). In the regression analysis, a weaker pattern of relationships emerged with only exposure to others' suffering ($\beta = .36$) and commitment to others ($\beta = -.25$) producing sizable regression weights.

In contrast to the findings obtained for follower-based appeals, use of logical appeals in communication was positively correlated with early exposure to events causing leaders to adopt an analytical orientation. More specifically, logical appeals were positively related to life themes linked to analysis ($r = .25$), evidential preference ($r = .19$), present focus ($r = .24$), and diversity ($r = .18$). Additionally, themes linked to risk taking ($r = .23$) and high performance expectations ($r = .20$) also proved to be positively related to the tendency of leaders to make logical appeals, suggesting that a focus on performance demands may engender in leaders a preference for logical appeals.

The regression analysis, like the correlational analysis, indicated that themes indicative of analysis ($\beta = .35$) and a focus on the present ($\beta = .24$) were positively related to logical appeals. Logical appeals, however, could also be stimulated by early exposure to injustice ($\beta = .22$), perhaps because exposure to injustice induces analysis of social problems. The negative relationship observed between environmental conflict and a leaders later use of logical appeals (β = −.23) may simply reflect the fact that people learn early on in their lives that logic does not work in a conflict-laden environment (Mumford & Van Doorn, 2001).

Political Tactics

Table 10.5 presents the results obtained when the rational influence dimension obtained in contrasting outstanding leaders with respect to their political behavior was correlated with, and regressed on, the themes evident in significant early life events. In the regression analysis, the multiple correlation obtained was .40. Events associated with a negative view of the self (β = .27) were found to be positively related to the use of rational-influence attempts, perhaps because they contribute to development of a skeptical orientation. Negative life themes, however, were negatively related to the tendency to employ rational influence (β = −.30). Apparently, when people are exposed to events lending to a negative worldview they see rational-influence tactics as relatively ineffective in an irrational, and potentially hostile, world. In the correlational analysis, whereas the overall pattern of findings was weaker, negative view of self, and the skepticism it entails, was again found to be positively related (r = .18) to the later use of rational-influence tactics.

Summary

The relationships observed between the life event themes and critical leader behaviors (problem-solving activities, leader–follower relations, communication strategies, and political tactics) indicated that later leader behavior is influenced by early experiences. Broadly speaking, the effects of early experiences were more pronounced for social-interactional behaviors, leader–follower relationships and communication strategies than for problem-solving activities and political tactics. With regard to interactional behaviors, life experiences contributing to a negative, controlling, narcissistic orientation were found to be particularly powerful influences on leader behavior, decreasing the likelihood that leaders would engage in productive activities such as prosocial argumentation, follower-based appeals, induction of intrinsic motives, shared direction, and team leadership.

CONCLUSIONS

In considering our observations with regard to the relationship between early life themes and later leader behavior, certain limitations of the present effort should be kept in mind. To begin, the measure of leader behavior applied in the present

TABLE 10.5
**Correlations and Standardized Regression Weights Obtained
in Regression Political Tactics Functions on Early-Career Life Themes**

Themes	Rational Influence	
	r	β
1) Belief Commitment	−.03	
2) Spirituality	−.02	
3) Injustice	.01	
4) Environmental Conflict	−.01	
5) Past Focus	−.02	
6) Uncertainty/Powerlessness	.01	
7) Negative View of Others	.02	
8) Negative View of Self	.18	.27
9) Power Motives	.04	
10) Negative Life Themes	−.05	−.30
11) Focus on Self	.08	
12) Analysis	−.07	
13) Evidential Preference	−.05	
14) Present Focus	.01	
15) Incremental Progress	−.03	
16) Exposure to Diversity	.02	
17) Positive View of Others	−.08	
18) Positive View of Self	.01	
19) Commitment to Others	−.05	
20) Exposure to Suffering	.01	
21) Exposure to Crises	−.04	
22) Future Focus	−.05	
23) Inspirational Communication	.02	
24) Performance Expectations	.04	
25) Personal Achievement	−.09	
26) Change Efforts	−.06	
27) Risk Taking	−.13	
28) Image Management	−.02	
Multiple Correlation		.40

Note. $r \geq .18$ significant at .05 level. β = standardized regression weight reported only if significant past .10 level.

study, the discriminant functions obtained in contrasting outstanding leaders with respect to problem-solving activities, leader–follower relationships, communication strategies, and political tactics, appeared to provide a systematic and reasonably comprehensive basis for examining the key behaviors involved in outstanding leadership. By the same token, however, it should be recognized that these dimensions describe leader behavior in only four domains. Thus, caution is called for in extrapolating our findings to other domains of leadership behavior such as decision making and empowerment (Yukl, 2002).

Along related lines, it should be recognized that these discriminant functions were expressly intended to account for differences, or variation, in the behaviors of different types of outstanding leaders. This point is of some importance for two reasons. First, our findings with regard to development speak not to outstanding leadership in general, but rather to different pathways to outstanding leadership. Second, it is possible that examination of alternative pathways, pathways outside the socialized and personalized and charismatic, ideological, and pragmatic pathways under consideration, might give rise to different variables that evidence different forms of relationships with early life experiences.

Our foregoing observations about early life experiences point to another characteristic of the present effort that should be noted. More specifically, in this study early experiences were assessed through thematic content of significant life events (Bluck & Habermas, 2001; Pillemer, 2001). Although use of this strategy allowed for a reasonably comprehensive examination of experiential influences, the processes by which developmental experience shapes later behavior (Baltes, 1997; Lerner, Freund, Stefanis, & Habermas, 2001) could not be examined using this thematic approach. Along related lines, these themes, as indicated by the different findings obtained in the correlational and regression analyses, represent interdependent and integrated sets of experiences. Accordingly, future research should examine how these themes operate together in shaping leader behavior.

Even bearing these limitations in mind, we believe that the results obtained in the present study have some important implications for understanding the nature and origins of different forms of outstanding leadership. To begin, experiences of leaders in late childhood, adolescence, and young adulthood apparently have a persuasive impact on subsequent leader behavior—effects that are evident in multiple domains. Moreover, these early career experiences give rise to differences in the expression of behaviors, such as prosocial argumentation, intrinsic versus extrinsic motivation of followers, team leadership, and external integration, that have been shown to be important influences on leader performance. This point is of some importance because it indicates that the influence of developmental experiences on subsequent leader performance may be mediated by leader behavior.

Of course, the question that arises at this juncture is exactly how early experiences operate to shape subsequent leader behavior. Perhaps the most clearcut conclusion that can be drawn in this regard is that the relationship between early experiences and subsequent leader behavior is quite complex. For example, initially we hypothesized that external integration would be positively related to experiences linked to interpersonal concern. Although this hypothesis seems reasonable, our findings in this regard indicated that external integration was more closely linked to experience leading to a lack of trust in others. In other words, external integration seems linked to experiences underscoring the need for self-protection in one's dealings with others.

Another example of the complex nature of these developmental effects may be found in the relationships obtained for prosocial argumentation and follower-based appeals. Initially, we hypothesized that experiences contributing to the development of interpersonal concern, by virtue of their influence on leaders' willingness to think about and address others' concerns, would influence subsequent use of communication strategies of the sort subsumed under the prosocial argumentation and follower-based appeals dimensions. In fact, the findings obtained for belief commitment, spirituality, and exposure to others' suffering provided some support for this proposition. By the same token, however, it appeared that exposure to negative events, events linked to a negative view of others, power motives, negative life themes, and a focus on the self, exerted powerful, asymmetrically powerful, negative effects on prosocial argumentation and follower-based appeals.

This general pattern of relationships was not specific to the communication strategies dimensions. As expected, social-interactional behavior, communication strategies, and leader–follower relationships were more strongly related to earlier life experiences than more cognitively oriented behaviors such as problem-solving activities and political tactics. In the case of these social-interactional behaviors, experiences linked to the acquisition of a negative view of others, power motives, negative life themes, and a focus on the self consistently produced strong negative relationships. Apparently, when experiences cause leaders to see others in a negative light, others who must be controlled, the likelihood of leaders evidencing effective interactional patterns is greatly diminished. Put more directly, bad leadership apparently emerges from bad experiences although good experiences do not ensure good leadership.

One explanation for the pattern of effects may be found in our earlier discussion of life narratives (Habermas & Bluck, 2000; Habermas & Paha, 2001; McAdams, 2001). Other people, especially significant others, are a salient core component of people's life narratives. When experience with people is inherently negative and controlling, narrative structures will be constructed that are built around negative cases—cases that may be especially important in shaping interpretations of events, particularly social events, due to recall and self-protection biases. Because leaders, in responding to crises, will reference these narratives, narratives where negative social experiences are salient components, the resulting interpretation of events will tend to generate counterproductive interpretations of others and their likely intentions. These expectations, in turn, will result in ineffective patterns of interaction.

Given the apparent impact of experiential themes such as negative views of others and negative life themes on the effectiveness of leaders' interpersonal behavior and the strong positive relationship observed between these social-interactional dimensions and subsequent leader performance, one must confront a paradox. Despite lacking critical behavioral skills needed to influence followers and ensure effective performance, personalized leaders, leaders evidencing a self-serving narcissistic orientation and a disdain for others, emerge

TABLE 10.6
Illustration of Personalized Leader's Use of Politics and Problem Solving

---

Lavrenti Beria—Personalized Ideologue

Once in his new post, Beria set about "cleansing" the NKVD of undesirable elements. In other words, he initiated a full-scale purge of the Exhovites, executing or imprisoning hundreds of officials. Even before his promotion Beria had moved against several NKVD officials who closely associated with Ezhov, such as M.I. Litvin, Leningrad NKVD chief, and A.I. Uspenskii, NKVD chief in the Ukraine. Another victim was Beria's olf boss, Stanislav reddens, who was serving at the time of his arrest as head of the NKVD in Kazakhstan. Reden's wife, Anna, who was the sister of Stalin's deceased wife Nadezhda ALliluyeva, reportedly went to see Beria in an effort to save her husband, but Beria told her that she would be wise to forget about her marriage, which had never been registered. Redens was shot shortly thereafter. Another victim was NKVD staffer Igor Kedrov, son of the old Bolshevik and former Chekist Mikhail Kedrov, who had complained about Beria in the 1920's. After Beria's appointment as NKVD chief, both Kedrovs addressed their negative views of Beria directly to Stalin. Igor was arrested and shot immediately, and his father was killed a few months later.

By early 1939 Beria had succeeded in arresting most of the top and middle-level hierarchy of Ezhov's apparatus, replacing these men with members of his Georgian group. It is possible to identify at least twelve Beria men—several of whom had been associated with him since the early 1920's—appointed to key NKVD posts between November 1938 and January 1939. . . . According to Merculov (a Beria man in an NKVD post) "so many of us came to Moscow from Georgia that later Beria had to send some back, because Stalin had noticed it."

Among Beria's associates who assumed republican and regional NKVD posts were Sergei Goglidze, appointed to head the Leningrad NKVD; Laventri Tsanava, who became NKVD chief in Belorussia; Grigorii Karanadze, NKVD chief in the Crimea; Aleksei Sadzhaia, in Uzbekistan. . . . This group of men, all of whom owed their allegiance to Beria, formed the core of his extensive power base within the NKVD.

Note. From *Beria: Stalin's First Lieutenant,* by A. Knight (1993, pp. 90–91). Copyright © 1993 by Princeton University Press. Reprinted by permission.

---

rather frequently. The findings obtained in the present effort, however, suggest one way this paradox might be resolved. More specifically, negative views of others, negative life themes, power motives, and a focus on the self were less strongly related to problem-solving activities and political tactics than were the social-interactional dimensions. Thus, given their exceptional willingness to work for power, and adequate problem-solving and political skills, personalized leaders can emerge despite an ineffective pattern of interactional behavior. An illustration of this point may be found in Table 10.6.

Not only do our findings have something to say about the emergence and performance of personalized as opposed to socialized leaders, they also have some noteworthy implications for understanding the origins of charismatic, ideological, and pragmatic leadership. Ideological leaders differ from charismatic and pragmatic leaders with respect to their willingness to share direction. The ability of ideological leaders to share direction, however, appears to lie in common hardships and a shared set of beliefs and values—beliefs and values such as spirituality that make it possible to deal with these hardships. An illus-

TABLE 10.7
Illustration of Bonding in Shared Direction by Ideological Leaders

Jane Addams—Socialized Ideologue

Ellen Gates Starr and Jane Addams were freshmen together in Rockford in 1877. Ellen Star flashed brilliantly through her first year, then left college to teach, first for a year at the little town of Mount Morris, Illinois, then in Chicago, at the famous old Kirkland School for Girls, fashionable but strenuously educational too. The reputation of Miss Kirkland as a teacher and director of the daughters of "old Chicago families" has never had a rival in that city. Ellen Starr taught English and "art"— not drawing and painting, but appreciation. Her preparation for such teaching was not remarkably extensive, but her delight in it was keen. She thrilled to beauty, then and all her life thereafter. For ten years she and Jane Addams maintained their girlhood acquaintance, until in 1887 they were abroad together. Ellen had gone to continue her study of "appreciation". When however, in Madrid, on Easter Day 1888, Jane confided in Ellen Starr her scheme for a house among the poor people somewhere in Chicago, Ellen embraced it at once, with that vivacity, sincerity, and confidence which have always been characteristic of her. She would live there too. Together they would live and work. And so they did, for forty years.

Note. From *Jane Addams: A Biography*, by J. W. Linn (1935, p. 130), New York: by Appleton-Century.

tration of the role of these bonding experiences in shaping the behavior of ideological leaders is provided in Table 10.7.

These observations, of course, underscore a point made earlier. Early life experiences, experiences occurring during late childhood, adolescence, and young adulthood, represent a powerful mechanism shaping the pathways people pursue to outstanding leadership. These experiences not only define narratives, and thus approaches to the crises that give rise to outstanding leadership, they also determine the repertoire of behavioral skills available to leaders. By conditioning available behavioral skills, these experiences may also act to determine when and where charismatic, ideological, and pragmatic leaders emerge.

11

Conclusions—Charismatic, Ideological, and Pragmatic Leaders: Different Paths to Outstanding Performance

Michael D. Mumford
Jill M. Strange
Samuel T. Hunter
The University of Oklahoma

It is difficult to dispute the impact of outstanding leadership on our lives and the broader social context that shapes the character of our lives. Martin Luther King changed the fundamental nature of racial relationships setting the course for a debate about integration rather than separation. Ronald Reagan initiated a strategy that brought an end to a conflict that literally put the world at risk. We drive to work every day on highways, highways that have shaped the fabric of our day-to-day lives, that in no small measure exist due to the efforts of Dwight D. Eisenhower.

Given the apparent impact of outstanding leadership on our lives, and our society, it is not unreasonable to argue that few topics in the social sciences warrant more attention. Yet, despite notable progress over the last 20 years (e.g., Conger & Kanungo, 1998; House, 1995), studies of outstanding leadership remain few and far between. The relative dearth of research on outstanding leadership is not attributable to a tendency to discount the importance of outstanding leadership. Instead, it is an epiphenomenon of the methodical approach applied in the social sciences.

Modern social science is, of course, a diverse, and multifaceted enterprise. Nonetheless, social science remains firmly grounded in the empirical, positivist, tradition. This tradition, and the methodological procedures it entails, make it difficult to study outstanding leadership in a systematic fashion. One reason for this difficulty is attributable to the fact that outstanding leaders are not readily available for study—outstanding leaders don't have the time to be "subjects." Another, perhaps somewhat more subtle, reason is that outstanding leaders,

leaders immersed in the conflict surrounding crises, are unlikely to reveal too much to anyone regardless of whether they are journalists, colleagues, lobbyists, or social scientists. Still another reason we find it difficult to study outstanding leadership is that ultimately outstanding leadership is a rare event—and it is only with the passage of time that it becomes possible to obtain a sufficient number of cases to permit quantitative analysis. Indeed, one might argue that it is only with the passage of time that one can say who was, and who was not, an outstanding leader.

The present book represents one attempt, hopefully a reasonably successful attempt, to overcome these challenges by conducting a quantitative analysis of the material drawn from multiple qualitative analyses of historically notable leaders. More specifically, in this book we attempted to apply a meta-analytic strategy where conclusions were drawn by aggregating observations across biographies, high-quality academic biographies, of multiple leaders. Our intent in this analysis was to provide some evidence that multiple pathways exist to outstanding leadership—pathways we have characterized as charismatic, ideological, and pragmatic. We sought, moreover, to determine how these three types of outstanding leaders differed with regard to critical behaviors—problem-solving activities, leader–follower relationships, communication strategies, political tactics, and development.

Limitations

As noted earlier, the quantitative analysis of multiple cases is not the only approach that might be used to study outstanding leadership. One might, for example, employ a dimensional-approximation approach (e.g., Jung et al., 2003; Lowe et al., 1996), experimental simulation (e.g., Kirkpatrick & Locke, 1996; Sosik et al., 1999), or qualitative case studies (e.g., Hunt & Ropo, 1995; Mumford & Van Doorn, 2001). The intent of the present study, the examination of cross-type differences, however, recommends the quantitative-case approach, in part because it represents the approach best suited to identifying the similarities and differences among different types of outstanding leaders and in part because it permits general conclusions to be drawn about typical behavior and experiences.

The quantitative-case approach applied in the present study was guided by an overarching hypothesis. More specifically, an attempt was made to confirm our hypothesis that the charismatic, ideological, and pragmatic types reflect distinct pathways to outstanding leadership that exist even when the distinction between socialized and personalized leaders (House & Howell, 1992) is taken into account. This theory-guided approach required a priori specification of the leaders who, at least apparently, had followed each of the pathways of interest. We suspect informed readers will, from time to time, dispute some of our classifications. Such disagreements are an inherent characteristic of this approach.

Indeed, in some cases, Malcolm X, for example (Mumford & Marcy, 2004), real and reasonable differences exist among scholars. In this regard, however, two points should be borne in mind. First, the classification of leaders in the present study does converge with the classification applied in other studies applying the quantitative-case approach (e.g., Fiol et al., 1999; O'Connor et al., 1995; Strange & Mumford, 2002). Second, error in classification of leaders decreases rather than increases the likelihood of finding expected cross-type differences. Thus, if we erred, it is an error that merely makes our findings more conservative.

A more significant limitation associated with the a priori specification of leader types arises from the constraints imposed by the selective, albeit systematic sampling, called for within this approach. Because we examined only leaders who illustrated each type, this study cannot rule out the potential existence of additional pathways to outstanding leadership beyond the charismatic, ideological, and pragmatic pathways. Along similar lines, the present study has little to say about the existence, and potential significance, of mixed-type leaders (Strange & Mumford, 2002). Finally, because we sought equal representation for each type, the present study does not have much to say about the "natural rate" with which charismatic, ideological, and pragmatic leaders emerge.

As is the case in most successful studies applying the quantitative case approach (e.g., Deluga, 2001; Emrich et al., 2001; Fiol et al., 1999; Strange & Mumford, 2002), the available qualitative data was not applied "as is." Instead, the approach applied herein involved the systematic abstraction of relevant behaviors from textual material accompanied by the application of coding procedures expressly developed to be appropriate with respect to representation of these behaviors in the material under consideration. The careful selection of textual material, the abstraction of relevant behavioral incidents, and the development of rating procedures appropriate to the material at hand may, in conjunction with the careful training of judges, account for the reliability and validity of the behavioral and experiential measures applied in the present investigation.

Despite the evidence accrued for the reliability and validity of the measures applied in examining the similarities and differences among charismatic, ideological, and pragmatic leaders, our conclusions in this regard might be questioned on other grounds, including reporting biases in biographical material, the kind of events typically considered in biographies, role differences, and so on. What should be recognized here, however, is that (a) an extensive set of control variables were developed and applied in the present set of studies, and (b) inferences about cross-type differences were drawn only after taking these controls, both general and study specific, into account. Thus many, although not all, of the biases associated with the use of qualitative biographical material were taken into account.

Nonetheless, one must remember that the biographical approach to the quantitative analysis of cases represents only one type of source data that might be used to characterize leaders' careers. For example, one might conceivably analyze the writings of contemporaries or examine leaders' autobiographies. We did not apply these approaches preferring to rely on the vetted, well documented, material presented in academic biographies. However, we would not rule out the value of these alternative sources for confirming the results obtained herein and for examining other phenomena, such as changes over time in perceptions of outstanding leaders.

Summary of Findings

As noted earlier, the primary concern in the present effort was demonstrating that behavioral and experiential differences exist among charismatic, ideological, and pragmatic leaders. Put more directly, we hoped to demonstrate that charismatic, ideological, and pragmatic leadership represent distinct pathways, viable pathways, to outstanding leadership. The significance of this objective is perhaps best understood by considering the current approach to outstanding leadership.

Traditionally, outstanding leadership is viewed as emerging from a single pathway. Here, of course, we refer to current theories of charismatic and transformational leadership (Bass, 1985, Conger & Kanungo, 1998; Shamir et al., 1993). Although theories of charismatic and transformational leadership evidence some noteworthy differences, they are bound together by the notion that outstanding leadership ultimately depends on the leader's effective articulation of a viable, future-oriented vision. Although the available evidence indicates that vision articulation has a profound impact on performance (e.g., Jacobsen & House, 2001; Kirkpatrick & Locke, 1996), the question remains as to whether there are alternative pathways to outstanding leadership.

This question is of some importance for three reasons (Foti & Miner, 2003). First, charismatic leadership may not prove universally effective across all settings and situations. Second, our nearly exclusive focus on charismatic leadership may have led us to lose sight of other attributes, or other strategies, that make possible the exercise of exceptional influence. Third, in our focus on vision and charisma, we may have created an overly restrictive model of outstanding leadership that leaves other talent to waste as we "force-fit" all leaders into a rigid charismatic model.

The present effort is based on the proposition that at least two other pathways to outstanding leadership exist—the ideological and pragmatic pathways—in addition to the charismatic pathway, which has been the primary focus of recent research on outstanding leadership. In our view, the origins of all three pathways lay in the fundamental nature of all forms of outstanding leadership. More specifically, we have argued that it is not vision per se that is the basis of outstanding leadership but rather the leader's construction of prescriptive mental models that provide a basis for sensemaking as people, and systems, grope for ways to cope with the crises that bring about the emergence of outstanding leaders (Drazin et al., 1999; Hunt et al., 1999; Weick, 1995).

Within this framework, articulation of a future-oriented vision is one way of using a prescriptive mental model to exercise influence. Another way prescriptive mental models might be used to exercise influence involves the construction and articulation of a vision that reinitiates a shared collective past vis-à-vis common beliefs and values—an ideological pathway. Still another way one might exercise exceptional influence is quite simply by using expertise and prescriptive models to resolve the various problems brought forth by a given crisis—a pragmatic pathway.

Taken as a whole, the results obtained in the series of studies conducted as part of the present effort provide some rather compelling evidence that these three alternative pathways to outstanding leadership, in fact, exist. In the present effort, we compared these three types in terms of four behavioral domains held to be critical to performance in the roles occupied by outstanding leaders: (a) problem-solving activities, (b) leader–follower relationships, (c) communication strategies, and (d) political tactics. Across all four of these domains, significant differences were observed in the pattern of behavior evidenced by charismatic, ideological, and pragmatic leaders, even when the distinction drawn between socialized and personalized leaders was taken into account.

Charismatic.   This observation, of course, brings to fore a new question: Exactly what do these behavioral differences tell us about the nature of charismatic, ideological, and pragmatic leaders? As might be expected (Yorges et al., 2001), the great strength of charismatic leaders, particularly socialized charismatics, lies in communication through follower-based appeals. Apparently charismatic leaders are unusually skilled at engaging others in the vision they are advocating vis-à-vis emotional persuasion, eloquence, a focus on followers' personal needs, and a focus on followers' social needs. Given the impact of creating a shared image of the future and building a consensus around this image, it is hardly surprising that follower based appeals would prove critical to defining the charismatic pathway.

Ideological.   What should be recognized in this regard, however, is that ideological leaders, particularly socialized ideologues, evidenced the same strength. In fact, it appears that ideologues were better able to make follower-based appeals than charismatic leaders, perhaps because such appeals could be framed around extant shared beliefs and values. The power and potential impact of ideological leadership, the power of shared ideals, was evident in two other ways in which ideological leaders differed from charismatic and pragmatic leaders. First, ideological leaders, in contrast to charismatic leaders who must maintain personal control in pursuing their unique vision of the future, were better able to share direction of the group with key lieutenants. In a sense, this finding is not especially surprising because the shared beliefs and values ideological leaders find in, or create in, their lieutenants provide a basis for effective delegation. What should be recognized here, however, is that the creation of an effective top-management team greatly enhances the potential impact of ideological leaders (Boal & Hooijberg, 2000). Second, ideological leaders, despite our stereotype of ideologues as thoughtless advocates of a given doctrine, in fact appear to display problem-solving skills that are substantially better than those of charismatic leaders; indeed, in some ways, their problem-solving skills come close to equaling those of pragmatic leaders. In fact, ideological leaders seem particularly skilled at conceptual integration—a finding that may reflect their concern with ideas and the need to integrate change and crises with the key communalities arising from shared beliefs and values.

Pragmatic. Not only was evidence accrued in the present effort for a distinct ideological pathway, a pathway that cannot simply be lumped under the rubric of charismatic leadership, substantial evidence was also obtained for the existence of a distinct pragmatic pathway. Pragmatic leaders relied on expertise, logical appeals, and rational persuasion—a pattern of behavior consistent with the earlier observations emerging from Mumford and Van Doorn's (2001) study of Benjamin Franklin. Pragmatics' use of expertise, logical appeals, and rational persuasion, in turn, suggests, consistent with our theory, that the success of pragmatic leaders is based in their ability to craft viable solutions to the problems posed by crisis or change. Although pragmatic leaders may not have the direct emotional impact of charismatic and ideological leaders, their ability to craft coherent solutions to the problems posed by crisis situations may allow them to exercise unusual influence through institution building—a point illustrated in our examination of performance differences.

Performance Differences

Leader Performance. The existence of distinct charismatic, ideological, and pragmatic pathways brings to fore a number of questions. Perhaps the most straightforward question in this regard concerns the existence of potential performance differences among charismatic, ideological, and pragmatic leaders. The findings obtained in our examination of the general outcome measures drawn from the epilogue, or prologue, chapters indicated that marked differences in overall performance were not observed among charismatic, ideological, and pragmatic leaders. Thus, in a general sense, it is fair to say that charismatic, ideological, and pragmatic leadership represent alternative, potentially equally viable pathways to outstanding leadership.

In this regard, however, it is important to note that the differences in pathways were linked to differences in the kind of outcomes pursued by leaders and the strategies used to bring about the attainment of these outcomes. Thus, pragmatic leaders did not initiate mass movements nor were they capable of exerting broad social impact. However, they did build institutions that were maintained over time at minimal social cost. This institution building was linked to skill in practical problem solving—problem-solving activities consistent with the value pragmatic leaders place on expertise and rational influence attempts. In contrast, ideological and charismatic leaders seemed to build their performance around others, exercising broad general social effects through communication and relationship building. In other words, charismatic and ideological leaders perform by moving people while pragmatic leaders perform by solving the problems of institution building.

Leader Emergence. These observations about performance strategies, in turn, bring to fore a new question: Are there differences in the conditions, or environment, giving rise to charismatic, ideological, and pragmatic leaders? Strictly speaking, the present effort has little to say about how the environment and local conditions shape performance requirements and the likely emergence of charismatic, ideological, and pragmatic leaders. The importance of this issue for future research, however, is underscored by one finding that emerged in the present effort. More specifically, different types of outstanding leaders emerge in different organizational settings. For example, ideological leaders are found in political and service organizations, whereas pragmatic leaders are found in military and business organizations. The tendency of certain types of outstanding leaders to emerge in certain organizational environments, however, broaches a number of other questions:

1. What environmental mechanisms (e.g., selection, socialization, performance demands) act to channel outstanding leadership along certain avenues?
2. Do followers perceive, and respond to, different types of outstanding leaders in different ways depending on the role, or setting, in which they are operating?
3. Is the nature of the crisis more important than setting, and follower expectations, in determining the type of outstanding leader likely to emerge?

These cross-organizational differences in leader emergence and performance, however, also imply that multiple different types of leaders will be interacting around select issues. This observation, in turn, suggests that there might be value in studies examining the nature of the interactions that occur among charismatic, ideological, and pragmatic leaders. In fact, these interactions might take a variety of different forms. It is possible that differences in leader types result in miscommunication and conflict. It is also possible that leadership teams may be able to capitalize on each others unique strengths and weaknesses resulting in synergistic effects. Finally, it is possible that different types of leaders emerge at different times depending on the degree of structure or chaos in the situation, with ideologues emerging relatively early and pragmatics relatively late in a cycle of crisis resolution activities. Although the present study could not address these leader by leader, and leader by time, interactions, there would seem to be value for further research along these lines.

Socialized Versus Personalized Leaders. The results obtained in the present effort not only confirm the existence of the charismatic, ideological, and pragmatic pathways, they point to the importance of the distinction drawn between socialized and personalized leaders (House & Howell, 1992; O'Connor et al., 1995). Although marked differences were not observed in the performance of charismatic, ideological, and pragmatic leaders, marked performance differences were obtained in contrasting socialized and personalized leaders on the general performance criteria drawn from the prologue and epilogue chapters. As might be expected, socialized leaders performed better, substantially better, than personalized leaders.

Traditionally, students of leadership have tended to construe the differences observed between socialized and personalized in terms of integrity or ethics. The results obtained in the present effort, however, indicated that integrity is not just another desirable characteristic for leaders, it is perhaps the single most important characteristic shaping leader performance. In keeping with this observation, it was found that variables discriminating socialized and personalized leaders were often the most powerful predictors of leader performance in the various regression analyses.

One explanation as to why socialized leaders are better performers than personalized leaders may be found in the results obtained in examining leader–follower relationships. Personalized leaders are less able than socialized leaders to create, and work with, teams in the management of complex crises. Given the controlling, narcissistic orientation of personalized leaders (O'Connor et al., 1995), this finding is not especially surprising. It is significant, however, in explaining the performance differences observed between socialized and personalized leaders because leader performance is known to depend on the development of a strong "top management" team (Boal & Hooijberg, 2000). In the case of outstanding leaders, moreover, this team of close followers may be essential for both dissemination and maintenance initiatives established by the leader. Lacking this support, the impact and performance of leaders will be limited.

The findings obtained in the present effort, however, point to two other factors that may act to undermine the performance of personalized leaders. First, personalized leaders, in contrast to socialized leaders, were found to motivate followers through extrinsic as opposed to intrinsic rewards. This lack of intrinsic motivation, in turn, implies that followers are unlikely to internalize the prescriptive mental model, or ideas, of the leader—making it difficult to maintain the leader's agenda over time. In fact, personalized leaders may be able to exercise influence only as long as they remain able to control rewards and contingencies thereby resulting in a transitory form of influence limited by the leader's current possession of a position of power.

Second, personalized leaders differed from socialized leaders in terms of prosocial argumentation. In their narcissistic concern with personal control, it becomes difficult for personalized leaders to grasp the needs and concerns of others. Their inability to understand the needs and concerns of others, in turn, makes it difficult for personalized leaders to craft communications that will evoke sustained positive action on the part of the followers. When the suboptimal communication, failure to induce intrinsic motivation, and lack of an effective top-management team are considered in light of the negative effects of a personalized orientation on information appraisal (Mumford, Espejo, Hunter, Bedell, Eubanks, & Connelly, 2005), it is not surprising that personalized leaders display poor performance when compared to socialized leaders.

This observation, given the frequency with which personalized leaders emerge across the pages of history, begs a question: How is it possible that history seems replete with personalized leaders? One answer to this question may be found in the fact that personalized leaders, in contrast to socialized leaders, seek power and control. This search for power and control, of course, may induce extraordinary effort to attain positions of influence. Another answer to this question, however, lies in the fact that problem solving and political tactics were not strongly related to leader orientation—socialized versus personalized. Thus, through political manipulation, and viable solutions to immediate pressing crises, personalized leaders may attain a position of local advantage that allows them to move into significant leadership roles. In fact, personalized leaders may create such crises as a vehicle to promote their advancement—a point illustrated in the early career of Adolf Hitler.

Theory and Development

The differences observed among charismatic, ideological, and pragmatic leaders, as well as the differences observed in comparing socialized and personalized leaders seem to provide some rather compelling support for the theory of outstanding leadership underlying the present effort. For example, consistent with the observations of Mumford and Van Doorn (2001), and the notion that pragmatic leaders formulate localized, problem-centered prescriptive mental models, pragmatic leaders were found to differ from charismatic and ideological leaders in problem-solving performance, their emphasis on the use of expertise, and the tendency to make rational appeals. Along similar lines, it was argued earlier that ideological leaders construct prescriptive mental models around shared beliefs and values (Strange & Mumford, 2002). In keeping with this proposition, it was found that capitalization on these common beliefs and values allowed ideological leaders to share direction of the enterprise.

Although other examples of this sort might be cited, the foregoing examples seem sufficient to make our basic point. The behavioral differences observed among the various types of outstanding leaders under consideration were, broadly speaking, consistent with the theory of outstanding leadership under consideration. Essentially, this theory holds that outstanding leadership is a leadership of crisis (Bligh, Kohles, & Meindl, 2004; Halverson, Holladay, Kazma, & Quionnes, 2004; Hunt et al., 1999) where crises are broadly defined as novel change events leading to decrements in organizational performance. The impact of outstanding leaders is, within this framework, contingent on their ability to help followers make sense of the crisis at hand (Drazin et al., 1999; Weick, 1995). These sensemaking activities provide followers with an understanding of the situation along with a framework that might be used to guide collective action in responding to the crisis.

The basis of sensemaking, however, is held to lie in the leader's construction of a prescriptive mental model (Mumford & Strange, 2002). The construction of prescriptive mental models, mental models that, in the case of ideological and charismatic leadership, provide the basis for vision formation (Strange & Mumford, 2005), is dependent on analysis of the causes of the crisis and the goals that should be pursued in crisis resolution. However, analysis per se is not a fully sufficient basis for crisis resolution, sensemaking, and construction of prescriptive mental models. Instead, the construction of prescriptive mental models is held to depend on the leader's reflection on these goals and causes in relation to the experiences they have encountered over the course of their careers.

The need for reflection on past experience suggests that the nature and content of prior life events, the events used to define life narratives (Habermas & Bluck, 2000; McAdams, 2001; Pillemer, 2001), will represent critical influences on the nature of the prescriptive mental models constructed by outstanding leaders. In fact, the way people apply life narratives in understanding and responding to events in their lives suggests that life narratives, or life stories, will play a critical role in sensemaking and the construction of prescriptive mental models. Life narratives provide people with a system for understanding and responding to complex, ambiguous events—and most crises are complex, ambiguous events. These narratives, moreover, provide a framework for guiding actions and communication with others. In fact, at least three pieces of evidence accrued in the present effort provide some support for these hypotheses with regard to the role of life narratives, and prescriptive mental models derived from reflection on these narratives, in shaping the pathways people follow to outstanding leadership.

First, people are exposed to a number of different kinds of significant events in the course of their lives—significant events that provide the keystones for narrative construction. In contrasting leaders with regard to significant events, specifically originating events, anchoring events, analogous events, turning point events, contaminating events, and redemptive events, it was found that different types of events took on special significance in the lives of different types of outstanding leaders—events that were consistent with the prescriptive mental model held to characterize a certain leader type. Thus, it was found that anchoring events, events defining core beliefs and values, appeared more frequently in the biographies of ideological leaders than charismatic and pragmatic leaders. Originating events, events defining goals, appeared more frequently in the biographies of pragmatic leaders than charismatic leaders and ideological leaders. Redemptive events were observed more frequently in the early lives of socialized leaders, and contaminating events were observed more frequently in the lives of personalized leaders.

Second, when the thematic content of significant events was examined, it was found that the content of these events was consistent with the general nature of the prescriptive mental models held to be applied by a certain type of outstanding leader. For example, in the case of ideological leaders, the themes evident in significant early life events stressed the importance of beliefs and values. The early experiences of pragmatic leaders, however, were characterized by themes that stressed the value of practical analytic problem solving and a certain skepticism about others.

Third, consistent with the general theoretical model under consideration, and the notion that life narratives provide guidelines for action, these themes were found to be strongly related to differences observed among various types of outstanding leaders in the discriminant analyses. Thus, spirituality and belief commitment were found to be related to the tendency of outstanding leaders to engage in shared direction—a common attribute of ideological leaders. Similarly, the use of logical appeals, a communication strategy found to characterize pragmatic leaders, was linked to early life events giving rise to an evidential preference, logical analysis, and a focus on the present. Taken as a whole, these findings not only confirm the distinctions drawn among the various types of outstanding leaders, they also underscore the role of personal experience, and reflection on this experience, in defining the pathways people follow to outstanding leadership.

Beyond this general conclusion, however, a number of other findings emerge in this analysis of developmental influences that warrant attention in further studies. One of these findings pertains to the nature of charismatic leadership. More specifically, charismatic leaders were less readily identified in terms of thematic content than were ideological and pragmatic leaders. Instead, the key to understanding charismatic leaders seemed to lie in their exposure to change events or turning point events—a finding that suggests that proactive individual adaptation to change may be critical to the development of charismatic leaders. Because change may be for good or ill, the role of turning point events in shaping the careers of charismatic leaders points to a pernicious problem. More specifically, excessive exposure to change events may result in attempts to manage uncertainty through control. In other words, charismatic leaders, even socialized charismatic leaders, may have a dark side, and a predilection to follow a personalized as opposed to a socialized path to outstanding leadership due to their need for personal control. Indeed, concern about this predilection was one force driving the framework of the U.S. Constitution (Ellis, 2001).

Finally, with regard to the development of socialized and personalized leaders, a noteworthy, potentially significant, asymmetry emerged. More specifically, contaminating events, especially events associated with a negative view of others and the need for control, exerted particularly strong effects on the behavior of personalized leaders—effects stronger than the influence of positive developmental events on the behavior of socialized leaders. Apparently, experience, bad experience, gives rise to personalized leaders. This observation, however, broaches the question. Why do negative experiences play such a powerful role in creating destructive behavior on the part of outstanding leaders?

Behavioral Dimensions of Outstanding Leadership

Not only has the present study provided us with an understanding of the nature and origins of outstanding leadership, it has also provided some important new information about the behavioral dimensions that make outstanding leadership possible. In fact, the dimensions obtained in the discriminant analyses contrasting outstanding leaders with respect to problem-solving activities, leader–follower relationships, communication strategies, and political tactics seem to paint a rather coherent picture of the requirements for outstanding leadership.

Outstanding leadership requires expertise and experience with the operations of the social system under consideration (Fleishman et al., 1991). Indeed, without expertise, it is difficult to see how someone could accurately appraise relevant goals and causes and construct a viable, plausible, prescriptive mental model. The findings obtained in examining problem-solving activities, however, indicated that expertise per se is not sufficient to ensure outstanding leadership. Outstanding leadership also requires conceptual integration and external integration. In other words, outstanding leaders must bring ideas together in such a way that they are consistent with the demands imposed by the external environment. Although it may not be surprising that outstanding leaders are integrators, what one must bear in mind in this regard is that integrative activities, both conceptual and external integration, are unusually demanding activities—intellectual demands a leader must be able to address if they are to make sense of the complex crises that give rise to the need for outstanding leadership (Jacques, 1976).

Outstanding leadership, however, is clearly not simply a matter of expertise, conceptual integration, and external integration. Outstanding leadership emerges in response to complex multifaceted crises—crises making demands that go well beyond any particular individual, however gifted. This point is of some importance because it suggests that outstanding leaders are not heroes working alone. Instead, their work, and the success of this work, will depend on a cadre of dedicated lieutenants. Our examination of the behaviors involved in leader–follower interactions indicated that to build this cadre of dedicated lieutenants, leaders cannot just reward followers, they must engage followers by building intrinsic motivation. Leaders must, moreover, put their egos aside, leading not as an individual but through a team with whom they are willing to share direction of the enterprise (Boal & Hooijberg, 2000).

The ability to involve others and share leadership, however, will not prove fully sufficient for outstanding leadership. Outstanding leadership requires that leaders be able to reach out to others through effective communication and the appropriate exercise of influence (Yukl, 2002). High-impact communication, however, requires prosocial argumentation (Fiol et al., 1999) as well as follower-based appeals and logical appeals. Thus, outstanding leadership requires the capacity to present arguments in a positive social context. Of course, communication, especially prosocial argumentation, is only one way to exercise influence. Another way leaders exercise influence is through political tactics. And, our findings with regard to political behavior indicated that outstanding leadership calls for rational influence. In other words, outstanding leaders do not force compliance; rather, they allow autonomy by seeking to shape people's personal decisions based on their articulation of the issues at hand.

Practical Implications

These dimensions of outstanding leadership are of interest for both practical and theoretical reasons. At a practical level, an understanding of these dimensions has much to say about how we might go about creating the capacity for outstanding leadership. For example, we might expressly seek leaders who have the background and basic capacities that make conceptual and external integration possible (Mumford, Zaccaro, Harding, et al., 2000). Alternatively, we might train leaders to use prosocial argumentation techniques. Finally, we might formulate strategies or procedures that help leaders motivate, manage, and share direction with other members of a top-management team.

Not only do the dimensions underlying outstanding leadership have some noteworthy practical implications, both the alternative pathways identified in the present effort and the mechanisms underlying the emergence of these pathways point to some potentially noteworthy applications. To begin, organizations have, at least historically, sought to identify a single type of ideal leader. The emergence of the charismatic, ideological, and pragmatic pathways, however, suggests that organizations confronting different conditions should seek out different types of leaders. Thus, in searching for leaders, organizations should examine the nature and structure of the crises at hand, or those likely to emerge, seeking out leaders following a pathway that will allow them to respond effectively to the demands imposed by these crises.

For example, in chaotic situations—and chaos often characterizes entrepreneurial organizations—ideological leadership may be necessary. Although it may, at first glance, seem strange to argue that entrepreneurs may often be ideologues, when one considers the careers of Scott McNealy and Bill Gates this notion may seem less farfetched. In contrast, in large stable organizations, it is not the ideologue or the charismatic who will be needed but rather the pragmatic leaders who can manipulate key causes to build an institution.

In addition to indicating the type of leader likely to prove effective in different settings, the results obtained in the present study remind us that organizations, if they are to avoid devastation, must minimize the advancement of personalized leaders. Clearly, personalized leaders undermine organizational performance. What should be recognized here, however, is that it is not problem-solving and/or political skills that allow us to identify personalized leaders but rather their relationships with others and their modes of communication. Clearly, relationships and communication strategies represent only one of a number of interpersonal behaviors that might be applied in attempts to identify and screen out personalized leaders.

The model underlying the present effort, and the results obtained in the developmental study, point to another noteworthy practical implication. We may know outstanding leadership when we see it, but it has proven singularly difficult to develop outstanding leaders (Strange & Mumford, 2005). However, the importance of sensemaking to outstanding leadership suggests that by developing procedures that help leaders analyze the causes of crises, identify critical goals, and select and reflect on relevant case models, we may do much to facilitate leader performance. Moreover, by providing leaders with viable case models, and the opportunity to reflect on these models, one may do much to make outstanding leadership a real possibility, especially if we can find ways to encourage reflection during the crises that often promote action in lieu of reflection.

Theoretical Implications

At a theoretical level, the findings obtained in the present study point to a need to reformulate the current paradigm applied in studies of outstanding leadership. One aspect of this paradigm derives from the influence of the romantic tradition. We tend to conceive of outstanding leaders as heroes—heroes acting alone. However, the findings obtained in examining leader–follower relationships suggest that far more attention needs to be given to the role of followers, and the nature of leaders' interactions with followers, in shaping the nature and success of outstanding leaders.

Another aspect of the paradigm currently applied in studies of outstanding leadership involves the decontextualization of the leader and his or her activities. In other words, we study the leader, not the context of the crisis giving rise to outstanding leadership or the life context in which the leader seeks to understand and resolve the crisis. What should be recognized here, however, is that prosocial argumentation, like the narratives around which leaders build their arguments, is inherently a contextual phenomenon. Thus, if we are to build a truly comprehensive understanding of outstanding leadership, we must begin to develop and apply models that expressly consider key contextual variables in attempts to describe and explain the behavior of outstanding leaders.

Another assumption evident in the paradigm currently applied in studies of outstanding leadership involves the tendency to explain outstanding leadership in terms of social-interactional behaviors (e.g., Shamir et al., 1993). Given the findings obtained in the present study, we do not wish to dispute the value of this approach. By the same token, however, in our focus on social interactions we appear to have lost sight of a more fundamental phenomenon. Ultimately, outstanding leaders must think—they must think about crises, ideas, relationships, and their lives to permit sensemaking, integration, and the construction of viable prescriptive mental models.

Current theories of outstanding leadership have, in my view, suffered due to a search for a single "magic bullet" that makes outstanding leadership possible. Here, of course, I refer to the emphasis placed on vision in attempts to understand and explain outstanding leaders. The results obtained in the present study, however, indicate that while vision may be important to outstanding leadership, visioning is not the only key characteristic of outstanding leadership. Outstanding leaders must build a cadre of followers, they must think integratively, and they must communicate. Until we recognize the inherent multidimensionality of outstanding leadership, it seems unlikely that we will develop truly viable models of this complex, multifaceted phenomenon.

More centrally, from a theoretical perspective we must, as a field, begin to try to understand outstanding leadership as it operates in a complex field. It is not to identify and understand the behaviors of outstanding leaders. We must understand how they make sense of crises, why they view these crises as significant, and how they create and articulate an understanding of complex, rapidly unfolding situations to others. Hopefully, the present effort will provide an impetus for further work intended to elucidate how leaders come to understand and appraise the complex crises that provide a basis for the sensemaking that underlies the charismatic, ideological, and pragmatic pathways to outstanding leadership.

Concluding Comments

This call for the need for greater complexity in our models of outstanding leadership is underscored by the broader conclusions resulting from the present effort. The key finding emerging from this effort is that there is not one way, or one set of behaviors, that makes outstanding leadership possible. Rather, the fundamental nature of outstanding leadership makes possible multiple alternative pathways to outstanding leadership. To make real progress in our understanding of outstanding leadership, we must begin to try to understand the origins and implications of these pathways. Hopefully, the present effort will provide an impetus for further research along these lines.

Appendix:
Reference List of Biographies Used in Content Analysis Studies

Alaexander, R. J. (1979). *Juan Domingo Perón: A history*. Boulder, CO: Westview Press.

Anderson, J., & May, R. W. (1952). *McCarthy: The man, the senator, and the "ism."* Boston: Beacon Press.

Anthony, K. (1954). *Susan B. Anthony: Her personal history and era*. New York: Doubleday.

Baker, L. (1969). *Felix Frankfurter*. New York: Coward-McCann.

Bar-Zohar, M. (1966). *The armed prophet: A biography of Ben-Gurion*. London: Arthur Barker. (Translated)

Bennett, L. (1976). *A biography of Martin Luther King, Jr.* Chicago: Johnson.

Bosanquet, M. (1968). *The life and death of Dietrich Bonhoeffer*. New York: Harper & Row.

Bosch, A. (1988). *Reagan: An American story*. New York: TV Books.

Bosworth, R. J. B. (2002). *Mussolini*. London: Arnold.

Brands, H. W. (1997). *T.R.: The last romantic*. New York: Basic Books.

Broderick, F. L. (1959). *W.E.B. DuBois: Negro leader in a time of crisis*. Stanford: Stanford University Press.

Brunk, S. (1995). *Emiliano Zapata: Revolution and betrayal in Mexico*. Albuquerque: University of New Mexico Press.

Byrne, J. A. (1999). *Chainsaw: The notorious career of Al Dunlap in the era of profit-at-any-price*. New York: HarperBusiness.

Byron, C. (2002). *Martha Inc.: The incredible story of Martha Stewart Living Omnimedia*. New York: Wiley.

Calic, E. (1982). *Reinhard Heydrich: The chilling story of the man who masterminded the Nazi death camps*. New York: Military Heritage Press. (Translated)

Caro, R. A. (1974). *The power broker: Robert Moses and the fall of New York*. New York: Knopf.

Chadha, Y. (1997). *Gandhi: A life*. New York: Wiley.

Chandler, D. P. (1999). *Brother number one: A political biography of Pol Pot*. Boulder, CO: Westview Press.

Chernow, R. (1998). *Titan: The life of John D. Rockefeller, Sr.* New York: Vintage.

Clark, C. M. (2000). *Kaiser Wilhelm II*. London: Longman.

Cohen, A., & Taylor, E. (2000). *American pharaoh: Mayor Richard J. Daley: His battle for Chicago and the nation*. Boston: Little, Brown.

Coogan, T. P. (1990). *Michael Collins: A biography*. London: Hutchinson.

Cook, B. W. (1992). *Eleanor Roosevelt: Volume one 1884–1933*. New York: Viking.

Cook, B. W. (1999). *Eleanor Roosevelt: Volume two 1933–1938*. New York: Viking.

Crassweller, R. D. (1966). *Trujillo: The life and times of a Caribbean dictator*. New York: Macmillan.

Crozier, B. (1973). *De Gaulle*. New York: Scribner's.

Davis, J. H. (1993). *Mafia dynasty: The rise and fall of the Gambino crime family*. New York: HarperPaperbacks.

Diederich, B., & Burt, A. (1991). *Papa Doc: Haiti and its dictator*. Maplewood, NJ: Waterfront Press.

Dinges, J. (1990). *Our man in Panama: How General Noriega used the United States—and made millions in drugs and arms*. New York: Random House.

Dubofsky, M., & Van Tine, W. (1986). *John L. Lewis: A biography*. Urbana: University of Illinois Press.

Duiker, W. J. (2000). *Ho Chi Minh*. New York: Hyperion.

Dykhuizen, G. (1973). *The life and mind of John Dewey*. Carbondale: Southern Illinois University Press.

Falk, C. S. (1984). *Love, anarchy, and Emma Goldman*. New Brunswick, NJ: Rutgers University Press.

Feiling, K. (1946). *The life of Neville Chamberlain*. London: Macmillan.

Felsenthal, C. (1993). *Power, privilege and the Post: The Katharine Graham story*. New York: Putnam.

Ferrell, R. H. (1994). *Harry S. Truman: A life*. Columbia: University of Missouri Press.

Fischer, L. (1964). *The life of Lenin*. New York: Harper & Row.

Fosdick, R. B. (1956). *John D. Rockefeller, Jr.: A portrait*. New York: Harper & Brothers.

Frank, K. (2002). *Indira: The life of Indira Nehru Gandhi*. Boston: Houghton Mifflin.

Franz, U. (1988). *Deng Xiaoping*. Boston: Harcourt Brace. (Translated)

Fraser, D. (1993). *Knight's cross: A life of Field Marshall Erwin Rommel*. New York: HarperCollins.

Fraser, N., & Navarro, M. (1980). *Eva Peron*. New York: Norton.

Garner, P. (2001). *Porfirio Diaz*. London: Longman.

Gelderman, C. (1981). *Henry Ford: The wayward capitalist*. New York: Dial Press.

Gilbert, M. (1991). *Churchill: A life*. New York: Holt.

Griswold del Castillo, R., & Garcia, R. A. (1995). *Cesar Chavez: A triumph of spirit*. Norman: University of Oklahoma Press.

Harlan, L. R. (1872). *Booker T. Washington: The making of a Black leader, 1856–1901*. New York: Oxford University Press.

Hart, B. H. L. (1932). *Foch: The man of Orleans*. Boston: Little, Brown.

Heckscher, A. (1991). *Woodrow Wilson*. New York: Scribner's.

Hennessee, J. (1999). *Betty Friedan: Her life*. New York: Random House.

Higham, C. (1993). *Merchant of dreams: Louis B. Mayer, M.G.M., and the secret Hollywood*. New York: Donald I. Fine.

Hirshson, S. P. (2002). *General Patton: A soldier's life*. New York: HarperCollins.

Hirst, D., & Beeson, I. (1981). *Sadat*. London: Faber & Faber.

Hyde, H. M. (1971). *Stalin: The history of a dictator*. New York: Farrar, Straus & Giroux.

Irving, D. (1989). *Goring: A biography*. New York: Morrow.

James, D. C. (1970). *The years of MacArthur*. Boston: Houghton Mifflin.

Kaufman, M. T. (2002). *Soros: The life and times of a messianic billionaire*. New York: Knopf.

Kaye, T. (1989). *Lech Walesa*. New York: Chelsea House.

Kessner, T. (1989). *Fiorello H. La Guardia and the making of modern New York*. New York: McGraw-Hill.

Knight, A. (1993). *Beria: Stalin's first lieutenant*. Princeton, NJ: Princeton University Press.

Kobler, J. (1992). *Capone: The life and world of Al Capone*. Greenwich, CT: Fawcett.

Krass, P. (2002). *Carnegie*. Hoboken, NJ: Wiley.

Lacouture, J. (1973). *Nasser*. New York: Knopf. (Translated)

Lasky, V. (1981). *Never complain, never explain: The story of Henry Ford II*. New York: Richard Marek.

Lenin, H. (1983). *Grand delusions: The cosmic career of John De Lorean*. New York: Viking Press.

Linn, J. W. (1935). *Jane Addams: A biography*. New York: Appleton–Century.

Lowenstein, R. (1995). *Buffett: The making of an American capitalist*. New York: Random House.

Lyon, P. (1974). *Eisenhower: Portrait of the hero*. Boston: Little, Brown.

Lyons, E. (1964). *Herbert Hoover: A biography*. Garden City, NY: Doubleday.

Lyons, E. (1966). *David Sarnoff*. New York: Harper & Row.

Maclean, F. (1980). *Josip Broz Tito: A pictorial biography*. New York: McGraw-Hill.

Manchester, W. (1968). *The arms of Krupp: 1587–1968*. Boston: Little, Brown.

Mandel, B. (1963). *Samuel Gompers: A biography*. Yellow Springs: Antioch Press.

Maney, K. (2003). *The maverick and his machine: Thomas Watson, Sr. and the making of IBM*. Hoboken, NJ: Wiley.

Mango, A. (2000). *Attaturk*. New York: Overlook Press.

McCauley, M. (1998). *Gorbachev*. London: Longman.

McDougal, D. (1988). *The last mogul: Lew Wasserman, MCA, and the hidden history of Hollywood*. New York: Crown.

McDougal, D. (2001). *Privileged son: Otis Chandler and the rise and fall of the L.A. Times dynasty*. New York: Perseus.

Morgan, T. (1985). *FDR: A biography*. New York: Simon & Schuster.

Mosely, L. (1982). *Marshall: Hero for our times*. New York: Hearst Books.

Mosely, L. (1985). *Disney's world*. New York: Stein & Day.

Moss, M. (1988). *Palace coup: The inside story of Harry and Leona Helmsley*. New York: Doubleday.

Murray, R. K. (1969). *The Harding era: Warren G. Harding and his administration*. Minneapolis: University of Minnesota Press.

Murray-Brown, J. (1973). *Kenyatta*. New York: Dutton.

Neff, J. (1989). *Mobbed up: Jackie Presser's high-wire life in the Teamsters, the Mafia, and the F.B.I.* New York: Atlantic Monthly Press.

Norris, R. S. (2002). *Racing for the bomb: General Leslie R. Groves, the Manhattan Project's indispensable man*. South Royalton, VT: Steerforth Press.

Padfield, P. (1990). *Himmler: Reichsfuhrer-SS*. London: Macmillan.

Payne, R. (1973). *The life and death of Adolf Hitler*. New York: Praeger.

Perret, G. (2001). *Jack: A life like no other*. New York: Random House.

Perry, B. (1991). *Malcolm: The life of a man who changed Black America*. Barrytown, NY: Station Hill Press.

Polmar, N., & Allen, T. B. (1982). *Rickover*. New York: Simon & Schuster.

Posner, G. (2002). *Motown: Music, money, sex and power*. New York: Random House.

Powers, R. G. (1987). *Secrecy and power: The life of J. Edgar Hoover*. New York: The Free Press.

Preston, P. (1994). *Franco: A biography*. London: Basic Books.

Pruessen, R. W. (1982). *John Foster Dulles: The road to power*. New York: The Free Press.

Rooney, D. (1988). *Kwame Nkrumah: The political kingdom in the third world*. New York: St. Martin's Press.

Salvatore, N. (1982). *Eugene V. Debs: Citizen and Socialist*. Urbana: University of Illinois Press.

Schwarzwaller, W. (1988). *Rudolf Hess: The last Nazi*. Bethesda, MD: National Press.

Seale, P. (1988). *Asad of Syria: The struggle for the Middle East*. Berkley: University of California Press.

Segal, R. (1979). *Leon Trotsky: A biography*. New York: Pantheon.

Shawcross, W. (1992). *Murdoch: The making of a media empire*. New York: Touchstone Press.

Short, P. (1999). *Mao: A life*. New York: Holt.

Sloane, A. A. (1991). *Hoffa*. Cambridge, MA: MIT Press.

Smith, G. I. (1980). *Ghosts of Kampala*. New York: St. Martin's Press. (Idi Amin)

Spence, H. (1969). *Marcos of the Philippines*. New York: World.

Sperber, A. M. (1986). *Murrow: His life and times*. New York: Freundlich Books.

Stein, J. (1986). *The world of Marcus Garvey: Race and class in modern society*. Baton Rouge: Louisiana State University Press.

Steinberg, A. (1975). *Sam Rayburn: A biography*. New York: Hawthorn Books.

Strouse, J. (1999). *Morgan: American financier*. New York: Random House.

Summers, A., & Swan, R. (2000). *The arrogance of power: The secret world of Richard Nixon*. New York: Viking.

Szulc, T. (1986). *Fidel: A critical portrait*. New York: Morrow.

Tilton, E. M. (1947. *Amiable autocrat: A biography of Dr. Oliver Wendell Holmes*. New York: Schuman.

Trimble, V. H. (1990). *Walton: The inside story of America's richest man*. New York: Dutton.

Ulam, A. B. (1989). *Stalin: The man and his era*. New York: Viking Press.

Unger, I., & Unger, D. (1999). *LBJ: A life*. New York: Wiley.

Urquhart, B. (1971). *Hammarskjold*. New York: Knopf.

Wall, J. F. (1990). *Alfred I. du Pont: The man and his family*. New York: Oxford University Press.

Warner, P. (1986). *Kitchener: The man behind the legend*. New York: Atheneum.

Watson, D. R. (1974). *Georges Clemenceau: A political biography*. New York: David McKay.

Williams, T. H. (1969). *Huey Long*. New York: Vintage Books.

Wyden, P. (1987). *The unknown Iacocca*. New York: Morrow.

Young, H. (1989). *One of us: A biography of Margaret Thatcher*. London: Macmillan.

Zaffiri, S. (1994). *Westmoreland: A biography of General William C. Westmoreland*. New York: Morrow.

References

Alea, N., & Bluck, S. (2003). Why are you telling us that? A conceptual model of the social function of autobiographical memory. *Memory, 11*, 165–178.

Amabile, T. M. (1988). A model of creativity and innovation in organizations. *Research in Organizational Behavior, 10*, 123–167.

Ammeter, A. P., Douglas, C., Gardner, W. L., Hochwarter, W. A., & Ferris, G. R. (2002). Toward a political theory of leadership. *Leadership Quarterly, 13*, 751–796.

Ansbacher, H. L., & Ansbacher, R. R. (1956). *The individual psychology of Alfred Adler*. Oxford, England: Basic Books.

Antonakis, J., & House, R. J. (2002). The full-range leadership theory: The way forward. In B. J. Avolio & F. J. Yammarino (Eds.), *Transformational and charismatic leadership: The road ahead* (pp. 3–34). Oxford, England: Elsevier.

Ashforth, B. A., & Lee, R. T. (1990). Defensive behavior in organizations: A preliminary model. *Human Relations, 43*, 621–649.

Avolio, B. J., Howell, J. M., & Sosik, J. J. (1999). A funny thing happened on the way to the bottom line: Humor as a moderator of leadership style effects. *Academy of Management Journal, 42*, 219–227.

Baltes, P. B. (1997). On the incomplete architecture of human ontogeny: Selection, optimization, and compensation as foundation of developing theory. *American Psychologist, 52*, 366–380.

Barclay, C. R. (1995). Autobiographical remembering: Narrative constraints on objectified selves. In D. C. Rubin (Ed.), *Remembering our past* (pp. 94–125). Cambridge, England: Cambridge University Press.

Barreto, M., Spears, R., & Ellemers, N. (2003). Who wants to know? The effect of audience on identity expression among minority groups. *British Journal of Social Psychology, 42*, 299–318.

Bartone, P. T., Snook, S. A., & Tremble, T. R. (2002). Cognitive and personality predictors of performance in West Point Cadets. *Journal of Military Psychology, 14*(4), 321–338.

Bar-Zohar, M. (1966). *The armed prophet: A biography of Ben Gurion*. London: Arthur Barker.

Bass, B. M. (1985). *Leadership beyond expectations*. New York: The Free Press.

Bass, B. M. (1990). *Bass and Stogdill's handbook of leadership: Theory, research, and managerial applications.* New York: The Free Press.

Bass, B. M. (1997). Does the transactional–transformational leadership paradigm transcend organizational and national boundaries. *American Psychologist, 52,* 130–139.

Bass, B. M., & Avolio, B. J. (1990). The implications of transactional and transformational leadership for individual, team, and organizational development. In W. Pasmore & R. W. Woodman (Eds.), *Research in organizational change and development* (pp. 231–272). Greenwich, CT: JAI.

Bass, B. M., & Steidlmeier, P. (1999). Ethics, character, and authentic transformational leadership behavior. *The Leadership Quarterly, 10,* 181–218.

Bauer, T. N., & Green, S. G. (1996). Development of leader–member exchange: A longitudinal test. *Academy of Management Journal, 39,* 1538–1567.

Baughman, W. A., & Mumford, M. D. (1995). Process analytic models of creative capacities: Operations involved in the combination and reorganization process. *Creativity Research Journal, 8,* 37–62.

Baum, R. J., Locke, E. A., & Kirkpatrick, S. A. (1998). A longitudinal study of the relationship of vision and vision communication to venture growth in entrepreneurial firms. *Journal of Applied Psychology, 83,* 43–54.

Beeghley, L., Bock, E., & Cochran, J. K. (1990). Religious change and alcohol use: An application of reference group and socialization theory. *Sociological Forum, 5,* 261–278.

Bennett, L. (1976). *A biography of Martin Luther King, Jr.* Chicago: Johnson.

Berger, R. M., Guilford, J. P., & Christensen, P. R. (1957). A factor-analytic study of planning abilities. *Psychological Monographs, 71,* 31.

Beyer, J. M. (1999). Taming and promoting charisma to change organizations. *Leadership Quarterly, 10,* 307–330.

Blank, T. (2003). Determinants of national identity in east and west Germany: An empirical comparison of theories on the significance of authoritarianism, anomie, and general self-esteem. *Political Psychology, 24,* 537–553.

Bligh, M. C., Kohles, J. C., & Meindl, J. R. (2004). Charisma under crisis: Presidential leadership, rhetoric, and media responses before and after the September 11th terrorist attacks. *Leadership Quarterly, 15,* 211–239.

Bluck, S. (2003). Autobiographical memory: Exploring its functions in everyday life. *Memory, 11,* 113–123.

Bluck, S., & Habermas, T. (2000). The life story schema. *Motivation and Emotion, 24,* 121–147.

Bluck, S., & Habermas, T. (2001). Extending the study of autobiographical memory: Thinking back about life across the life span. *Review of General Psychology, 5,* 135–147.

Bluck, S., & Staudinger, V. M. (2000). *Looking back and looking ahead: The role of the past and the future in present life evaluations.* Unpublished manuscript.

Bluedorn, A. C. (2002). *The human organization of time: Temporal realities and experience.* Stanford, CA: Stanford Business Books.

Bluedorn, A. C., Johnson, E. A., Cartwright, D. K., & Barringer, B. R. (1994). The interface and convergence of the strategic management and organizational environment domains. *Journal of Management, 20,* 201–262.

Boal, K. B., & Hooijberg, R. (2000). Strategic leadership research: Moving on. *Leadership Quarterly, 11,* 515–550.

Bolman, L. G., & Deal, T. E. (1991). *Reframing organizations: Artistry, choice, and leadership.* San Francisco: Jossey-Bass.

Bond, M. H., Kwan, V. S., & Li, C. (2003). Decomposing a sense of superiority: The differential social impact of self-regard and regard for others. *Journal of Research in Personality, 34,* 537–553.

Bosch, A. (1988). *Reagan: An American story.* New York: TV Books.

Brands, H. W. (1997). *T.R.: The last romantic.* New York: Basic Books.

Brass, D. J. (2001). Social capital and organizational leadership. In S. J. Zaccaro & R. J. Klimoski (Eds.), *The nature of organizational leadership: Understanding the performance imperatives confronting today's leaders* (pp. 132–152). San Francisco: Jossey-Bass.

Brewer, U. F. (1986). What is autobiographical memory? In D. C. Rubin (Ed.), *Autobiographical memory* (pp. 25–49). New York: Cambridge University Press.

Broderick, F. L. (1995). *W.E.B. DuBois: Negro leader in a time of crisis.* Stanford, CA: Stanford University Press.

Burns, J. M. (1978). *Leadership.* New York: Harper & Row.

Calantone, R. J., & Schatzel, K. E. (2000). Strategic foretelling: Communication-based antecedents of a firm's propensity to preannounce. *Journal of Marketing, 64,* 17–30.

Campbell, R. J., & Bray, D. W. (1993). Use of an assessment center as an aid in managerial selection. *Personnel Psychology, 46,* 641–649.

Chadha, Y. (1997). *Gandhi: A life.* New York: Wiley.

Chandler, D. P. (1999). *Brother number one: A political biography of Pol Pot* (Rev. ed.). Boulder, CO: Westview Press.

Chernow, R. (1990). *The house of Morgan: An American banking dynasty and the rise of Morgan Finance.* New York: Group Press.

Chernow, R. (1998). *Titan: The life of John D. Rockefeller, Sr.* New York: Vintage.

Collison, C., & MacKenzie, A. (1999). The power of story in organizations. *Journal of Workplace Learning, 11,* 38–40.

Conger, J. A. (1989). *The charismatic leader: Behind the mystique of exceptional leadership.* San Francisco: Jossey-Bass.

Conger, J. A. (1999). Charismatic and transformational leadership in organizations: An insider's perspective on developing streams of research. *Leadership Quarterly, 10,* 145–180.

Conger, J. A., & Kanungo, R. S. (1988). Toward a behavioral theory of charismatic leadership in organizational settings. *Academy of Management Review, 12,* 637–647.

Conger, J. A., & Kanungo, R. S. (1998). *Charismatic leadership in organizations.* Thousand Oaks, CA: Sage.

Connelly, M. S., Gilbert, J. A., Zaccaro, S. J., Threlfall, K. V., Marks, M. A., & Mumford, M. D. (2000). Exploring the relationship of leadership skills and knowledge to leader performance. *Leadership Quarterly, 11,* 65–86.

Conway, M. A. (1995). *Flashbulb memories.* Mahwah, NJ: Lawrence Erlbaum Associates.

Conway, M. A. (1996). Autobiographical memory. In E. L. Bjork & R. A. Bjork (Eds.), *Memory* (pp. 165–194). San Diego, CA: Academic Press.

Coogan, T. P. (1990). *Michael Collins: A biography.* London: Hutchinson.

Cox, C. M. (1926). *Genetic studies of genius: The early mental traits of three hundred geniuses.* Stanford, CA: Stanford University Press.

Crowell, L. (1936). Franklin D. Roosevelt's audience persuasion in the 1936 campaign. *Speech Monographs, 14,* 48–64.

Dansereau, F., Graen, G. B., & Haga, W. J. (1975). A vertical dyad linkage approach to leadership within formal organizations: A longitudinal investigation of the role making process. *Organizational Behavior and Human Performance, 13,* 46–78.

Dansereau, F., Kim, K., & Kim, I. (2002). Extending the concept of charismatic leadership: An illustration using Bass's categories. In B. J. Avolio & F. J. Yammarino (Eds.), *Transformational and charismatic leadership: The road ahead* (pp. 143–172). Oxford, England: Elsevier.

Day, D. V. (2000). Leadership development: A review in context. *Leadership Quarterly, 11,* 581–613.

Day, D. V., & O'Connor, P. M. G. (2003). Leadership development: Understanding the process. In S. E. Murphy & R. E. Riggio (Eds.), *The future of leadership development* (pp. 11–28). Mahwah, NJ: Lawrence Erlbaum Associates.

Deluga, R. J. (2001). American presidential Machiavellianism: Implications for charismatic leadership and rated performance. *Leadership Quarterly, 12,* 334–363.

Den Hartog, D. N., House, R. J., & Hanges, P. J (1999). Culture specific and cross-culturally generalizable implicit leadership theories: Are the attributes of charismatic/transformational leadership universally endorsed? *Leadership Quarterly, 10,* 219–256.

Dienesch, R. M., & Liden, R. C. (1986). Leader–member exchange model of leadership: A critique and further development. *Academy of Management Review, 11*, 618–634.

Dockery, R. M., & Steiner, D. N. (1990). The role of initial interaction in leader–member exchange. *Group and Organization Studies, 15*, 395–413.

Doerner, D., & Schaub, H. (1994). Errors in planning and decision-making and the nature of human information processing. *Applied Psychology: An International Review, 43*, 433–453.

Drazin, R., Glynn, M. A., & Kazanjain, R. K. (1999). Multi-level theorizing about creativity in organizations: A sensemaking perspective. *Academy of Management Review, 24*, 286–329.

Duarte, N. J., Goodson, J. R., & Klich, N. R. (1994). Effects of dyadic quality and duration on performance appraisal. *Academy of Management Journal, 37*, 499–521.

Dubofsky, M., & Van Tine, W. (1986). *John L. Lewis: A biography.* Urbana: University of Illinois Press.

Dvir, T., Eden, D., Avolio, B. J., & Shamir, B. (1999, April). *Impact of transformational leadership on follower development and performance: A field experiment.* Paper presented at the meeting of the Society for Industrial Organizational Psychology, Atlanta, GA.

Eisenberg, N., & Miller, P. A. (1987). The relations of empathy to prosocial and related behaviors. *Psychological Bulletin, 10*(1), 91–119.

Eisenhardt, K. M. (1989). Building theories from case study research. *Academy of Management Review, 14*, 532–550.

Ellis, J. J. (2001). *Founding brothers: The revolutionary generation.* New York: Knopf.

Emmons, R. A. (1981). Relationship between narcissism and sensation-seeking. *Psychological Reports, 48*, 247–250.

Emrich, C. G., Brower, H. H., Feldman, J. M., & Garland, H. (2001). Images in words: Presidential rhetoric, charisma, and greatness. *Administrative Science Quarterly, 46*, 527–557.

Ericsson, K. A., & Charness, N. (1994). Expert performance: Its structure and acquisition. *American Psychologist, 49*, 725–747.

Erikson, E. H. (1957). *Childhood and society.* New York: Norton.

Erikson, E. H. (1959). Identity and the life cycle. *Psychological Issues, 1*, 18–164.

Erikson, E. H. (1968). *Identity, youth, and crisis.* New York: Norton.

Estes, Z., & Ward, T. B. (2002). The emergence of novel attributes in concept modification. *Creativity Research Journal, 14*, 149–156.

Fairholm, G. W. (1993). *Organizational power and politics: Tactics in organizational leadership.* Westport, CT: Praeger.

Fedor, D. B., & Maslyn, J. M. (2002). Politics and political behavior: Where else do we go from here? In F. J. Yammarino & F. Dansereau (Eds.), *Research in multi-level issues: The many faces of multi-level issues* (pp. 271–285). Oxford, England: Elsevier.

Feldhusen, J. F., & Pleiss, M. K. (1994). Leadership: A synthesis of social skills, creativity, and histrionic ability? *Roeper Review, 16*, 293–294.

Feldman, D. H. (1999). The development of creativity. In R. J. Sternberg (Ed.), *Handbook of creativity* (pp. 169–186). New York: Cambridge University Press.

Ferris, G. R., Adams, G., Kolodinsky, R. W., Hochwarter, W. A., & Ammeter, A. P. (2002). Perceptions of organizational politics: Theory and research directions. In F. J. Yammarino & F. Dansereau (Eds.), *The many faces of multi-level issues* (pp. 179–254). Oxford, England: Elsevier.

Fiedler, F. E., & Chemers, M. M. (1982). *Improving leader effectiveness: The leader match concept.* New York: Wiley.

Finke, R. A., Ward, T. B., & Smith, S. M. (1992). *Creative cognition: Theory, research, and applications.* Cambridge, MA: MIT Press.

Finkelstein, S. (2002). Planning in organizations: One vote for complexity. In F. J. Yammarino & F. Dansereau (Eds.), *Research in multi-level issues: The many faces of multi-level issues* (pp. 73–80). Oxford, England: Elsevier.

Fiol, C. M., Harris, D., & House, R. J. (1999). Charismatic leadership: Strategies for effecting social change. *Leadership Quarterly, 10*, 449–482.

Fiol, M. C., O'Connor, E. J., & Aguinis, H. (2001). All for one and one for all? The development and transfer of power across organizational levels. *Academy of Management Review, 26,* 224–242.

Fitzgerald, C., & Kirby, L. K. (1997). *Developing leaders: Research and applications in psychological type and leadership development: Integrating reality and vision, and mind and heart.* College Park: University of Maryland Press.

Fitzgerald, J. M. (1995). Intensive meanings of reminiscence in adult development and aging. In D. C. Rubin (Ed.), *Remembering our past* (pp. 360–393). Cambridge, England: Cambridge University Press.

Fleishman, E. A., & Harris, E. F. (1962). Patterns of leadership behavior related to employee grievances and turnover. *Personnel Psychology, 15,* 43–56.

Fleishman, E. A., Mumford, M. D., Zaccaro, S. J., Levin, K. Y., Hein, M. B., Korotkin, H. L. (1991). Taxonomic efforts in the description of leadership behavior: A synthesis and functional interpretation. *Leadership Quarterly, 2,* 245–287.

Fleishman, E. A., & Quaintance, M. K. (1984). *Taxonomies of human performance: The description of human tasks.* Orlando, FL: Academic Press.

Foti, R. J., & Miner, J. B. (2003). Individual differences and organizational forms in the leadership process. *Leadership Quarterly, 14,* 83–112.

Franz, U. (1988). *Deng Xiaoping.* Boston: Harcourt Brace. (Translated)

Fromm, E. (1973). *The anatomy of human destructiveness.* New York: Holt, Rinehart & Winston.

Gardner, H. (1993a). *Creative minds: An anatomy of creativity as seen through the eyes of Freud, Einstein, Picasso, Stravinsky, Eliot, Graham, and Gandhi.* New York: Basic Books.

Gardner, H. (1993b). *Multiple intelligences: The theory in practice.* New York: Basic Books.

Gardner, W. L., & Avolio, B. J. (1998). The charismatic relationship: a dramaturgical perspective. *Academy of Management Review, 23,* 32–58.

Gardner, W. L., & Cleavenger, D. (1998). Impression management strategies associated with transformational leaders at the world-class level: A psychohistorical assessment. *Management Communication Quarterly, 12,* 3–41.

Gelderman, C. (1981). *Henry Ford: The wayward capitalist.* New York: Dial Press.

Gerring, J. (1997). Ideology: A definitional analysis. *Political Research Quarterly, 50,* 957–994.

Gerstner, C. R., & Day, D. V. (1997). Meta-analytic review of leader–member exchange theory: Correlates and construct issues. *Journal of Applied Psychology, 82,* 827–844.

Gessner, J. E., O'Connor, J. A., Clifton, T. C., Connelly, M. S., & Mumford, M. D. (1993). The development of moral beliefs: A retrospective study. *Current Psychology, 11,* 236–254.

Gilbert, M. (1991). *Churchill: A life.* New York: Holt.

Goodstadt, B. E., & Hjelle, L. A. (1973). Power to the powerless: Locus of control and the use of power. *Journal of Personality and Social Psychology, 27,* 190–196.

Graen, G. B., & Cashman, J. F. (1975). A role-making model of leadership in formal organizations: A developmental approach. In J. G. Hunt & L. L. Larson (Eds.), *Leadership frontiers* (pp. 143–165). Kent, OH: Kent State University Press.

Graen, G. B., & Schiemann, W. (1978). Leader–member agreement: A vertical dyad linkage approach. *Journal of Applied Psychology, 63,* 206–212.

Graen, G. B., & Uhl-Bien, M. (1995). Relationship-based approach to leadership: Development of leader–member exchange (LMX) theory of leadership over 25 years: Applying a multi-level multi-domain perspective. *Leadership Quarterly, 6,* 219–247.

Graen, G. B., & Uhl-Bien, M. (1998). Relationship-based approach to leadership: Development of leader–member exchange (LMX) theory of leadership over 25 years: Applying a multi-level multi-domain perspective. In F. Dansereau & F. J. Yammarino (Eds.), *Leadership: The multiple-level approaches* (pp. 103–134). Stamford, CT: JAI.

Habermas, T. (2001). History and life stories. *Human Development, 44,* 191–194.

Habermas, T., & Bluck, S. (2000). Getting a life: The emergence of the life story in adolescence. *Psychological Bulletin, 126,* 748–769.

Habermas, T., & Paha, C. (2001). The development of coherence in adolescent's life narratives. *Narrative Inquiry, 11,* 35–54.

Hackman, J. R., & Walton, R. E. (1986). Leading groups in organizations. In P. S. Goodman (Ed.), *Designing effective work groups* (pp. 118–132). San Francisco: Jossey-Bass.

Halberstam, D. (1986). *The reckoning.* New York: Avon Books.

Halbesleben, J. R. B., Novicevic, M. M., Harvey, M. G., & Buckley, M. R. (2003). Awareness of temporal complexity in leadership of creativity and innovation: A competency based model. *Leadership Quarterly, 14,* 433–454.

Haleblain, J., & Finkelstein, S. (1993). Top management team size, CEO performance, and firm performance: The moderating effects of environmental turbulence and discretion. *Academy of Management Journal, 36,* 844–863.

Halverson, S. E., Holladay, C. C., Kazma, S. M., & Quionnes, M. A. (2004). Self-sacrificial behavior in crisis situations: The competing roles of behavioral and situational factors. *Leadership Quarterly, 15,* 211–240.

Hambrick, D. C., & Finkelstein, S. (1987). Managerial discretion: A bridge between polar views of organizations. In L. L. Cummings & B. M. Staw (Eds.), *Research in organizational behavior* (Vol. 9, pp. 346–406). Greenwich, CT: JAI.

Hambrick, D. C., & Mason, P. (1984). Upper echelons: The organization as a reflection of its top managers. *Academy of Management Review, 9,* 193–206.

Hammond, K. J. (1990). Case-based planning: A framework for learning from experience. *Cognitive Science, 14,* 385–443.

Havinghurst, R. (1953). *Human development and education.* New York: Longmans.

Heckscher, A. (1991). *Woodrow Wilson.* New York: Scribner's.

Hennessee, J. (1999). *Betty Friedan: Her life.* New York: Scribner's.

Hersey, P., & Blanchard, K. H. (1984). *The management of organizational behavior.* Englewood Cliffs, NJ: Prentice-Hall.

Hershey, D. A., Walsh, D. A., Read, S. J., & Chulef, A. S. (1990). The effects of expertise on financial problem-solving: Evidence for goal-directed, problem-solving scripts. *Organizational Behavior and Human Decision Processes, 46,* 77–101.

Hirshon, S. P. (2002). *General Patton: A soldier's life.* New York: HarperCollins.

Hogan, R., & Dickstein, E. (1972). A measure of moral values. *Journal of Consulting and Clinical Psychology, 39,* 210–214.

Hogarth, R. (1980). *Judgment and choice.* New York: Wiley.

Holyoak, K. J., & Thagard, P. (1997). The analogical mind. *American Psychologist, 52,* 35–44.

Hoskisson, R. E., Hitt, M. A., Wan, W. P., & Yiu, D. (1999). Theory and research in strategic management: Swing of the pendulum. *Journal of Management, 25,* 417–457.

Hosman, L. A., Huebner, T. H., Sictanen, S. A. (2002). The impact of power-of-speech style, argument strength, and need for cognition on impression formation, cognitive responses, and persuasion. *Journal of Language and Social Psychology, 21,* 361–379.

House, R. J. (1971). A path–goal theory of leader effectiveness. *Administrative Science Quarterly, 16,* 321–338.

House, R. J. (1977). A 1976 theory of charismatic leadership. In J. G. Hunt & L. L. Larson (Eds.), *Leadership: The cutting edge* (pp. 189–207). Carbondale: Southern Illinois University Press.

House, R. J. (1995). Leadership in the 21st century: A speculative inquiry. In A. Howard (Ed.), *The changing nature of work* (pp. 411–450). San Francisco: Jossey-Bass.

House, R. J. (1988). Power and personality in complex organizations. In B. M. Staw & L. L. Cummings (Eds.), *Research in organizational behavior* (Vol. 10, pp. 305–357). Greenwich, CT: JAI.

House, R. J., & Howell, J. M. (1992). Personality and charismatic leadership. *Leadership Quarterly, 3,* 81–108.

House, R. J., & Podsakoff, P. M. (1994). Leadership effectiveness: Past perspectives and future research. In J. Greenberg (Ed.), *Organizational behavior: The state of the science* (pp. 45–82). Hillsdale, NJ: Lawrence Erlbaum Associates.

House, R. J., Spangler, W. D., & Woycke, J. (1991). Personality and charisma in the U.S. presidency: A psychological theory of leader effectiveness. *Administrative Science Quarterly, 36,* 364–396.

Howell, J. W., & Hall-Merenda, K. E. (1999). The ties that bind: The impact of leader–member exchange, transformational and transactional leadership, and distance in predicting follower performance. *Journal of Applied Psychology, 84,* 686–694.

Hunt, J. G. (2004). Consideration and structure. In J. M. Burns, G. R. Goethals, & L. Sorenson (Eds.), *Encyclopedia of leadership* (pp. 196–204). Great Barrington, MA: Berkshire/Sage.

Hunt, J. G., Boal, K. B., & Dodge, G. E. (1999). The effects of visionary and crisis responsive charisma on followers: An experimental examination of two kinds of charismatic leadership. *Leadership Quarterly, 10,* 423–448.

Hunt, J. G., & Ropo, A. (1995). Multi-level leadership: Grounded theory and mainstream theory applied to the case of General Motors. *Leadership Quarterly, 6,* 379–412.

Ireland, E. D., & Hitt, M. A. (1999). Achieving and maintaining strategic competitiveness in the 21st century: The role of strategic leadership. *Academy of Management Executive, 13,* 43–58.

Isenberg, D. J. (1986). Thinking and managing: A verbal protocol analysis of managerial problem-solving. *Academy of Management Journal, 29,* 775–788.

Jacobs, T. O., & Jaques, E. (1987). Leadership in complex systems. In J. Zeidner (Ed.), *Human productivity enhancement* (Vol. 2, pp. 7–65). New York: Praeger.

Jacobs, T. O., & Jaques, E. (1991). Executive leadership. In R. Gal & A. D. Mangelsdorff (Eds.), *Handbook of military psychology* (pp. 161–189). Chichester, England: Wiley.

Jacobsen, C., & House, R. J. (2001). Dynamics of charismatic leadership: A process theory, simulation model, and tests. *Leadership Quarterly, 12,* 75–112.

Jacques, E. (1976). *A general theory of bureaucracy.* London: Heinemann.

Jenkins, R. (2001). *Churchill: A biography.* New York: Farrar, Straus & Giroux.

Jick, T. D., & Murray, V. V. (1982). The management of hard times: Budget cutbacks in public sector organizations. *Organizational Studies, 3,* 141–169.

Johnson-Laird, P. (1983). *Mental models.* Cambridge, MA: Harvard University Press.

Jones, E. E., & Pittman, T. S. (1982). Toward a general theory or strategic self presentation. In J. Suls (Ed.), *Psychological perspectives on the self* (pp. 231–262). Hillsdale, NJ: Lawrence Erlbaum Associates.

Jung, D. I., Chow, C., & Wu, A. (2003). The role of transformational leadership in enhancing organizational innovation: Hypotheses and some preliminary findings. *Leadership Quarterly, 14,* 525–545.

Kacmar, K. M., & Ferris, G. R. (1991). Perceptions of organizational politics scale (POPS): Development and construct validation. *Evaluation and Psychological Measurement, 51,* 193–205.

Kazanjian, R. K., Drazin, R., & Glynn, M. A. (2000). Creativity and technological learning: The role of organization, architecture, and crisis in large-scale projects. *Journal of Engineering and Technology Management, 17,* 273–298.

Kazdin, H. (1980). *Research design in clinical psychology.* New York: Harper & Row.

Keane, M. T. (1996). On adaptation in analogy: Tests of pragmatic importance and adaptability in analogical problem-solving. *The Quarterly Journal of Experimental Psychology, 49,* 1062–1085.

Kedia, B. L., Nordtvedt, R., & Perez, L. M. (2002). International business strategies, decision-making theories, and leadership styles: An integrated framework. *Competitiveness Review, 12,* 38–53.

Keller, J. (2003). Parental images as a guide to leadership sense making: An attachment perspective on implicit leadership theories. *Leadership Quarterly, 14,* 141–160.

Kessner, T. (1989). *Fiorello H. La Guardia and the making of modern New York.* New York: McGraw-Hill.

Kihlstrom, A., & Israel, J. (2002). Communicative or strategic action—an examination of fundamental issues in the theory of communicative action. *International Journal of Social Welfare, 11,* 210–218.

Kipnis, D., Schmidt, S. M., & Wilkinson, I. (1980). Intra-organizational influence tactics: Explorations in getting one's way. *Journal of Applied Psychology, 65,* 440–452.

Kirkpatrick, S., & Locke, E. A. (1996). Direct and indirect effects of three core charismatic leadership components on performance and attitudes. *Journal of Applied Psychology, 81,* 36–51.

Klein, K. J., & House, R. J. (1998). On fire: Charismatic leadership and levels of analysis. In F. Dansereau & F. J. Yammarino (Eds.), *Leadership: The multiple-level approaches* (pp. 3–22). Stanford, CT: JAI.

Knight, A. (1993). *Beria: Stalin's first lieutenant.* Princeton, NJ: Princeton University Press.

Kolodner, J. (1993). *Case-based reasoning.* San Mateo, CA: Morgan Kaufman.

Komaki, J. L., Desselles, M. L., & Bowman, E. D. (1989). Definitely not a breeze: Extending an operant model of effective supervision to teams. *Journal of Applied Psychology, 74,* 522–529.

Korte, J. (1995). *White gloves: How we create ourselves through memory.* New York: The Free Press.

Krass, P. (2002). *Carnegie.* New York: Wiley.

Lalonde, C. E. (2003). Counting the costs of failures of personal and cultural continuity. *Human Development, 46,* 137–144.

Largan-Fox, J., & Code, S. (2000). Team mental models: Techniques, methods, and analytical approaches. *Human Factors, 42,* 242–271.

Lasch, C. (1991). *The true and only heaven: Progress and its critics.* New York: Norton.

Lemann, N. (2000). *The big test: The secret history of the American meritocracy.* New York: Farrar, Straus & Giroux.

Lerner, R. M., Freund, A. M., Stefanis, I. D., & Habermas, T. (2001). Understanding developmental regulation in adolescence: The use of the selection, optimization, and compensation model. *Human Development, 44,* 29–50.

Liden, R., Sparrowe, R. T., & Wayne, S. J. (1997). Leader–member exchange history: The past and the potential for the future. *Research in Personnel and Human Resource Management, 15,* 47–119.

Liden, R. C., Wayne, S. J., & Stillwell, D. (1993). A longitudinal study on the early development of leader–member exchanges. *Journal of Applied Psychology, 78,* 662–674.

Linn, J. W. (1935). *Jane Addams: A biography.* New York: D. Appleton–Century.

Lockhart, R. S. (1989). Consciousness and the function of remembered episodes. In H. L. Roediger & F. I. Craik (Eds.), *Varieties of memory and consciousness* (pp. 423–430). Hillsdale, NJ: Lawrence Erlbaum Associates.

Lord, R. G., de Vader, C. L., & Alliger, G. M. (1986). A meta-analysis of the relation between personality traits and leadership perceptions: An application of validity generalization procedures. *Journal of Applied Psychology, 71,* 402–410.

Lowe, K. B., Kroeck, K. G., & Sivasubramaniam, N. (1996). Effectiveness correlates of transformational and transactional leadership: A meta-analytic review of the MLQ literature. *Leadership Quarterly, 7,* 385–425.

Lowenstein, R. (1995). *Buffett: The making of an American capitalist.* New York: Random House.

Lubart, T. I. (2001). Models of the creative process: Past, present and future. *Creativity Research Journal, 13,* 295–308.

Madison, D., Allen, R., Porter, L. W., Renwick, P., & Mayes, B. (1980). Organizational politics: An exploration of managers' perceptions. *Human Relations, 33,* 79–100.

Mainemelis, C. (2002). Time and timelessness: Creativity in (and out of) the temporal dimension. *Creativity Research Journal, 14,* 227–238.

Manchester, W. (1968). *The arms of Krupp: 1587–1968.* Boston: Little, Brown.

Maney, K. (2003). *The maverick and his machine: Thomas Watson, Sr. and the making of IBM.* Hoboken, NJ: Wiley.

Marta, S., Leritz, L. E., & Mumford, M. D. (2005). Leadership skills and group performance: Situational demands, behavioral requirements, and planning. *Leadership Quarterly, 16,* 97–120.

Martin, J., Scully, M., & Levitt, B. (1990). Injustice and the legitimation of revolution: Damning the past, excusing the present, and neglecting the future. *Journal of Personality and Social Psychology, 59,* 281–290.

Maslyn, J., & Uhl-Bien, M. (2001). Leader–member exchange and its dimensions: Effects of self and other effort on relationship quality. *Journal of Applied Psychology, 86,* 647–708.

McAdams, D. P. (2001). The psychology of life stories. *Review of General Psychology, 5,* 100–123.

McAdams, D. P., Hoffman, B. J., Mansfield, E. D., & Day, R. (1996). Themes of agency and communion in significant autobiographical scenes. *Journal of Personality, 64,* 339–378.

McClane, N. D. (1991). The interaction of leader and member characteristics in the leader–member exchange (LMX) model of leadership. *Small Group Research, 22,* 283–300.

McClelland, D. C. (1975). *Power: The inner experience.* New York: Irvington.

McGourty, J., Tarshis, L. A., & Dominick, P. (1996). Managing innovation: Lessons from world class organizations. *International Journal of Technology Management, 11,* 354–368.

McKeon, B., & Thomas, D. (1988). *Q-Methodology.* Beverly Hills, CA: Sage.

Meindl, J. R. (1990). On leadership: An alternative to the conventional wisdom. *Research in Organizational Behavior, 12,* 159–203.

Merrifield, P. R., Guilford, J. P., Christensen, P. R., & Frick, J. W. (1962). The role of intellectual factors in problem-solving. *Psychological Monographs, 76,* 1–21.

Miller, P. J. (1994). Narrative practices: Their role in socialization and self-construction. In V. Neisser (Ed.), *The remembering of self-construction: Accuracy in the self-narrative* (pp. 158–179). Cambridge, England: Cambridge University Press.

Mills, C. W. (1967). *The Marxists.* New York: Dell.

Mintzberg, H. (1979). *The structuring of organizations.* Englewood Cliffs, NJ: Prentice-Hall.

Mintzberg, H. (1983). *Power in and around organizations.* Englewood Cliffs, NJ: Prentice-Hall.

Mintzberg, H. (1990). The manager's job: Folklore and fact. *Harvard Business Review, 68,* 163.

Mobley, M. I., Doares, L. R., & Mumford, M. D. (1992). Process analytic models of creative capacities: Evidence for the combination and reorganization process. *Creativity Research Journal, 5,* 125–156.

Morgan, T. (1985). *FDR: A biography.* New York: Simon & Schuster.

Morris, E. (1979). *The rise of Theodore Roosevelt.* New York: Coward, McCann, & Geohegen.

Morris, E. (2001). *Theodore Rex.* New York: Random House.

Moss, M. (1989). *Palace coup: The inside story of Harry and Leona Helmsley.* New York: Bantam Dell.

Mumford, M. D. (2001). Something old, something new: Revisiting Guilford's conception of creative problem-solving. *Creativity Research Journal, 13,* 267–276.

Mumford, M. D. (2002). Social innovation: Ten cases from Benjamin Franklin. *Creativity Research Journal, 14,* 253–266.

Mumford, M. D., Baughman, W. A., Supinski, E. P., & Anderson, L. E. (1998). A construct approach to skill assessment: Procedures for assessing complex cognitive skills. In M. D. Hakel (Ed.), *Beyond multiple choice: Evaluating alternatives to traditional testing for selection* (pp. 75–112). Mahwah, NJ: Lawrence Erlbaum Associates.

Mumford, M. D., Baughman, W. A., Supinski, E. P., & Maher, M. A. (1996). Process-based measures of creative problem-solving skills: II. Information encoding. *Creativity Research Journal, 9,* 77–88.

Mumford, M. D., Connelly, M. S., & Gaddis, B. (2003). How creative leaders think: Experimental findings and cases. *Leadership Quarterly, 14,* 411–432.

Mumford, M. D., Connelly, M. S., & Leritz, L. E. (2005). Integrity in professional settings: Individual and situational influences. In F. Columbus (Ed.), *Advances in psychology research* (pp. 319–345). Hauppauge, NY: Nova Science Publishers.

Mumford, M. D., Espejo, J., Hunter, S. T., Bedell, K., Eubanks, D., & Connelly, M. S. (2005). *The sources of leader violence: A multi-level comparison of ideological and non-ideological leaders.* Norman, OK: The University of Oklahoma.

Mumford, M. D., Feldman, J. M., Hein, M. B., & Nago, D. J. (2001). Tradeoffs between ideas and structure: Individual versus group performance in creative problem-solving. *Journal of Creative Behavior, 35,* 1–24.

Mumford, M. D., & Gustafson, S. B. (1988). Creativity syndrome: Integration, application, and innovation. *Psychological Bulletin, 103*, 27–43.

Mumford, M. D., & Licuanan, B. (2004). Leading for innovation: Conclusions, issues, and directions. *Leadership Quarterly, 15*, 217–221.

Mumford, M. D., & Manley, G. G. (2003). Putting the development in leadership development: Implications for theory and practice. In S. Murphy & R. R. Riggio (Eds.), *The future of leadership development* (pp. 237–262). Mahwah, NJ: Lawrence Erlbaum Associates.

Mumford, M. D., & Marcy, R. T. (2004). Malcom X. In J. M. Burns, G. R. Goethals, & L. Sorenson (Eds.), *Encyclopedia of leadership* (pp. 939–944). Great Barrington, MA: Berkshire/Sage.

Mumford, M. D., Marks, M. A., Connelly, M. S., Zaccaro, S. J., & Reiter-Palmon, R. (2000). Development of leadership skills: Experience and timing. *Leadership Quarterly, 11*, 87–114.

Mumford, M. D., Mobley, M. I., Uhlman, C. E., Reiter-Palmon, R., & Doares, L. (1991). Process analytic models of creative capacities. *Creativity Research Journal, 4*, 91–122.

Mumford, M. D., Peterson, N. G., & Childs, R. A. (1999). Basic and cross-functional skills: Taxonomies, measures, and findings in assessing job skill requirements. In N. G. Peterson, M. D. Mumford, W. C. Borman, P. R. Jeanneret, & E. A. Fleishman (Eds.), *An occupational information system for the 21st century: The development of O*NET* (pp. 49–70). Washington, DC: American Psychological Association.

Mumford, M. D., Reiter-Palmon, R., & Redmond, M. R. (1994). Problem construction and cognition: Applying problem representation tactics in ill-defined domains. In M. A. Runco (Ed.), *Problem finding, problem solving, and creativity* (pp. 3–39). Norwood, NJ: Ablex.

Mumford, M. D., Schultz, R. A., & Van Doorn, J. R. (2001). Performance in planning: Processes, requirements, and errors. *Review of General Psychology, 5*, 213–240.

Mumford, M. D., Scott, G. M., Gaddis, B., & Strange, J. M. (2002). Leading creative people: Orchestrating expertise and relationships. *Leadership Quarterly, 13*, 705–750.

Mumford, M. D., Stokes, G. S., & Owens, W. A. (1990). *Patterns of life adaptation: The ecology of human individuality.* Hillsdale, NJ: Lawrence Erlbaum Associates.

Mumford, M. D., & Strange, J. M. (2002). Vision and mental models: The case of charismatic and ideological leadership. In B. J. Avolio & F. J. Yammarino (Eds.), *Charismatic and transformational leadership: The road ahead* (pp. 109–142). Oxford England: Elsevier.

Mumford, M. D., Strange, J. M., Scott, G. M., & Gaddis, B. (2004). Creative problem-solving in leadership: Directions, actions, and reactions. In J. C. Kaufman & J. Baer (Eds.), *Faces of the muse: How people think, work, and act creatively in diverse domains* (pp. 212–236). Mahwah, NJ: Lawrence Erlbaum Associates.

Mumford, M. D., Supinski, E. P., Baughman, W. A., Costanza, D. P., & Threlfall, K. V. (1997). Process-based measures of creative problem-solving skills: V. Overall prediction. *Creativity Research Journal, 10*, 77–85.

Mumford, M. D., Supinski, E. P., Threlfall, K. V., & Baughman, W. A. (1996). Process-based measures of creative problem-solving skills: III. Category selection. *Creativity Research Journal, 9*, 395–406.

Mumford, M. D., & Threlfall, K. V. (1992). Quantifying genius: A review of Dean Keith Simonton's *Psychology, Science, and History: An Introduction to Historiometry. Contemporary Psychology, 37*, 216–218.

Mumford, M. D., & Van Doorn, J. R. (2001). The leadership of pragmatism: Reconsidering Franklin in the age of charisma. *Leadership Quarterly, 12*, 279–309.

Mumford, M. D., Wesley, S. S., & Shaffer, G. S. (1987). Individuality in a developmental context, II: The crystallization of developmental trajectories. *Human Development, 30*, 291–321.

Mumford, M. D., Whetzel, D. L., & Reiter-Palmon, R. (1997). Thinking creatively at work: Organization influences on creative problem solving. *Journal of Creative Behavior, 31*, 7–17.

Mumford, M. D., Zaccaro, S. J., Harding, F. D., Jacobs, T. O., & Fleishman, E. A. (2000). Leadership skills for a changing world: Solving complex social problems. *Leadership Quarterly, 11*, 11–35.

Mumford, M. D., Zaccaro, S. J., Johnson, J. F., Diana, M., Gilbert, J. A., & Threlfall, K. V. (2000). Patterns of leader characteristics: Implications for performance and development. *Leadership Quarterly, 11*, 115–133.

Murray, A. I. (1989). Top management group heterogeneity and firm performance. *Strategic Management Journal, 10*, 125–141.

Neimeyer, G. J., & Metzler, R. E. (1994). Personal identity and autobiographical memory. In V. Neisser & R. Fivush (Eds.), *The remembered self: Accuracy in the self narrative* (pp. 105–135). New York: Cambridge University Press.

Nelson, K., Plesa, D., & Henseler, S. (1998). Children's theory of mind: An experimental interpretation. *Human Development, 41*, 7–29.

Nidich, S. I., Nidich, R. J., & Alexander, C. N. (2000). Moral development and higher states of consciousness. *Journal of Adult Development, 7*(4), 217–225.

Noice, H. (1991). The role of explanations and plan recognition in the learning of theatrical scripts. *Cognitive Science, 15*, 425–460.

O'Connor, J. A., Mumford, M. D., Clifton, T. C., Gessner, T. E., & Connelly, M. S. (1995). Charismatic leaders and destructiveness: An historiometric study. *Leadership Quarterly, 6*, 529–555.

O'Hair, D., Friedrich, G. W., Wiemann, J. M., & Wiemann, M. O. (1995). *Competent communication*. New York: St. Martin's Press.

Okuda, S. M., Runco, M. A., & Berger, D. E. (1991). Creativity and the finding and solving of real world problems. *Journal of Psychoeducational Assessment, 9*, 145–153.

Oyserman, D., & Markus, H. R. (1990). Possible selves and delinquency. *Journal of Personality and Social Psychology, 59*, 112–125.

Parnes, S. J. (1967). *Creative behavior*. New York: Scribner.

Payne, R. (1973). *The life and death of Adolf Hitler*. New York: Praeger.

Perkins, D. N. (1992). The topography of invention. In R. T. Weber & D. N. Perkins (Eds.), *Inventing minds: Creativity in technology* (pp. 238–250). New York: Oxford University Press.

Perret, G. (2001). *Jack: A life like no other*. New York: Random House.

Perrewé, P. L., Ferris, G. R., Frink, D. D., & Anthony, W. P. (2000). Political skill: An antidote for workplace stressors. *Academy of Management Executive, 14*, 115–123.

Perrewé, P. L., Zeccars, K. L., Ferris, G. R., Rossi, A. M., Kacmar, C. J., & Ralston, D. A. (2004). Neutralizing job stressors: Political skill as an antidote to the dysfunctional consequences of role conflict. *Academy of Management Journal, 47*, 141–152.

Pillemer, D. B. (1998). *Momentous events, vivid memories: How unforgettable moments help us understand the meaning of our lives*. Cambridge, MA: Harvard University Press.

Pillemer, D. B. (2001). Momentous events and the life story. *Review of General Psychology, 5*, 123–134.

Pillemer, D. B. (2003). Directive functions of autobiographical memory: The guiding power of the specific episode. *Memory, 11*, 193–202.

Popper, M. (2000). The development of charismatic leaders. *Political Psychology, 21*, 729–744.

Popper, M., & Mayseless, O. (2002). Internal world of transformational leaders. In B. J. Avolio & F. J. Yammarino (Eds.), *Transformational and charismatic leadership: The road ahead* (pp. 203–230). Oxford, England: Elsevier.

Popper, M., Mayseless, O., & Castlenovo, O. (2000). Transformational leadership and attachment. *Leadership Quarterly, 11*, 267–290.

Porter, L. W., Allen, R. W., & Angle, H. L. (1981). The politics of upward influence in organizations. In L. L. Cummings & B. M. Staw (Eds.), *Research in organizational behavior* (Vol. 3, pp. 109–149). Greenwich, CT: JAI.

Post, J. M., Ruby, K. G., & Shaw, E. D. (2002). The radical group in context: I. An integrated framework for the analysis of group risk for terrorism. *Studies in Conflict and Terrorism, 25*, 73–100.

Priest, R. F., & Swain, J. E. (2002). Humor and its implications for leadership effectiveness. *Humor, 15*, 169–189.

Qin, Y., & Simon, H. A. (1990). Laboratory replication of scientific discovery processes. *Cognitive Science, 14*, 281–312.

Reiter-Palmon, R., & Illies, J. J. (2004). Leadership and creativity: Understanding leadership from a creative problem-solving perspective. *Leadership Quarterly, 15*, 55–78.

Rejai, M. (1991). *Political ideologies: A comparative approach.* Armonk, NY: M.G. Sharpe.

Rivera, J. B. (1994). *Visionary versus crisis-induced charismatic leadership: An experimental test.* Unpublished doctoral dissertation, Texas Tech University, Lubbock.

Robinson, S. L. (1996). Trust and breach of the psychological contract. *Administrative Science Quarterly, 41*, 574–599.

Rouse, R. B., Cannon-Bowers, J. A., & Salas, E. (1992). The role of mental models in team performance in complex systems. *IEEE Transactions on Systems, Man, and Cybernetics, 22*, 1290–1308.

Runco, M. A. (2003). Idea evaluation, divergent thinking, and creativity. In M. A. Runco (Ed.), *Critical creative processes* (pp. 64–94). Cresskill, NJ: Hampton Press.

Russ, S. W. (2003). Creativity research: Whither thou goest. *Creativity Research Journal, 15*, 143–147.

Sagie, A. (1996). Effects of leader's communication style and participative goal setting on performance and attitudes. *Human Performance, 9*, 51–64.

Samaras, J. T. (1980). Two-way communication practices for managers. *Personnel Journal, 59*, 645–648.

Sarbin, T. E. (1986). *Narrative psychology: The storied nature of human conduct.* New York: Praeger.

Schriesheim, C. A., Castro, S. C., & Cogliser, C. C. (1999). Leader–member exchange (LMX) research: A comprehensive review of theory, measurement, and data-analytic procedures. *Leadership Quarterly, 10*, 63–114.

Schwarzwaller, W. (1988). *Rudolf Hess: The last Nazi.* Bethesda, MD: National Press.

Schwenk, C. R. (1995). Strategic decision making. *Journal of Management, 21*, 471–493.

Scott, G. M., Lonergan, D. C., & Mumford, M. D. (2005). Conceptual combination: Alternative knowledge structures, alternative heuristics. *Creativity Research Journal, 17*, 79–98.

Sederberg, P. C. (1984). *The politics of meaning: Power and explanation in the construction of social reality.* Tucson: University of Arizona Press.

Sein, M. K., & Bostrom, R. P. (1989). Individual differences and conceptual models in training novice users. *Human–Computer Interaction, 4*, 197–229.

Shamir, B., House, R. J., & Arthur, M. B. (1993). The motivational effects of charismatic leadership: A self-concept based theory. *Organizational Science, 4*, 577–594.

Shamir, B., & Howell, J. A. (1999). Organizational and contextual influences on the emergence and effectiveness of charismatic leadership. *Leadership Quarterly, 10*, 257–284.

Shawcross, W. (1992). *Murdoch: The making of a media empire.* New York: Touchstone Press.

Short, P. (1999). *Mao: A life.* New York: Holt.

Shrout, P. E., & Fleiss, J. L. (1979). Interclass correlations: Uses in assessing rater reliability. *Psychological Bulletin, 86*, 420–428.

Simonton, D. K. (1990). *Psychology, science, and history: An introduction to historiometry.* New Haven, CT: Yale University Press.

Singer, J. A., & Bluck, S. (2001). New perspectives on autobiographical memory: The integration of narrative processing and autobiographical reasoning. *Review of General Psychology, 5*, 91–100.

Song, J. H. (1982). Diversification strategies and the experience of top executives of large firms. *Strategic Management Journal, 3*, 377–380.

Sosik, J. J., Kahai, S. S., & Avolio, B. J. (1999). Leadership style, anonymity, and creativity in group decision support systems: The mediating role of optimal flow. *Journal of Creative Behavior, 33*, 227–256.

Sproule, J. M. (1989). Progressive propaganda critics and the magic bullet myth. *Critical Studies in Mass Communication, 63*, 225–246.

Sternberg, R. J. (1988a). A three facet model of creativity. In R. J. Sternberg (Ed.), *The nature of creativity* (pp. 125–147). Cambridge, England: Cambridge University Press.

Sternberg, R. J. (1988b). *The triarchic mind: A new theory of human intelligence.* New York: Viking.

Sternberg, R. J., Kaufman, J. C., & Pretz, J. E. (2003). A propulsion model of creative leadership. *Leadership Quarterly, 14,* 455–474.

Strange, J. M., & Mumford, M. D. (2002). The origins of vision: Charismatic versus ideological leadership. *Leadership Quarterly, 13,* 343–377.

Strange, J. M., & Mumford, M. D. (2005). The origins of vision: Effects of reflection, models, and analysis. *Leadership Quarterly, 16,* 121–148.

Strouse, J. (1999). *Morgan: American financier.* New York: HarperCollins.

Szulc, T. (1986). *Fidel: A critical portrait.* New York: Morrow.

Taylor, S. E., & Schneider, S. K. (1984). Coping and the simulation of events. *Social Cognition, 7,* 174–194.

Thomas, J. B., & McDaniel, R. R. (1990). Interpreting strategic issues: Effects of strategy and the information processing structures of top management teams. *Academy of Management Journal, 33,* 286–306.

Tierney, P., & Farmer, S. M. (2002). Creative self-efficacy: Its potential antecedents and relationship to creative performance. *Academy of Management Journal, 45,* 1137–1148.

Trimble, V. H. (1990). *Walton: The inside story of America's richest man.* New York: Dutton.

Tushman, M. L., & Anderson, P. (1986). Technological discontinuities and organizational environments. *Administrative Science Quarterly, 31,* 439–465.

Tushman, M. L., & O'Reilly, C. A. (1997). *Winning through innovation; A practical guide to leading organizational change and renewal.* Cambridge, MA: Harvard Business School Press.

Tyler, L. E. (1964). *The psychology of human differences.* Englewood Cliffs, NJ: Prentice-Hall.

Valle, M., & Witt, L. A. (2001). The moderative effort of teamwork perceptions on the organizational politics—job satisfaction relationship. *Journal of Social Psychology, 14,* 379–388.

Vincent, A. S., Decker, B. P., & Mumford, M. D. (2002). Divergent thinking, intelligence, and expertise: A test of alternative models. *Creativity Research Journal, 14,* 163–178.

Volpe, C. E., Cannon-Bowers, J. A., Salas, E., & Spector, P. (1996). The impact of cross-training on team functioning. *Human Factors, 38,* 87–100.

Ward, T. B., Patterson, M. T., & Sifonis, C. M. (2004). The role of specificity and abstraction in creative idea generation. *Creativity Research Journal, 16,* 1–10.

Weber, M. (1924). *The theory of social and economic organizations.* New York: The Free Press.

Weber, M. (1947). *The theory of social and economic organization* (T. Parsons, Trans.). New York: The Free Press.

Weick, K. E. (1995). *Sensemaking in organizations.* Thousand Oaks, CA: Sage.

Weisberg, R. W. (1999). Creativity and knowledge: A challenge to theories. In R. J. Sternberg (Ed.), *Handbook of creativity* (pp. 226–250). Cambridge, England: Cambridge University Press.

Winter, D. G. (1987). Leader appeal, leader performance, and the motives profile of leaders and followers: A study of American presidents and elections. *Journal of Personality and Social Psychology, 52,* 196–202.

Woike, B. A. (1995). Most memorable experiences: Evidence for a link between implicit and explicit motives and social cognitive processes in everyday life. *Journal of Personality and Social Psychology, 68,* 1081–1091.

Xiao, Y., Milgram, P., & Doyle, D. J. (1997). Planning behavior and its functional role in interactions with complex systems. *IEEE Transactions on Systems, Man, and Cybernetics, 27,* 313–325.

Yammarino, F. J., & Tosi, R. J. (2004). CEO charisma, compensation, and firm performance. *Leadership Quarterly, 15,* 405–420.

Yorges, S. L., Weiss, H. M., & Strickland, O. J. (1999). The effects of leader outcomes on influence, attributions, and perceptions of charisma. *Journal of Applied Psychology, 84,* 428–436.

Young, H. (1989). *One of us: A biography of Margaret Thatcher.* London: Macmillan.

Yrle, A. C., Hartman, S., & Galle, U. P. (2002). An investigation of relationships between communication style and leader member exchange. *Journal of Communication Management, 6,* 257–268.

Yukl, G. (1999). An evaluation of conceptual weaknesses in transformational and charismatic leadership theories. *Leadership Quarterly, 10,* 285–305.

Yukl, G. (2000). *Leadership in organizations.* Upper Saddle River, NJ: Prentice-Hall.

Yukl, G. (2001). *Leadership in organizations.* Upper Saddle River, NJ: Prentice-Hall.

Yukl, G. (2002). *Leadership in organizations.* Upper Saddle River, NJ: Prentice-Hall.

Yukl, G., & Falbe, C. M. (1990). Influence tactics and objectives in upward, downward, and lateral influence attempts. *Journal of Applied Psychology, 75,* 132–140.

Yukl, G., & Tracey, J. B. (1992). Consequences of influence tactics used with subordinates, peers, and the boss. *Journal of Applied Psychology, 77,* 525–535.

Zaccaro, S. J., Gilbert, J., Thor, K. K., & Mumford, M. D. (1991). Leadership and social intelligence: Linking social perceptiveness and behavioral flexibility to leader effectiveness. *Leadership Quarterly, 2,* 317–331.

Zaccaro, S. J., Gualatieri, J., & Minionis, D. (1995). Task cohesion as a facilitation of team decision making under temporal urgency. *Military Psychology, 7,* 77–93.

Zaccaro, S. J., & Klimoski, R. J. (2001). *The nature of organizational leadership: Understanding the performance imperatives confronting today's leaders.* San Francisco: Jossey-Bass.

Zaccaro, S. J., Mumford, M. D., Connelly, M. S., Marks, M. A., & Gilbert, J. A. (2000). Assessment of leader problem-solving capabilities. *Leadership Quarterly, 11,* 37–64.

Zanzi, A., & O'Neill, R. M. (2001). Sanctioned versus non-sanctioned political tactics. *Journal of Managerial Issues, 13,* 245–262.

Zhou, J., & George, J. M. (2001). When job dissatisfaction leads to creativity: Encouraging the expression of voice. *Academy of Management Journal, 44,* 682–696.

Author Index

Subject Index